The Young Max Weber and German Social Democracy

Historical Materialism Book Series

The Historical Materialism Book Series is a major publishing initiative of the radical left. The capitalist crisis of the twenty-first century has been met by a resurgence of interest in critical Marxist theory. At the same time, the publishing institutions committed to Marxism have contracted markedly since the high point of the 1970s. The Historical Materialism Book Series is dedicated to addressing this situation by making available important works of Marxist theory. The aim of the series is to publish important theoretical contributions as the basis for vigorous intellectual debate and exchange on the left.

The peer-reviewed series publishes original monographs, translated texts, and reprints of classics across the bounds of academic disciplinary agendas and across the divisions of the left. The series is particularly concerned to encourage the internationalization of Marxist debate and aims to translate significant studies from beyond the English-speaking world.

For a full list of titles in the Historical Materialism Book Series available in paperback from Haymarket Books, visit: www.haymarketbooks.org/series_collections/1-historical-materialism.

The Young Max Weber and German Social Democracy

The 'Labour Question' and the Genesis of Social Theory in Imperial Germany (1884–1899)

Victor Strazzeri

Haymarket Books
Chicago, IL

First published in 2022 by Brill Academic Publishers, The Netherlands

Published in paperback in 2023 by
Haymarket Books
P.O. Box 180165
Chicago, IL 60618
773-583-7884
www.haymarketbooks.org

ISBN: 978-1-64259-989-3

Distributed to the trade in the US through Consortium Book Sales and Distribution (www.cbsd.com) and internationally through Ingram Publisher Services International (www.ingramcontent.com).

This book was published with the generous support of Lannan Foundation and Wallace Action Fund.

Cover art and design by David Mabb. Cover art is a detail from *Painting 26, Rhythm 69, (William Morris Block Printed Pattern Book, with Hans Richter Storyboard, developed from Richter's Rhythmus 25 and Kazimir Malevich's film script Artistic and Scientific Film – Painting and Architectural Concerns – Approaching the New Plastic Architectural System)*. Paint and wallpaper on canvas (2007).

Printed in the United States.

10 9 8 7 6 5 4 3 2 1

Library of Congress Cataloging-in-Publication data is available.

Contents

PART 3
Imperialism and the Nexus of Class, Race and Culture in Max Weber's Early Thought (1894–8)

Acknowledgements

This book is a heavily edited version of the PhD thesis I submitted to the Political Science department of the Free University of Berlin in mid-2017. My sincere thanks go, first of all, to my advisors, Wolf-Dieter Narr (*in memoriam*), Klaus Roth and Jan Rehmann, who happen to be among the kindest, most generous (and patient) scholars I met in Germany. Wolf-Dieter's health did not allow him to continue as first advisor – though his fingerprints are found throughout my work – and Jan Rehmann agreed to step in at an advanced stage of the research. The discussion of an early manuscript at his New York home remains one of the most exhilarating intellectual exchanges I have experienced and I continue to profit from our collaboration in the editorial work for the *Historical-Critical Dictionary of Marxism*. My sincere thanks also goes to Wolfgang Fritz Haug, the HCDM's founder, who responded to an email of mine in 2012 asking for advisor suggestions; his prompt referral to Narr, Rehmann and Wolfgang Küttler set this whole adventure in motion and opened up a world of critical knowledge (and friendship) in the circle of gifted people that help make the dictionary project a reality. Stefan Berger also answered that email and has been a valuable *Gesprächspartner* ever since. The exchanges with Darko Suvin over the years, in turn, have been eye-opening and inspiring. My thanks also go to Sara Farris for the advice, insight and support. Finally, it is hard to put into words how much I learned from José Paulo Netto, without whose support and encouragement – alongside Leila Escorsim – this work (and the journey that led to it) would not have been possible.

The research for this book benefited immensely from the decades of painstaking work that resulted in the recently-concluded *Max Weber-Gesamtausgabe*; even more so, from the generosity and openness of many of the scholars associated with the project; above all, I would like to thank Rita Aldenhoff-Hübinger, Gangolf Hübinger and Edith Hanke. Sam Whimster, Joshua Derman, Álvaro Morcillo-Laiz and Sérgio da Mata have inspired me with their commitment to and knowledge of Weber's work. The researchers of the Weber Scholars Network have also left their mark in this book.

My research in Berlin would not have been possible without a doctoral fellowship from the DAAD, which also enriched my time in Germany with the various activities it organises and the support from my contact Maria Salgado, to whom my heartfelt thanks goes. In my final year I also benefited from an FUBright grant for a six-week stay at the History department of the George Washington University, and from a semester as a guest researcher at the Institute of Sociology at the Albert-Ludwigs-Universität Freiburg. Angela

Zimmerman and Manuela Boatcă, my hosts in Washington, DC and Freiburg i.B., respectively, have been incredibly generous and inspiring influences on my work ever since.

I attended many conferences in these years, but both the yearly *InkriT-Tagung* in Berlin and the *Historical Materialism* meetings in London (and Athens) have been the absolute highlights. Though I changed topics, period and discipline after moving to Switzerland in September 2017, the reworking of the thesis profited much from all I have learned from my host in Berne, Brigitte Studer. Thomas Barfuss has brought friendship and perspective. Wolfram Adolphi, defiance and critical insight (with much humanity and kindness mixed in).

I would also like to thank Sebastian Budgen and the editorial team at Historical Materialism for the opportunity to publish my dissertation alongside so many fantastic authors in the HM series and for their support during the manuscript preparation.

I am lucky to have made so many valuable acquaintances since moving to Europe in April 2014 that I will name only the cities where most of these dear friends are: Berlin, Barcelona, Tampere and Athens; I also miss my friends in Brazil, who have managed to be present throughout these years, despite that Atlantic in between; Jéssica, João Victor e Rodrigo, *vocês representam todos esses fazedores de saudades*. I would also like to thank with all my heart my father Eduardo, mother Luciana and brother Filipe, *por inspirar, amar e acolher. E* Ana Carolina, *que é parte insuprimível dessa* (*e da minha*) *história.*

Abbreviations

ADAV	*Allgemeiner Deutscher Arbeiterverein* [General German Workers' Association]
DFP	*Deutsche Fortschrittspartei* [German Progressive Party]
EB	*Editorischer Bericht* [Editorial commentary][1]
Einleitung	[Introduction][2]
ESK	*Evangelisch-Sozialer Kongress* [Protestant Social Congress]
FG	Roth, Guenther 2001, *Max Webers Deutsch-englische Familiengeschichte: 1800–1950*, Tübingen: Mohr Siebeck.
HKWM	*Historisch-kritisches Wörterbuch des Marxismus* [Historical-Critical Dictionary of Marxism], edited by Wolfgang Fritz Haug, Frigga Haug, Peter Jehle und Wolfgang Küttler, Hamburg: Argument Verlag, 1994 f.[3]
HSA	Heine, Heinrich, *Säkularausgabe. Werke, Briefwechsel, Lebenszeugnisse*, Berlin: Akademie-Verlag, 1970 f.
LB	Weber, Marianne 1984 [1926] *Max Weber: Ein Lebensbild.* Tübingen: Mohr.
LB-E	Weber, Marianne 1975 [1926], *Max Weber: a biography*, New York: Wiley.
MEW	*Marx-Engels-Werke*, Berlin: Dietz, 1956–1989.
MWG	*Max Weber-Gesamtausgabe* [Max Weber's collected works]. Edited by H. Baier et al., Tübingen: Mohr: 1984–2020. Abteilung I: Schriften und Reden [Section I: Writings and Speeches]; Abteilung II: Briefe [Section II: Letters]; Abteilung III: Vorlesungen und Vorlesungsnachschriften [Section III: Lessons and Lesson Transcripts] – See bibliography for precise volume information.[4]
QGdS	*Quellensammlung zur Geschichte der deutschen Sozialpolitik 1867 bis 1914. II. Abteilung: Von der Kaiserlichen Sozialbotschaft bis zu den Februarerlassen Wilhelms II. (1881–1890)* [Sourcebook on the history of German social policy, 1867 to 1914. Section II: From the Kaiser's social pronouncement to Wilhelm II's February Decrees]. Edited by Hans Joachim Henning und Florian Tennstedt. (See bibliography for precise volume information).

1 Each article in the MWG contains detailed editorial-philological notes on a given text's genesis, context and archival basis. For their authorship, see the editor and collaborator information on each MWG volume in the bibliography.

2 Each volume of the MWG contains an interpretative introduction by its respective editor(s). See bibliography for more details.

3 See the website of the Berlin Institute for Critical Theory for precise volume information: http://www.inkrit.de/neuinkrit/index.php/en/hcdm/index-of-volumes

4 For reasons of space, I do not provide the individual titles of material from Max Weber quoted from the *Max Weber-Gesamtausgabe*. Detailed information on each volume and their contents can be found in the Mohr Siebeck website at: https://www.mohrsiebeck.com

SAP	Sozialistische Arbeiterpartei Deutschlands [Socialist Workers' Party of Germany]
SpCb	*Socialpolitisches Centralblatt* [Central Journal for Social Policy]
SPD	Sozialdemokratische Partei Deutschlands [Social Democratic Party of Germany]
Verein	Verein für Socialpolitik [Association for Social Policy, founded in 1872].

Introduction

> The hero of my book, its true hero, is the social movement.
>
> HEINRICH HEINE, 1852

∴

A seemingly inconsequential family anecdote provides the first clues to Max Weber's relationship to German Social Democracy. As Marianne Weber recounts, his birth had been difficult and had left his mother Helene too weak to breastfeed:

> This was done by another woman, the wife of a Social Democratic carpenter ... When later his social and democratic views developed in opposition to the political heritage of his ancestors, the family used to joke that 'Max drank his political views with his nurse's milk'.[1]

While the veracity of this family story is entirely reliant on Marianne's account, it is suggestive of Max Weber's trajectory – and its historical backdrop – in a number of ways. Firstly, it points to the fact that, in spite of its profound social divides, class society in Prussia-Germany still saw instances of direct, even intimate exchange between the working class and ruling strata. Magnified to the societal level, the anecdote uncovers the working class as a hidden protagonist in the process of social and economic transformation that would propel a soon to be founded Imperial Germany to one of the world's leading industrial nations by the end of the nineteenth century. Finally, the reference to Weber's 'social and democratic views' invites an approach to his work that has been seldom engaged with in the research, namely, how his thought and trajectory were informed by the social struggles and, more specifically, by the foremost political organisation of the working class of his time, i.e., German Social Democracy.[2] In the chapters that follow, I leverage these insights into the conflictive, asymmetrical, yet somehow intimate relationship between the

---

1 LB-E, p. 31.

2 In his seminal *Max Weber and German politics* (2004 [1959]), Wolfgang J. Mommsen addresses above all Max Weber's criticism of the labour movement and German Social Democracy. He is also the author of the only essay solely dedicated to the topic in the vast secondary literature

working class and the liberal bourgeoisie in *fin-de-siècle* Imperial Germany to shed light on an overlooked, but decisive driver of Max Weber's intellectual and political development.

Overlooked, partly because many key remarks on and instances of dialog with Social Democracy fall in a period of Weber's trajectory – his student and legal clerkship years in the 1880s and first decade of scholarly activity (as a political economist) in the 1890s – that has received comparatively little attention in the scholarship. This is explained, first of all, by the fact that Weber's canonical works all date from a later period of his intellectual output, one that happens to coincide with his (partial) recovery from a bout of mental illness that left him unable to teach, write or pursue any manner of social activity between mid-1898 and late-1902. Second, and most crucial, however, is the fact that the writings from 1903/4 onwards boast not only significant thematic departures with regards to the early production, but also embody an attempt at an objective, value-free social science that has often been contrasted to the more evidently engaged (and controversial) writings of the 1890s.

The resulting schematic division of Weber's development as an intellectual into two distinct, fairly disconnected stages with unequal scientific value has, for one, discouraged many experts from a systematic confrontation with what was in fact an extraordinarily fruitful first decade of output; setting off with his doctoral work on medieval trading companies in 1889, it encompasses writings on Mediterranean antiquity, the stock exchange and, in particular, agrarian sociology,[3] the overarching theme of the early period and the one I will be focussing on as well. Besides the scholarly worth these writings possess in their own right, I hope to demonstrate that they can also shed light on many aspects of the 'mature' Weber's intellectual physiognomy, especially when framed as elements of a continuous, if non-linear 'learning process' which, in Weber's case, just as in Marx's, never found an endpoint in their lifetimes.[4] Along these

on Weber (see his 'Max Weber and German Social Democracy' in Mommsen 1987, pp. 90–105 and – slightly altered – in Mommsen 1989, pp. 74–86). The relationship of Weber to Eduard Bernstein and Karl Kautsky, respectively, were discussed in the highly readable articles of John Breuilly and Dick Geary for a collective volume edited by Mommsen and Schwentker (1988). More recently, Jan Rehmann's (2015) Gramscian analysis of Weber approached the matter in ways that have decisively shaped my own work. Finally, a recent *Max-Weber Gesamtausgabe* [MWG] volume containing Weber's hitherto unpublished lectures and materials on the labour movement and the 'labour question' (MWG III/4) – a product of Rita Aldenhoff-Hübinger's keen editorial work – has brought invaluable new material on the topic (see Strazzeri 2015 and chapter 11, below).

3 For an overview of how these different scholarly pursuits were related and for clues as to their place in Weber's overall trajectory, see Mommsen 2005, pp. 185–190.

4 The concept of 'learning process' was introduced by Wolfgang Fritz Haug to shed light on the

lines, instead of the dichotomisation of Weber's writings along an axis ranging from 'engaged' (the early work) to 'value-free' (the post 1903/4 production), in a gesture akin to the direct transposition of Weber's attempt to keep his politics at arm's length from his scholarship to the chronology of his life, I will repurpose Weber's exhortation that every intellectual must face up to the 'demands of the day, both personally and professionally',[5] as a formula to decipher his own trajectory and work.[6]

In Max Weber's lifetime, as in ours, one overarching phenomenon was ultimately responsible for rearing these 'demands', i.e., the capitalist economic order which, '[n]ext only to bureaucracy', forms the 'central topic of [his] scholarly and public work'.[7] From his lasting intellectual confrontation with this 'immense cosmos', Weber is best known for having theorised its connections to a rationalised 'life conduct' and a methodical work ethic; he is understood to be less concerned about the mechanisms behind modern class formation and social inequality, especially when compared to Marx's critique of political economy. As Erik Olin Wright put it in a seminal essay,

> If theoretical frameworks are identified as loudly by their silences as by their proclamations, then one of the defining characteristics of class analysis in the Weberian tradition is the virtual absence of a systematic concept of exploitation.[8]

While this glaring absence says much about Max Weber's conceptualisation of capitalism, it does not necessarily indicate that the social ills of modern class society had no bearing in his trajectory and outlook. In fact, Max Weber makes

---

self-reflective dynamic underlying Marx's distinct 'phases' and 'periods' and as a rejoinder to scholars who have recently attempted to 'correct Marx with Hegel' and who claim that, when he reached his forties, Marx's 'theoretical acumen ... went downhill' (see Haug 2006). The concept can also help to cast doubt on the notion that Weber's early period was a self-contained 'phase' he will entirely surpass, and that the writings of the 1890s are at most flawed attempts at his later achievements.

5 As Weber stated at the end of his 1917 lecture, *Science as vocation* (Weber 2012 [1917], p. 353).

6 I will return to the question of the breaks and continuities between the 'young' and 'mature' Weber in the epilogue to this work. For more nuanced and compelling treatments of the issue of partisanship and scholarship in his trajectory from the recent Weber-scholarship, see Aldenhoff-Hübinger 2004, Bruhns 2009, Palonen 2010 and Paré 1999. Ironically, the taint of political engagement has also been employed lately to dismiss Marx's *late* thought, identified with 'so-called "labour-movement Marxism" typically regarded with a certain distaste' (Haug 2006, p. 573).

7 Mommsen 2005, p. 185.

8 Wright 2002, p. 832.

a surprise appearance in a recent essay by Pankaj Mishra dedicated to the question of why German elites have historically attached a larger importance to the social insurance system as a pillar of state power than their equivalents in the UK and the US:

> Weber was among the conservative German nationalists *who saw the social question as a matter of life or death.* Military and economic rivalry with Britain was a daunting enough prospect for their fledgling state. But, as disaffection increased among the classes uprooted and exploited by industrial capitalism – a political party representing the interests of the working classes emerged in Germany decades before it did in Britain – the fear of socialist revolution also preyed on the minds of German leaders.[9]

Mishra is referring, of course, to the threat posed by Social Democracy to the status quo of Weber's Imperial Germany, with vast ramifications not only for its domestic politics, but also to its emerging status as a leading power on the world stage. The quote accurately conveys how the urgency of the so-called 'social question' was a function of the combined phenomena of a 'radically new dynamic of poverty' which, 'for the first time in recorded history, *grew in direct proportion to the increase in the social capacity to produce wealth*' and of its 'social-political ramifications'.[10] In other words, 'it was from the effective prospect of a toppling of the bourgeois order that pauperism was designated as the "social question"'.[11] Establishing how the 'social question' and its refractions shaped Max Weber's development as an intellectual, from the time he was a 20-year old law student (1884) to when he was forced to interrupt his activities in 1898/9, is precisely the aim of this book.

The decision not to extend my research question beyond this time span is not a function of its diminished relevance for Weber from the 1900s onwards, but rather of the fact that his trajectory up to that point offers more than enough to unpack on the subject for a book-length study, not least because of a revolution in the available source material. Thanks to the recently concluded critical edition of Max Weber's writings, letters and course materials (the *Max Weber-Gesamtausgabe* [MWG]), research into his early trajectory can now rely

9 Quoted from Pankaj Mishra's July 2020 essay 'Flailing states' for the *London Review of Books* v. 42, n. 14, available online at https://lrb.co.uk/the-paper/v42/n14/pankaj-mishra/flailing-states

10 Netto 2001, pp. 42–3.

11 Netto 2001, p. 43.

on an exhaustive and meticulously annotated set of sources. As a result, old questions such as 'did he really read Marx' and, if so, which works did he privilege, can now be answered with a fair amount of certainty: yes, he not only read Marx, he *taught* Marx; we even know which elements of *Capital* he found most compelling – the portrayal of power relations between employer and worker, the general trends towards capital concentration and formation of an industrial reserve army – and those he (symptomatically) ignored or dismissed, as in the case of the analysis of the commodity and value-forms. Max Weber read Engels closely too, appropriating the concept of 'labour aristocracy' from him long before Lenin had popularised the term;[12] finally, we learn he was surprisingly knowledgeable about the classics of European socialist and anarchist thought. As is often the case with a critical edition of a classic, the MWG does not tell keen Weber readers much that they did not already know or at least suspect, but, as in these and many other examples over the next chapters, it helps fill a lot of gaps.

Which brings me to the age-old Marx/Weber 'problem'. In this work, the questions surrounding Max Weber's reception of the ideas of Karl Marx, which, between Löwith (1932) and Löwy (2013), have by now received more than eight decades of scholarly attention, will be set against the historical backdrop that first raised them. In other words, Weber's reading of Marx will be reconsidered from the standpoint of its concrete mediator, German Social Democracy, whose triumph over repression and rise to a key political actor – and foremost organisation of the international workers' movement – by the 1890s constituted a seismic event in Imperial German politics and society. This era-defining occurrence made a tremendous impact – across class lines – on an entire generation of young intellectuals that was coming of age in those years, including Max Weber. One scholar has even termed his cohort the 'generation of 1890', in reference to the rise of the 'social question' to a central issue of public debate that year.[13] In this sense, the fact that the young Weber's political convictions, to return to Marianne Weber's words quoted above, eventually came to be at odds with those of his immediate forebears on matters '*social* and *democratic*' in nature, evoked a very concrete meaning in Imperial Germany:

> The vilifying label 'Social Democrat' constitutes one of the most important constants of the Reich's internal politics from its foundation to the First World War; branded 'enemies of the Reich', 'unpatriotic' [*Vaterland-*

12 See Chapter 11.

13 Repp 2000, pp. 19–20.

> *slose*] and 'antinational' since 1871, Social Democrats were excluded from the nation, which the bourgeoisie thoroughly identified with.[14]

Yet, does this mean that Weber considered 'joining the underdogs'? Wolfgang J. Mommsen raised this question in the title of an essay on Weber's relationship to the SPD, subsequently answering in the negative.[15] Similarly, this book does not argue that Weber, a self-professed 'class conscious bourgeois', was ever, even on some deep level, a Social Democrat, just as little as Marianne intended to with her anecdote. What she was drawing attention to – and what I will examine systematically in Part 1 – are the set of issues which precipitated Max Weber's break with the previous generations of German liberals, of which his father Max Sr. and especially his uncle Hermann Baumgarten were notable figures. The hypothesis I advance is that the presence of Social Democracy in Imperial Germany is a decisive contributor to the fact that this rupture – and Weber's ensuing attempt to set German liberalism on a new course – took place precisely along the fault line of the 'social question'. Yet, just as in the issue of Marx's impact on Weber's ideas, my argument for the SPD's role in Weber's trajectory raises the complicated question of assessing 'influence' in the development of an intellectual.

As Lucien Goldmann argued several decades ago, considered in isolation, '*influences* of all manner explain very little – if anything at all – *in intellectual history*'. Hence, rather than establishing if a thinker was influenced by another – or, in this case, impacted by a social movement – Goldmann maintained it was more important to ask '*why* they suffered *precisely this influence at this particular time in their history and trajectory*'.[16] Making good on this methodological proposition with regards to the young Weber's relationship to the labour movement means taking a closer look at the social setting that marked his formative years, i.e., his family's home in Charlottenburg, then a municipality adjacent to Berlin. Though Max Weber is frequently identified with South-West Germany – he took a teaching position in Freiburg i.B. in 1894, then Heidelberg in 1897, both of which were in the Grand Duchy of Baden – he spent most of his childhood and youthful years in the greater Berlin area. In other words, though not remembered as such, Max Weber *was a Berliner*. More specifically, Weber grew up in a liberal bourgeois milieu that, according to his biographers, shaped him decisively.[17] In the words of Wolfgang J. Mommsen,

14 Groh 1974, p. 62.
15 See Mommsen 1989 (page references in note 2 above).
16 Goldmann 1952, p. 89.
17 See Käsler 2014, pp. 64–85, Kaube 2014, pp. 19–26.

> Max Weber grew up in the orbit of the German liberalism of the late Bismarck period; leading men of German National Liberalism, but also prominent representatives of the Progressive Party [so-called left-liberals – V.S.] … frequented Max Weber's parental home alongside not a small segment of the intellectual luminaries of the Berlin of the time.[18]

Though Weber owed his early political education and enduring aspects of his worldview to this liberal milieu and the (male) notables that populated it, as I will discuss in Chapters 1 and 2, this insight should not overshadow the fact that his thought-world and politics boasted *significant departures* with regards to his forebearers. This is in no small part due to the fact that Weber came of age at a time of profound crisis for German liberalism. As Geoff Eley has stressed, '[t]he 1890s were a vital decade of political flux, in which one pattern of politics began to be replaced by another'.[19] From a top-down 'politics of notables' that relied on social prestige and high-level connections with barely any interaction with constituencies and little in the way of organisational and electoral structures, a time of mass politics had arrived with its hard-fought campaigns, press controversies and a greater role to public opinion and popular mobilisation.[20] Liberals, who were mostly unwilling to adapt to the new reality, found themselves on the losing side of this transition. Consequently, if 'between the 1860s and the end of the 1880s the dominant fraction in the Bismarckian power bloc had been liberal', 'by the start of the 1890s this liberal predominance was already starting to decompose, and by 1900 it was in fragments'.[21] The more conservative National Liberal Party, of which Max Weber's father, Max Sr. was lifelong member and long-time Reichstag representative, suffered the greatest setback, considering that the political role that had defined it, the alliance with Bismarck dating back to the process of unification in 1866, had been broken by the chancellor in 1878/9 on account of a dispute over protectionist tariffs. This left the party looking for a political identity precisely at a time of heightened competition in the electoral arena and when burgeoning social conflict favoured more radical forms of politics to the left and right.

This literally hit close to home in Max Weber's case, not only because of his father's ties with the party, but also because his uncle, the historian Hermann Baumgarten (1825–93), had played an important role in the ideological preparation of the liberal compromise with Bismarck through his 1866 pamphlet *Ger-*

18 Mommsen 1993, p. 34.
19 Eley 1980, p. 19.
20 See Eley 1980, pp. 19–40.
21 Eley 1980, p. 19.

man liberalism: a self-critique. The work not only sang the praises of Prussian aristocracy as a political and historical actor, highlighting its vocation to unite the German nation, it depicted the bourgeoisie as a fundamentally prosaic and industrious class by nature, one that was unfit for rulership. Baumgarten was the main political interlocutor of the young Max Weber and their ample correspondence and running political commentary on the Reich's politics between 1884 and 1891 are key sources for Part 1 of this work. By those years, Baumgarten had become a critic of Prussian dominance over Imperial Germany, yet he did not seem able to offer a new political horizon for his nephew and his generation. The young Weber, in turn, was intent on finding avenues of renewal for German liberalism.

A key element of this effort – which seems to take a conscious form already in the late 1880s, when he was not yet twenty-five – is precisely Weber's awareness of the need for German liberals to face the 'social question', which meant developing a renewed perspective on the labouring classes, both urban and rural, as well as on 'state social policy' [*Sozialpolitik*]. Chapter 3 will argue Max Weber could, once again, find inspiration for this insight at home, more specifically from his mother Helene's commitment to charitable and poor relief efforts in Charlottenburg. Though often portrayed as a bucolic and tranquil bourgeois enclave in the Weber scholarship, Berlin's neighbouring municipality was a large industrial city in its own right, with all the social contrasts this implied. The 'social question' was, hence, in no way circumscribed to the endless tenement buildings of the Berlin periphery; in fact, it showed itself right at the Webers' Charlottenburg doorstep, as Helene reported in 1885: 'now that it is cold, one poor, one hungry family after the other appears at the door, one jobless man after the other'.[22] Interestingly, despite Helene's monarchical convictions, Christian piety and overall more conservative worldview than the secular and liberal Max Sr., her social engagement and impact in institutional poor relief efforts only grew as the turn of the century approached. She was, in a way, more in line with her epoch's trends than her liberal husband and she no doubt played a role in the young Weber's growing awareness of social issues as of the late 1880s. But the aforementioned generational break was visible in his relationship to his mother too. Her social engagement and views of workers were strictly patriarchal, meaning that, while she was not opposed to the alleviation of poverty, the ultimate goal of her charitable work was the moral reform *of the poor themselves*, seen as fundamentally passive players in the process. Max Sr.'s involvement in poor relief authorities and in a number

22 Cited in FG, p. 516.

of charitable associations, as befitted a bourgeois notable, took place on similarly paternalistic grounds. A patriarchal view was incompatible, however, with a state social policy that addressed old-age, disability, childbirth, joblessness etc., as structural issues, rather than as instances of hardship to be overcome on an individual basis through the benevolence – and 'positive example' – of bourgeois philanthropists. Patriarchalism also ruled out working-classes politics as a legitimate response to the 'social question'. On both counts, therefore, this strand of social intervention was fast becoming out of sync with the times, considering the introduction of state social policy initiatives by Bismarck in the mid-to-late 1880s and the growing role of German Social Democracy.

Chapters 4 and 5 approach the progressive detachment of the young Weber's outlook from those of his immediate family members in the context of major political and social transformations in Imperial Germany between 1887 and 1890/1. If there is truth to Marianne Weber's assessment that by the time her husband was twenty-four – i.e., in April 1888 – 'he was a man whose basic structure was complete and self-contained, a man whom insights and experiences could enrich but no longer remould',[23] that would mean that when the death of the old Kaiser Wilhelm I in March of 1888 triggered a period of sea change in Imperial German politics, Weber's intellectual and moral foundations were already in place. In fact, by this juncture he had already largely outgrown the National Liberalism of his father and uncle and was seeking other platforms for his political intervention. In line with Marianne's remark, however, Weber's maturation in this period pertains less to his evolving viewpoint than to a change in his interlocutors – from his immediate family to young social reformers and political economists – and to a transition from detached commentator on the Reich's politics to *active* participant in its social reality. This process is also reflected in Weber's accelerated personal and career development; if Otto Baumgarten reports that his cousin Max appeared to be 'suffering strongly from a lack of initiative and determination in life' in the autumn of 1887,[24] this is precisely when Weber took the decision, after some hesitation, to 'pursue an academic track', even if 'it remained to be seen' whether he could 'achieve anything [of worth] in this regard'.[25]

This overcoming of passivity evokes the *second element* of Lucien Goldmann's critical take on assessing 'influence' in intellectual history, namely, the

23 LB-E, p. 85.
24 Cited in FG, p. 513.
25 MWG II/2, pp. 122–3.

active part played by thinkers themselves in *choosing* to incorporate a particular intellectual source or inspiration: 'the active role of the individual and social subject expresses itself not only in the choice of a manner of thinking [*pensée*] that they identify themselves with, but also in the transformations they effect on it'.[26] This insight, in turn, is the key to understanding why Weber's personal and intellectual development kicked into high gear precisely as a series of events were set in motion that would fundamentally alter Imperial Germany's political landscape; the 'three-Kaiser year' of 1888, which fatefully ended with a young Wilhelm II ascending to the throne, was followed by the reactivation of the labour movement in spectacular fashion with the mass Ruhr miners' strike of 1889. Finally, an eventful 1890 began with the non-prolongation of the repressive 'Law against the Socialists' – heralding Social Democrats' triumph at the polls – and culminated with Bismarck's dismissal by the Kaiser. Hence, more significant than Max Weber's thoughts on all of these occurrences – which I detail in Chapter 5 – is what he decided to do next in terms of his scholarly work and engagement. After submitting his two academic qualification works on medieval trading companies (1889) and Roman agrarian history (1891), respectively, which drew high praise, and having also concluded his legal clerkship, Weber chose to immediately commit to a prominent role in the Verein für Socialpolitik's empirical survey on the situation of rural labour in the Empire. Weber came on board the collective research effort in early 1892 and was charged with writing the report on East Elbian Germany, based on the responses of its large landowners to two questionnaires sent by the Verein. This was a politically sensitive task as the region was the seat of Junker power, i.e., of Prussian aristocracy. Weber was finished with his book-length analysis by late summer 1892 and would continue to be primarily engaged with agrarian policy for the two subsequent years, writing numerous essays and giving a series of lectures on the subject.

Part 2 of this work consists of the systematic analysis of these writings and other materials, marking a shift in the primary source material away from Weber's private correspondence and onto his socio-political interventions in the German public sphere. In terms of my research interests, the relevance of this output stems not only from the fact that in it Weber confronts the 'labour question' and associated phenomena – i.e., Social Democratic agitation, workers' grievances, cross-border labour migration – openly and exhaustively, but also from the fact that this phase of his work was a veritable laboratory for his developing perspective on social life more generally. In other words, I claim

26 Goldmann 1952, p. 89.

crucial aspects of the novel analytical standpoint on social reality that Weber would later become known for have their genesis precisely in his 'rural labour' writings.

Because innovations in terms of method and in political outlook were strictly intertwined at this point of his trajectory, Weber's key analytical advance, i.e., his engagement of workers' standpoint to understand their drivers and motivations, was in a direct relationship with his (conditional) recognition of their status as legitimate political actors. This not only enabled Weber to present a unique perspective on the 'labour question', but also represented a break with deep-rooted patriarchal stances on workers prevalent in the German upper classes. Chapter 6 attempts precisely to contextualise the significance of this break by tracing back the three-way debate between conservatives, liberals and socialists on the legitimacy of working-class politics in the German lands from the *Vormärz* (or pre-1848) period to the 1890s. Given this contentious historical backdrop, Chapter 7 approaches the analytical dilemmas and the political stakes underscoring the Verein's 'rural labour' survey of 1891/2. My strategy to tease out Weber's specific contribution and peculiar approach to this collective research endeavour is anchored on contrasting it to a second survey on rural workers, organised by the *Evagelisch-Sozialer Kongress* [ESK – Protestant Social Congress]. Max Weber was directly involved in the preparation and execution of this subsequent initiative and because it was aimed at addressing the blind spots and omissions of the Verein's effort, it gives an ideal basis for comparison. Chapter 8 delves into Weber's analysis proper, reconstructing his gradual articulation of a novel standpoint on the 'labour question' predicated on the consideration of workers' 'ethical-ideal drivers' as decisive causal factors for large-scale transformations in the German Eastern countryside. I argue it is this engagement with the standpoint of the lowly rural worker that marks the genesis of Weber's social theory (rather than his later study of the ethics of ascetic Protestant entrepreneurs), because it gave him the first empirical demonstration of the centrality of culture as a driver of human agency. In turn, Chapter 9 details how at the conference organised by the Verein to discuss the survey's results, Weber went head to head not only with established political economists, but also with Social Democrats. I show how Weber's novel take on the 'labour question' ultimately shaped the overall debate during the proceedings, considering deliberations converged precisely on the issue of the adequate *standpoint* on the matter, which his report had stressed. The survey's organisers were chiefly concerned with large landowners' interests – i.e., assuring the availability of labour power, worker discipline etc. – and anchored the entire research effort on their portrayal of rural workers' situation; on the opposite end of the conference's political spectrum were Social Democrat intellectuals demanding that the 'labour question' be approached through direct recourse to workers – instead of through intermediaries – with a view to resolving it in their interest (through collectivisation of land, the abolition of remaining feudal-like duties, unionisation) and by means of their own agency.

Max Weber, in turn, posited that the first thing to consider was, indeed, the 'standpoint of *workers*', that is, 'what in *their* eyes is the practical problem ... and its solution'.[27] Yet, his analysis was predicated on reaching a higher level of generalisation on the problem through what he termed 'the standpoint of state reason', i.e., the 'analysis of what the problem and its solution are in the eyes of the *state* and of *politicians*'.[28] As he phrased it in one of his lessons on the labour movement and the 'labour question' in 1895:

> 'The economic science is sovereign'! It therefore has the right to pass judgement on the development of the labour relation [*Arbeitsverhältnis*], in so far as it *measures it up against an ideal*. It does not construct this ideal from the standpoint of any party or interest group – instead it places *national interest* at the very top as its ideal.[29]

In other words, by ascribing 'national interest' to its virtual carriers (the state and its political personnel), Weber found a platform of analysis that he claimed approached the 'labour question' beyond the one-sided standpoints of both landowners and workers. This instance did not, however, intend to eliminate class horizons altogether; Weber construed 'state reason' as the embodiment of a hegemonic order that was clearly based on a particular class constellation. In terms of the social structure of the countryside, for instance, he criticised patriarchal landlords for wanting to hold on to their feudal-like prerogatives while at the same time demanding to have access to a cheap, disposable labour force; on the other hand, he did not defend the unleashing of capitalist modernisation in the German East to such an extent that it would leave only a reduced number of agrarian capitalists and a mass of rural proletarians in its wake. Weber favoured, instead, fostering the conditions for a stable middle strata of tenant farmers and small landowners to emerge, with access to enough land of their own to lead an autonomous existence, but whose surplus labour power could also be employed in the large estates. The rearing of such strata by means of state-led agrarian reform would not only provide

27 MWG III/4, p. 76.

28 Ibid.

29 MWG, III/4, p. 251, my emphasis.

a horizon of upward social mobility for landless workers, it would also prevent further social polarisation in the German East (thus curbing the threat of social-democratic agitation). Last and certainly not least, these measures would tie native workers to the land, 'safeguarding German culture' (and the German infantry's preferred reservoir of manpower) from 'excessive' Polish migration.

The urban complement to this (projected) social rearrangement was equally predicated on fostering middle-strata, more specifically, the 'labour aristocracy'. Weber saw the emergence of this 'higher-standing' segment of workers as strategic because it effectively split the working class socially and politically, providing the most dynamic segments of the German industrial bourgeoisie with an ideal ally in its modernisation efforts. If the role Weber envisioned for the 'labour aristocracy' in this new power bloc was clearly subaltern, membership in it came with important concessions, such as the right to collective bargaining and to a greater say in the political affairs of the nation.

Weber, therefore, did not hold the sheer maximisation of output, efficiency and competitiveness to be the absolute goals of state intervention in the social structure and in economic life; it was, rather, *power considerations* that structured his viewpoint, more specifically the combined objectives of *fostering social coherence* within Imperial Germany and creating the ideal conditions for its *projection outwards*. Jan Rehmann pioneeringly interpreted this modernising standpoint as a strategy of passive revolution[30] aimed at counteracting both the reactionarism of Prussian aristocracy and the formation of a revolutionary labour movement in Imperial Germany:

> Weber reveals himself to be an early exponent of Fordist 'populations rationalisation'. His way of posing the problem splits society into two opposed socio-economic blocs. What is decisive is not the opposition, analysed by Marx, between societal labour and its capitalist form, but the one between industrial modernisation and 'traditionalist' counterforces: on one side stand the 'prebendary strata' and all their congenial parties with a stake in 'economic stagnation'; on the other side stands the alliance between 'organisationally high-ranking entrepreneurs' and the working

30 As Antonio Gramsci puts it in *The Prison Notebooks*, the formulas of 'passive revolution' [*rivoluzione passiva*] and 'revolution-restauration' express 'the historical fact of the absence of popular initiative in the development of Italian history, and the consequent fact that "progress" would consist of a reaction of dominant classes to the sporadic subversive activities of popular masses through "restorations" that incorporate a part of popular demands' ([Q.8, § 25] available at: http://dl.gramsciproject.org/quaderno/8/nota/25.html).

> class, both of whom have an interest in the 'maximum rationalisation of work', an interest that coincides 'principally' with the 'political interest in preserving the nation's international standing'.[31]

In the passage, Rehmann is referencing Antonio Gramsci's conceptualisation of 'Americanism' and its most advanced expression in terms of 'production and manner of working', i.e., Fordism. In Gramsci's own words, 'Americanism' presupposed what 'could be characterized as "a rational demographic composition", which consists in the absence of numerous classes lacking an essential function in the productive world, that is, purely parasitic classes'.[32] This aspect of 'Americanism', says Rehmann, strongly coincides with Weber's projection of a new hegemonic configuration for Imperial Germany; once more, his writings on the 'rural labour question' from 1892–4 provide the fundamental insights that would feed into this '*proto*-Fordist' horizon.[33]

Part 2 concludes with an assessment of Weber's ambiguous relationship to Prussian aristocracy and with a consideration of the most controversial aspect of his early production, his anti-Polish agitation and defence of a closed-border policy for the German East. I argue that, far from a simple bias or outgrowth of his nationalism, Weber's stance on Polish migration provides an important clue to the normative core of his concept of culture and how the latter related to his understanding of class and labour. Weber, namely, saw culture as a function of 1) social stratification, with the upper classes – but also high-standing workers – as its fundamental bearers, and 2) of how class status interacted with the standing of the nation-state in the world economy. The conjugation of these two factors is crucial, considering that, to Weber, capitalist development was not necessarily synonymous with cultural development:

> It is not possible for our workers to compete with Polish workers. German workers would have to climb down a cultural level [*Kulturstufe*] in their needs in order to do so; it is very much the same with our agricultural

31 Rehmann 2015, pp. 118–19.

32 Gramsci 1966 [1934], pp. 312–13.

33 I will term Weber's modernising perspective *proto*-Fordist, because the historical phenomenon proper, i.e., Henry Fords' rationalisation of production and popularisation of the assembly line, dates from the early years of the twentieth century in the United States and only found an enthusiastic reception in Europe after the First World War (See Jakob Tanner, 'Fordismus', HKWM, 1999, 580–8). Weber's early acquaintance with Fordist (and Taylorist) principles, as Jan Rehmann keenly points out, is explained by his visit to the seat of an important precursor to their broad application, i.e., Chicago's stockyards (or meatpacking district), during his US trip in the summer of 1904 (see Rehmann 2015, pp. 24–9).

> enterprises who are noncompetitive because they would have to climb down a cultural level in order to compete with those of Russia, Argentina and America. There is a certain situation in capitalistically-disorganized national economies, according to which the higher culture not only is not superior in the struggle for existence, but is, in fact, weaker vis-à-vis a culture with a lower standing.[34]

The solution Weber presented to the dilemmas of an age of globalised capitalism consisted in the formula of 'social imperialism',[35] according to which geopolitical and economic ascendancy in the world stage is channelled by the nation-state to temper social polarisation, yet still allowing it to profit from the increase of wealth and accelerated technical innovation that only a fast-expanding capitalist economic order can conjure.

These topics are fleshed out in the concluding Part 3 of this work, which delves into what I argue is Weber's fundamentally global standpoint on culture and economic life in his writings of the 1890s. Chapter 10 attempts to conjugate my findings on Weber's understanding of labour, class and culture with recent critical appraisals of his work from postcolonial and world-system theory approaches. My analysis identifies Weber's concept of culture as a normative – rather than relativist – construct, one that is structured on a fundamental level by a crystallisation of the hierarchies of class and 'nationality' (i.e., race/ethnicity) of the Imperial age. In other words, cultural achievement emerges as a function of a nexus of social and global inequalities, which Weber naturalises in a spiteful rejection of what he termed Social Democrats' 'dream of racial and cultural equality'.[36]

Chapter 11, in turn, examines Weber's recently published teaching materials on the labour movement and the 'labour question' (MWG III/4) to unearth his hidden dialogue with Friedrich Engels, whose writings he leveraged – alongside those of Lujo Brentano – to a surprising degree as a source for his appraisal of the historical trajectory of British imperialism and society. In light of his peculiar interpretation of the British model, Weber arrives, in fact, at a possible 'solution' to the 'labour question', whose primary condition he explicitly declares to be: breaking the 'solidarity of *all* the oppressed'.[37] This is to be achieved less by the repression of the workers' movement, than by what Weber suggests is a

---

34 MWG I/4, pp. 182–3.

35 For my definition of the term, relying on Geoff Eley's considerations (Eley 1976), see section 9.6.

36 MWG I/4, p. 724.

37 MWG III/4, p. 195.

fostering of the latter's natural 'maturation'; the aforementioned development of a 'labour aristocracy' is the key here, as this segment of workers is expected to take on the role, alongside the entrepreneurial class and a modernised large landowner segment, of bearer of the nation's political stability and of its outwards (i.e., imperialist) expansion.

Considering the widespread notion in the scholarship that both this imperialist stance and its accompanying normative concept of culture are overcome by Weber, together with his illness, in 1903/4, I have added an *epilogue* that briefly discusses how these and other findings of my work can be relevant in deciphering Weber's later, 'canonical' trajectory as well.

∵

A note on the genesis and makeup of this book: This work is a significantly revised version of a PhD thesis I submitted to the Department of Political Science at the Free University of Berlin in mid-2017, first with Wolf-Dieter Narr, then with Jan Rehmann and Klaus Roth as supervisors. It began as a Marxist-inspired 'social history of ideas' in the tradition of Georg Lukács, Lucien Goldmann and, more recently, Michael Löwy, whose two early works of critical intellectual history from the 1970s – on the young Marx and young Lukács,[38] respectively – have remained models for my own portrayal of Weber's early trajectory. In fact, Löwy's description of his *The Theory of Revolution in the Young Marx* – incidentally, the first book about Marx I read as an undergraduate – closely conveys the makeup of my work:

> It is basically an attempt at a Marxist interpretation of Marx, that is, a study of his philosophical and political evolution in the historical context of social struggles in Europe during the decisive years of 1840–48, and in particular of his relationship with the experiences of the emerging working class and the early socialist labour movement.[39]

If one switches Marx for Weber in the first sentence, the decisive years to 1884–94 and the relationship's addressees to *Imperial Germany*'s emerging working-class and socialist labour movement, one has the basic argument for *Max Weber and German Social Democracy*. These (some might say antediluvian) references, which I continued to draw and learn from until the very end of

38 See Löwy 1970 and 1976.

39 Löwy 2005, p. vi.

the manuscript revision, are rooted in my contact with a gifted generation of Brazilian Marxist intellectuals (alongside Löwy, José Paulo Netto, Carlos Nelson Coutinho and many others) during my studies. Their political and scholarly education coincided with the anti-dictatorship struggles of the 1960s and 1970s and, having experienced repression followed by exile in Europe, they returned to the country in 1979 to subsequently rebuild its social sciences tradition from a critical perspective during the country's (ever unfinished, now threatened) redemocratisation. I was fortunate to have these scholars and thinkers as teachers back home and they have remained a reference point – not only in research – ever since.

My arrival in Germany in Spring 2014 and subsequent move to Switzerland in Autumn 2017 meant the exposure to other traditions of critical thought in the humanities, but also to different disciplines and fields than those I had engaged with in Brazil. The book's topic, for one, inspired an engagement with representatives of both the Marxist and the Weberian traditions in the Northern Hemisphere, many of whose representatives – see the Acknowledgements above – I had the pleasure to interact with and learn from in the last years.

I mention this dual set of dialogue partners to illustrate a key goal of this book, namely, to cater to different readers and interests, both in terms of theoretical and political orientations, but also with regards to thematic and disciplinary focus. The book is hence set up to invite different *ways of reading* – *Lesarten* is the German term – by being, on the one hand, straightforward about its own methodological grounding in a critical Marxist tradition, yet nevertheless delivering as much material and variety of perspective for the reader, so that they can come away with their own conclusions and utilise my findings for other intellectual purposes. To this end, I have made a point of quoting Weber extensively and of entering into dialogue with a wide sample of scholars who have engaged with his work in ways that were relevant to my approach and topic; moreover, a lot of the material the reader will find here has either only recently become available in German or has never been translated into English and/or the romance languages.

The production and reworking of the manuscript also coincided with my own disciplinary shift from political and social theory to history, though my aim with the book is, once more, to address those working in each of these fields with their distinctive priorities. In this sense, historians of Imperial Germany will find nothing new in Part 1, which situates the young Weber's development in the context of the crisis of German liberalism and the rise of Social Democracy; yet they will perhaps discover how Weber's work – which many historians still draw from – emerged from that contentious historical landscape. Those interested in theory, on the other hand, might profit more from my description of German society and politics in the late nineteenth century and especially from my effort to trace back the genesis of Weber's influential paradigm in the social sciences at least in part to his encounter with the 'rural labour question' (Part 2).

Part 3, in turn, is a product of many eye-opening readings from a new generation of scholars combining Marxism with postcolonial, feminist and world-system perspectives. I'll mention only Angela Zimmerman, Sara Farris and Manuela Boatcă, not only because they embody such approaches, but because of their generosity in exchanging ideas and commenting on parts of this manuscript. For all its challenges – personal and intellectual – my years of PhD and early postdoctoral research have coincided with a compressed journey of learning that has been a tremendous joy to experience. The book's three parts, written consecutively, convey precisely this pathway, which has also made me return to (and better understand) a lot of the insights my teachers in Brazil had patiently tried to convey. The epilogue to the book tries to bring all the threads of the work into a critical synthesis that also displays where my writing on Weber, and research more generally, is headed next. The story begins, however, with two letters from a twenty-year old Max Weber on the political situation of the Reich from the mid-1880s. *Boa leitura!*

PART 1

The Young Max Weber and Imperial German Politics: Between the Crisis of Liberalism and the Challenge of German Social Democracy (1884–1891/2)

CHAPTER 1

The Young Weber's Diagnosis of the Political Situation in Imperial Germany (1884–5)

Introduction

> We do not want the votes of Social Democrats; the Social Democrat, who consciously seeks no objective, is our direct adversary, even more so than the conservative. … As independent men we must place ourselves in opposition to both the government above and the menacing masses below.
>
> RUDOLF VON VIRCHOW at the German Progressive Party convention of 1878, cited in Cioli 2003

•••

> German liberalism's predicament corresponds to the early rise of Social Democracy.
>
> THOMAS NIPPERDEY 1993

∴

When Max Weber turned twenty in 1884, his correspondence started to regularly feature commentary on the political situation of Imperial Germany. There was ample material for him to work with. A decade after unification, the Reich was a cauldron of political strife, pitting various shades of conservative, catholic, liberal and socialist against one another. Major disputes involved the relationship of the state to religion – the so-called *Kulturkampf* – taxation and free-trade, social policy, migration and colonialism. This was also a time of major geopolitical tensions, which saw the Reich increasingly at odds with France and its ally to the East, Tsarist Russia. Otto von Bismarck, still the towering personality of German political life in the mid-1880s, seemed to be perpetually manoeuvring so as to balance these conflicting vectors of political and social conflict. His goal: safeguarding the conservative constitution of the German Empire – despite rapid industrialisation and modernisation – and asserting its status as a major player in the international arena.

My analysis of the young Weber's political education in this context will focus on two phenomena, namely the crisis of liberalism and the growing centrality of the 'social question' in Imperial Germany. The compound of political and social issues conjured by the feverish expansion of capitalist relations of production (mass proletarisation, urbanisation, pauperism etc.), and which also extended to the countryside, had fundamentally challenged the old liberal 'notable politics' that had helped forge unification in 1870/71. The pragmatic National Liberal Party that had once thrived as the main ally of Prussian Conservatism in the establishment of the Reich now struggled to find a new role with the splitting of this alliance in the late 1870s (over a dispute with Bismarck on trade policy) and in light of Social Democracy's mounting challenge to it from below. The period under consideration in Part 1 starts, then, with Bismarck's break with the National Liberals in 1878 and the introduction of an anti-Socialist exception law that same year; it continues through to Bismarck's pioneering state social policy initiatives in the 1880s and ends with his dismissal by the new Kaiser Wilhelm II which, added to German Social Democracy's triumph over repression and electoral success, signalled the arrival of a new political era for Imperial Germany in 1890/91.

While this was not evident at first, including to Weber, these processes, i.e., German liberalism's decline (and ensuing fragmentation) and the emergence of a mass workers' movement headed by the SPD and its affiliate free-union movement, were connected. Weber's gradual shift of focus in his correspondence from one topic to the other across the 1880s reflects a growing awareness of their interdependence and of the need for the enlightened sectors of the German bourgeoisie to provide a *coherent political response* encompassing both issues.

But before he could arrive at this new political synthesis – which he would anchor on an equally novel standpoint on social life – Max Weber needed to outgrow the strand of moderate liberalism his father, Max Weber Sr., and especially his uncle Hermann Baumgarten had helped forge in the context of unification. Its mantra had been 'Realpolitik', i.e., the 'realist' alliance of enlightened liberals with Prussian aristocracy, embodied by Bismarck and Kaiser Wilhelm I, to achieve a modern German state that not only instantly became a major player in continental politics and the world stage, but also provided a fertile arena for capitalist entrepreneurship. One condition for the alliance proved fateful: German liberals chose to abandon the democratic strands – republican and socialist – of the 1848 moment in the name of the greater goal of unification and in the expectation of a gradual (and top-down) constitutionalisation of the Empire. This not only put German liberals increasingly at odds with the emergent workers' movement, but also in a significant programmatic bind, as advances towards a liberal constitution very quickly stalled after unification as a result of conservative retrenchment. Meanwhile, socialists had become the standard bearers of a republican and democratic Germany. This conundrum deepened as the National Liberal Party was either complicit with or actively supported repression against both Catholics and socialists. A case in point, the aforementioned *Sozialistengesetz* or 'Law against the Socialists', which outlawed German Social Democracy and its affiliate unions in 1878, was approved with National Liberal support. Yet, this did not prevent Bismarck from dealing a major blow to his erstwhile allies by introducing protectionist tariffs that same year.

Part 1 of this work seeks precisely to reconstruct the young Weber's intellectual and political development set against the convoluted social backdrop of Imperial Germany between 1878 and 1890/1. My main argument is that his engaged perspective on this period and the lessons he drew from it hold the key for his subsequent outlook on 1) workers as societal subjects and political actors and 2) Social Democracy and its associated union movement as key cogs in a reformed power structure for the Reich. Beyond the formation of Weber's political thought, however, I argue that this conjuncture also helped shape his budding analytical perspective on social life – examined in detail in Parts 2 and 3. My goal, in other words, is to demonstrate how Weber's framing of the 'social question' ultimately contributed to the genesis of his social theory. While the literature has consistently combed Weber's early correspondence for clues on his later development, an approach stressing his relationship to German Social Democracy (and labour more generally) is mostly absent; the chapters that follow aim to address this gap.

1 German Liberalism after 1878: Between the 'Greek Gift' of Universal Suffrage and Anti-Socialist Repression

The young Max Weber's most cited remarks on Imperial German politics are his considerations on universal suffrage from a letter to his uncle Hermann Baumgarten dated 8 November 1884.[1] Elections to the Reichstag had taken place two weeks before and Weber comments on the disastrous results for left-liberals who, after considerable success in the previous ballot in 1881, had suffered the biggest regression amongst all parties. Were it not for the 'capriciousness of universal suffrage', which he was convinced had been 'demonstrated' in years prior, 'the future of liberalism would seem rather bleak'.[2]

1 MWG II/1, pp. 468–77. The letter was started on 8, but continued on 10 November 1884.
2 MWG II/1, p. 471.

The 'capriciousness' of the ballots likely refers to how the National Liberals' success throughout the 1870s had turned into bitter defeat in the 1881 elections, when a splinter group – the so-called 'Secession' – scored a huge victory alongside left-liberal Progressives. This had now been followed by a minor recovery by the National Liberals in the 1884 vote, accompanied by heavy losses by the newly united left-liberals. The growth of Social Democrats in 1884 had also been a significant occurrence of those elections.[3]

The 'fundamental mistake', as Weber remarked, had been the 'Greek gift of Bismarckian Caesarism', namely, 'universal suffrage … the clearest assassination of the equal status of all in the true sense of the term'.[4] The critique of formal equality in the sense of Aristotle[5] is not a surprise coming from a twenty-year-old knowledgeable about politics in Antiquity. What is revealing is Weber's awareness that the introduction of universal suffrage 'from above' by Bismarck in 1866 was an offensive measure disguised as a concession. It is not difficult to infer who the Trojans to Bismarck's Greeks are, i.e., German liberalism. With the introduction of universal suffrage, the Prussian chancellor had hoped both to fragment the opposition to his left and to constitute a broader base of support for conservatism with the votes of the masses, especially in the countryside. As far as splitting the opposition, this tactic had achieved the desired effect. But only insofar as another political actor, organised labour, had re-entered the stage in Germany and undercut not only liberals' expectation of leading the forces of progress and modernisation, but Bismarck's own projection of working-class voting tendencies.

The damaging nature of the 'Greek gift' of universal male suffrage to German liberals can indeed only be understood with reference to the 'reawakening' of working-class politics in the late 1850s in the German lands, galvanised by Lassalle's founding of the General German Workers' Association [Allgemeiner Deutscher Arbeiterverein] in 1863 and its subsequent unification with the 'Eisenach socialists' led by August Bebel and Wilhelm Liebknecht in 1875 to form the Social Democratic Workers' Party [Sozialdemokratische Arbeiterpartei Deutschlands – SAP].

If Lawrence Scaff is correct to point out that, of all the key political and intellectual trends of Max Weber's youth, 'none was more far-reaching and troublesome for turn-of-the-century politics than the complexities associated with liberalism and its travails',[6] the situation of Germany's liberals at this

3 Nipperdey 1993, p. 412.
4 MWG II/1, p. 471.
5 See *Politics* 1282b–83a.
6 Scaff 1989, p. 11.

juncture is incomprehensible without reference to the 'social question' and to working-class politics. Bismarck's move had, in this sense, only exposed his liberal opponents' ambiguous relationship to democracy and, most of all, to the so-called 'fourth estate', which dated back to the experiences of the failed revolutions of 1848–9. As Gustav Mayer put it in a classic essay on the subject:

> With the goal of breaking away the broad popular masses from the Progressive Party, Bismarck engraved his banner with the two democratic demands that the former had left out of their foundational program, i.e., universal, equal and secret suffrage rights and state aid for the unpropertied. In doing so, the great demagogue explicitly raised the claim of being the first to once again unfurl the banner of [18]48er democracy, which had been rolled up thirteen years prior.[7]

Yet, workers' ability to vote and elect their own representatives was only one element to foster what Mayer famously termed the 'separation of bourgeois and proletarian democracy' in the German lands. The 1860s and 1870s had seen the rise of workers as autonomous political actors on multiple levels: organisational, cultural, ideological and in terms of political aims. While German liberals did not trail a 'peculiar' path in their suspicion of universal suffrage – in this respect they were very much in line with nineteenth-century liberalism's general tendency to favour restrictions to the right to vote[8] – their trajectory cannot be understood without considering the nature of the challenge they faced from organised labour. There is no mistaking, however, that the possibility to elect parliamentary representatives – first in the North-German Confederation, then the Empire – gave Social Democrats a decisive platform for organising and agitating. This would prove vital especially in the years of the 'Law against the socialists' (1878–90), when taking part in Reichstag elections was, paradoxically, the only avenue of legal political action the party had left.[9]

The *Sozialistengesetz* was Bismarck's chief attempt to countervail the challenge posed by the rising labour movement to the newly established political and social order of unified Germany.[10] It made Social Democratic labour unions, associations and political organizations effectively illegal and outlawed all press and literature considered to originate from their ranks or advertise their goals. Crucially, however, it did not affect workers' right to vote in national elec-

7 Mayer 1969 [1911], p. 114.
8 See Gagel 1958; Losurdo 1993; Kahan 2003.
9 See Anderson 2000, pp. 286–94.
10 See Pöls 1960 and Tennfelde 2001, pp. 111–35.

tions, and nor did it prohibit Social Democrats from running for seats in the Reichstag. This created a peculiar situation in which arrests, deportations and the closing down of Social-Democratic newspapers and organisations ran parallel to the party's growing success at the polls.

The elections of 1884 delivered electoral growth to the SAP for the first time since the introduction of the repressive measures in 1878, with the party doubling its mandates[11] in comparison to the previous vote. This curious dynamic can perhaps clarify why a letter commenting on universal suffrage also contains Weber's first significant (known) remarks on Social Democracy. They refer precisely to the lack of effectiveness of the 'Law against the Socialists' in light of Social Democrats' electoral success. In Weber's view, there had been good reasons for implementing the repressive law:

> If one were to defend it, one would have to take the likely not all too mistaken position that, without the law, a quite significant limitation of many achievements of public life – free speech, freedom of assembly, rights of association – would be very much inevitable. Social Democrats were indeed in the process of fundamentally compromising essential institutions of public life through their form of agitation. Should one, broadly put, restrict these fundamental rights considered indispensable for public liberty or, rather, attempt to use the double-edged sword of repressive exception measures? The latter was arguably worth the try.[12]

From Marianne Weber's depiction to contemporary biographies,[13] 'young man' Weber has been tied to the liberal and bourgeois milieu he grew up in and more specifically to the moderate National Liberal circles to which his father belonged as a career politician in the party. When addressing the letter above and the political views of the young Weber, Wolfgang J. Mommsen,[14] for example, traces them back to the influence of Hermann Baumgarten and Max Weber Sr.[15] With regards to the *Sozialistengesetz*, it seems a fair assumption considering that during Max Sr.'s – ultimately unsuccessful – campaign in the aforementioned 1884 Reichstag elections, he declared himself in favour of prolonging the 'Law against the socialists'.[16]

11 Compared to 1881, the 1884 elections saw the number of Social-Democrat-held seats go from 12 to 24 and the percentage of the vote from 6.0 to 9.7% (Nipperdey 1993, p. 315).

12 MWG II/1, p. 471.

13 See Kaesler 2014; Kaube 2014.

14 Mommsen 2004, pp. 7–8.

15 Mommsen 2004, p. 4.

16 See Roth 2001 [FG], p. 422.

As is clear from the quote above, the young Weber showed reservations, but ultimately supported the repressive law; it was the 'lesser evil' in terms of safeguarding the fundamental rights of the majority, whilst still combatting Social Democrats' 'forms of agitation'. This stance was not only in line with his father's views, but more generally with those of other moderate National Liberals, such as Eduard Lasker. Addressing the merits of the law in the Reichstag session of 29 May 1878, i.e., when the first draft of the *Sozialistengesetz* was put to a vote, the veteran liberal characterised it in terms akin to the young Weber's. The objects of repression were not the aims or 'pursuits'[17] of Social Democracy, which many liberals would recognise as their own, but the methods they used:

> The fundamental mistake in the government draft is ... that it seeks to combat the aims of Social Democracy. The representative Bennigsen ... correctly retorted yesterday that *a large part of these goals will always and necessarily have to be defended by all cultivated persons in every society, so that progress is possible.* What must be rejected and repressed are the *methods* with which Social Democracy seeks to achieve its alleged goals.[18]

Despite voting against the law in that opportunity, Lasker's arguments left open the possibility for a change of position. After the National Liberals' poor performance in the elections of July 1878, called after a second attempt on the Kaiser's life, the aforementioned reservations no longer prevented Lasker or his party from voting in favour of the 'Law against the Socialists'. The law was passed in October 1878 with 221 votes from National Liberals and Conservatives against 149 from Left-Liberals, Social Democrats and the Catholic Centre.[19]

As Weber does not clarify what he meant by the Social Democrats' objectionable 'form of agitation', the similarity of his arguments to those of Lasker's make the latter's more detailed considerations on the subject of interest here. According to the prominent National Liberal, the 'methods' of social democrats should be condemned because they directed 'the entire social movement towards hatred and hostility between the classes, envy of the weak against the strong, of the poor against the wealthy'.[20] According to this perspective, Social Democrats' appeal to class struggle culminated in the revolutionary call

---

17 The full title of the exception law was, in fact, *Gesetz gegen die gemeingefährlichen Bestrebungen der Sozialdemokratie*, i.e., 'Law against the socially dangerous *pursuits* of Social Democracy', which is what Lasker alluded to in his speech.

18 Eduard Lasker cited in Cioli 2003, pp. 126–7.

19 See Wehler 1995, pp. 904–5.

20 Lasker 1910, p. 9.

to bring down the entire established order, therefore meriting a repressive response.[21] This constituted a common refrain on the part of conservatives and liberals in light of the antagonistic refractions of the 'social question' in Imperial Germany; while admitting the need to improve the situation of the working classes, they rejected Social Democracy's efforts in this regard, refusing to recognise the party's status as a legitimate political actor and representative of working people's interests.

This stance was not without consequence, something the young Weber was aware of. His likening of the repressive measures to a 'double-edged sword' indicates the belief that, by supporting the *Sozialistengesetz*, German liberalism did not come out unscathed. In another section of the 1884 letter, he seems to recognise that the policy of making concessions to Bismarck in the name of gradual progressive advances since unification had, in this case, gone too far:

> At times, it dawns on me, however, that the equality of rights for all indeed comes before all other rights, and that it would be better to put a muzzle on everyone, than to completely chain a few.[22]

Such a breach with fundamental principles had a precedent in the National Liberal's support for the political persecution of Catholics during the years of the *Kulturkampf* (see Chapter 5 below). But this had taken place in the immediate aftermath of unification, when the party still played an important role in the parliamentary majority and had key posts in government. Furthermore, such an illiberal measure could be partially justified by the greater goal of separation between Church and state and by the need to prevent papal meddling in German affairs.

Bismarck's recruitment of the National Liberals' support for the *Sozialistengesetz*, in turn, was a clear defeat for Max Weber Sr.'s party. As Hans-Ulrich Wehler stressed, the recourse to 'open class-antagonism and legally-sanctioned persecution' dispelled any semblance of a 'defensive stance' vis-à-vis Social Democracy and marked 'a deep rupture in liberal rule of law culture', culminating in a 'dangerous weakening of political liberalism'.[23] Hence, while the end of the alliance with the National Liberals is usually tied to Bismarck's decision to introduce protectionist tariffs and to his partial reconciliation with Catholics, approval of the *Sozialistengesetz* equally signalled that a new period had

21 See Pack 1961, pp. 8–11.
22 MWG II/1, p. 471.
23 Wehler 1995, p. 906.

begun in Imperial German politics as of 1878, one that coincided with a general decline of liberalism. Further parliamentarisation of the Reich, the gradual achievement of which had been the main justification for the National Liberals' compromises with Bismarckian conservatism after unification, now seemed unlikely.[24]

Repression against Social Democrats at this juncture was also, it must be stressed, a function of their recent success. The unification of the two main socialist currents at Gotha heralded the 'meteoric rise of organized labour', an event that, according to one historian, made 1875/76 – not 1878/79 – the 'epochal year' in the history of the Reich's party politics. In fact, 1875 had also marked the founding of the German Conservative Party, which broadened Bismarck's power base and coalition possibilities.[25] From this point on, finally, each step in German liberalism's decline was compounded by the growing success of Social Democracy,[26] which the *Sozialistengesetz* would fail to curb for long.

2 The 1884 Reichstag Elections and the Emerging Role of German Social Democracy

This turning point in the history of German liberalism left a deep mark in the young Weber's developing political awareness; indeed, the dilemma of how to breathe new life into a declining liberal camp would occupy him for the next several years. That a new stance regarding the 'social question' was a key stepping stone in this regard is an insight he would only arrive at later, around 1890. As of 1884/5 his concerns still reflected a National Liberal outlook, i.e., the condition of workers remained a peripheral issue at best. This did not prevent Weber from showing a surprising degree of interest in the electoral fortunes of Social Democracy. In fact, his references to the party in the letter quoted above go beyond the issue of the *Sozialistengesetz* and approach the SAP's political development in recent years. Most notable was their unprecedented willingness to pledge electoral support to National Liberal candidates in a number of run-off votes.

> The views of Social Democracy, as well as a part of its personnel, have anyway changed completely. Following an official declaration to this effect,

24 See Nipperdey 1993, p. 382 f.
25 Jansen 2001, p. 95.
26 Cioli 2003, p. 101.

did Social Democrats not vote for the National Liberals against a Centre Party candidate in Cologne? Something previously unheard of![27]

While sources on the SAP's activities in Cologne during the *Sozialistengesetz* are scarce,[28] and the Centre Party came out ahead in the 1884 elections there,[29] a similar case elsewhere suggests Weber's remarks were not only accurate, but that he had spotted an important development. In Munich, the Bavarian capital, the 1884 election marked the first time that a Social Democrat was elected thanks to *National Liberal support* – with Social Democrats' votes securing, in turn, the success of the National Liberal candidate.[30] Thanks to an electoral alliance in the run-off vote, Georg von Vollmar (SAP) and Johann Seldmayr (NLP) took both Munich districts, defeating the incumbents from the Catholic Centre Party – which won the vast majority of remaining seats in the Kingdom of Bavaria.[31]

The dominating presence of the Catholic Centre is a not insignificant motivating element of the alliance there, and this common enemy[32] most likely explains the Cologne example given by Weber as well.[33] In the Protestant and more conservative North of Germany, this would not easily be the case,

27 MWG II/1, p. 471.

28 See Nyassi and Köster 1979, pp. 152–3.

29 Though it isn't clear to which district Max Weber was referring, the Catholic Centre managed to sweep all six districts of the greater Cologne region in the Prussian Rhine Province. Nevertheless, Social Democratic support had produced notable results for National Liberals in the Cologne region, considering they went from 5.3% of the 1881 vote to 17.7% in the 1884 elections, i.e. tripling their results (See Ritter and Niehuss 1980, p. 80).

30 See Resch 2012, p. 180.

31 See Ritter and Niehuss 1980, pp. 237–8.

32 Heinrich Meister of the SAP was also elected in Hannover in 1884 through support from National Liberals. As in the cases of Cologne and Munich, where the Centre Party was hegemonic, support to a Social Democrat was likely only considered because a third anti-liberal political force played a dominant role. The common adversary in this case was the Deutsch-Hannoversche Partei – known simply as the Welfs – the bitterly anti-Prussian party of the former ruling Hanoverian nobility. A virtual tie in the first round between Meister and the Welfian candidate (37.3% vs. 37.9%) turned into a narrow victory for the Social Democrats with decisive support from National Liberals, who, according to a historian of the Hanoverian Social Democracy, 'ironically ... supported the class enemy in order to vanquish the Welfs' (Schulz 1990, p. 30).

33 Both the regions of Cologne (more than 80%) and Oberbayern (above 90%), where the two Munich districts were located, were predominantly Catholic (Cf. Ritter and Niehuss 1980, p. 80 and p. 84). The fact they also had a powerful Centre Party constituency and relative mild application of the *Sozialistengesetz*, especially after 1881 (see Brunn 1986, p. 56 and Resch 2012, p. 104f.), makes them comparable in terms of the question of alliances between National Liberals and Social Democrats.

as National Liberals, Left-Liberals and Social Democrats vied for many of the same voters in the middle and working classes. According to Eduard Bernstein's account of the situation in Berlin at the time of the 1884 elections, the 'sharply pronounced party and class antagonisms [there] left no room for political convergences'.[34]

Nevertheless, the 1884 elections provided clear indications that collaboration between National Liberals and Social Democrats could bring positive electoral results for both parties. Max Weber would, in fact, champion an alliance between moderate socialists – such as Georg von Vollmar and later Eduard Bernstein – and enlightened liberals with social sensibilities from the 1890s onwards. The 1884 letter shows the first traces of this stance in Weber's trajectory. As it matured into a political project, it would carry two caveats; first, that liberalism should be in a position to play the dominant role in such a partnership; second, that if Social Democracy was to become a legitimate party of government, it should isolate and ultimately shed its revolutionary wing (I return to this topic in Part 3).

It is no coincidence that the ambivalent status of German Social Democracy as a party of both progressive social reform and revolution first erupted in this juncture. The *Sozialistengesetz* 'had a twofold, self-contradictory effect: in terms of awareness it produced a radicalization of theory; in terms of method it steered the party towards the practical work of achieving reform through parliament'.[35] In other words, while repression confirmed, to some, the need to overthrow the political and social order of Imperial Germany to achieve working-class emancipation, the sudden centrality of parliamentary politics for the SAP – an unforeseen consequence of the exception law – and the party's electoral successes led others, most notably the Bavarian Georg von Vollmar,[36] to push for a more gradualist stance on social change and to consider an alliance with liberals. To go back to Weber's letter, this is what he (optimistically) meant by the SAP having 'changed completely'.

---

34 Bernstein 1907, p. 146.

35 Miller and Pothoff 1986, p. 37.

36 As Christian Ude surmised, Vollmar's life mirrors 'the early history of his party from its radical beginnings to its first reformist propositions' (1992, p. 61). Vollmar had started out in the radical wing of the SAP in the late 1870s, which led him to prison and finally exile in Switzerland. His return to Bavaria's relatively less repressive milieu and his election to both the Reichstag and the Sachsen Landtag in the 1880s, when he became increasingly involved with parliamentary tasks of considerable responsibility, led to a gradual change in his political stance. The end of the *Sozialistengesetz* was the defining moment for his adoption of a moderate reformism and it also signalled to him that the time was ripe for a similar change to the party's orientation as a whole.

The boost to moderate Social Democrats was also a function of the so-called period of 'milder enforcement' of the *Sozialistengesetz*,[37] whose start broadly coincided with Bismarck's first attempts to win over worker support through the introduction of social policy measures in the aftermath of the 1881 elections; the supposed reprieve lasted until the subsequent vote in 1884, when Social Democrats' success led to a renewed 'tightening' of the law. The notion of a milder period must be taken with a grain of salt, however, as enforcement of the *Sozialistengesetz* was by definition arbitrary[38] and varied immensely according to regional and local specifics. Indeed, this was the advantage of the exception law: authorities could step up or decrease repression according to the political climate. Bavaria, Cologne and Prussian Berlin – from where Weber was writing – were very different worlds.

This point raises another question. Considering that the young Weber had spent his first two years of study (spring of 1882 to summer 1884) in Heidelberg and Strasbourg, respectively, it is noteworthy that he somehow found a way to keep track of the activities of Social Democrats in Berlin. There was good reason to do so as 1883 marked the first time the SAP had seriously conducted a campaign for Berlin's municipal council of representatives, the *Stadtverordnetenversammlung*.[39] This was something of a watershed for the party[40] considering its strong results – five mandates won – came despite repression and the tiered system of voting based on property and income that underscored the Reich's municipal elections. Though the young Weber was in Alsace from 1 October 1883 on – thus missing both rounds of voting[41] – he had an insider source at hand: Max Weber Sr. was himself a Berlin city counsellor at this time. His close interaction with Social Democrats from that point on no doubt came to his son's attention, as Weber would later [1907] recall:

> It always left a deep impression on me when my father, who was most surely no admirer of Social Democracy – as Reichstag representative here

37 See Bernstein 1907, p. 111 f.

38 The arbitrariness of authorities in cases of arrest and deportation as well as in the breaking up of political meetings bordered on the absurd, as most descriptions of the period richly illustrate. For Berlin, cf. Bernstein 1907; for Cologne, see Nyassi and Köster 1979, p. 136 f.; for an example from Bavaria where the arbitrariness of the police led to the death of a Social Democrat, see Resch 2012, p. 167.

39 Bernstein 1907, p. 114.

40 Bernstein gives a detailed account of the 1883 municipal elections (1907, p. 113 f.). For a recent account, see Weipert 2013, p. 42 f.

41 First round and run-off voting took place, respectively, on 18.10.1883 and 29.12.1883, see Bernstein 1907, p. 118 f.

> in Magdeburg he had to grapple with Social Democracy and no less so as a city counsellor in the Berlin municipality – would nevertheless tell me again and again that, when it came down to it in Berlin's public works commission, his firmest support was city counsellor [and prominent SAP leader – VS] Paul Singer.[42]

These recollections and the remarks from the 1884 letter provide the first indications that, despite the class and 'milieu' divide that separated a young man brought up in the affluent municipality of Charlottenburg from the working masses in Berlin's northern districts, the gulf was not wide enough to completely insulate Weber from the broader ramifications of Social-Democratic agitation in the Reich's metropolis.

In fact, despite entire semesters spent elsewhere for his studies and the military call-ups that would send him to Alsace and the German East, Weber's vantage point stayed firmly rooted in Berlin throughout the 1880s. In terms of understanding the young law student's development, this is a significant point as the political dynamics of the Prussian capital in this decade in many ways prefigure the contours of German politics of later decades. In his 8 November 1884 letter, Weber mentions, for instance, the 'great excitement regarding the fate of the run-off vote [to the Reichstag elections – V.S.] in Berlin'. The stakes were high, as Court Chaplain Adolf Stoecker, an archconservative and anti-Semite,[43] 'unfortunately had good chances', a prospect Weber found 'very unpleasant'. This remark is followed by the correct assertion that the 'Social Democrats were becoming ever more decisive in more and more electoral districts'.[44] In the three districts[45] still up for grabs in Berlin, the run-off vote pitted Progressives against Anti-Semites; as Social Democracy had garnered a significant amount of votes in the first round, they would likely tilt the scales in the final one.

42 MWG I/8, p. 306.

43 Adolf Stoecker, Imperial Court Chaplain and founder of the 'Christian Social Workers Party', sought to bridge the divide between the Protestant religious establishment and workers through a mix of state socialism, anti-Semitism and appeals to religious and nationalist sentiments. He made a strong impact on the political scene in Berlin ever since his appointment to the Imperial court in the late 1870s (see Brakelmann et al. 1982). He would later go on to play an important role as an adversary to the young Weber's wing of the Protestant Social Congress, as Part 2 will discuss.

44 MWG II/1, p. 474.

45 A run-off vote was also necessary for the sixth district, but since the SAP's Wilhelm Hasenclever had just barely missed a first round victory, no serious challenger appeared in the second round of voting, see Bernstein 1907, pp. 148–9.

Indeed, the issue had been discussed avidly in SAP meetings and an initial policy of neutrality in the run-off ballot, proposed by Paul Singer, gradually gave way to the idea that Adolf Stoecker, who was competing in the second district against Rudolf Virchow, should not be allowed to win.[46] Anti-Semites even attempted to spoil a voter rally from Social Democrats, leading Singer – a Jew and resident of the second district, who had been slandered by Stoecker in days prior – to make 'against Stoecker!' the party's slogan in the run-off elections of 13 November.[47] Virchow won the district with 23.797 votes against Stoecker's 15.850, with Social Democrats' votes playing a decisive role in the victory.

The changing political landscape of Imperial Germany was, in this sense, not only a function of Social Democrats' growth, but included the emergence of organised factions within conservatism[48] and of new far-right groups espousing ultra-nationalist and anti-Semitic views.[49] While these developments suggested the splintered German liberal camp needed to consider possible alliances to its left, Weber reports Max Sr. did not take well to the idea: 'Social Democrats increasingly tip the balance in more and more districts; that even National Liberals must take heed of them now, is not very much to my father's joy'.[50]

The young Weber, in turn, did not seem to dread the enlarged role of Social Democrats in electoral politics as of 1883–84. If he already seemed open to an alliance of liberals and socialists, a deeper break with the positions of his father and uncle had, however, not yet transpired.

3 The Crisis of the Liberal Parties and the 'Right-Wing Turn' of National Liberals in 1884

Not all twenty-year old university students were as attuned to politics as the young Weber, a fact he pointed out himself in a long letter to Hermann Baumgarten from 14 July 1885.

---

46 See Bernstein 1907, pp. 149–50.

47 Bernstein 1907, p. 150.

48 See Nipperdey 1993, p. 333 f.

49 For an overview of the rise of the radical right in the Kaiserreich, see McGowan 2014, pp. 16–42; for an account of early political Anti-Semitism in Berlin and Stoecker's role, see Pulzer 1988, pp. 83–97.

50 MWG II/1, p. 474. Weber makes reference to the situation in Kassel, remarking that National Liberals had recommended abstention between Conservatives and Social Democrats in the run-off vote there. It is perhaps the only case in which the young Weber was either mis-

> To my odd contemporaries the relationship to these things [i.e., to politics – VS] is limited either to dabbling in some Anti-Semitism – which is also practiced out of 'politeness' by those who would otherwise not care about anything at all but cards and billiards; or, and this is the higher stage, they venture to *call* themselves 'Bismarckians *sans-phrase*' ...[51]

Weber was also bothered by his fellow students 'phenomenal ignorance of the history of this century'; to them, he remarked, 'domestic politics exists only after 1878'.[52] This meant that they downplayed or ignored the internal political struggles that characterised the period between 1866 and the mid-1870s, likely overlooking the National Liberals' contribution to the processes of German unification and creation of the Reich. Bismarck now eclipsed his erstwhile liberal allies and was the sole recipient of a cult-like awe by Weber's peers.[53] As Lawrence Scaff has indicated, Weber would continue to refer to 1878 as a turning point for German history into his later writings.[54] A part of recent historiography has converged with the young Weber on this point by stressing the achievements that resulted from the willingness of a section of German liberalism to enter into a compromise with Bismarck in the 1860s,[55] even if this alliance proved short-lived.[56] In the 1885 letter, however, the young Weber was more preoccupied with what lay ahead for German liberalism and, especially, for the National Liberal Party. Since Bismarck had unilaterally dissolved the compromise that had defined the organisation, the question was what alternative role would enable them to come back to prominence, something that still was not clear by the mid-1880s.

> Even Mr. von Bennigsen seems, in many ways, to no longer maintain that earlier firm standpoint in his views. If the party will ever again win the confidence of the people is very questionable. Folks' memories are short and no one knows anymore what the party once achieved.[57]

---

informed or behind the pace of events. While Left-Liberals supported the SAP, National Liberals ended up endorsing the conservative candidate with decisive consequences, as the vote was won by the latter by a mere 94-vote difference. (See Frenz and Schmidt 1989, pp. 37–8).

51 MWG II/1, p. 527.

52 MWG II/1, p. 528.

53 MWG II/1, p. 527.

54 Scaff 1989, p. 15f.

55 See Langewiesche 2001, pp. 73–90.

56 I examine the more problematic parts of this legacy and how Weber confronted it in Chapter 2 below.

57 MWG II/1, p. 525.

Weber's disappointment with Rudolf von Bennigsen, a leading moderate amongst National Liberals, was probably due to the latter's inability to countervail the process of fragmentation that not only his party, but German liberalism overall had been experiencing ever since Bismarck's aforementioned policy reorientation in the late-1870s. A decade after German liberals had split on the matter of supporting Prussian-led national unification, the issue of tariffs on foreign goods had produced further division.[58] Bennigsen had thus been charged in the early 1880s with creating common ground within a liberal camp polarised, on one side, by free-marketers that flatly rejected the protectionist measures – i.e., most Progressives and the 1880 'left' splinter of the National Liberals (the 'Secession') – and a conservative wing that, rallying behind Bismarck, accepted the tariffs and had been in favour of the *Sozialistengesetz* from the start.[59] In terms of Bismarck's newly proposed state social policy measures, the problem was the almost uniform suspicion – if not outright rejection – it met with from the entire spectrum of German liberalism:

> Both left-wing and right-wing National Liberals … turned against social reform, considering it limited free enterprise and its 'natural' balancing mechanisms (by subjecting them to bureaucratic regulations) and interfered with social hierarchies.[60]

With Conservatives pledging their support to state social policy and given Social Democrats' radical critique of the ills of class society, liberals risked being side-lined completely in the debate on the 'social question'. Bennigsen's attempt to find a middle ground regarding these dilemmas culminated in his *Berliner Erklärung* [Berlin Declaration] of 29 May 1881,[61] which recognised that dissonant views on protective tariffs existed, but argued they should not lead to splits. It also conceded that some measure of governmental intervention on the 'social question' would be acceptable. In other words, it opened the door to liberal backing of Bismarck on both issues, without fully committing to any one stance.

---

58 As Rita Aldenhoff-Hübinger has pointed out, one of Bismarck's goals with the introduction of the tariffs was precisely to split the National Liberals in order to weaken liberal opposition (2002, p. 117).

59 There had also been an earlier split to the right of National Liberals. In 1879, 15 parliamentarians – the most notable of which was historian Heinrich von Treitschke – left the party. This emerging conservative wing of German liberalism was however internally diverse, as support for protective tariffs and repression of Social Democrats was not always identical with acceptance of state social policy and vice-versa; see Kieseritzky 2002, p. 187.

60 Nipperdey 1993, p. 322 – also in this direction, see Cioli 2003, p. 37.

61 See Kieseritzky, 2002, p. 184f.

It is not a coincidence that the *Erklärung* was made public during the parliamentary debates on Bismarck's first proposal of accident insurance for workers. Bennigsen wanted to associate the National Liberals with the proposed social policy measures, but he shared the disquiet of the entire liberal camp regarding Bismarck's strong interventionist turn, which to many was tantamount to 'state socialism'. In fact, debates on the law saw liberals and conservatives clash over the role that private actors were to play in the institutions of social protection (if any) and, crucially, over who would shoulder the payment of insurance premiums (the state, employers and/or workers).[62] The lack of consensus on these matters led Bismarck to dissolve the Reichstag at the end of June 1881 and to call for fresh elections.[63]

The vote, which took place on 27 October of that same year, was quite plainly a referendum on the new government policies, especially on the proposed social insurance measures. If the 1878 elections had been marked by the effects of the assassination attempts on the Kaiser and the introduction of the *Sozialistengesetz*, Bismarck saw the 1881 elections as a barometer on how the working class – and not the 'eloquent and ambitious journalist-types' who desired to lead it – actually felt about the measures he had brought forth to the Reichstag for approval. 'With the next elections we will have the first evidence of whether the worker … has developed a stance on this', said Bismarck in an April 1881 speech.[64]

The 1881 elections led to a bitter defeat of National Liberals, who lost more than half of their mandates[65] as did the Free Conservatives, i.e. the two key parties of Bismarck's former parliamentary majority. Bismarck and his allies had clearly failed to build ample support for the change of course since 1878, a setback that benefited left-liberal parties greatly in the elections. The spectacular results for the opposition are also attributable to the fact that Bismarck's policy shift – specifically the introduction of protective tariffs for heavy industry and agriculture and the rejection of direct taxation in favour of continued taxation on consumption – benefited newly-organised interest groups within the ruling classes, urban and rural, but offered no benefit to the middle-class and workers. Conversely, the social policy measures meant to show the government's engagement with the 'social question' (and expose left-liberals lack of commitment on the issue) had not yet had the desired effect. To their

62 For an insightful overview of the genesis and makeup of the first round of social legislation introduced in Imperial Germany in the 1870s and 1880s, as well as the various actors involved, see Kott 2014, pp. 23–51.

63 See Loth 1996, pp. 68–9 and Kieseritzky, 2002, p. 219.

64 Bismarck 1981 [1881], p. 211.

65 See Bendikat, 1988, p. 25 f.

credit, left-liberals had not rejected the accident insurance bill, but proposed a revised version (with more participation of the private sector and local administration), which Bismarck's supporters voted down.

Ultimately, the dissolution of the Reichstag following the standoff on the law only served to underline Bismarck's disregard for decisions reached by parliamentary majority. Taken together, these factors were all to the benefit of left-liberalism's stance against protectionism, excessive taxation of the urban classes and defence of parliamentary prerogatives. The fact that the elections took place in the most repressive phase of the enforcement of the *Sozialistengesetz*, in turn, meant that left-liberals did not need to worry about competition from Social Democrats. According to Eduard Bernstein, they fully took advantage of the situation, presenting themselves as 'defenders of the people in the face of Bismarck's monopoly projects and other reactionary measures'.[66] National Liberals, on the other hand, having suffered splits to their right and left in the run-up to the elections and still wavering in their views, took the greatest losses.

The defeat led to a renewed search for popular support on Bismarck's part, symbolised by the two presiding themes of the 1881–4 period, social policy and the defence of colonial expansion.[67] The period also marked key shifts within the National Liberal Party. These were epitomised by the 'Heidelberg declaration' of 29 March 1884, drafted by Johannes von Miquel. It signalled a shift from Bennigsen's policy of compromise and a decided move to the right in the form of an endorsement of Bismarck's arguments for colonialism as well as his stances on social and economic policies.[68] Thus, the realignments within German liberalism after 1878 had not led to a united liberal camp in opposition to Bismarck, as some had hoped, but rather to further polarisation as the free-market enthusiasts which made up the 'Secession' fused with the orthodox Progressives, while the National Liberal Party – freed from most of its more orthodox liberal members – took a decided step towards conservatism.

These developments provide the backdrop to the young Weber's pessimistic evaluation of the prospects of German liberalism, as we learn from his letters of November 1884 and July 1885 to Hermann Baumgarten. Indeed, they impacted the Weber household directly, as Max Sr., a National Liberal 'centrist' who had remained with the party in spite of all the previous splits, now ended up isolated, very much against his will, on its 'left'[69] (likely because he

66 Bernstein 1907, p. 71.
67 Bendikat 1988, p. 26.
68 See Cioli 2003, p. 105 and Bendikat 1988, p. 31f.
69 MWG II/1, p. 524.

opposed an unconditional rapprochement with Bismarck). This was a move the young Weber also dreaded, considering no liberalising measures were in sight as compensation, and he feared a further 'right-wing slide' by his father's party.[70]

Having learned the lesson that questions of taxation and tariffs strained the party internally and made it unpopular with public opinion, the National Liberals had, nevertheless, finally put social policy at the forefront of their parliamentary activity. No concrete proposals came from the party on the issue, but their supportive stance was enough to associate them with Bismarck and distinguish them from left-liberals, who remained highly critical of the measures.[71]

In the 1885 letter, Weber notes how this shift to the right by National Liberals had also led to a growing incorporation of anti-Semitic elements into the party and that if and when there was a change of course in politics, 'the Progressives would be the only ones left to lead it, and their capacity for constructive political action continuously diminishes'.[72] The two wings of German liberalism now increasingly embodied the opposing yet complementary political stances Weber would criticise throughout his life: an opportunism devoid of values that conforms to whichever trend is strong at a particular time – epitomised, in this case, by the National Liberals' incorporation of anti-Semitic discourse and submission to Bismarck – and the dogmatic purism of holding on to certain values or positions regardless of circumstances or broader political aims – which Progressives embodied in the 1880s.

The young Weber sought, instead, to assess the situation of German liberalism beyond a factional perspective – i.e., unlike his father. In effect, he felt Max Sr. underestimates the 'ominous significance' of left-liberals' defeat in the 1884 elections.[73] Their loss was nothing to be celebrated if it meant National Liberals would more than ever be at the mercy of Conservatives and increasingly distant from their erstwhile liberal principles: 'For, what happens to the role of counterweight to the right-wing, on account of which the middle party would once again be able to take up a decisive position?'[74]

Though rejecting left-liberal orthodoxy, it is important to highlight that the young Weber did show adherence to 'free-market' principles in this juncture, including when it came to elementary worker welfare measures. In this sense, he commended Bismarck's rejection of a motion to prohibit work on Sundays

70 MWG II/1, p. 474.
71 Bendikat 1988, p. 43.
72 MWG II/1, p. 525.
73 MWG II/1, p. 475.
74 Ibid.

in the so-called 'Sunday rest' speech of January 1885.[75] This is no surprise, considering Bismarck's stance on the matter is mostly a throwback to the years when he worked closely with National Liberals. As a benchmark for the views on labour in the Weber household in the mid-1880s, the speech is worth a closer look.

Bismarck starts it by stressing that the recent measures of governmental intervention in the market – i.e., the introduction of taxes to protect German agriculture – did not make governmental regulation of labour relations any more legitimate. If the tariffs' immediate goal was to protect the workers in the agricultural sector from foreign competition, they equally had had the economic goal of strengthening the consumer base for industry.[76] German industry, however, needed to export its commodities to survive, which meant that limiting the workday or prohibiting Sunday work would put it at a competitive disadvantage. This would be detrimental not only to the nation, but to the workers themselves, Bismarck argued, as they would face unemployment and lower wages if the government forced employers to reduce their working hours.[77]

In typical demagogic form, Bismarck repeatedly argues that if the reduction of the workday did not bring all these economic disadvantages, his concern for the welfare of workers would have already led him to outlaw Sunday work. This patriarchal tone, present whenever Bismarck referred to workers' toils, must surely have appealed to liberal sensibilities, as did his remark that there could be no Chinese Wall around Imperial Germany, meaning it could never hope to become economically self-sufficient.[78] This corresponded with National Liberal views at the time, whose commitment to social policy had taken a step forward since the early days of liberalism in the German lands, but had neither deep roots nor a clear expression in terms of political programme:

> In the 1870s, liberals attempted, in contrast to their predecessors in the *Vormärz* period [i.e., the run-up to the 1848 revolutions – VS], to provide an adequate solution to the social question, though this did not lead to open parliamentary engagement on this front. The consideration of the social question, to the extent that it affected the political dimension of liberalism, remained above all limited to the theoretical realm.[79]

75 MWG II/1, p. 526.
76 Bismarck 1895, pp. 227–8.
77 Bismarck 1895, p. 230.
78 Bismarck 1895, pp. 230–1.
79 Cioli 2003, p. 37.

The young Weber would eventually overcome this 'purely theoretical' stance on the 'social question', a shift already palpable in his period of legal clerkship in Berlin starting in 1887.[80] This meant breaking with the liberal political culture he grew up immersed in, and especially reassessing National Liberal legacy. Weber's uncle, Hermann Baumgarten, had, in fact, been a key player in the genesis of this strand of liberalism in Germany. The young Weber's close relationship and lively intellectual dialogue with the old liberal provides, in this sense, a key window into his political education and relationship to the bourgeois 'milieu' in which he grew up. Weber's subsequent engagement with the 'social question' and workers' standpoint in the 1890s (see Part 2) gains starker contours when set against this particular point of departure, as I will approach below.

80 See Chapter 4.

CHAPTER 2

Hermann Baumgarten and the Young Max Weber: The Ambiguous Legacy of National Liberalism

1 A Direct Conduit to the Dilemmas of the German Liberal Bourgeoisie

No description of Max Weber's intellectual development during his student years can overlook the central role played by his uncle Hermann Baumgarten (1825–93). While Max Sr. was a lifelong professional politician of middling stature who left no significant writings and, thus, no clear record of his worldview, Hermann Baumgarten was a scholar and publicist, whose biography is acutely representative of the post-1848 trajectory of his class, the enlightened bourgeoisie or *Bildgungsbürgertum*, and in particular of the fate of National Liberalism, a political current he helped found. If the younger Max Weber was, as Jürgen Kaube has framed it, 'born into the intellectual conflicts of the German bourgeoisie',[1] he found in his uncle one of its historical spokespersons.

This chapter aims precisely to situate Baumgarten's dialogue with the young Weber against the backdrop of intellectual and political-strategic debates from the mid-1860s to the mid-1880s, i.e., from when the 'national question' loomed to when the 'social question' emerged as a key issue in the German lands. Baumgarten's decisive influence on the young Weber is a matter of consensus in the scholarship; what is at times overlooked and what I aim to emphasise, instead, is just how ambiguous the liberal legacy Baumgarten sought to entrust his nephew with had become by the 1880s.

For, if Baumgarten no doubt helped the young Weber 'free himself from the one-sided National Liberal point of view of his parents' home',[2] the old liberal had been one of the chief architects of the policy of bourgeois compromise with Prussian aristocracy that enabled the 'lesser-German' or *kleindeutsch* pathway to national unification in the first place (i.e., from 'above' and in exclusion of Austria). In similar fashion, if it is safe to assume Baumgarten 'opened [the young Weber's – V.S.] eyes to the internal weakness of the Bismarckian

1 Kaube 2014, p. 61.

2 Mommsen 2004, p. 7.

system',[3] he presented no viable alternative to his nephew's generation that might lead out of the deep crisis German liberalism faced in the 1880s – which explains his own political isolation.

This nuanced relationship must be emphasised if Baumgarten's place in Max Weber's development is to be gauged correctly. He was, in this sense, less a clear-cut role model and more a personification of the political dilemmas Weber's generation of liberals had to solve. A balanced account of the twists and turns of the old liberal's own trajectory is the first step to reconstruct this ambiguous role. Portraying Baumgarten from the standpoint of the time he interacted with the young Weber in the mid-1880s, i.e., when he had converted himself into a sharp critic of Bismarck, tends to overshadow the fact that he had, twenty years earlier, been the main ideologue of liberalism's turn to Bismarck and Prussia in the name of the greater goal of unification. Baumgarten's pamphlet *German Liberalism: a Self-critique* from 1866 was, as Guenther Roth put it, a type of 'foundational manifesto of the National Liberal Party'. And though by the time the young Weber was in Strasbourg for his military service (1883–4) his uncle was involved in a bitter debate with conservative historian Heinrich von Treitschke, the latter had published Baumgarten's pamphlet in his *Preußische Jahrbücher*, at a time when the two men were still friends and close collaborators.[4] Indeed, in about a decade and a half, Baumgarten had gone from regarding himself and Treitschke as two 'Prussian outposts in Baden' who 'shared a common disdain for South German mentality'[5] to a Bismarck detractor and advocate of objectivity in historical scholarship.[6]

This is not to say that Baumgarten was inconsistent in his trajectory; much had changed in German political life in the twenty years since he had penned his political manifesto; Bismarck's break with the National Liberals in 1878 was just one realignment amidst several seismic shifts that liberals seemed especially unable to adapt to and navigate as Imperial Germany's political arena was reconfigured not even two decades into its existence. These new circumstances no doubt helped create the divide between the worldviews of uncle and nephew. It is Max Weber's response to this new setting, however, both in terms of novel theoretical production and a revised political programme for German liberalism, that would give lasting status to his contribution long after its genesis in the 1890s and early 1900s.

3 Ibid.
4 FG, p. 283.
5 Ibid.
6 See Biefang 1996, pp. 399–405.

What phenomena characterised the changed political landscape of the mid-1880s and why did it pose a particular challenge to German liberals? For starters, the party-form of both its Progressive and National Liberal wings, i.e., one based on the rule of bourgeois-patrician notables, was fast becoming outdated.[7] As Jonathan Sperber has stressed, '[h]istorians have tended to view the 1890s as the dividing line, when a political system characterized primarily by notables' politics gave way to one dominated by mass politics'.[8] The SPD was at the forefront of this transformation, though repression under the *Sozialistengesetz* delayed its progress until the 1890s. Mass politics was, nevertheless, eventually 'taken up by the other parties, starting with the Catholic party, the Centre, then the conservatives and, finally and *most reluctantly*, by the liberal parties'.[9]

This delay was a function of German liberals deep-seated elitism and top-down understanding of politics. Faced with the dilemma of 'being, on the one side, reliant on the people', but, on the other, 'rejecting it as irrational and corruptible', liberals did not move to 'strengthen their party organization and, therefore, their propaganda-work' returning, instead, to 'their old conceptions', i.e. to the imperative of 'subjugating the mobilizing masses'.[10] According to Frank Möller, this had been 'conditioned by the events of the 1860s',[11] i.e., by the political dynamics of the process of German unification.

Hermann Baumgarten embodied a direct link vis-à-vis his nephew Max Weber to the liberal contribution to this epochal shift. The next sections will examine why this legacy had become a riddle for the young Weber to solve.

2 *German Liberalism, a Self-Critique*: National Liberalism's Foundational Manifesto of 1866

According to Thomas Nipperdey, Hermann Baumgarten belonged to the right wing of Prussian liberalism which, in broad terms, meant he favoured 'revolution from above instead of below' and 'unity before freedom'.[12] As Baumgarten argued in his *German Liberalism: a Self-Critique* of 1866, in order to achieve the supreme goal of national unity, the first hurdle to overcome was the ideolo-

7 See Eley 1980, pp. 19–40 and Cioli 2003, pp. 103–5.
8 Sperber 1997, p. 19.
9 Ibid. – my highlights.
10 Möller 1996, p. 11.
11 Ibid.
12 Nipperdey 1993, p. 314.

gical rigidity and 'particularism' – or 'small-state' mentality – rampant within German liberalism's own ranks. This meant accepting the leadership of Prussia – and the consequent exclusion of Austria – in the process of unification, as well as the leadership of the Prussian *nobility* in the entire process. Many more conservative liberals shared this point of view at the time, but it was Hermann Baumgarten who most coherently articulated this particular alternative to the question of unification; in other words, he was the one to provide a set of historical and theoretical justifications that suggested the 'inevitability' of the 'lesser-German' pathway to unification and, consequently, the pointlessness of alternative courses. That not only meant leaving Austria out, but also denying the possibility of unification on a republican basis, i.e., against the dynasties altogether.

To make this argument, Baumgarten's pamphlet retraced German politics from the time of the Reformation focusing on the question of the bourgeoisie's political role and its relationship to the aristocracy and ruling dynasties. He claimed to have found not only a set of patterns which explained Germany's failure to rise to a great European power until that point, but also the roots of its constant upheavals and unrest. The first determining factor was a mode of political engagement overly hampered by 'moral concerns' and characterised by 'diligent proficiency in small matters ... but narrow-minded idleness when grand things are at stake'.[13] Though Baumgarten traced this stance all the way back to the 'Lutheran princes', it was the German bourgeoisie that had recurrently embodied it ever since.

Baumgarten believed this paralysing dichotomy had been overcome at a few key historical junctures, either due to external threat and/or by the action of a few 'isolated men' who were granted the 'God-given strength' to rise above such limitations; these men almost always 'belonged to the same state', i.e., Prussia.[14] The 'wars of liberation' against Napoleon had been a prime example;[15] the initial defeat and ensuing French occupation had, in Baumgarten's words, been a 'flogging which we direly needed and our people were taught through an iron fist that aesthetic accomplishment and philosophical knowledge did not make up the sum of man's tasks'.[16] The eventual uprising against the French occupiers is one of the few instances in his narrative of three centuries of German history where the German working masses play any sort of role. But it

13 Baumgarten 1974 [1866], p. 26.

14 Baumgarten 1974 [1866], p. 27.

15 On the importance of the wars of liberation as a historical analogy to this generation of pragmatic liberals, see Becker 2001, pp. 306–21 and Möller 2003, pp. 84–9.

16 Baumgarten 1974 [1866], p. 32.

is not the only one where workers, along with liberals, are said to have been taught a lesson. It is not a coincidence that, according to Baumgarten, the 'wars of liberation' signal a moment when not only regional differences but also *all class antagonisms* were subsumed under a national banner, leading 'the glory of Germany ... to rise again'.[17] With 'national liberation' equated to narrow anti-French resentment and deprived of any emancipatory content whatsoever, this brand of nationalism easily slid into chauvinism, as Georg Lukács pointed out.[18] In fact, the absolute primacy of the achievement of national unity in Baumgarten's narrative meant that it was severed from any programme of social change and/or democratic reform. As Frank Möller has more recently stressed, for Baumgarten's generation, the 'liberation war symbolized only the struggle for the "nation's unity"; the opposition to the Monarchs was no longer emphasized'.[19]

Baumgarten's portrayal of the 'Constitutional Conflict', that is, the struggle between Monarch and parliament over control of the budget in early-1860s Prussia that culminated in Bismarck's rise to power, is exemplary of this stance. He framed it as 'the first great political struggle undertaken on German soil, without the aid of a revolution'.[20] The German Progressive Party's (henceforth DFP) refusal to bow to the interests of the Prussian crown on the question of military financing is brushed aside by Baumgarten as immaturity. Bismarck is portrayed as the moderate party willing to make compromises, but dealing with an inflexible DFP – the main liberal organisation at the time – that was intent on forcing the government to break with the constitution.[21] The rejection of any compromise was, according to Baumgarten, typical of German liberals.[22] And though the DFP's refusal to approve the budget was anchored on the fair principle of the rule of the majority – which it held in the Prussian parliament – Baumgarten argued that in politics such principles were only the starting point of a struggle, not its end, and agitation could only go so far.[23]

At bottom, Baumgarten argued liberals lacked the 'political strength' to realise their 'grandiose objectives' in 1862; symptomatically, however, Baumgarten criticised the German Progressives for threatening to overstep the boundaries of the law,[24] but seemed to have had no problems when Prussian authorities

17 Baumgarten 1974 [1866], p. 34.
18 Lukács 1954, p. 37.
19 Möller 2003, pp. 87–8.
20 Baumgarten 1974 [1866], p. 112.
21 Baumgarten 1974 [1866], p. 110.
22 Baumgarten 1974 [1866], pp. 110–11.
23 Baumgarten 1974 [1866], p. 113.
24 Baumgarten 1974 [1866], p. 114.

actually did so, as in 1849, to end the conflict. Baumgarten's message was clear, i.e., imposing one's political will was acceptable, as long as this did not involve mobilising support from below (i.e., from the masses). In fact, the labour movement is an entirely missing actor in the narrative of German history laid out in *Der deutsche Liberalismus: eine Selbstkritik*.

It is easy to argue, as Baumgarten did, that one's view of the role of revolutionary change in history was not essential in the absence of such a possibility ('A people that becomes richer by the day, doesn't make revolutions'),[25] yet what he seemed to effectively be suggesting was that revolution was not possible in the German context at all. According to Baumgarten, liberal deputies put democracy in discredit when they threatened ultimate measures, but did not follow up on them,[26] and it begs the question if it would have been better served by acquiescence to Prussian arbitrariness.

The historical significance of this line of argumentation consists in the fact that it laid the ideological foundations for a segment of German liberalism to accept a compromise with Bismarck and the Prussian crown in the name of national unification. Notably, Max Weber would never look back at the ensuing split within the liberal camp as a mistake, nor dispute the notion that the chosen pathway to unification was the only one available (a point I will return to later in this work).[27] In fact, he would continue to regard the period that culminated in the formation of the Reich as one of glory for its liberal protagonists, in spite of his later criticism of Bismarckian politics and of the pernicious role of Prussian aristocracy in Imperial Germany. The young Weber's repeated assertion that his was a generation of political 'epigones'[28] refers precisely to the events that led to unification and the founding of Imperial Germany, not – as the commentary to the English translation of his political writings suggests – to the 'Age of Goethe'.[29]

Yet, even if Max Weber converged with his uncle on the appraisal of liberalism's role in the unification process, this does not mean he reproduced the *understanding* of history and the conceptual framework that underscored Baumgarten's 1866 pamphlet. A good example for Weber's *selective* appropriation of the ideas of the previous generation of German liberals pertains to

25 Baumgarten 1974 [1866], p. 115.
26 Baumgarten 1974 [1866], p. 116.
27 See section 9.6.
28 For instance, in Weber's 1893 lecture to the *Verein für Socialpolitik* (MWG I/4, p. 195), but most famously in his Freiburg inaugural lecture of May 1895, see MWG I/4, p. 569. On Weber's use of this peculiar term and its roots in his reception of Nietzsche, see Majul 2018.
29 See Weber 1994, p. 24.

the notion of politics as *Beruf*, i.e., as a profession *or* vocation. While mostly associated with Weber's work, it already figured in Baumgarten's 1866 pamphlet: 'Politics are a profession [*Beruf*] like jurisprudence and medicine, and indeed the most elevated and difficult profession that a man can devote himself to'.[30] This passage of *German Liberalism: a Self-critique* is quoted often in Weber scholarship,[31] especially as evidence of Baumgarten's direct influence on his nephew's own conceptualisation of political practice. There are, however, telling differences between them.

For starters, Baumgarten's concept of politics as 'vocation' – or *profession*, the more adequate translation to his use of the term – is conceptualised in class terms. In other words, he attributes each social class with a specific vocation with regards to political life (or they might lack it altogether). He argued, for instance, that '[i]n all monarchical states, the nobility is the true political class [*Stand*]'. 'The burgher', conversely, 'is fit to work, not for rulership, yet the essential task of the statesman is to rule'.[32] According to Baumgarten, the dutifulness of the self-made bourgeois allowed him to play a role in local politics, where practical matters such as building a sewage system or paving a road were the main tasks at hand. The diligence required by the bourgeois individual's search for economic success, on the other hand, prevents the acquisition of the vital skills of the ruler, skills which the nobility cultivates from an early age, i.e., in the sense that they are groomed for power, or receive the necessary training for it. This is a far cry from Weber's later understanding of *Beruf* as calling or vocation, that is, as an ethical devotion to political life that is tempered by a sense of responsibility.

Weber conceptualised the traits that constitute a political 'calling' in terms of the individual personality, i.e., they were *in principle* accessible to all men (and women?) of politics regardless of class or ideology. The caveat that only some individuals were able to successfully negotiate the tension between politics' ultimate ethical mandates – conviction and responsibility – which suggests an aristocratic or elitist component in Weber's conceptualisation, does not bring it any closer to his uncle's somewhat mechanical attribution of political vocation according to class. For Baumgarten derived the aptitude for politics *directly* from sociological determinants; the bourgeois, for instance, due to his socialisation through work, was a 'democrat at heart'. This put him, therefore, at a disadvantage in the task of ruling over other men and in the power struggles that characterise the higher spheres of politics.

30 Baumgarten 1974 [1866], p. 45.

31 For instance (Kaesler 2014, pp. 236–37 and 239; FG, pp. 286–87).

32 Baumgarten 1974 [1866], pp. 42–3.

Hermann Baumgarten's concept of *Beruf* has, in this sense, less to do with the ideal drivers of action, as in Weber's later conceptualisation, and more with a rigid understanding of social stratification, according to which each class plays a complementary role in an organic whole. In Baumgarten's normative conception of social hierarchy, the aristocracy and the monarchy are, in fact, permanent fixtures and have a specific set of qualities. This leads him to make puzzling generalisations. For instance, that in those countries where the nobility had not been the political protagonist, little had been achieved in terms of 'orderly political freedom'. The neighbouring Dutch and Swiss cases, not to speak of France, are somehow absent from the frame. Baumgarten's attempt to substantiate his claim is indicative, rather, of a highly deterministic and teleological conception of history:

> The unchangeable nature of circumstances is the cause of this phenomenon, which arises in the same form everywhere, i.e., that monarchical states have the choice either to achieve a moderate constitution through the aid of the nobility or to remain under the rule of a bureaucratic, more or less absolutist government.[33]

In other words, Baumgarten foreshadowed the notion of a German 'peculiar path' into modernity, though he made it a historical archetype, not a deviation. Germany's post-1848 political and social makeup (the preponderance of the aristocracy despite the take-off of capitalist development, a politically subdued bourgeoisie etc.) had, in Baumgarten's framework, a *universally valid character*, verifiable throughout continental Europe and even in Britain. The only German anomaly was the lack of a unified state.

The effort to understand Baumgarten's influence on Max Weber must, therefore, go beyond deceiving resemblances and inquire, rather, what historical factors contributed to their dissonant worldviews. More interesting than pointing out similarities is the fact that Weber would make his mark as a social thinker precisely due to those aspects of his perspective that most clearly diverged from his uncle's. This is true for Weber's ethics-centred understanding of political vocation, but also for his critique of positivistic and organicist conceptualisations of social reality, like Baumgarten's. In fact, if Weber appropriated certain elements from his uncle's writings, he did so by setting his ideas and concepts on an entirely new (epistemological, analytical but also political) basis, fit to respond to the challenges of the new situation the Ger-

33 Baumgarten 1974 [1866], p. 42.

man bourgeoisie faced from the 1880s onwards, not least the rise of a well-organised socialist labour movement. Baumgarten's considerations on *Realpolitik* – another oft-cited element of the latter's influence on Max Weber – throws this generational shift into sharp relief.

3 'Realpolitik' and Positivism

In Frank Möller's generational depiction of 1848 liberals,[34] Hermann Baumgarten (1825–93) would have belonged to the youngest cohort. One of his role models, Georg Gottfried Gervinus, belonged, in turn, to those 'moderate liberals' born around 1800 to whom the rhetoric of 'realist' or 'practical' action was already a hallmark.[35] In the context of the revolution, as Möller puts it, this meant diverging both from the 'freedom *pathos*' of the St. Paul's Church left and from the firmer principles of the older, more orthodox, liberals. For the 'realist' wing of 1848 liberals, just as for Baumgarten later on, this meant 'success in the question of national unification was placed above one's own constitutional program'. Hence, given Prussia's 'position of power', it was only logical for this camp to eventually extend it a '"vocation" [*Beruf*] for leadership in Germany', not least in forging national unity.[36]

A full commitment to 'political realism' or *Realpolitik* had, nevertheless, not yet transpired in Gervinus' generation (assuming here that unification under Prussian leadership was the 'realist' course to take).[37] The bond to liberal traditions of the *Vormärz* period was too strong, the belief they represented public opinion and possessed a moral duty to it too deep to allow for a compromise with Prussian aristocracy, the sworn enemies of freedom and constitutional government, even for the greater goal of national unification.[38] That would change in the mid-1860s and it fell precisely upon Hermann Baumgarten to play the role of ideological standard-bearer of German liberalism's definitive turn to 'realist' politics. His basic argument is summarised in the following passage of his 1866 pamphlet:

---

34 Möller 2003, pp. 71–91.

35 See Hübinger 1984, pp. 131–3.

36 Möller 2003, p. 76.

37 On Gervinus's subsequent rejection, in the early 1850s, of the notion that bourgeois subservience to the Prussian monarchy was the only 'realist' position available (and the serious personal and political consequences that he faced for defending a democratic notion of progress), see Hübinger 1984, pp. 198–203.

38 Möller 2003, pp. 73–7.

> *Liberalism must become fit to rule.* Whomever sees it as a shrinking of liberal greatness to accomplish little while in government, instead of placing infinite demands while in the opposition, I obviously cannot help.[39]

This is a statement that could have come from Max Weber, a lifelong critic of fidelity to absolute principles at the expense of any consideration of circumstances or consequences. Yet, in the concrete case of the process of German unification, the weighing of the possible, the viable and the worthwhile is still a hotly contested issue in historiography.[40] This is reflected in the divergent reception of *German Liberalism: a Self-Critique*. On the one hand, when contrasted to the fruits of National Liberals' pragmatism – which opened the door to their contribution to the process of unification and the constitution of the German Reich –, the limited impact of the German Progressive Party's more principal-centred politics seems to vindicate the path defended by Baumgarten in 1866. As one historian has stressed, the 'victory of the non-liberal Bismarck would ultimately serve liberal goals'.[41] However, the role of Hermann Baumgarten in this juncture cannot be oversimplified into that of the 'responsible *Realpolitiker*, who sought concrete ways to bring his political ideas into fruition', as one recent Weber biographer described him.[42] In fact, as Adolf Birke stressed in his introduction to Baumgarten's essay, ever since its publication, 'historical judgement has swayed between the condemnation of the [author's] "worship of success" and the overestimation of his "pragmatic [*realpolitisch*] discernment"'.[43]

Crucial to the proper historical perspective on Baumgarten's argument for compromise with Prussian aristocracy is the 'before' and 'after' of his publication. The founding of the German Progressive Party [DFP] had, it must be stressed, already marked a turn away from the decided liberalism of the *Nationalverein* [National Association] and a step towards *Realpolitik*.[44] 'Having learned from the crushing defeat of 1849', liberals were, in Gustav Mayer's words, 'ready to make compromises'. This was a reference to the fact that, when the DFP was formed in Prussia in 1861, its founders had left the demand for universal suffrage out of its programme and disregarded social issues alto-

39 Baumgarten [1866] 1974, p. 149.

40 The fact that no history of the National Liberal Party, a key player in German unification, has been written to this day – while there are dozens of histories of the SPD – is perhaps indicative of how divisive the matter still is.

41 Nipperdey 1993, p. 314.

42 See Kaesler 2014, p. 238.

43 Birke 1974, p. 7.

44 See Möller 2003, p. 82.

gether.[45] This is precisely what led Mayer to see the formation of the DFP (and its subsequent National Liberal split in 1866/67) as key drivers behind the 'separation between proletarian and bourgeois democracy in Germany'. As neither wing of liberalism sought to take into account worker's interests, the political field was open to Lassalle and the later rise of Social Democracy.[46]

Baumgarten's 'realism' is, in this sense, a function of historical perspective; i.e., it requires setting off from the premise that the only viable path to German unity was 'from above' and led by Prussia. Baumgarten's 'demand for an alliance between bourgeoisie and Junker' is, therefore, a realist stance only to the extent that it 'corresponded to the social and economic preconditions of Bismarck's path for the foundation of the *Reich*'.[47] Yet, liberals' sacrifice of core democratic and liberal values came at a price. It implied a 'voluntary and fundamental abdication of a political leadership role' and, fatefully, 'discharging (civil) society from political responsibility'.[48] The 'realist' stance of National Liberals, as Frank Möller has stressed, betrayed an over-reliance on state power and was clearly predicated on the abandonment of mass politics:

> That, with Bismarck's successes, liberals simply gave up their most significant party creation, the *Nationalverein*, can be explained from this utter underestimation of public opinion. They had blocked their own pathway to an effective mass politics.[49]

The notion that mass support and political participation were expendable in light of the greater goal of unification is tied to many liberals' (ultimately unfulfilled) expectation that post-unity conditions would, *in and of themselves*, counteract any attempts at reactionary retrenchment on the part of conservatives and the Prussian Monarch. As Baumgarten argued, if 'certain absolutist, aristocratic and bureaucratic traditions held sway over the Prussian state ... these traditions would not be able to prevail within the framework of the remaining Germany that is to be won'. This was the key wager behind Baumgarten's appeal to liberals to 'bury the hatchet' with Prussian aristocracy in 'a decided outwards projection of power' that was 'both in the interest of the state as of the liberal party itself'.[50]

---

45 Mayer 1969 [1911], pp. 109–10.
46 Mayer 1969 [1911], p. 108f.
47 Birke 1974, p. 18.
48 Birke 1974, p. 21.
49 Möller 2003, p. 83.
50 Baumgarten 1974 [1866], pp. 130–1.

Just as in this thinly veiled acknowledgement of militarism and imperialism as the ultimate prizes the German bourgeoisie would collect from unification, Baumgarten extended liberals only a supporting role in actively fostering the new circumstances he saw as their best safeguard. Hence, if no aristocrats bearing the vocation to lead were found, it was the 'duty of enlightened liberal politics to aid in this transformation of the nobility'; liberals could engage in such a task with a clear consciousness as Germans had the benefit of lacking the 'envious levelling' tendencies of the French.[51]

Despite its paucity, this nod to an active role for liberals was still an outlier in Baumgarten's fundamentally *deterministic* narrative; progress was to him much more a function of the development of economic forces and the expansion of state power than of contingent political action. From the vantage point of Baumgarten's historical optimism, a unified Germany under the aegis of Prussia would provide enough wealth and opportunities to harmonise any serious conflicts between the nobility and the bourgeoisie. The new conditions, i.e., 'the joy in finally having firm and safe ground under our feet will surely and before long uproot our bad habits'.[52]

The notion of the nation-state as a well-functioning organism epitomised Baumgarten's expectations for a united Germany. For, if in previous periods, the 'limbs added to the ailing backbone's burden by pulling in opposing directions', the achievement of unification 'after centuries of erring in the desert of statelessness', was equivalent to a 'deliverance that began an entirely new development', i.e., one 'where all parts would work together'.[53]

As one historian has pointed out, the fact that 'this process could also be used to secure a long-term conservative state order, was something the realist liberals did not expect'.[54] This miscalculation was a direct result of the blind trust in the achievement of statehood as the best safeguard against the reactionary tendencies of Prussian aristocrats:

> But are we not allowed to hope, that the distorted state of our public conditions so far bears the fundamental blame not only for the terrible stance of our nobility, but also for the aberration of liberalism and, consequently, that the beneficial steering of a real state, the only space for a real aristocracy, will quickly separate the true noble perspectives and aims from the miserable Junker, the putrid fruit of entirely unhealthy political conditions?[55]

51 Baumgarten 1974 [1866], p. 150.
52 Baumgarten 1974 [1866], p. 146.
53 Baumgarten 1974 [1866], p. 147.
54 Möller 2003, pp. 83–4.
55 Baumgarten [1866] 1974, p. 150.

This deterministic understanding of social progress marks a fundamental difference between Baumgarten's and the mature Max Weber's perspective on the historical process. As Dirk Kaesler has stressed, to Baumgarten,

> history can be flipped open like a book, from which one can derive purpose and aim ... [I]n the history of mankind, or at least of Prussia-Germany there reigns a teleology ... which reveals itself to the attentive historian when it has reached its supposed destination.[56]

This teleological understanding of history is just one of several positivist elements of Baumgarten's standpoint. His organic analogies are, in this sense, more than useful metaphors; they are rather a symptom of the deterministic basis of his outlook on social development. Rather than the result of a serene analysis of actual historical trends, as would be expected of a 'realist', Baumgarten's political prescriptions emerge as the product of a normative understanding of German conditions after 1848/9 grounded on a positivistic epistemology. Understood in this light, the old liberal's salient role in the context of unification takes on a different meaning for historical interpretation. Baumgarten emerges less as a realist than as the timely conveyor of a specific narrative of German history; as such, its effectiveness correlated rather with its functionality to the class constellation that coalesced around a Prussian-led solution to German unification, as opposed to the empirical accuracy of his portrayal.

If Baumgarten's pamphlet is framed as a partisan intervention in a fundamentally open historical setting – rather than as a 'realist' assessment of a heavily predetermined outcome – then the terms of his relationship to Max Weber accordingly take on a new light. The uncle-nephew influence question emerges, from this vantage point, as equivalent to the legacy of a particular political-strategic programme, namely, that an alliance between Prussian aristocrats and bourgeois liberals was the class constellation most suited to anchor capitalist development and political modernisation in a united Germany.

Framing Baumgarten's proposition as *partisan* is also consistent with the fact that it was contested in the 1860s, i.e., that there were alternatives to it. One contemporary of the old liberal, August Bebel – to mention just one key representative of working-class politics and democracy in early-1860s Germany – had a radically different set of expectations for a united Germany under Prussian aegis.

56 Kaesler 2014, p. 235.

In the suggestively titled chapter of his autobiography that recounts the time of the Austro-Prussian war ('The catastrophe of 1866'), Bebel recalls having met the possibility of a 'lesser German' solution to the question of unification with the following words:

> And it is on this Prussia of Mr. von Bismarck with his contempt for law and constitution that the German people is to place their trust? Surely not! And it is this Prussia that is to be placed on the pinnacle of Germany, the state that, throughout its entire history and only with the exception of the period from 1807 to 1810, when it lay in shatters, has never been a liberal state and shall *never* be one! Those who think otherwise do not know Prussia.[57]

4 'Realpolitik' as Ideology

If Hermann Baumgarten's 1866 work is framed as a crystallisation of the ideology of the post-1848/9 period for a segment of the German liberal bourgeoisie to whom unification on a conservative basis was the supreme goal, then the nature of the legacy he sought to entrust the young Max Weber with, and with which the latter would ultimately break, assumes a different meaning. As Guenther Roth pointed out, the historical constellations underlying the uncle's and nephew's lifetimes were 'radically different'.[58] This is the key to understand why this cross-generational dialogue produced a series of mismatches in outlook, despite the unquestionable influence the uncle had on his admiring nephew. Baumgarten's outlook had by the 1880s become unwieldy. For this reason, in his attempt to face up to the questions raised by his historical time, Weber would need to negotiate the elements he would incorporate and reject from the received liberal worldview of previous generations. The central issue was no longer how to achieve national unification – i.e., whether 'from above' or through a democratic revolution – but how to face up to the 'social question' in an 1880s context where *transnational* trends – cross-border migration, global trade flows, colonialism etc. – played an increasing role.

57 Bebel 1995 [1910–14], p. 116.

58 This insight is at the same time an effective rebuttal to Roth's own subsequent claim that 'Weber's triad of passion, sense of responsibility and clarity of judgement' differed from that of Baumgarten's 'only in the choice of terms' (FG, p. 287). On the contrary, as in the case of the notion of politics as *Beruf* I approached earlier, the convergence in

The interface between historical time and perspectives on social reality is the key here. Baumgarten belonged to a generation of liberals to whom the growing economic power of the bourgeoisie and its increasing relevance to the nation-state led to the assumption that the final prevalence of liberal values and the achievement of moderate reforms would arrive without the need for political unrest or involvement of the masses.[59] It is, therefore, no coincidence that August Ludwig von Rochau, the first major liberal thinker of *Realpolitik*, had grounded his appeal to realism in the early 1850s on the basis of 'general laws of state life', which he claimed could be established as in the natural sciences.[60] This was a key trait of the outlook on politics of Baumgarten's and Max Weber Sr.'s generation of moderate liberals, one that must be highlighted if the path-breaking nature of Weber's methodological innovations and engagement with workers' standpoint are to be put into proper perspective.

By the 1880s, it had become clear that the ever-greater economic power of the bourgeoisie would not translate automatically into its political preeminence within the Reich; indeed, Bismarck's policy-shift in 1878 meant a *regression* in liberal influence in public affairs, despite the galloping process of industrialisation and modernization the German economy was experiencing. This does not mean the situation was unproblematic for the Reich's conservative elites. In his Inaugural Lecture [*Antrittsrede*] of 1895, Max Weber stressed that the changes in economic structure spurred by unification – which Bismarck had striven for – had led to demands for a political order that were anathema to Bismarck's own 'Caesaristic nature'.[61] Thus, if 'external' unification had been achieved between 1866 and 1871, the task that Weber attributed to his generation consisted in the 'internal unification of the nation',[62] i.e., the need to anchor political power on a new class constellation to effectively establish bourgeois hegemony in Imperial Germany.[63] Significantly, this projected class constellation – which was to replace the alliance between nobility and bourgeoisie that Hermann Baumgarten had helped forge – extended to the higher strata of the working class the role of key, if subaltern, allies of the bour-

the concepts employed by uncle and nephew are telling not because of their superficial resemblance, but primarily due to the striking difference of historical perspective they reveal upon closer examination.

59 See Möller 2003, pp. 78–9.

60 Möller 2003, p. 78. Rochau's concept of *Realpolitik* and the young Weber's views on the matter will be approached in Chapter 4.

61 MWG I/4, p. 567.

62 See Ibid.

63 See Rehmann 2015, p. 54.

geoisie. Weber's chief aim during the 1890s would be consequently to bridge this class divide not only from a political, but also from a theoretical and ideological standpoint (see Parts 2 and 3). If Baumgarten provided the ideological mortar to the class constellation behind 'external' unification in 1866–71, Weber aimed to do the same with regards to the 'Fordist' social arrangement he believed would propel Germany's 'internal' unification at the turn of the century.

Max Weber's youthful letters indicate he was aware of the need for this new hegemonic synthesis at an early stage in his trajectory. Indeed, his efforts at apprehending the actual balance of forces in German society and politics that colour his early correspondence were no doubt a vital step towards this goal. Yet, beyond a grasp of historical trends, forging a novel political-strategic programme for his class required the adoption of a new outlook on social life, i.e., a new epistemological and conceptual framework. In particular, it required overcoming the naturalistic determinism and faith in progress that had characterised the previous generation of bourgeois liberals and was at the core of Hermann Baumgarten's political 'realism'.

According to Karl-Georg Faber, 'the interpretation of social occurrences as natural phenomena in the broadest sense was a general tendency of the period [i.e., the 1860s – V.S.], even though the concepts of "nature" and "development" at use were not clearly established'.[64] In fact, it is this epistemology centred on notions of 'necessity' and 'unbreakable laws' that had ultimately provided the basis for the 'ideological or ... doctrinaire character of so-called *Realpolitik*'.[65]

From this vantage point, the old liberal's call for a compromise with Prussian power in the name of 'realism' was more than a politically expedient stance adequate for the years of unification; it also had a set of historically conditioned epistemological premises, which supported its claim to veracity and accurateness. As Faber indicated, the mid-1860s saw the rise of a political and social variation of Darwinism that the events of 1866 seemed to validate: 'in the eyes of many contemporaries, the year 1866 subsequently acquired the same function as a natural experiment'.[66] More recent scholarship has upheld this argument, namely, that the Prussian military victory over Austria was not only central to the legitimation of the 'lesser-German' solution to unification, but that it also contributed to the sedimentation of a positivistic outlook on social development:

64 Faber 1966, p. 26.
65 Faber 1966, p. 20.
66 Faber 1966, p. 17.

> Whoever could attain the organizational, administrative and technical achievements necessary to conclude a war of this magnitude in a matter of weeks and with startling success could also demand a political leadership role for themselves.[67]

Along with the shared experience of the failed revolution of 1848/9, Prussian military successes in the 1860s catalysed certain previously given – though unclear – notions, providing the evidence needed for them to harden into a consistent ideology.[68] Hermann Baumgarten helped give shape to this perspective with his 'self-critique' of 1866.

Max Weber, on the other hand, would need to forge new methodological tools to face up to a transformed historical reality. In fact, he made his mark as a thinker precisely by breaking with the naturalistic understanding of social phenomena which his uncle had adhered to. Weber scholarship has historically traced this back to his Neo-Kantian influences – i.e., has made it strictly an issue of methodological 'affiliation' – and, more recently, to his legal education – which would have attuned Weber to contingent forms, rather than 'iron laws'.[69] The vantage point I propose here stresses, instead, the social determinants of Weber's epistemology.[70] In line with my analysis of the social and historical underpinnings of Hermann Baumgarten's thought, I argue it is the mounting social strife Weber witnessed as a young man in Imperial Germany (see Chapter 5) that helped propel his break with positivistic conceptions; his uncle's notion that social classes are articulated within the nation-state as the limbs of an organism, for instance, had become untenable by the late 1880s. Not surprisingly, Weber articulated an almost diametrically opposed outlook on social struggle, conceptualising it as a permanent fixture of societal reality. As he put it in 1896:

> Whoever wants to conduct worldly [*irdische*] politics, must above all be free of all illusions and recognize the one fundamental fact, the unavoidable eternal struggle of man with man on this Earth, as it effectively takes place.[71]

67 Becker 2001, p. 156.
68 See Faber 1966, pp. 39–40.
69 See Ghosh 2014. For a critique of Weber's retreat behind 'formal rationality' as a strategy to rationalise and legitimise capital's 'substantive irrationality', see Mészáros 2010, pp. 63–5 and the epilogue to this work.
70 Again, in line with Mészáros 2010.
71 MWG I/4.2, p. 622.

This insight is what provided the basis for Weber's own notion of political 'realism'. Instead of a deterministic and teleological conception of history that prescribed certain courses of political action, Weber maintained that economic power *did not* necessarily coincide with a given class's ability to rule, i.e., with what he would call 'political maturity', in a passage foretelling Gramsci's later theorisation of hegemony:

> What is dangerous and in the long run incompatible with the nation's interest is when an economically declining class maintains its hold on political rulership. Even more dangerous, however, is when classes, towards which economic power and, with it, the entitlement to political rulership, gravitate, are not mature enough politically to take the reins of the state. Both conditions threaten Germany at this time and this is the key to the current perils of our situation.[72]

Weber's proposal for a new balance of forces in Imperial Germany, i.e., a new power bloc led by the bourgeoisie and integrating the upper strata of the working class,[73] demanded an effort of political education of these incumbent hegemonic rulers; this task required, in turn, forging a *novel epistemological basis* or 'worldview' that broke with the problematic premises underlying his uncle's synthesis of 1866.

The young Weber's increasing awareness of the crisis of German liberalism as a political force and of the worldview that informed it notwithstanding, his most immediate confirmation of Baumgarten's significant misjudgement of the post-unification pathways of Imperial Germany was the latter's own isolation in the 1880s.[74] Its highpoint was Baumgarten's break with his erstwhile fellow enthusiast of Prussian power and leadership, historian Heinrich von Treitschke, in a public spat centred on the second volume of the latter's *Deutsche Geschichte* [German History].[75] Baumgarten termed the work a mere 'Prussian history' due to its one-sided, highly partisan perspective which recast German historical development in light of Prussia's later pre-eminence.[76] In other words, he lambasted Treitschke for a brand of teleology in historical narrative he had himself engaged in in his 1866 pamphlet. The conflict with Treitschke was, nevertheless, a clear effort at self-critique by Baum-

72 MWG I/4, p. 566.
73 See Rehmann 2015, pp. 7–8.
74 Biefang 1996, pp. 398–99.
75 Biefang 1996, pp. 399–405.
76 Biefang 1996, p. 401.

garten.[77] The controversy, which took place in 1882/83, i.e., shortly before the intensification of the uncle-nephew correspondence, is arguably a key precedent to Weber's own conceptualisation of objectivity in the social sciences and social policy – which I will return to later in this work.[78] As historian Gustav Mayer, who like Weber had been a student of Treitschke's at the University of Berlin in the late-1880s, remarked:

> The main driver of his development had been the unification of Germany; the new tasks that emerged after this objective was accomplished, he was no longer able to devise.[79]

While this statement referred to Treitschke, it could very well be extended to the Baumgarten of that period, despite the fact that the former had embraced the conservative turn in German politics after 1878 (including an adherence to Anti-Semitic notions),[80] while the latter had recanted to a more principled liberal stance. What they had in common – and what characterised liberalism more generally as a political current in 1880s Imperial Germany – was a considerable decline in relevance, the result of a combination of an outdated understanding of society and politics and a declining ability to intervene in current affairs. Marianne Weber called this the 'tragic' fate of this generation of liberals:

> The task that would have been proper for this liberal middle-class generation of patriots – participation in the internal development of the Reich, whose external form they helped to create – was denied to them.[81]

German liberalism found itself from the late-1870s onwards at a crossroads, just as it had in 1866. Rather than the issue of its relationship to the nobility and the German dynasties, it was once more the question of its stance towards an increasingly active and autonomous working-class movement that characterised its dilemmas. The young Weber's awareness of this shift would, however, only consistently emerge in his correspondence as of the late-1880s (for reasons I will explore in Chapter 5).

When he subsequently offered his take on the question of the German bourgeoisie's relationship to the working class as a young intellectual in the 1890s,

77 Biefang 1996, p. 403.
78 See section 9.5.
79 Mayer 1949, p. 22.
80 cf. Biefang 1999, p. 505.
81 LB-E, p. 81.

Weber was by no means breaking new ground. Germany's urban elites had already become aware of and begun experimenting with ways to intervene in the 'social question' since the pre-1848 or *Vormärz* period, that is, shortly after the genesis of modern capitalist relations of production and budding industrialisation in the German lands. Crucially, those early stages of modern economic development were embodied not only by urban growth, factory buildings and puffing chimneys, but also by the emergence of a new class of property-less wage laborers – the modern proletariat – which by the 1840s had become impossible to ignore due to mounting pauperisation and the first episodes of revolt.

Weber had a direct connection to the patterns of charitable intervention that arose in that context, especially through his mother Helene Weber's many initiatives in this regard, but also through Max Sr.'s activities as city counsellor. While the clearly gendered natured of social work in nineteenth-century Germany helps explain middle-class women's major role in its philanthropic arm, municipal poor relief's institutional structure remained exclusively male terrain until the 1900s. The main traits of the 'patriarchal' brand of social engagement that both of Weber's parents consequently engaged in and a discussion of how it might have impacted his own outlook on the 'social question' form the topics of the next chapter.

CHAPTER 3

The Webers and the 'Social Question': The German Bourgeoisie's 'Patriarchal' and Gendered Engagement with the Contradictions of Modern Class Society

1 Contextualising Helene Weber's Influence in Max Weber's Development[1]

In late 1884, after a year of military service in Alsace, Max Weber resumed his legal education in Berlin, where he would remain for the better part of the ensuing decade. Notably, this return was not to the Reich's capital per se, but to its then adjacent municipality of Charlottenburg, where the family household was located and where he had grown up and attended the *Gymnasium*. The Weber family's high social standing – enabled mainly by the wealth from his mother's side – as well as Charlottenburg's reputation as seat of a prosperous, liberal-minded bourgeoisie seem to tie in perfectly with the strong bourgeois identity Max Weber is associated with. While this depiction of his 'social milieu' is not entirely misleading, it is, however, rather one-sided. Villas of affluent merchants had dotted the city since the eighteenth century, but the received image of Charlottenburg as a purely bourgeois enclave – in contrast to the royal palaces of Potsdam and the endless tenement complexes of the working poor to the northwest and southeast of Berlin – is problematic.[2] Charlottenburg saw the arrival of industrial activity as early as the 1830s and between 1850 and 1880 went on to become a city with a strong contingent of workers (who, it must be said, mostly worked in neighbouring Berlin). The population, in fact, more than doubled between 1870/1, when the city's inhabitants totalled some 20,000, and 1885, when the number of dwellers rose to 42,000.[3] Commenting on this period

1 Though it does not quote them directly – as they do not approach the German case – this chapter is informed by José Paulo Netto's considerations on the genesis of social work as a profession (see Netto 1992) and its relationship to the so-called 'social question' (see Netto 2001) in the context of transformations to the capitalist mode of production in nineteenth-century West Europe and North America.

2 See Bergler 2011, pp. 47–52.

3 See Ludwig 2005, pp. 109–10.

of strong growth, Andreas Ludwig points out that it corresponded to the development of a typical young industrial city in Imperial Germany.[4]

This growth phase coincides with the period stretching from when the Weber family relocated to Charlottenburg in late 1872 – after roughly three years residing in the centre of Berlin[5] – and Max Weber's return home to resume his legal education in the autumn of 1884. The family thus experienced first-hand the latter stages of the transformation of Charlottenburg into what at the time constituted a *Großstadt*, a large city in Imperial Germany. This transformation brought a shift in local political leanings (from monarchical to liberal)[6] and increasing urbanisation. It also brought land speculation and increasing social contrasts, especially after the introduction of a series of mass transportation links to Berlin, first through the 'Hobrecht plan' of 1862 – which laid out the urban framework of the booming Prussian metropolis[7] – then through the completion of a metropolitan ring-railroad (*Ringbahn*) in 1877 and an East-West elevated thoroughfare, the 'city railway' (or *Stadtbahn*), in 1882.[8]

The member of the household most connected to local life was undoubtedly Max's mother, Helene Weber, born Fallenstein (1844–1919), who was an active philanthropist and thus very much aware of the increasing social contrasts that rapid industrialisation in the greater Berlin region had generated:

> Often all the misery that exists around us unseen and unheard, as well as the helplessness with which we face this misery, weigh so heavily on my [heart] that any enjoyment, any possession appears to me like an injustice. I must so often think of our mother, and I am glad that she did not have any real insight into the conditions and spiritual filth such as surround us in Charlottenburg because of the proximity of the big city. She would not have been able to bear it.[9]

In this chapter I will approach how Helene Weber's religious convictions and philanthropic engagement in Charlottenburg can offer a glimpse into a dimension of the young Weber's development that is usually overlooked in the scholarship. My hypothesis is that Helene played a significant role in Max's polit-

4 Ludwig 2005, p. 110.
5 See FG, pp. 505–06 and Kaesler 2014, p. 148.
6 See Ludwig 2005, pp. 115–16.
7 See Bernet 2004.
8 See Ladd 1990, pp. 80–81; Ludwig 2005, pp. 112–13; Scarpa 1995, pp. 206–7; Escher 1985, pp. 225–40; Schulz 1887, pp. 218–24 and 253 f.
9 Helene Weber cited in LB-E, p. 95.

ical education as of his return to Berlin in late 1884, especially by bringing the more visible refractions of the 'social question' to her eldest son's attention, a task in which she was aided by her like-minded sister Ida and nephew Otto Baumgarten in Strasbourg. Max Weber's awareness of social issues and interest in social policy would only later become visible, especially after 1887. The exchanges between mother and son that are reported after his return from Alsace in 1884 are, however, a plausible component of his gradual coming to terms with the growing urgency of the 'social question' in Imperial Germany.

Helene's imprint on the young Weber would seem to be in a tense relationship – if not downright antagonism – to the one left by Max Weber Sr. on their son. The Weber matriarch clearly possessed a divergent set of values regarding those of her husband, who, for instance, did not share her religious piety. Their relationship would, in fact, grow increasingly acrimonious with the years, leading Max Weber to eventually intervene – taking the side of his mother – when domestic tensions came to a head in the mid-1890s. Regarding their stance towards the 'social question', it would, nevertheless, be inaccurate to paint Helene Weber as the ideological polar opposite of Max Sr.

Helene's charitable activities and outlook on poverty are representative of a manner of addressing social ills that was quickly becoming outdated in the 1880s. The decade marked not only a transition in both local and central government policies regarding the 'social question' – i.e., the shift towards an institutionalised social security regime[10] – but also the return of working-class politics to German soil. In this respect, Helene found herself very much in an analogous position to that of Max Sr., considering both embodied a bourgeois stance whose genesis predated national unification and feverish industrialisation and was no longer compatible with prevalent social trends, be it in a 'patriarchal' view towards the lower classes or in the attachment to a 'politics of notables' [*Honoratiorenpolitik*]. Yet, because social and economic transformations in late nineteenth-century Germany occurred in a scenario of continued disenfranchisement of working people in most arenas of civil society and political representation, changing conditions did not, in and of themselves, result in democratic gains or in a corresponding rooting out of views belonging to different times. On the contrary, reliance on private individuals to conduct welfare measures and the 'old-liberal' stance towards the lower classes – with its moralistic overtones and restrictive notion of citizenship – would both survive into the twentieth century. This meant the young Max Weber experienced views

10 See Kott 2014, pp. 26–47.

and practices tied to an earlier phase of bourgeois engagement with the working masses and the poor in Germany, while already being confronted by new conditions which called for their renewal.

Helene's role with respect to her son's maturing outlook was thus in many ways akin to Max Sr.'s or Hermann Baumgarten's, that is, it represented a model that could be admired in its own terms, but needed to be overcome; this analogous role notwithstanding, it does not seem each of Weber's parents impacted him to the same extent. Despite arguably being politically more conservative than her husband, two elements of Helene Weber's social intervention suggest her role in shaping Weber's later political intervention went beyond that of Max Sr.'s moderate liberalism, within the framework of which the 'social question' represented a very weak link. For one, her general involvement, concern and interaction with the Berlin poor appears to have been much more consistent and central to her life than it ever was to her husband. Second, the exclusion of women from citizenship in Imperial Germany – which arguably went further than that of male members of the working class, who could at least vote in the Reichstag elections – meant that Helene's engagement for more female participation in poor relief authorities took on a growing political (and progressive) significance as the turn of the century approached. In fact, while Max Weber Sr. is more or less unceremoniously turfed out of office in the municipality of Berlin in 1893,[11] Helene Weber's political role in Charlottenburg would only grow around the 1900s, that is, as she entered her late 50s.

This chapter's focus on Max Weber's immediate family might suggest a biographical framing of his development, as championed by Arthur Mitzman's psychoanalytical *The Iron Cage* (1970) and Guenther Roth's more recent *Familiengeschichte* (2001), an intricate genealogical study of the Webers. While these works remain fundamental references for Weber scholarship, I will take a different pathway and decentre the family microcosm, highlighting, rather, the wider social trends in which it was embedded. In this sense, if the crisis of German liberalism in the 1880s was the backdrop to the young Weber's relationship to the political legacy of his father and uncle, it is the evolution of bourgeois charity and poor relief activities that help provide the context of Helene's impact in shaping her son's worldview. The ideas and practices that informed the German bourgeoisie's intervention on the 'social question' – as well as how the Webers appropriated them – will thus provide the main topics of the following sections.

11 See FG, p. 390.

2 The Reign of the Bourgeois: Local Administration and the 'Social Question' in the German Lands until the 1880s

The sphere of politics where the German liberal bourgeoisie held most sway was no doubt at the local (*Gemeinde*) level. Despite the many transformations of Prussia-Germany in the same period, this would remain valid from the 1850s well into the end of the nineteenth century. A number of factors explain this phenomenon: the relative autonomy of local administration vis-à-vis provincial and central authorities;[12] growing urbanisation, which meant the extension of areas over which the landed aristocracy did not exert the same level of influence as in the higher levels of government and rural districts; finally, the maintenance of various forms of suffrage restriction, most notably the 'three-class' voting system, which – along with other forms of exclusion of workers and the poor from political participation and civil life – shielded the bourgeoisie from competition from below.

The bourgeois pre-eminence at the local level carried important consequences for policies of poor relief. As Florian Tennstedt has stressed, because the principle that buttressed local autonomy was that of the 'citizen collective' [*Bürgergemeinde*] instead of the 'dweller collective' [*Einwohnergemeinde*], and citizenship was based on paying taxes, its exercise remained a privilege of the propertied classes, i.e., was off-limits to the unpropertied wage-labourer.[13] George Steinmetz has raised this point even more forcefully, affirming that, in this period, 'the German bourgeoisie created a system of urban social policy in its own image', which 'allowed capitalist social-policy needs to be transmitted directly to the public agenda'.[14] This dynamic was particularly evident in poor relief 'with its individualizing and market-oriented features'.[15]

The period comprised between the 1850s and 1880s marks a specific phase of intervention on the 'social question' in Prussia-Germany. It results from the interplay between two factors: first, the rising social antagonisms resulting from a *new form* of pauperism and destitution, which had been brought forth by industrialisation and was compounded by the ongoing effects of the gradual capitalist transformation of the German countryside since the 1820s.[16] Second, the response at the local level to this dynamic by liberal notables and the bureaucracy.

---

12 See Steinmetz 1993, pp. 150–1.

13 Tennstedt 1983, p. 378.

14 Steinmetz 1993, p. 154.

15 Steinmetz 1993, pp. 46–7.

16 See Sachße and Tennstedt 1998, pp. 257–60.

Social conflict and political upheaval also played their role in the genesis of social policy; early so-called 'hunger' uprisings and the revolution of 1848/9 were, in this sense, not only the first expressions of German labour as a political force, but also triggered an institutional response from bourgeois social reformers and the state, i.e. a diversified policy of poor relief [*Armenpolitik*] and the introduction of 'worker policy' [*Arbeiterpolitik*].[17] The necessary consideration of these two sets of policies is, in fact, precisely what set apart modern social intervention from responses to pauperism dating from the middle-ages. On the one side, the dismantlement of the feudal social order and the introduction of freedom of movement in Prussian-Germany in the 1840s meant there was mounting demand for measures of poor relief. No longer tied to the recipient's location of origin, aid could be claimed – after a mandatory waiting period, among other restrictions – from the municipality the individual chose to move to, which put pressure on urban and industrial locations. The provision of poor relief was, however, in permanent tension with 'worker policy', given that it could not be so generous as to 'discourage' individuals from work (especially in the factories), nor overburden local finances. Hence, the traditional means of assuring the fundamental needs of a municipality's citizens, namely 'poor relief', was negatively determined by 'worker policy'.[18]

This tension was responsible for a chronically insufficient response from local authorities to the emerging 'social question' which, in turn, required private philanthropy to fill the gaps. As a result, intervention on the 'social question' in late nineteenth-century German municipalities was a public-private tapestry ranging from tax-funded measures of municipal government to private philanthropy, with a variety of institutions – such as foundations (*Stiftungen*), associations (*Vereine*) and the Churches – as key players in between.

The bearers of these various initiatives, public and private, often overlapped. In fact, this mode of addressing the 'social question' was rooted in a particular understanding of citizenship:

> Although early liberals demanded that the scope of state activity be limited to an absolute minimum and be only negative in nature, this view of the state did not diminish the moral obligation of the community toward the needy, and the conviction that individual citizens should be personally responsible for all the matters of public concern that lay outside the proper scope of state activity … [this] made voluntary social engagement

17 Tennstedt 1983, p. 232.
18 Tennstedt 1983, pp. 232–3.

> the logical counterpart to the minimal state and a distinguishing characteristic of nineteenth-century notions of citizenship.[19]

The upshot of this notion of 'personal responsibility' coupled with a citizenship status tied to property was the almost complete disenfranchisement of recipients of poor relief: 'Workers were legally disempowered by poor relief, which presented itself in the form of a handout rather than a right'.[20] In other words, social aid was framed in moral terms, the confrontation with the refractions of the 'social question' consisting primarily in rehabilitating the individual to work and to lead an orderly Christian life. This outlook was shared both by advocates of workers' 'self-help' associations and by social reformers favouring private charitable initiatives.[21] Above all, the notion of poor relief as a right was to be rejected lest the 'work ethic of the poor' be undermined and 'lead them to make unlimited claims on the property of others, and thus turn class against class'.[22]

Which brings us to the question of the social carriers – as opposed to recipients – of poor relief. A rapidly changing social structure coupled with the aforementioned restrictive concept of citizenship of mid-nineteenth-century Prussia-Germany meant that mandatory (unpaid) social work was performed by members of the middle classes and was a key element of their intervention in the public sphere. The growing awareness of social contrasts – and accompanying fear of revolution – was a further driver for this kind of engagement as well as for the philanthropic activity which characterised the more affluent bourgeois strata. Moreover, even though women were excluded from direct participation in poor relief activities conducted by local authorities (as a result of their own disenfranchisement), bourgeois women nevertheless sought to fulfil their civic duty through private charity, where they played 'a predominant role ... that they often conceived as a direct correspondent to the military obligations of the men'.[23]

The exclusion of the wage-labourer from citizenship, in turn, meant their engagement with charitable activities, not to mention political militancy in the labour movement, were viewed as illegitimate forms of tackling the 'social question' and, therefore, did not play a role in the combined framework of state aid and philanthropic support to the poor. As a result, the bourgeoisie and local

---

19 Frohman 2008, pp. 54–5.
20 Steinmetz 1993, p. 163.
21 See Frohman 2008, pp. 72–9.
22 Frohman 2008, p. 78.
23 Tennstedt 1983, p. 233.

state officials were its undisputed carriers. Their patriarchal stance towards the poor – often buttressed by monarchical and Christian convictions in an odd mix with free-market principles – was, in turn, the main ethical driver of social intervention. It built, alongside the hunger for cheap labour power of the new political economy of capital, the perpetuating mechanisms of the whole system.

This particular configuration of intervention into the 'social question' found its clearest expression in the so-called *Elberfeld System*. It originated in the Wuppertal region – Friedrich Engels's birthplace – in the 1850s, where, due to precocious industrialisation for German standards, social ills were also quick to emerge. The system consisted in the combination of existing forms of poor relief based on the engagement of voluntary overseers and the 'individualised' control of recipients – as established in the cities of Hamburg and Berlin – with a market- and efficiency-oriented approach. It not only aimed to lower the costs of poor relief to public authorities, but also to convert assistance to the poor into an effective tool of proletarianisation in terms of increasing the availability of workers for industry. It was put into effect through a decentralised system of control over the poor on a block to block level. The delivery of benefits was dependent on the proof of inability to work or, in the case of the 'workable poor', 'proper behaviour' certified by home visits by middle-class unpaid (male) overseers.[24] This meant a much cheaper and more 'effective' system than the establishment of workhouses, one that also supposedly contributed to the 'moral elevation' of the recipients (and to their maximum availability to work) as a result of the contribution of bourgeois overseers exercising their duties as citizens.[25]

Though bourgeois women played an important role in the complex of state-led and private initiatives that constituted the *Elberfeld System*, the tasks they were allowed to perform were conditioned by their own limited citizenship status at the time. Thus, they could neither hold public office in the Armendirektion – the municipal department responsible for managing poor relief – nor exercise any of the voluntary activities with a direct link to public administration, such as the role of house visitor.[26] The consequence was not a lower level of engagement on the part of middle-class women, but rather their focus on a highly gendered form of private charitable intervention, directed especially at poor women, with the goals of instilling proper forms of domesticity, motherhood and religious observance.

24 Sachße and Tennstedt 1993, pp. 215–216; Frohman 2008, p. 87f.
25 See Tennstedt 1983, p. 235.
26 See Steinmetz 1993, pp. 166–7.

It is within this matrix of local poor relief institutions and private philanthropy that Max Weber Sr. and Helene Weber developed their activities of social intervention. How they performed them under the specific conditions of post-unification Berlin and Charlottenburg, will be the subject of the next section.

3 Max Weber Sr.'s Patriarchal Engagement with the 'Social Question' in the Berlin Metropolis

Before turning to Helene Weber, it will be instructive to approach Max Weber Sr.'s own engagement with the 'social question'. It took place primarily in the framework first of Erfurt's, then Berlin's Armendirektion, but also encompassed his membership in a number of civil-society organisations dedicated to social issues. My aim in this section is not to argue that Max Sr. was any manner of champion of social reform nor that the situation of Germany's lower classes were among his foremost concerns. On the contrary, Max Sr.'s dealings with the offshoots of the 'social question' reflect, above all, an engagement on the grounds of tradition and social decorum in line with the mode of bourgeois social engagement I outlined in the previous section. His involvement in the authorities administrating poor relief was, in this sense, less a function of his convictions and more a consequence of the typical career ladder of a liberal politician in nineteenth-century Germany.

The peculiarity of performing these activities in Berlin lies in the fact that the city boasted an early version of the *Elberfeld System*. In fact, by 1823, i.e., relatively soon after the introduction of the administrative reforms that extended local authorities the task of dealing with poor relief in Prussia, Berlin had already introduced a similar scheme, modelling it after the pioneering Hamburg experiences that had emerged as early as 1787.[27]

This is the institutional backdrop to Max Sr.'s very first political appointment as an (unpaid) member of Berlin's Armendirektion in the autumn of 1861.[28] At this point, he was a young liberal law-graduate navigating a Berlin political landscape marked by the 'Constitutional Conflict'.[29] His participation in poor relief authorities was typical to the extent that it corresponded to entering public administration via its lowest echelon. In September of 1862, Max Weber Sr.

27 See Scarpa 1995, pp. 24–33.

28 See FG, p. 376, n. 12 and p. 380.

29 See FG, pp. 374–5 and Kaesler 2014, pp. 82–4. See section 2.2 above for a short discussion of the events that constituted the 'Constitutional Conflict'.

was elected city counsellor [*Stadtrat*] of the city of Erfurt, i.e., he became a representative at the city's executive body. By 1863 he had also joined the local Armendirektion, becoming chair of the commission in early 1864.[30] Finally, in late 1868, Max Weber Sr. was elected *Stadtrat* to Berlin; he justified the early interruption of his mandate in Erfurt by stressing his desire to join 'one of the biggest municipal authorities in the world'. Upon arrival, he would resume the duties he performed in Erfurt, including a return to Berlin's Armendirektion.[31]

In 1869, i.e., shortly after moving back to Berlin, Max Sr. will also join what was the main liberal organisation for social reform in Germany until the founding of the Verein für Socialpolitik in 1872, i.e., the 'Central Association for the Welfare of the Laboring Classes' [Centralverein für das Wohl der arbeitenden Klassen].[32] The Centralverein had been established in 1844 as a direct consequence of the Silesian weaver uprisings of June that year, and more generally, as an attempt to address the rising pauperism which accompanied the end of serfdom and the beginnings of industrialisation in Germany. After a drawn out process, it suggestively obtained legal status from Prussian authorities on 31 March 1848, i.e., immediately after the first wave of revolutionary activities in Berlin broke out.[33] While it is not clear exactly why Max Weber Sr. joined the Centralverein, or what his duties within it were, a closer look at the makeup of the organisation and its activities can illuminate the typical 'patriarchal' stance of German elites regarding the working classes.

It consisted in the attempt to bring workers into a harmonious relationship with a rising bourgeois social order through education and 'moral elevation', especially by means of the emulation of ruling-class values, social roles and mores. While a certain improvement in the deplorable material conditions of the working class is also a goal of 'patriarchal' intervention vis-à-vis the 'social question', it had to be pursued in conjunction with workers' 'spiritual and moral uplifting'.[34] The part workers were expected to play was restricted to the organisation of savings funds and strictly excluded the building of trade-unions or raising demands for greater political and civil participation. The achievement of harmony between the classes as well as the maintenance of social order were the fundamental goals of this brand of social reform. In this sense, it was in direct opposition to any horizon of worker emancipation and autonomy and rejected all notion of struggle with established authorities.[35]

---

30 FG, pp. 384–85.

31 FG, p. 390, n. 40.

32 See *Einleitung* in MWG I/4, p. 43.

33 See Reulecke 1983, p. 143.

34 Reulecke 1983, p. 150.

35 See Reulecke 1985, p. 50.

The inherent tension between the goal of social reform and the refusal to significantly transform the established order gave the Centralverein, as one historian put it, a Janus face.[36] For while it aimed to improve the livelihood of the labouring classes, it did so in complete disregard of workers' own viewpoint and agency. In the same vein, while it strove for a modernisation of local administration, it did so in the name of traditional 'patriarchal' values which debased workers' status as subjects. Examining the drivers of the unpaid engagement of bourgeois notables in both public and private initiatives of poor relief, Ludovica Scarpa also found a contradictory 'mix of liberal convictions and typical corporatist functions, paternalism and modernity'. In this sense,

> the citizenship impulse that drove notables to spend their free time in poor relief and education commissions, in the executive committee of child-welfare institutions, hospitals and orphanages etc. and in local chapters and educational associations of the *Centralverein*, had paradoxically a two-faced character: their championing of local autonomy and of the modernization of civil society stood in the best tradition of corporatist tutelage.[37]

Its goal of achieving social harmony notwithstanding, the Centralverein was still the object of repression by Prussian authorities and the organisation experienced a drop in membership with the reactionary turn in German politics in the 1850s. The 1860s and 1870s marked, in turn, a period of renewed growth and it is in this context that Max Sr. would join. In these decades the number of members would more than quadruple from a low of 152 in 1863 to 635 in 1875[38] – though these figures show to what extent this was truly an organisation of 'notables'. According to Jürgen Reulecke, there was one major factor contributing to the association's return to relevance at this juncture:

> It was the challenge of the resurgent autonomous labour movement in the 1860s that first led to a new inflow of members, who discovered in the Centralverein a potentially peace-making institution, a role which in the 1870s they correspondingly began to cultivate.[39]

36 Reulecke 1985, pp. 53–4.
37 Scarpa 1995, p. 112.
38 See Reulecke 1983, p. 257.
39 Reulecke 1983, p. 257.

While Max Weber Sr.'s outlook on the 'social question' is hard to reconstruct, his career path within the ranks of National Liberalism and the organisations he took part in throughout his life suggest that the trajectory of the Centralverein and the patriarchal views of its members can offer some clues to his own stance. The fact that Berlin was the setting of his political activities is another factor that can help elucidate how the 'social question' was framed in the Weber household. As Andrea Bergler has stressed, the staple of liberal notables in charge of public authorities in the Prussian metropolis – of which Max Sr. was a member for two decades – was especially resistant to more professional and (less patronising) assistance to the poor. Symptomatically, they also took longer to admit women into the ranks of the Armendirektion than other municipalities.[40] The Centralverein was also a testament to the endurance of patriarchal stances on social reform on the part of liberal notables; its statutes remained unaltered from the 1840s until 1914. Calls for the organisation to change its patriarchal perspective on workers as late as 1895 – by Gustav Schmoller no less – went unheeded.[41]

Yet, it was not in poor relief that Max Sr. made his biggest contribution to local politics in Berlin; it was, instead, in the city's public works commissions, which he joined in the early-to-mid 1870s and eventually came to preside.[42] Considering this was a period of explosive urban growth in the greater Berlin area, these activities no doubt impacted the everyday lives of many of the metropolis' inhabitants.[43] In fact, there was also an unmistakable social component to Max Sr.'s running of Berlin's public works initiatives on account of the direct connection between the 'housing question' and the 'social question'.[44] Not surprisingly, Max Sr. would also join the 'Association for the improvement of small dwellings' [Verein zur Verbesserung kleiner Wohnungen][45] founded in 1888, which indicates his awareness that poor housing conditions were one of the most dramatic expressions of the mounting social contrasts in the bourgeoning metropolis of Berlin.

Set against the backdrop of these activities, Max Weber Sr.'s engagement with the 'social question' and patriarchal stance towards the working classes emerges as not all that distinct from Helene Weber's, which the next item will

40 See Bergler 2011, p. 73 and pp. 86–7.

41 Reulecke 1985, pp. 51–2.

42 FG, pp. 390–1.

43 I plan to delve deeper into this facet of Max Sr.'s activities, and how they connect to the young Weber's development, in an upcoming essay entitled *Max Weber in Berlin*.

44 See Ladd 1990, p. 139f.

45 FG, p. 392.

examine. Despite the evident contrast between Max Sr.'s secular and liberal outlook and Helene's Christian values, their social intervention was rather complementary in the sense that they both performed the typical gendered roles that characterised the dealings of the urban bourgeoisie with the working classes in Imperial Germany.

This form of engagement nevertheless meant that liberal-bourgeois notables like Max Sr. would struggle to adapt to the new implications of the 'social question' in late nineteenth-century Imperial Germany. Both the rise of the labour movement to a significant political force and the growing centrality of the state for social policy ran counter to their deep-rooted practices and beliefs. In this regard, the Christian social-reformism of Helene Weber paradoxically built a better platform and stepping stone for Max Weber's own political and social engagement than his father's brand of social reform. Hence, when the young Weber became active in the debate on the 'rural labour question' in the 1890s, he did not do so within the framework of liberal organisations, but rather in the 'state socialist' Verein für Socialpolitik and the Christian-led Protestant Social Congress.[46]

4 Monarchical Convictions and Christian Philanthropy: Helene Weber's Social Engagement

According to the available research, Helene Weber's (1844–1919) political convictions were monarchical and conservative and her forms of social engagement were, above all, an extension of these leanings as well as of her religious piety.[47] Nevertheless, this did not prevent her from playing an increasingly active, even progressive role as she entered her 50s. This is visible in Helene's striving for more recognition of the contribution of middle-class women in poor relief efforts, but also in her support of the young theologians behind the more progressive wing of the Protestant Social Congress, founded in 1890; these included Friedrich Naumann and Paul Göhre, both of whom Max Weber would strongly engage with in the 1890s, but also Helene's nephew Otto Baumgarten (1858–1934). Son of the old liberal Hermann, the young theologian would eventually play a key role in the Congress's purge of its reactionary wing led by Adolf Stoecker.[48]

---

46 See Part 2 below.

47 FG, p. 520f.

48 See Part 2 for a closer discussion of the organization and Max Weber's role in it in the early 1890s.

An 1887 letter from Baumgarten offers an interesting glimpse into the dynamics of the Weber household and, in particular, into Helene's peculiar stance. The then aspiring pastor mentions, for instance, being struck by the Weber matriarch's 'very left-leaning sympathies'. He recounts how she saw in non-Christian environments the potential starting point of 'a moral – if amorphous – stance towards Christianity'. He attributed these views to a 'dictate ... of her love', which moreover, 'saved, even in [Max Sr.] a modest amount of tolerance regarding these [religious? – V.S.] needs of ordinary people'.[49] These remarks notwithstanding, Guenther Roth argues that 'Helene's growing social engagement remained tied to a traditional perception of "lower" and "higher-standing" [individuals], which was coherent with her monarchism'.[50]

Beyond Helene Weber's religious values and ethical commitment, her awareness of social issues was likely heightened by the fact that 'urban elites were even more exposed to and aware of social pressures than the state', as George Steinmetz has argued.[51] In this sense, if Max Sr. had, from an institutional standpoint, a greater level of responsibility with regards to addressing the 'social question' as a public representative in the Berlin municipality, Helene was in direct contact with its refractions as a consequence of her charitable activity. The setting of Charlottenburg is also relevant in this respect. The Berlin-adjacent city only made the transition from a brand of local administration centred on the rule of bourgeois notables (and dating back to the 1830s and 1840s)[52] to a more bureaucratised and centralised mode of operation from the late-1880s onwards:[53]

> Clothing, nutrition, housing and education – these recognized fundamental needs were only covered by Charlottenburg's poor relief at a very low level between 1850 and 1880. From the standpoint of the municipality these responsibilities meant above all a burden to the local finances, even if the modern roots of poverty were gradually recognized and the first attempts at solving them took place.[54]

That meant Charlottenburg's public authorities remained very reliant on private philanthropy to address social issues, which became increasingly acute as

49 Cited in FG, p. 512.
50 FG, p. 522.
51 Steinmetz 1993, p. 155.
52 Frohman 2008, pp. 55–6.
53 Ludwig 2005, pp. 18–19 and pp. 194–5.
54 Ludwig 2005, p. 124.

the city's social landscape was transformed from the time the Weber family settled there (1872) up to the turn of the century. The shift in the population's social makeup is visible in the changes to the distribution of voters across the three classes of the municipal electorate. In 1869, the first and second classes (in terms of property owned) represented 9.1% and 27.5% of the electorate, which was rounded up by 63.4% of third-class voters; by 1906/07 the numbers were 1.57%, 12.22% and 86.21%, respectively, indicating a much higher degree of inequality, one that was in line with prevalent conditions in Prussia.[55]

As Max Weber returned home for his studies in the mid-1880s, the city was thus right in the middle of a major demographic transition. While this changing landscape made the reform of local authorities a growing need, and Helene Weber would play an integral part in them later on, at this time she was engaged primarily with private charity initiatives, as befitted the gendered role of a bourgeois notable's wife. The main organisation Helene was involved in was the Elisabeth-Frauenverein, a women's association that (likely) dated back to 1838 and focused above all on the care of poor married women who had recently given birth. The Frauenverein supplied them with basic hygiene supplies as well as a number of free soups, cooked in the kitchens of its affluent members.[56] There was thus a close connection between bourgeois women's gendered everyday realities, anchored in domestic life, and the forms of their charitable intervention. They were, in this sense, expected to 'educate' young proletarian women to fulfil a notion of motherhood modelled according to the conventions and values predominant in the villas of Charlottenburg. This element of 'moral improvement' by means of personal example also characterised male-exclusive dimensions of poor-relief such as in the house visits central to the *Elberfeld System*. The main difference was in the aim of bourgeois women's intervention, that is, it was centred less on discipline towards work and more towards fostering a particular type of domesticity.

Besides the issue of charity as a conduit for gender and class roles, the care for recent proletarian mothers also involved a number of debates in which moral stances and sanitary concerns overlapped. In H. Albrecht's *Handbook of Social Welfare Assistance* [*Handbuch der sozialen Wohlfahrtspflege*] of 1902, for instance, the care for recent mothers is presented with reference to the question of whether women in poverty should deliver at their own homes – with the assistance of a midwife sent by the charity organisation – or if they should be

55 Ludwig 2005, p. 113, n. 20.
56 See Ludwig 2005, p. 153 and p. 278 and Schultz 1887, pp. 286–7.

brought to centralised institutions that could assure proper hygiene and care, remaining there with the new-born for some time.[57]

The debate on the best setting for childbirth highlighted how the situation of working-class women was less a function of individual cases of hardship than of broader social issues, such as the Berlin metropolitan area's aforementioned housing shortage and the appalling living conditions of its proletarian inhabitants. The question of whether it was 'morally advisable' for proletarian women to give birth away from their families was hotly contested. The *Handbook*'s author mentions the existence of a handful of 'fanatics' intent on making a norm out of childbirth in an institutional setting.[58] This critical position was mirrored by the Elisabeth-Frauenverein, which also supported childbirth at home. If the primary argument related to the welfare of the mother, as Marianne Weber recounts, it also encompassed the notion that the father had to be made aware of his duties in the family as soon as possible, something the shared experience of the 'life and death struggle' of childbirth was expected to foster. This was an issue of principle for Helene, who thought child-birth away from home would shield the father from his responsibilities and encourage him to 'replace the wife with a "girlfriend", while the former is away at the clinic'.[59]

That these forms of charitable activity were driven by more than altruism and embodied the moral considerations and class outlook of its bourgeois carriers was reflected in the Frauenverein's policy of providing assistance only to *married* proletarian women. Single mothers or those bearing children out of wedlock were not encompassed by the organisation's activities. In part due to the impact of such restrictions, the mortality of new-borns was twice as high in the case of unmarried women when compared to married ones at the time.[60]

5 The 'Social Question' and National Liberal Legacy

After Max Weber returned to Berlin in late 1884, he engaged in discussions on religion and morality with his mother spurred by common theological readings. In the context of these mother-son exchanges, their contrasting views on the working class were also externalised, as Helene reports in a letter:

57 See Albrecht 1902: pp. 350–1.
58 Albrecht 1902, p. 352.
59 LB, p. 515.
60 Bergler 2011, p. 54.

> Max has become acclimatised again very nicely, and his inner development during the past year is a great joy to me. He is so much more understanding and communicative, and I suppose he is fully aware that this gives me pleasure. Before he had to attend lectures we read Channing for an hour each morning ... particularly on adult education and self-culture. This greatly interested and delighted us, although Max and I proceed from very different points of view, since I cannot share his theory that some people exist only to work for others and mechanically earn their daily bread.[61]

Just as in the case of his relationship to the National Liberal legacy of his father and uncle, the young Weber finds himself in a 'transitional stage' in the mid-1880s in terms of his views on workers and his stance regarding the 'social question'. As Chapters 4 and 5 will show, both questions would merge into a single problem by the decade's close. The remarks above serve, however, as a useful benchmark for the development of the young Weber's views. This stance on workers dates from 1884, when he was midway through his law degree; the contrast to his outlook in 1892, i.e., when he concluded his academic education and made his first interventions in the public sphere, is considerable. The notion that some people 'exist only to work', or that the 'unqualified affirmation of a culture ... demands the sacrificing of the masses for its purposes', reported by Helene, harken back to the liberal elitism he would (mostly) distance himself from by the early 1890s.[62] The trajectory in between these two points builds the subject-matter of the final two chapters of Part 1.

Before moving on to them, an important methodological question merits some attention. The issues of the legacy of German liberalism and the growing centrality of the 'social question' have so far been approached as they were refracted by the young Weber's key family references, i.e., Max Sr., Hermann Baumgarten and Helene Weber. My purpose was not, however, to derive the affective or psychological drivers of the young Weber's development from his family microcosm. The merits of such an approach notwithstanding, my goal was, instead, to illuminate the wider intellectual and societal context that informed these relationships. In order words, the fact that Weber's maturation was mediated by his family relations should not overshadow the broader social circumstances which framed his gradual learning process. It was in confronting the questions of his time, some of which concretely impacted his close family

61 Cited in LB-E, pp. 94–5.

62 LB-E, p. 95.

circle, that Weber found his particular pathway not only to scientific production, but also to political activism and a prominent role in the public debates of the 1890s.

In framing family relationships as a prism for broader societal questions, I take a cue from Max Weber himself. As befits his status as a foundational figure of social thought, when looking back at the domestic tensions that characterised his parents' relationship, Weber conceptualised them in social and political terms. A clear example is a letter from 1910 to his brother Arthur, in which he addresses his mother's social engagement and father's lack of comprehension for concerns of this kind:

> Mother desired to have free recourse to a small part of the interest payments on her estate so that she could cover her needs and also pursue her social goals … Father's very lively nature strongly opposed this perspective. He had grown up in a rigid old liberal time, which had not yet known these social problems, and the notion of handing out his wife her own money without supervision went against all the established traditions of his family, even though he was a naturally kind-hearted man. And so the inner conflicts increased from year to year.[63]

Weber situated his parents' marital conflicts within the wider scope of liberalism's decline, mounting social conflict and shifting gender roles. Attributing his father's views to a 'rigid old liberal time' when 'social problems' were 'not known' – or, rather, could still be mostly ignored by liberals – indicates Max Weber understood *those times had passed* by the 1880s. While Helene's worldview was not any less patriarchal and old-fashioned than her husband's, she was not only able to maintain her social engagement in the 1890s and beyond, she widened her scope of intervention. This marks a stark contrast to Max Weber Sr.'s fading political role in the same period; after more than two decades of service, he left his post in the Berlin local authorities without great fanfare in 1893.

As for Helene Weber, her engagement with the young theologians behind the Christian-Social movement and especially her struggle for the greater participation of women in the poor relief authorities in Charlottenburg meant she was able to remain a relevant actor into the twentieth century. She became an official (unpaid) member of the Armendirektion in the early 1900s, subsequently earning the right to participate and vote in its deliberations.[64]

63 For the full contents of the letter, see MWG II/6, pp. 762–4.

64 Ludwig 2003, p. 195.

The recognition of the centrality of the 'social question' was, therefore, the dividing line regarding the ability of Weber's parents to remain active in public life as they reached the later stages of their biographies. 'Social problems' also separated the years of National Liberal pre-eminence in German politics from the party's decline in the 1880s. In a letter from April 1914, Max Weber showed he recognised the personal merits of his father, yet also understood there were broader circumstances behind the latter's failures and unfulfilled expectations. These failings were, in fact, those of an entire generation of German liberals:

> We all see him more fairly nowadays and can rejoice about who he was in his atypically firm and pure bourgeois sense [*Bürgersinn*]; we know that the ruptures in his life corresponded to the tragic fate of his whole generation, which never came fully into its own in terms of their ideals – political or otherwise – and which never fulfilled its hopes, which *were also not taken up by the younger generation*; his was a generation that had lost the old belief in authority, but still thought about certain things in an authoritarian way that we no longer could accept.[65]

As in the previous letter, Max Weber emphasises here the impossibility of the upcoming generation – his own – to follow in the same pathway of his father and his liberal contemporaries, despite all their achievements. Indeed, as this chapter has indicated, conscious of its crisis, Weber already held a sceptical distance to what he termed the 'old-liberal' perspective during his student years in the mid-1880s. It is, however, only in the period following his definitive return home to Charlottenburg upon conclusion of his studies and first round of legal examinations in 1887 that this process of 'generational detachment' will come to a head. Put differently, it was only when the broader historical drivers that would permanently shape Weber's further intellectual and political trajectory erupted in full force, that his own personal transformation shifted into high gear. These articulated processes of social change and individual maturation form the topics of Chapters 4 and 5, covering the years of 1887 to 1891/2.

65 Quoted in LB: 522–3.

CHAPTER 4

Outgrowing National Liberalism (1887)

1 From Political Commentator to Historical Actor

In January 1887, Otto von Bismarck attempted to instrumentalise a war scare to gain an edge in the upcoming elections of late February. They would be held early, since Bismarck had dissolved the Reichstag over the unwillingness of left-liberals, of members of the Centre Party and Social Democrats to approve the military budget for the next seven years, the '*Septennat*'. As a consequence of the supposedly tense relations with France in those early months of 1887, 72.000 reservists were called up for military exercises in the Alsace region.[1] Among them was the young Max Weber. He reports being called up in a 22 January 1887 letter to F. Frensdorff, a legal scholar at Göttingen with whom he'd been in frequent contact in the winter term of 1885–6, and who had offered to be his doctoral advisor. Max Weber indicated that his prospects of undertaking doctoral studies were unclear at that moment,

> ... because my legal activities will be interrupted for the foreseeable future thanks to my call-up for military service with the 47th Regiment in Strasbourg, Alsace. I will thus be required to exchange my study for the coloured jacket during eight weeks – if peace holds, that is.[2]

While tensions with France never boiled over into a conflict and Max Weber was safely home by Easter, a March 1887 letter from Strasbourg to his mother shows how convinced he was of the threat of war. That things were quiet in mid-March despite the apprehension that had surrounded the call-up of reservists in no way indicated that the danger had been overplayed all along, he stressed. Anyone who had 'experienced what took place there in military terms' could only consider the accusation by left-liberals that it had all been just a government ploy for electoral purposes to be 'malicious nonsense'.[3]

Besides his willingness to give credence to Bismarck, Max Weber's remarks on the 1887 military tensions show to what extent the increasing shifts in German political life began affecting him first-hand. The ensuing years would, in

1 Loth 1996, p. 79.
2 MWG II/2, pp. 42–3.
3 MWG II/2, p. 54.

fact, do more than provide Weber with plentiful political and social upheaval to work into his maturing appraisal of the Reich's situation and prospects; they also coincided with a transition in his own role as a historical actor. From youthful observer and commentator of political life, who experienced societal phenomena primarily through the lens of how they affected his family members, he began to get actively involved in the historical process. This shift triggered, on the one hand, the effective surpassing of the National Liberal tradition of his forebearers; nevertheless, neither Weber's relationship to the legacy of his father and uncle nor his stance towards Bismarck would be free from important ambiguities, as this chapter aims to show.

The first palpable effect of this new disposition as an historical actor was Weber's overcoming of the passivity and indecision that had marked the end of his legal studies and the start of his time as a *Referendar* – or legal clerk – back in Berlin in 1886–7. In an autumn 1887 letter from Otto Baumgarten, in which the latter reports on the domestic situation of the Webers, we learn that his cousin Max 'lives quite withdrawn and appears to me to be suffering strongly from a lack of initiative and determination in life'.[4] This diagnosis would not hold for long, as the closing years of the 1880s mark the start of a frenzied decade of work and activity for Max Weber, interrupted only by the onset of his illness in the century's twilight years.

Max Weber would himself characterise the time between 1884 and 1887 as 'relatively long' and 'very rich in external events and internal transformations'.[5] The 'external events' of the ensuing period, which culminated in the crucial year of 1890, would no doubt outdo the previous juncture in intensity and significance, fast-tracking the young Weber's maturation in the process. It was not just the tempestuous political conjuncture set off by the death of the old Kaiser in 1888 that would grab Weber's attention, as Chapter 5 will discuss; German Social Democracy and the labour movement in Imperial Germany began to figure more prominently in his political commentary in this period as well, with key consequences for his overall worldview. This coincided with Weber's definitive outgrowing of National Liberalism.

4 Cited in FG, p., 513.
5 MWG II/2, p. 69.

2 A Balance Sheet of Liberal 'Realpolitik': Reflecting on the *Kulturkampf* amidst a Ramp Up of Repression against Socialists

This chapter begins, just as previous ones in Part 1, by providing an overview of political debates in Imperial Germany so as to unlock the significance of Weber's many utterances on current events in his youthful letters. The difference of the period starting in 1887 is, as mentioned above, the fact that the intertwinement of personal and career issues, intellectual developments and social phenomena will become more immediate and acute. This is not only due to the very palpable reach of political and social shifts into Max Weber's life, as in the case of the war scare with France. The young Weber will from this point on progressively leave the role of passive observer and student and start looking for ways to intervene concretely as well as to shape his scholarly interests more autonomously.

Despite the key significance of these years for Max Weber's development, his views on political developments in the 1880s have not received much attention from researchers, especially if compared to his considerations on the process of unification and on Wilhelmine Germany, respectively. In his history of German liberalism, to name one example, Dieter Langewiesche correctly points out that in the much-quoted essay of 1917, 'Parliament and Government in a Reconstructed Germany', the late Max Weber was at once a 'sharp-tongued critic of the Wilhelmine bourgeoisie's lack of will to power' – a standpoint he had already held since his Freiburg Inaugural Lecture of 1895 – and someone who 'found understanding words' for the National Liberals' policy of compromise stemming from 'their predicament' between 1866 and 1877.[6] Max Weber would indeed, then as in his youth, see the achievements wrought in the years of the so-called 'Liberal Era' in a very positive light. But how did Weber appraise German liberalism and its bourgeois bearers in the time *between* the two periods referred to by Langewiesche? That is to say, how was Weber able to reconcile his positive appraisal of moderate liberal politics until 1878, on the one hand, and his biting criticism of the bourgeoisie under the reign of Wilhelm II, i.e., after 1890, on the other? The decade or so in-between constitutes, in fact, the decisive juncture for Weber's own maturation, namely, the period stretching from the late 1870s to the late 1880s.

As in his student years, Imperial Germany's political life figured prominently in the young Weber's correspondence from 1887 to 1891, especially – but not exclusively now – in the letters to Hermann Baumgarten. That being said, while

6 Langewiesche 1988, p. 166.

the elections of 1884 had deserved a long reflection,[7] no commentary on the following ballot, which took place on 21 February 1887, is to be found in his available correspondence. The fact that Max Weber was stationed in Alsace readying for war, and what's more, that the vote took place only days after a period Weber describes as of 'feverish activity' on the forts, probably explains his silence on this event.[8] The 1887 election counts one significant development, namely, the formation of a new majority encompassing both conservative factions alongside a now more right-leaning National Liberal Party. The so-called 'Kartell' had been a long sought-after parliamentary base of Bismarck's and marked the return of the National Liberals to a 'ruling' parliamentary majority; the price had been further sacrifice to the party's liberal platform.

Building the scenario that led to the victory of the *Kartell* had demanded a series of moves from Bismarck, one of them being a return to the 'hard enforcement' of the anti-Socialist law, as well as the aforementioned channelling of external tensions into the electoral discussion. The Reich's relations with Russia had deteriorated since 1885–6 due to a dispute over Bulgaria between the great powers;[9] tensions with France, in turn, rose as result of the appointment of General Boulanger as war minister.[10] Though the political movement behind the general in late 1880s France was highly contradictory – he would find support among both the republican far left and the royalists[11] – a key element of *Boulangisme*'s rapid rise was its nationalist component and professed refusal to bow to German will in continental politics.[12] The actual threat posed by France to Imperial Germany was questionable at that point, and was immediately refuted by its own diplomats;[13] conveniently, however, the peak of the crisis was reached on 31 January, i.e., just in time for the electoral period.[14]

This context meant that the 1887 elections, whose campaign period was exceptionally short,[15] was monopolised by debates on the expansion of the peacetime military contingent and the seven-year budget that accompanied it. The only other issue brought up, and only by the opposition, were the Reich's finances and the tax burden on German workers and peasants. As military

7 See section 1.1.
8 See MWG II/2, p. 54f.
9 See Engelberg 1990, pp. 456–62.
10 See Ulrich 2007, pp. 100–1.
11 Seager 1969, p. 5.
12 See Bendikat 1988, pp. 376–81 and Seager 1969, p. 50f.
13 Seager 1969, p. 51.
14 Seager 1969, p. 56.
15 Bendikat 1988, p. 296.

spending comprised 70% of the Imperial budget since 1881, these were by no means unrelated issues. Bismarck and the *Kartell* parties, in turn, led a one-dimensional campaign centred on military affairs and foreign policy issues;[16] they accused left-liberals and Centre party members – who did not reject military funding, seeking only to shorten its duration from seven to three years – of putting the nation at risk and of placing parliamentary prerogatives ahead of patriotism and security.[17]

German Social Democracy, the only party to openly denounce militarism and the manipulative character of the campaign, was incidentally the only political force to have put out a full electoral programme,[18] but was severely hampered by arrests and the aforementioned end of the 'mild enforcement' of the *Sozialistengesetz*. If the law's initial blanket repression had already been denounced as fruitless by the young Weber in 1884, the year 1886 would mark a new strategy of persecution, with the targeting of social-democratic leadership, including its parliamentarians, many of whom would spend the better part of a year in prison following the Freiberg trials of late 1886.[19] Finally, because of decrees put in place by arch-conservative Interior Minister Robert von Puttkammer in this period, workers had to contend with an escalation in the suppression of strikes and labour organising, even when unrelated to party activities.

Under these extreme circumstances and with the recent conservative turn of the National Liberals, one of the objects of most interest for the young Weber in the 1884 elections, namely the role of Social Democrats in run-off votes and the exchanging of support with National Liberal candidates, was not a matter of concern in 1887. The electoral tactic of the Social Democrats was now based on the support of the parties opposing the *Septennat* (i.e. the Centre and Progressives) on the run-offs. While Social Democrats managed to slightly raise their total percentage of the vote to 10.4%, a considerable feat given the circumstances, they lost more than half of their seats (from 24 to 11) due to imbalances in the electoral weight of urban and rural districts and the lack of support for their candidates by left-liberals (though the latter had themselves strongly profited from the support of the Social Democrats).[20]

Despite his silence on the 1887 elections, it would not take long for Max Weber to once again take up his running commentary of the current polit-

---

16 See Wehler 1995, p. 992.

17 See Bendikat 1988, pp. 296–309.

18 See Bendikat 1988, p. 299; Lidtke 1966, pp. 254–60 and Engelberg 1990, p. 484.

19 Lidtke 1966, p. 248 f.

20 See Lidtke 1966, pp. 259–60.

ical situation of the *Kaiserreich* in two letters to Hermann Baumgarten, dated 25 April[21] and 29 June 1887.[22] In the first letter, Weber produces an assessment of 'realist politics' that, coincidentally or not, is addressed to its former champion within the German liberal bourgeoisie. It was Baumgarten's birthday and the young Weber's choice of gift was a collection of poems from Heinrich von Treitschke, his uncle's now bitter rival; a 'bizarre idea', he admitted.[23] In his attempt to justify it, Weber started by conceding the 'ungratifying effect' of Treitschke's influence 'on the serenity of judgement, on the capacity of judgment and on the sense of fairness of the members of his generation'.[24] Yet, he also reported having experienced a 'certain joy' upon reading the poems, and in finding in them a 'fundamental ideal undercurrent' which the 'hapless man never seems to shed entirely'.[25] Weber then goes on to argue that, while Treitschke's activities as a professor had 'ominous' consequences, the blame for this lay 'mainly on the shoulders of his audience'.[26] A similar dynamic, he argued, presided over the nation's relationship to Bismarck:

> If only the nation knew how to deal with and utilize the latter correctly, that is, to stand firm against him when the moment calls for it and to put trust in him where he has earned it – I should say, had the nation understood this all along, because now it's too late – the in so many respects devastating consequences of his personal politics would never have taken on the scale they have.[27]

Weber's reference to the 'nation's' unwillingness to stand up to Bismarck was likely directed at German liberals' failure in this regard. This did not apply only to National Liberals' continued willingness to compromise with conservatism, however, but also to Progressives' decision to place their hopes for a favourable change in the political direction of the Reich in the 'liberal-leaning' Crown Prince Friedrich. Not surprisingly, neither alternative was especially attractive to Weber's youthful contemporaries, who seemed to gravitate to a more aggressive notion of *Realpolitik*. As he recounts, were his classmates

21 MWG II/2, pp. 69–74.
22 MWG II/2, pp. 90–5.
23 MWG II/2, p. 70.
24 Ibid.
25 Ibid.
26 Ibid.
27 Ibid.

> not so intoxicated with ruthlessness, military or otherwise, i.e., with the culture of 'realism' … then they might be able to take more away from Treitschke's classes than the countless, often crudely biased statements, the impassioned struggle against diverging opinions and the fondness … for what one calls *Realpolitik* today.[28]

These remarks notwithstanding, the young Weber's critique of Treitschke's teaching did not mean he favoured restraint on the lectern at this point. Even the old professor's excesses were something to value 'and take home with', if regarded as a symptom of his 'impassioned striving for ideal foundations'.[29] In fact, the affirmation of ideals seemed to the young Weber an antidote to a reverence of 'realism' that by the late-1880s had gone from political credo to a broader cultural phenomenon impacting both artistic and philosophical currents in Imperial Germany.[30] Non-coincidentally, this is also the period when naturalism had its short peak phase in German literature, a development Georg Lukács traced back to a general reverence of naked and crude reality by young writers that, despite sympathetically drawing attention to mounting poverty and destituteness, nevertheless limited themselves to a superficial portrayal of things 'as they were'.[31]

Against this backdrop, Treitschke's forceful expression of ideals was to Weber a refreshing contrast to the cult of 'realism' and opportunism prevalent at the time. The young Weber's stance towards Treitschke betrays, in this sense, some of the same drivers of the upcoming enthusiastic reception of Friedrich Nietzsche in Imperial Germany. As Lukács argues, the discovery of the philosopher's writings would both complement and partially negate naturalism's coarse perspective on social reality. The critique of present conditions remained, yet the means for their transformation had shifted; the call for collective forms of social change, often culminating in support for Social Democracy among young writers and the intelligentsia, gave way to the notion that 'a genuine individual can only realize his deepest potentialities *apart from* or *in opposition to* present society'.[32]

In his search for an ethical alternative to crude 'realism', the young Weber reflected the ongoing cultural transformation of his middle-class contemporaries. His backhanded praise of Bismarck and Treitschke as figures who, for all

28 Ibid.
29 MWG II/2, pp. 70–1.
30 See Le Rider 2008, pp. 7–20.
31 Lukács 1947, pp. 19–22.
32 Lukács 1947, p. 24, my emphasis.

their faults, nevertheless held on to strong ideals also foreshadows his later emphasis on the value-based drivers of individual agency. In terms of the 1887 letter, as mentioned previously, the targets of his critique were less his callous classmates and more the forces that had not 'stood firm' against Bismarck's personal politics. The cult of the Chancellor and that of *Realpolitik* were parallel phenomena in this sense. Considering this was a letter to Hermann Baumgarten, the erstwhile champion of 'realist' politics, no less, and that Weber still saw politics from the vantage point of German liberalism, it is fair to deduce that liberals bore the most blame for the 'devastating consequences' of Bismarck's personal politics in Weber's eyes.

Crucially, while Hermann Baumgarten was the ideologue behind the 'pragmatic' split of the pro-Prussian elements from the German Progressive Party, the infatuation of many German liberals with 'political realism' preceded his intervention of 1866; in fact, the thinker who had first popularised the concept in the German lands had also been a liberal, August Ludwig von Rochau (1810–73), with his 1853 pamphlet entitled *Grundsätze der Realpolitik* or 'Foundations of *Realpolitik*'.

Rochau's trajectory was emblematic of an entire generation of German liberals. His revolutionary activities in the 1830s forced him into exile in France until 1848. Back on German soil, he attempted to synthesise the lessons of the defeated revolution of 1848–9 in its immediate aftermath by pointing to the fundamental centrality of power in politics[33] (though he did not defend subservience to the strongest as a value in itself).[34] Whatever criticism of Prussian dominance was still present in the initial 1853 edition of the book gave way, however, to the praise of Bismarckian power politics in its 1869 reworking, which also called for the repression of socialists and Catholics and dismissed women's rights.[35] The rejection of expanded suffrage as harmful to liberalism was also in line with then emerging National Liberalism.[36]

Weber's discussion of *Realpolitik* and how to best face up to Bismarckian conservatism from his 1887 letter came precisely at a time when National Liberals had renewed their policy of compromise with the Reich's Chancellor in return for membership in the ruling parliamentary coalition. The move harkened back to the party's genesis in the 1860s, which likely prompted Weber's reflections on the topic.

---

33 See Rochau 1972 [1869], pp. 25–37.
34 Wehler 1972, p. 15.
35 Wehler 1972, pp. 18–19.
36 Rochau 1972 [1869], pp. 227–8.

While a segment of contemporary scholarship has stressed that liberal politics in Germany up to 1878 should not be understood 'exclusively as a rapid succession of compromises leading precipitously to the feeble refusal of a share in power',[37] the balance sheet of liberals' renewed alliance with Bismarck in the late-1880s leaves little room for silver linings. Hence the crucial, even existential question for the young Weber in that period, namely, whether there was any political space available for the reassertion of some manner of liberal influence in the Reich. To historian Dieter Langewiesche, 'that they [National Liberals – V.S.] would be denied the harvest they hoped to reap, i.e. a parliamentary government, they could not foresee. And exacting this harvest was something they could not do'.[38] In other words, Langewiesche frames National Liberals as having done their best given the circumstances. In his historical portrayal, Thomas Nipperdey also put National Liberals in a rather positive light, as he stressed that the 1878 break with Bismarck was the result of an 'assertive' – rather than 'governmental' – liberalism. According to this view, 'National Liberals were neither heroes nor victims … and also no sinners or traitors'. Yet, what Nipperdey argued defined these liberals' legacy still suggests a strong air of inevitability: 'They were victims of their time. And they were victims of Bismarck'.[39]

The unfavourable conditions for liberals did not only pertain to the political sphere, considering the economic downturn – of global proportions – that had started in 1873 would only be overcome in the mid-1890s.[40] To Hans-Ulrich Wehler, the sputtering economy made German liberalism's erosion more acute; only a political achievement as substantive as the introduction of true parliamentary rule could have counterbalanced its downward turn.[41]

These were the stakes for German liberalism in the late-1880s. Given that the young Weber was taking his first steps towards political and social engagement at the time, he was heavily invested in finding possible openings regarding liberalism's dilemmas. The second major topic of his 1887 letters to his uncle was, incidentally, the so-called *Kulturkampf*, i.e., the 'culture war' unleashed soon after unification by Reich authorities against Catholicism and supposed Papal meddling in German affairs. Historians' aforementioned stressing of the unfavourable circumstances faced by liberals in this juncture crucially do not apply in this case, considering the *Kulturkampf* received enthusiastic National Lib-

37 Langewiesche 1988, p. 176.
38 Ibid.
39 Nipperdey 1993, p. 402.
40 See Wehler 1995, p. 575 f.
41 Wehler 1995, p. 954.

eral support. More than any other political development in the early trajectory of Imperial Germany, it highlighted the ambiguous legacy of liberals' allegiance to a process of national unification devoid of any democratising thrust. The persecution of Catholics and the ensuing repression of Social Democracy and the labour movement later in the 1870s were, in this sense, indicative of the more ominous consequences of the liberal policy of 'political realism' that contemporary scholarship – focusing rather on its 'achievements' – often choses to ignore or at least downplay. In contrast to these stances are Leo Kofler's remarks to the effect that:

> The subjection of society as a whole to the rule of the *Junker* State and its needs did not comprise merely the economy, the bureaucracy and the political sphere; it also strongly left its mark in cultural and moral respects.[42]

The *Kulturkampf* consisted, to put it briefly, in a ostensible struggle for institutional secularisation that was, nevertheless, aimed mainly against Catholicism – painted by Reich authorities as a 'foreign' element in German society. The young Weber seemed clearly aware of the ambiguous balance-sheet of the *Kulturkampf* for German liberals. Beyond the fact that 1887 is considered to mark the end of the *Kulturkampf*, the fact that (Protestant) liberals played a key role in promoting it likely gave him reason to pause. Hence, after praising the manner in which Bismarck ended the conflict in a recent speech, Weber remarked that:

> It is nevertheless sad, this unceremonious 'peace'; and in any case there lies an admission of injustice, indeed of grave injustice, when it is now said that, from our side, the struggle has had only 'political' reasons.[43]

Weber's dreary tone on the outcome of the *Kulturkampf* is reminiscent of his reservations over the persecutory component of the *Sozialistengesetz*, expressed in an 1884 letter I examined earlier.[44] Just as on that occasion, however, there is *no clear condemnation* of the repressive measures either. It is a telling sign of the young Weber's relationship to and, indeed, identification with Protestantism that he seemed to have no problems with a (state-backed) struggle

---

42 Kofler 1966, pp. 275–6.
43 MWG II/2, p. 72.
44 See section 1.1.

against Catholicism if it had, as he put it, remained an issue of 'consciousness against consciousness',[45] as if that would have constituted any less of a violation of religious freedom.

Nevertheless, the young Weber did seem more troubled by the repercussions of the *Kulturkampf* for German liberalism than he had been by the fallout of the persecution of Social Democrats. Unlike the 'Law against the Socialists', which National Liberals voted for only after pressure from Bismarck and an electoral defeat broke their initial resistance, the *Kulturkampf* constituted, if not a creation of liberals, then a struggle they identified with and ultimately propelled out of deep-seated conviction. Furthermore, its peak coincides with the 'glory years' of liberals' alliance with Bismarck, the so-called 'Liberal Era'.

Setting off soon after unification in 1871/72, the *Kulturkampf* involved a series of measures to discipline the Catholic clergy, diminish Papal authority over the Catholic Church hierarchy in Germany as well as the latter's influence over German society. This was pursued through the introduction of civil marriage, the limitation of religious influence in education and by facilitating the process of leaving the Church.[46] There were also measures of open religious persecution, such as the exiling of numerous members of the clergy, banning of the Jesuits, and suppression of part of the Catholic press amidst a general rise in hostility toward the entire Roman Catholic population. Especially from a liberal vantage point, there was no way around the two-pronged nature of the *Kulturkampf*, as it both raised the banner of secularisation and legitimised state persecution of the Reich's citizens. Finally, it was highly inconsistent in its sparing of the Lutheran Church and arguably helped stoke nationalism through the conspiracies of Papal interference in German affairs spread throughout the struggle – including by authorities.

The contemporary scholarship on the period reflects these ambiguities; it stresses the many modernising advancements brought by the *Kulturkampf*, but also highlights its damaging effects, not only for the religious freedom of Catholics and their integration into the newly-founded Empire, but also for German liberalism. If liberals took on the role of ruthless enforcers, they were, as Social Democrats criticised, highly selective ones, as their secularising drive stopped short of addressing the influence of the Lutheran Church in German public life.[47]

The *political* motivations behind National Liberals' support for the *Kulturkampf* were clear, and, therefore, all the more discrediting for the liberal

45 MWG II/2, p. 72 – see complete quote below.

46 Wehler 1995, pp. 894–97.

47 See Prüfer 2002, pp. 160–1.

camp as the years passed. The emergence of the Catholic Centre Party in the early 1870s and the process of political reorganisation of conservatism from around the middle of that decade onwards, had enabled Bismarck to become independent of National Liberals in the question of parliamentary majorities. By engaging in the anti-Catholic struggle and doubling down on Bismarck's own claim that Catholic clergy and their supporters were 'enemies of the Reich', National Liberals aimed to keep the Chancellor tied to them, in terms of constituting the only suitable partners for moderate ('free') conservatives in the Reichstag. The bottom-line was that liberals had been complacent with rights violations for purposes of political convenience or, as the young Weber put it, for 'reasons of an external nature':

> If [the *Kulturkampf* – V.S.] was not an issue of conscience, but only one of opportunism, then we have obviously, as the Catholics claim, violated the conscience of the Catholic people – to the mass of Catholics it was indeed an issue of conscience – due to reasons of an external nature. If so, what we have always maintained, i.e., that it was a matter of conscience against conscience, was obviously not the case.[48]

The *Kulturkampf* had been taken up so eagerly, as Thomas Nipperdey surmised, because it allowed National Liberals to fulfil two roles, that is, to lead a struggle in the name of their core values and to cooperate with the government all at once.[49] Admitting to a 'political' motivation was damaging, in this sense, because it confirmed that the means – reliance on State repression, securing the alliance with Bismarck – employed to achieve secularisation were in fact themselves the overbearing *aims* of the struggle. In the young Weber's assessment, the end result for liberals, beyond attempts to commemorate 'what we have', was 'very uncomfortable', also in its implications for any treatment of the issue of religion and the state in the future. As he put it: 'We have thus acted unconscionably and come out morally defeated as well'.[50]

Hence, instead of achieving the double aim of liberalising the German Empire and politically binding Bismarck to them, German liberals became more and more dependent on the Chancellor as the struggle went on; furthermore, every constitutional achievement reached at the expense of repressive measures had, in a way, a tainted nature to it that undermined future

48 MWG II/2, p. 72.
49 Nipperdey 1993, p. 379.
50 MWG II/2, p. 72.

advances.[51] If hard anti-clericalism was by no means an exclusively German phenomenon, French republicans' struggle for secularisation, to name one example, had a different meaning in the context of a republic,[52] in that it at least did not help bolster an authoritarian political framework. The bottom-line, as Nipperdey has argued, is that 'liberals themselves changed due to the *Kulturkampf*'.[53] The dependence on Bismarck, the willingness to instrumentalise core principles for political goals and the growing difficulty of playing any type of progressive, modernising role was coupled with growing political isolation and fragmentation from the late-1870s onwards, culminating in the National Liberals' conservative turn in the 1887 elections.

Left-liberals, in turn, place their hopes for an opening up of the political system squarely on the pending rise to the throne of enlightened Crown Prince Friedrich and the English-born Princess Victoria. Succession was imminent as Wilhelm I had entered his nineties, and the Progressive Party's expectation was that the future Kaiser would loosen Bismarck's grip on state power. If a 'resolutely' liberal party relying on the royal family to further its goals was not contradictory enough, the young Weber was also appalled by the left-liberal leadership's 'servility' towards the Crown Prince, with regards to whom, as Weber correctly foresaw, 'they were most likely fooling themselves'.[54] If the young Weber had still thought of liberalism's two wings as part of the same political camp in his 1884/85 letters, his hostility towards Progressives was on the rise in 1887. In a letter from June that year, a very upset young Weber emphasises the 'unbelievable ways in which the left-liberal deputies compromise liberalism',[55] as they had seemed to display a 'the worse things are, the better for us' attitude regarding the approval of new taxes to fund increased military expenditures.

If a reunited liberalism did not present the answer, there were no other clear alternatives either. The stability of the Reich's politics would, however, soon be severely shaken. If Max Weber did not seem content with the prospects of German liberalism in 1887, the following years were to dramatically change the German political landscape. An attentive Weber would follow these developments closely.

51 Langewiesche 1988, p. 184.
52 Nipperdey 1993, p. 380.
53 Nipperdey 1993, p. 379.
54 MWG II/2, p. 73.
55 MWG II/2, p. 92.

CHAPTER 5

Witness to the End of an Era: The 'Three-Kaiser Year', Mass Strikes and Bismarck's Fall (1888–1891/2)

1 Introduction

The year 1888 is known in German history as the 'year of three Kaisers'. As it began, Wilhelm I still occupied the throne; by mid-June, his 29-year old grandson, Wilhelm II, had been crowned emperor, his father, Friedrich III, having reigned for a mere 99 days. The cycle of change triggered in Imperial Germany by the events of 1888 went, however, far beyond the rapid succession of monarchs. As the old Kaiser passed away on 9 March, however, there were no indications of the upcoming turmoil. In fact, a situation of relative stability seemed to prevail. The hopes associated with the liberal-leaning Crown Prince's ascent to the throne had dampened, especially in light of the advanced stage of his illness – larynx cancer – which foretold a short reign; moreover, the liberal-conservative Reichstag majority – the *Kartell* – gave Bismarck the means to neutralise any gestures towards left-liberals the new Kaiser might have attempted.[1] Yet, almost exactly two years to the date of Wilhelm I's death, on 15 March 1890, Bismarck would be ousted from office, following the rejection of a new extension to the *Sozialistengesetz* and the *Kartell*'s tremendous defeat in the February elections.

Fuelled by the social and political unrest of these years, the young Weber's own stance on the 'social question' and the future of German liberalism, which he would increasingly see as related, became sharper and more coherent. This shift in perspective would, in turn, propel his pursuit of various forms of political and scholarly engagement during the 1890s. The years 1888–91, as the next sections will argue, represent, therefore, a clear turning point in Max Weber's trajectory, one in which societal change and personal maturation combined to forge lasting aspects of his personality and thought.

1 See Loth 1996, p. 81 and Ulrich 2007, p. 110.

2 Taking Stock of Bismarck's Legacy amongst the Berlin Masses

The old Kaiser's death on 9 March 1888 prompted a reflection by Weber in a letter sent to Hermann Baumgarten four days later. Contrary to his customary dispassionate political analyses, this time Weber reflects on the event's repercussions from the standpoint of first-hand experience. He had attended the mass vigil outside the Imperial Palace in central Berlin and, rather than focusing on the intrigues raging within the court, Weber provides an eyewitness account of public sentiment in the evening of 8 March centred on 'how the popular masses conducted themselves'.[2]

According to Weber, views amongst the crowd gathered at Unter den Linden on the eve of the Kaiser's death ranged from the belief that Wilhelm I still had many years ahead of him to speculation he was already dead. Weber assured his uncle 'the optimistic party was not short on crude Berliner jokes'.[3] Yet, when confronted with enraged reactions to this behaviour, probably from members of his own class, as well as with accusations that Berliners did not express enough grief, Weber 'vigorously objected'.[4] He stressed, instead, how 'inside a mass, men are peculiar things',[5] and how, on the morning of the 9th, as the flag at half-mast over the Palace announced the Kaiser's death, there was a 'deep silence' that 'left a very grave impression'. Indeed, he found 'the behaviour of city dwellers' had been nothing if not 'exemplary'.[6] Considering 'the usual mores of the Berlin populace regarding the police', this had made their jobs easier as well, he added.[7]

Weber's light-hearted comments indicate an unusual proximity to the ordinary Berliners gathered at Unten den Linden; he remarked, in fact, that 'the most significant aspect' of the entire experience 'was to be as one with individuals from entirely different intellectual spheres'.[8] This 'cross-class' or 'cross-cultural' insight was, in fact, a tell-tale sign of the young Weber's changing perspective on workers at this juncture. The remainder of the letter, and especially the ensuing one to Baumgarten, mark a return to the detached mode of political commentary that had characterised the uncle-nephew correspondence so far. Yet, there was an important change; the working class now figured as a relevant political

2 MWG II/2, p. 146.
3 Ibid.
4 MWG II/2, p. 147.
5 Ibid.
6 Ibid.
7 Ibid.
8 MWG II/2, p. 148.

actor in Weber's considerations. Whether this shift in vantage point had any relation to his interactions with workers, like the one reported above, is a key question for this section and chapter.

The following letter to Baumgarten, dated 30 April 1888,[9] turned to the political implications of the Kaiser's passing. Weber reports 'thinking incessantly about public matters';[10] this was understandable considering that the reign of Kaiser Friedrich III was expected to be short and Crown Prince Wilhelm was known for his reactionary tendencies. As Weber reports, the latter was often in the 'company of high-ranking military personnel' and of 'feudal and high Church circles', and his views were knowingly influenced by these sectors.[11] This meant that Bismarck's role took on a new connotation for moderate liberals. If previously they had grown critical of his overbearing influence in the Reich's politics, they now saw the Chancellor as the only possible 'counterweight' to the future Kaiser's 'feudal tendencies'.[12]

The young Weber's own ambiguous stance towards Bismarck, discussed briefly in the previous chapter, is again on display in the letter. In terms of Weber's generation, now coming of age politically, this was far from an anomaly. Ernst Engelberg highlighted how a number of 'opposition writers' belonging to roughly the same cohort as Weber were increasingly torn between a fascination with the rising labour movement and a remaining admiration for Bismarck:

> The oppositional writers of the eighties, drawn into the societal conflicts in the Prussian-German Reich, found themselves in an intermediary position not only in social terms; they were also politically and ideologically torn. On the one hand, they were attracted to the labour movement, which had been gaining strength under the *Sozialistengesetz*; on the other, they had difficulty letting go of their childhood impressions from the 'great period' of the Reich's foundation and its imposing founder.[13]

In Weber's case, the notion of Bismarck as the only credible bulwark against the reactionary tendencies of the future Kaiser threw this ambiguous stance into sharp relief. As he put it,

9 MWG II/2, pp. 151–9.
10 MWG II/2, p. 151.
11 MWG II/2, p. 152.
12 MWG II/2, p. 149.
13 Engelberg 1990, p. 529.

> That Bismarck did not foster these tendencies as an end in themselves is beyond doubt. He does not ignore how dangerous they are; the only questionable thing in his politics is that he attempted to use them to further his own aims, which cannot take place entirely without him also being used by them.[14]

Bismarck's channelling of reactionary currents had, in fact, been a tool to weaken German liberals in the recent past. The result was the 'decadence', to use Weber's term,[15] of the political party landscape in the late 1880s, embodied in liberalism's fragmentation and decline. This situation likely explains why Weber did not share his uncle's initial optimism that Friederich III's reign could herald a return to the status quo of the 1867–77 period,[16] i.e., of fruitful liberal cooperation with Bismarck and the ruling dynasty in the name of gradual modernising achievements. Baumgarten's 'realist' liberal politics, it seemed, were no longer in tune with the times.

3 Weber's Generation Confronts a Liberal Camp Divided between Opportunists and Fundamentalists

A declining liberal tradition was, however, not the only factor to announce that a generational shift was unfolding within the German bourgeoisie; new voices were springing up from it, which Max Weber not only paid attention to, but seemed to identify with. His April 1888 letter signals, in this sense, a change in the interlocutors of his political analysis, from his father and uncle's cohort to 'acquaintances his age, with more or less conservative leanings'.[17] Weber reports hearing from them how left-liberals still nurtured hopes of seeing Bismarck dismissed by the new Kaiser – signalling a lack of 'clarity in political judgement' – and that 'positive cooperation' between National Liberals and the sectors that split from it (as a result of the party's conservative turn) was unlikely.[18] Indeed, the polarisation between an opportunistic National Liberal Party on the one hand, and a left-liberal camp with unreasonable demands, on the other, was now at its peak:

14 MWG II/2, p. 153.
15 Ibid.
16 MWG II/2, p. 151.
17 MWG II/2, p. 155.
18 Ibid.

> The notion of one day engaging in constructive politics with these people [i.e., left-liberals – VS] must be dropped entirely; and so the division of liberalism is made permanent, as are, to its discredit, the antics of stereotypical fanatical demagogues on one side, and blind Bismarckians, on the other.[19]

This polarisation and the weakness in the liberal parties' respective positions made the prospect of a moderate coalition uniting representatives of both wings of German liberalism far-fetched. As a result, Weber anticipated a scenario in which the 'radical parties of the left and right would alternate control over German politics by allying themselves with the [Catholic] Centre'. The radical parties, he argued, would prefer to split votes with either the Centre Party or even their own polar opposites, as long as the 'middle parties' lost ground. This would be the equivalent of having 'French circumstances' prevail in Imperial Germany.[20]

What political forces was Weber referring to here and why did he draw a comparison to contemporary France? The 'middle-parties' are the moderate segments of both the National Liberals and the Free Conservatives [*Reichskonservativen*], the radicals are likely the High Conservatives [*Deutschkonservativen*], on one side, and left-liberals, on the other, with the Catholic Centre as the possible coalition partner in between. While an alliance of Catholics and left-liberals would have been implausible, that was the only centre-radical 'left' combination available, considering Social Democrats did not figure in Weber's analysis of the political spectrum at all here. As for the reference to French conditions, it indicates he feared a rapid succession of coalition governments formed by various combinations of radicals, opportunist republicans and conservatives. France had had, in fact, seven different ruling majorities from 1885 to 1889, a phenomenon that had contributed to the rise of the movement behind General Boulanger.[21] The parallels with the French system would, however, become less apt with the electoral breakthrough of Social Democrats in 1890; French socialists would not play a comparable role in electoral politics until the 1900s.[22] Nevertheless, the young Weber's compar-

---

19 Ibid.

20 Ibid.

21 See Bendikat 1988, pp. 310–15 and pp. 355–65.

22 See Ducange 2020, p. 113f. It was only in 1905 that different French socialist currents converged to form the *Section Française de l'Internationale Ouvrière – Partie Socialiste*: 'Socialist unity was finally achieved, thirty years after the formation of the German Social-Democratic Party' (Ducange 2020, p. 114).

isons between Imperial Germany and France suggest a degree of apprehension of one key component affecting the political dynamic across the Rhine, i.e., mass politics – and the instability and polarisation Weber associated it with.

Weber believed that if divisions in German politics came to a head, 'all the experiences of the end of the fifties and sixties would be lost'.[23] By that he meant all the experiences of the 'Constitutional Conflict', i.e., when liberals – then united within the German Progressive Party – made use of their majority in the Prussian parliament to vote against the military budget only to be overruled by Bismarck's first significant intervention as chancellor. As approached in section 2.2. above, the ensuing split in the liberal camp and the emergence of the question of German unity culminated in the 'realist' compromise politics of the breakaway National Liberal Party. The notion of a parallel situation in the late 1880s signals that Weber feared a new showdown with Bismarck on the part of left-liberals. He likely favoured a return to a policy of compromise by the 'middle parties' at this point, fearing, perhaps, conservative retrenchment in the event of an open liberal challenge to the status quo. Such a radical challenge would, nevertheless, soon take place – but it would be led by a party Weber did not seem to consider a relevant actor in Imperial German politics as of April 1888, i.e., German Social Democracy.

Seemingly subdued by the *Sozialistengesetz*, Social Democrats did not merit the same attentions as the recently-crowned Friedrich III, whose short reign dashed left-liberal hopes, but produced at least one significant change regarding the situation of progressive forces in general. Arch-conservative interior minister Robert von Puttkamer was let go on 8 June 1888, a week before the Kaiser's death, and with this change, which was already expected – including by Weber[24] – the continuity in Bismarck's running of domestic politics had finally been broken.[25] Wider changes seemed, therefore, to be on the horizon, though it was not clear what would trigger them.

Max Weber apparently recognised this and – contrary to his uncle – did not feel pessimistic about the turbulence that lay ahead. He did not see a regression in the constitutional order of the Reich as a likely outcome, especially because of the trust he placed in the new generation – his own – whose political and practical intervention in Germany was just beginning.[26] Which is not to say there were no worrying signs in terms of political orientation within his cohort

23 MWG II/2, p. 155.
24 MWG II/2, p. 149.
25 See Seeber [ed.] 1977, pp. 217–19.
26 MWG II/2, pp. 156–7.

as well; ever since returning to Berlin in 1886, Max Weber had become acquainted with the rising popularity of anti-Semitism and ultra-nationalism amongst his contemporaries:

> Surely there are those self-important fellows who are anti-Semites, if for no other reason, as a matter of decorum; there are many idealists, who through Treitschke get caught up in a kind of mythical national fanaticism, and others still who merely adopt the supposed gentlemanly boasting and the supposed realism of the new school.[27]

This quote is well-known because of Weber's clear rejection of anti-Semitism. Yet, it also shows Weber's understanding of the range of types that made up his generation of bourgeois intellectuals. The dual critique of blind idealism on one side, and of an equally narrow veneration of 'realism' – now complemented by a socially prescribed level of bigotry – on the other, emerge as the fundamental poles of the young Weber's budding views on the relationship between politics and ethics. There were, however, 'other elements' in his generation that he actually identified with. In fact, he had 'gradually become convinced' that they 'would prevail in the future', due to being 'both more lucid and more energetic towards themselves'. Weber meant those contemporaries of his who had

> … shaken off anti-Semitism and other related excrescences of recent years; those that, despite having an essentially distinct position from the National Liberalism of the [eighteen-]seventies, are nevertheless just as free from a desire for status and from High-Church tendencies as it was; and who are, furthermore, entirely free from careerism or other materialist considerations. In short, those to whom I can ascribe intellectual freedom. They also see the period between 1867 and 1877 in an entirely different light as one is accustomed to do.[28]

In other words, Weber had found other young bourgeois intellectuals that, just like himself, rejected the reactionary demagoguery of figures such as Court Chaplain Stoecker, but who, on the other hand, were not lacking in values and ideals. They drew the young Weber's admiration despite holding 'essentially distinct' positions from those of his role models, i.e., the triumphant National Liberals of the 1860s and 1870s. Where these young contemporaries – 'mostly

---

27 MWG II/2, p. 156.
28 Ibid.

political economists and social policy experts' – tellingly differed from National Liberalism was in their 'greater appreciation of state intervention in the so-called social question as would seem justified for most, given the current situation'.[29] This statement prompts, in turn, a surprisingly candid admission by Weber of German liberalism's poor track-record on social issues from the time of unification to the present:

> The now indisputable fact that [eighteen-]seventies liberalism extended less importance to the social tasks of the state than would now seem justified or than we now consider normal ... or the fact that liberals today still only endure social legislation with a – sure enough – often valid, but mostly merely passive mistrust instead of intervening in order to remedy some of its truly problematic aspects ... all of this leads these politicians to see the National Liberal era as solely a transitional phase to a time of greater tasks of the state and to underestimate the legislative work done in those years.[30]

This key remark deserves closer attention. It shows Weber wrestling with his own interpretation of National Liberal heritage, having found a section of his contemporaries who did not value the constitutional achievements of his uncle's and father's generation as much as he did, but whom he nevertheless admired on ethical and political grounds. The fact that he was drawn by their concern for the 'social question' marks, in turn, a true watershed in Weber's trajectory. As he put it, whereas this 'school' – 'if one can call it that at all' – was grounded on different 'value judgements' than his own and had a certain bureaucratic tendency, it was nevertheless 'not difficult to come to terms with them in many respects'.[31]

It is not clear what young acquaintances Weber is concretely describing here so admiringly. Nevertheless, they share some of the typical traits of those young social reformers he would closely interact with from 1891/92 onwards in the framework of two organisations: the Protestant Social Congress and the Verein für Socialpolitik (Association for Social Policy). In both instances, Weber would be a leading figure of an up- and coming youthful wing that would promptly be at odds with the more established members of these organisations, which included the anti-Semite Adolf Stoecker in the case of the Congress.[32]

29 MWG II/2, pp. 156–7.
30 MWG II/2, p. 157.
31 Ibid.
32 See Part 2.

In fact, the young Weber rejected his uncle's accusation that the younger generation had gone 'through Treitschke to Stoecker', stressing that the 'politically responsible' among them were turning away from the latter.[33] This was indeed the case, and Stoecker would fail in his aim of channelling anti-Semitism into a mass-movement in the 1880s[34] (alas, others would, of course, be successful in this pursuit later on). The young Weber did, however, temper his optimism by recognising that 'Caesarist rule would not be without consequences', and that much depended on whether Bismarck would start the search for a successor 'as soon as normal circumstances returned'. The young Weber hoped Bismarck would choose someone worthy of the status of 'statesman' in time to prevent an alliance of Junkers and Catholics (which he considered would represent a regression of the 'national element' in the Reich).[35] But Bismarck would not move in the direction favoured by the young Weber and, above all, 'normal circumstances' would not return for a number of years. The reason for this was re-emergence of the labour movement in 1889, as the next item will detail.

4 The Resurgent Working Class: The Ruhr Miners' Strike of 1889 and the Expansion Of State Social Policy

The instability of the power structure centred on Bismarck became more pronounced in 1889. For starters, the *Kartell* parties, i.e. Conservatives, Free Conservatives and National Liberals, were proving an ever less reliable basis of support for the chancellor's rule.[36] In the elections to the Prussian chamber of representatives in late-1888, for example, the constituents of the *Kartell* all acted according to their own interests and in direct competition with each other. The result – which did not break conservative hegemony, but gave National Liberals more seats – only made tensions between the respective political camps greater.[37] Hence, instead of a cohesive base to counteract the instability of transitioning to the reign of yet another new Kaiser, the *Kartell* was torn between its right-wing – High Conservatives determined to prevent even moderate reforms and reverse previous ones – and the National Liberal left

33 MWG II/2, p. 158.
34 See Pulzer 1988, pp. 83–97.
35 MWG II/2, p. 158.
36 See Nipperdey 1993, p. 418, Wehler 1995, p. 994; Seeber [ed.] 1977, pp. 218–19.
37 Wehler 1995, p. 992.

who wished to resume the introduction of modernising measures.[38] There was hardly a coherent core between these positions and mistrust of Bismarck's manoeuvring, even by his allies, was higher than ever.[39]

Besides the pending issue of whether to prolong the 'Law against the Socialists' once more, the key development in political debate was social policy's return to the foreground in late-1888. Conditions were ripe given the desire of young Kaiser Wilhelm II to present himself as a friend of working people, but also due to the fact that the previous election had weakened the main opposition to state-led intervention in the 'social question', i.e., left-liberals, while disciplining ambiguous National Liberals as to the growing relevance of social policy for the broader public.[40] This time the measures under discussion were old age and disability provisions, considered an essential complementary piece of legislation to the measures of health and accident insurance introduced in 1883 and 1884. The main issues were, once more, who would bear the burden of the system – Bismarck pushed for a federally-funded framework while left-liberals favoured one based entirely on worker contributions – and whether it would be administered locally, regionally or centrally and by whom (state authorities at different levels or cooperatives).[41]

The question of the different needs of urban workers and their rural counterparts played an important role in debates, as many conservatives claimed their 'patriarchal welfare' rendered centralised old-age and disability insurance schemes unnecessary and would, instead, only undermine their authority and time-old relation of trust to their workers. By the late 1880s, however, it had become evident that growing industrialisation and the spread of capitalist relations of production into the countryside had 'made a societal issue out of the individual process of ageing'. The network of corporatist and patriarchal organisations that had been employed to face up to the 'social question' no longer encompassed a large share of workers who had 'severed their ties to them long before'.[42] The legislation on old-age and disability insurance was a watershed moment for social policy – not only in Imperial Germany, but in the European

38 Seeber [ed.] 1977, p. 233. These measures included the introduction of direct taxation encompassing large landed estates and the extension of modern municipal administration to rural townships east of the river Elbe, both of which directly affected the economic and political foundations of Junker power.

39 Wehler 1995, pp. 994–5.

40 See QGdS II/6, p. XXIII.

41 See Kieseritzky 2002, pp. 313–25; Kott 2014, pp. 53–60; Seeber [ed.] 1977, pp. 256–62 and Wehler 1995, p. 913.

42 See QGdS II/6, p. XXI.

context as a whole – to the extent that it 'finally recognised the negative consequences of impersonal and structural labour conditions, without making the individual responsible for his hardship – as was previously the case – by means of moral categories'.[43]

That does not mean capitalist industrialists welcomed the measures. In fact, many of them held patriarchal views not far removed from those of East-Elbian landowners and would rather see matters of insurance and support to workers be solved through their own initiatives on a company by company basis. In addition, the threat of German Social Democracy and, more significantly, the irruption of a mass strike by Ruhr coal miners in May 1889 – stretching to other mining areas in the whole of the Reich by July and involving, at one point, a hundred thousand workers – gave issues of social policy, workers' insurance and collective bargaining rights considerable urgency and an unmistakable political edge.[44]

Given the repressive climate under the *Sozialistengesetz*, the strike started by Ruhr miners quickly took on the character of a revolt. For the socialist labour movement this was, in Friedrich Engels's own words, 'an immense event'; and an unexpected one at that, considering that the suddenly rebellious workers of the Ruhr were known as 'good subjects, patriotic, obedient, and religious, and furnishing some of the finest infantry for the VII. Army corps'. 'I know them well', Engels added, 'my native place is only 6 or 7 miles south of the coalfields'.[45] Furthermore, the quite recent (1854) transfer of mining enterprises to private entrepreneurs meant relations between workers and mine owners remained mired in patriarchal practices. This included military-like discipline and a peculiar kind of piece wage [*Akkordlohn*] with a complex set of rules determining a worker's earnings.

The young Weber commented on the Ruhr miner strike in his letters, as expected, and its impact on him appears to have been considerable. More specifically, the dilemmas that it raised as a concentrated – and antagonistic – expression of the 'social question' in Imperial Germany would feed directly into his work and political engagement in the 1890s. It is no accident that topics such as the patriarchal stance of both German landowners and industrialists, the 'situation' of workers – i.e., their living and working conditions – and not

43 Wehler 1995, pp. 913–14. For a detailed analysis of the old-age and disability insurance effectively introduced in the Reich and a comparison with its European equivalents, see Kott 2014, pp. 54–8.

44 Kieseritzky 2002, p. 374.

45 See Engels's article 'The Ruhr Miners' Strike of 1889', published in June that year and available at marxists.org.

least workers' right to collective bargaining would all figure into his research in the following decade; the mass strike had forcefully pushed these questions to the centre of public debate in Imperial Germany.

In a 30 May 1889 letter, Weber writes to his mother about how two Sundays before, that is, at the height of the strikes, his regular meeting with friends and acquaintances to discuss political economy and play billiards and cards featured none of the latter. Instead, 'an animated political conversation emerged about strikes, the Law against the Socialists, Stoecker and so on, with a worrying preponderance of the "enemies of the Reich" [i.e. Social Democrats – V.S.]'.[46] The conversation only stopped because participants had to run to take the last trains and horse-drawn trams. While Weber does not provide any more details on the discussion that night, it hardly seems to have culminated in the one-sided condemnation of strikers and Social Democrats, i.e., the expected reaction in bourgeois circles. That this regular meeting of young scholars had been started to discuss political economy is also relevant; Weber's interest in the discipline would parallel his growing engagement with the 'labour question' in the following years.

In a letter of mid-July 1889 to his cousin Emmy Baumgarten, Weber offers a window precisely into how the strike movement was framed within the higher echelons of Imperial Germany's bourgeoisie. He mentions having met a certain Mrs. von Schubert, the daughter of an actual manager of a mine in the Ruhr area. In this occasion,

> the topic of the latest large strike in the region came up, and I was quite taken aback by her. Not because she seemed to place the wrongdoing almost exclusively on the shoulders of the workers and was outraged about what took place, but because of how consistently she took the standpoint of formal law. As a consequence, the work stoppages were reprehensible to her not primarily due to the profound destitution they subjected married workers to, but due to the injustice which the worker commits by breaking the contract with his employer.[47]

If Weber stops short of taking the side of workers, his remarks make it clear he did not share the point of view of mine owners either. More significant, perhaps, considering his legal background, was his rejection of a stance based on 'formal law' alone. Indeed, as Weber correctly recalled, the main argument of the mine owners' association to characterise the strike as illegal was the sup-

46 MWG II/2, pp. 196–7.

47 MWG II/2, p. 193.

posed 'one-sided breach of contract' on the part of the workers (aggravated by the fact it occurred on a mass scale). As a letter addressed to Bismarck on 13 June 1889 from Dortmund's Chamber of Commerce details, employers also claimed that the attempt to interfere with the 'plentiful and normal supply of labour' – i.e., to impose 'a monopoly price' for it through reductions to the working day and overtime – were both illegal and 'thoroughly social-democratic'.[48] As a result, mine owners demanded changes to the legal code that would allow the criminal prosecution of workers engaging in 'mass contract breaches' – and of those inciting them – as well as swift and decisive use of the military to suppress the strikes.[49]

Though there was indeed open repression by authorities – resulting in striking workers wounded and killed and labour leaders imprisoned – state violence only amplified the strike and was condemned even in the bourgeois press; while the strike petered out in late May and early June, it resulted in a number of concessions and culminated in the founding of the first miners' trade-unions in the Ruhr area.[50] Finally, the strike finally forced German liberals to reconsider their foot-dragging stance on social policy.[51] This literally hit 'close to home' in Max Weber's case, as his final comment on Ms. von Schubert's perspective makes clear:

> Hearing this from a young woman was especially surprising to me and again made me think how dependent we are regarding the direction of our moral judgement, and how the latter is connected to the habitual circles (*Lebenskreise*) we originate from.[52]

The question of how the capacity for moral judgement is tied to class background had already appeared two years earlier in Weber's correspondence, more specifically in a letter of July 1887 to the same addressee (Emmy Baumgarten). The topic emerges as part of a reflection on how much 'circumstances [*Verhältnisse*] have an influence on people'. To his own surprise, Weber concluded at the time that their weight was 'relatively minor'. It's worth quoting his words in full here:

---

48 See QGdS II/ 4, p. 410.

49 QGdS II/4, p. 411.

50 For an exhaustive account of the 1889 strike and its achievements, see the Friedrich Ebert Foundation's timeline: https://library.fes.de/fulltext/bibliothek/tit00148/00148023.htm#E323E53.

51 Kieseritzky 2002, p. 376.

52 MWG II/2, p. 193.

> The enormous gap in our circumstances with regards to those of a part of the lower classes – in the external living conditions almost as broad as the one between man and beast, considering some animals lead an almost more dignified existence – *does not mean*, in relative terms – obviously only in relative terms! – *that there is just as great a gap in moral consciousness*. The development of the intellect [*Verstand*], the sense of beauty etc. suffers greatly under these circumstances, but not moral judgment, whose purity within individual members of these classes is no more variable, in relative terms, than it is within the individual members of our class. Obviously, only in comparison to the enormous gap that exists in other areas. What is weakened is the essential capacity to resist those influences contrary to moral judgement, *not the faculty of judgement itself*.[53]

In 1887, therefore, Weber's argument had been that, despite the wide disparity in living circumstances, a worker's capacity for moral judgement was not necessarily different from that of members of the bourgeoisie. Crucially, Weber stopped short of declaring all men as equal bearers of moral consciousness on that occasion, repeatedly stressing any parity in this regard across class divides was only valid in relative terms; in other words, if social status did not entirely determine the 'purity' of moral judgement to the Weber of July 1887, he still believed that 'circumstances' favoured its development in the upper classes. In the August 1889 letter, in turn, Weber reversed the poles in the connection of social class and moral judgements, tracing the bias – or even impairment – of this faculty on the part of a bourgeois woman back to her *privileged* social background. Hence, the stress now was on how different social segments could have divergent moral perspectives, the case in point being how class interests had warped the judgement of a member of the elites, just as poor living conditions had an unfavourable bearing on workers' intellect. Though not incompatible, a comparison of the two stances shows an important shift in vantage point, one that built a key stepping stone to Weber's subsequent engagement with workers' perspective in his studies of the 'rural labour question' of 1892–4.[54]

Amongst the many far-reaching ramifications of the mass strike of 1889 – which include a sharp rise in labour conflict in Imperial Germany in the ensuing years – was the thrusting of workers' own voices and demands into the centre of debate on the 'social question' (in spite of continued muzzling of Social Democrats). The young Weber was not the only one to have been im-

53 MWG II/2, p. 105 – my emphasis.

54 See Chapters 7 and 8 below.

pacted by these developments within the liberal bourgeoise. As one historian has highlighted, the sudden awareness of the 'actual disposition of workers produced a shock within the liberal camp'.[55] This contributed to a shift in the position of a segment of liberals, not only with regards to state social policy, but also to the now decade-old – and increasingly ineffective – repression of German Social Democracy through the *Sozialistengesetz*.

5 After the *Sozialistengesetz*: The 1890 Elections and the Fall of Bismarck

As the end of 1889 neared, two issues took centre stage in political debate in Imperial Germany, namely, the question of whether the *Sozialistengesetz* should be extended once more and the upcoming elections to the Reichstag in February 1890. In light of the Ruhr strike, growing differences began to emerge between Bismarck and segments of the *Kartell* regarding the best way to deal with the challenge of Social Democracy and of a resurgent labour movement.

Bismarck's proposal was to either prolong a harsher version of the law indefinitely or to make changes to the criminal code so that the exception measures were incorporated on a permanent basis to the Reich's legal edifice.[56] In terms of his coalition partners, these measures were seen as both too mild by arch-conservatives and too harsh by many moderate ones and especially by liberals, who feared such legal changes would, in fact, threaten some of the more outspoken members in their own camp.

There was thus a growing consensus that the exception law was no longer effective, yet even within Bismarck's parliamentary majority there were widely diverging stances on what the best alternative to it was. As National Liberals did not wish to commit to a harsher version of the exception law on the eve of the elections, the last attempt at prolonging the *Sozialistengesetz* failed to reach a majority in the Reichstag on 25 January 1890, i.e., less than a month before Germans went to the polls. Bismarck now had a new coalition in view – made up of both wings of conservatism and, for the first time, the Catholic Centre – and hoped to reap the benefits of the insecurity generated by the exception law's pending loss of effect in October 1890. There is no relevant correspondence from Max Weber in 1890, probably due to his intense preparation for the second round of his state legal exams. Nevertheless, just before temporarily sus-

55 Kieseritzky 2002, p. 376.
56 Seeber [ed.] 1977, p. 251, n. 195.

TABLE 1 The young Weber's predictions for the 1890 elections and the actual results

Political parties	Weber's predictions	Results on *20.2.1890/ 01.03.1890 (run-off)*
Social Democrats	'significant strengthening'	seats = more than triple (11–35) votes = + 9.6 % (to 19.7 %)
DFP (*left-liberals*)	'small gain'	seats = almost double (32–66) votes = + 3.0 %
National Liberals	'considerable weakening'	seats = lost over half (97–41) votes = – 5.9 %

SOURCE: RITTER AND NIEHUSS 1980

pending his running commentary on the Reich's political life – as he had done in 1886 for similar reasons – he would send a letter to Hermann Baumgarten on 31 December 1889, which contained his predictions for the coming election. After commenting that 'it seemed liberalism had unfortunately not reached its low point',[57] he called the upcoming election in the following manner.

Social Democrats, he believed, would see a significant strengthening (at least a doubling) of their votes, with left-liberals experiencing a small rise – which amounted to a defeat – and National Liberals suffering a considerable fall. As can be seen in the table above, Weber was very close to actual results, even though his prediction of a marginal rise in the votes for left-liberals resulted in a jump in their seats.

The ramification of these results, Weber added, would nevertheless remain unclear until Bismarck's death delivered the real test of strength for the parties. Weber also hoped that, by the time this occurred, the young Kaiser would have gained a firmer grip on his role.[58] The fact that Weber had called the election results before the extension of the *Sozialistengesetz* came up for approval in the Reichstag on 25 January 1890 is also telling. It means that, independent of whether the exception law would be extended or not, Weber felt the winds were in favour of the 'outlawed party'. That the extension would not pass on that January session and that a whirlwind of changes would follow this development shows how volatile the political situation of the *Kaiserreich* was.

57 MWG II/2, p. 213.
58 Ibid.

Following the non-extension of the law and mere weeks before the 20 February vote, the Kaiser published his two 'February decrees' [*Februarerlasse*] which, in essence, recognised the need to improve labour conditions and worker protection. The decrees were a mix of resilient patriarchal views on workers and concerns about the realities of the world market. Hence, due to the imperative of safeguarding the competitiveness of German industry, the Kaiser's condition to introduce a reduction to the working day would be an agreement on the matter among all industrial powers in Europe. Wilhelm II organised an international conference on labour protection to this effect that same February 1890, which, while ineffective in terms of this goal, did draw visibility to Germany's model of social policy on the continent.[59] The 'February decrees' are, indeed, known less for their concrete results than for marking the beginning of Wilhelm II's short-lived aspiration to establish a 'social reign'. There were, to be sure, consequential measures, such as the appointment of Hans von Berlepsch as Prussian Minister of Commerce. As president of the Düsseldorf administrative district – which encompassed part of the Ruhr area – Berlepsch had refused to call on the military to repress the miners' strike in the previous year.[60] The Kaiser's gestures also helped make 1890 the year in which the 'social question' unmistakeably took centre stage in the German public debate. Added to the veritable political earthquake of Bismarck's ouster from power, the 'February decrees' marked the beginning of the so-called *Neuer Kurs* or 'New Course' in Imperial German politics. This was a short phase stretching only to the middle of the 1890s, but it would nevertheless play a decisive role in Max Weber's trajectory, as the next chapters will discuss.

When the elections of 20 February 1890 finally arrived, efforts at strengthening the *Kartell* through the aforementioned opening to social reform were, instead, capitalised by a resurgent Social Democracy. Its electoral results registered a spectacular jump: double the votes and more than triple the seats in comparison with 1887.[61] The political forces in the Reich had, in fact, begun a phase of significant realignment and there was no clear end in sight to the period of change inaugurated in 1888. An often-quoted metaphor by the young Weber from the letters of these years points to his awareness of the ongoing transition and to where he believed the biggest source of instability was. The metaphor first appears in the letter of 31 December 1889, in which he also called the election results, and came after his considerations on the erratic young Kaiser:

---

59 See Kott 2014, pp. 66–7.

60 See Bernstein 1910, pp. 288–9.

61 See Table 1 above.

> These boulangist-bonapartist kind of pronouncements are really undesirable. One has the impression, as if one were latched onto a train moving at great speed, but had doubts whether the next set of tracks would be correctly put in place.[62]

The quote not only points to a considerable apprehension regarding the reign of the new Kaiser, but also to the fact that Weber's growing consideration of the 'social question' was accompanied by the fear, if not outright rejection, of mass politics. In other words, the breathtaking speed of events was concerning to Weber no doubt due to the inexperience of Wilhelm II as a leader, but especially due to the mass component of the latter's politics. The term 'boulangist-bonapartist' – as per Weber's previous remarks on French politics[63] – made direct reference to a high-ranking figure attempting to channel (and steer) the desires of the masses. In similar fashion, Weber's growing engagement with workers' standpoint from this point onwards in his trajectory would always be accompanied by concerns regarding the unforeseen ramifications of working-class political agency (and by the question of how to best subdue it in the interest of shoring up bourgeois hegemony), as I will approach later on in this work.[64]

6 1891: Assessing a New Political Reality

The young Weber's second use of the fast-moving train metaphor comes a little over a year later, in a letter of 3 January 1891 to Hermann Baumgarten, again as a comment on the new Kaiser. The fear inspired by the train ride was tied, this time around, to 'entering a section of the railways with newly-hired switchmen'.[65] This was not only a reference to the young Kaiser, but also to his new chancellor, Leo von Caprivi, and perhaps to the uncertainty surrounding a significantly altered political landscape in the space of a few years.

At least the developing 'political judgement' of his bourgeois contemporaries would, as Weber remarked, benefit from the fact that 'Bismarck did not die while in power, but left the scene for other reasons'.[66] In fact, Weber once more showed optimism about the 'true liberals of the young generation', who

---

62 MWG II/2, p. 213.
63 See 5.3 above.
64 See Part 3.
65 MWG II/2, p. 231.
66 MWG II/2, p. 229. Bismarck had been dismissed by the Kaiser in March 1890.

while not very numerous, were 'more moderate than before' – i.e., less prone to the verbal radicalism of left-liberals. In line with his considerations in the April 1888 letter analysed above,[67] Weber believed the new-found prominence of the 'social question' presented a particular challenge to German liberalism.

> As long as economic and social issues maintain centre stage so exclusively as they have, i.e., as long as a situation in which division according to interest sectors prevails, there will only be a limited sphere of influence for liberalism. All the more if it remains itself split into interest groups.[68]

The young Weber believed nonetheless that when 'essentially political questions' were at stake, liberals fared much better. By 'essentially political' he meant constitutional or administrative measures that directly impacted the unfinished modernisation of the Reich. According to his own examples, these were measures that secularised public life (the issue of religious influence over schools – [*Volksschulgesetz*]) or pushed back Junker authority – and arbitrariness – in the rural districts (as in the *Landgemeindeordnung* approved in 1891).[69] In other words, those that harkened back to the achievements of the 'Liberal Era' until the mid-1870s and had the virtue of uniting both liberal parties as well as Social Democrats against conservatives and Catholics.

While this view of liberalism's strong points was in line with the perceptions of the previous generation, Weber differed from the latter in his awareness that the 'social question' – and Social Democrats – were now a permanent fixture of the political landscape. Hence, liberals had to provide an adequate response on both counts, rather than continue to underplay or ignore these phenomena. The future was thus not necessarily 'all too bleak for liberalism',

> ... as long as it did not make mistakes on politics at the federal level, including not taking part in earnest in the present movement for social policy, which, as much as it gives reason for concern, has likely reached its peak anyhow.[70]

67 See section 5.3.
68 MWG II/2, p. 231.
69 Ibid.
70 Ibid.

7 Conclusion of Part 1: 'The Existence Of Social Democracy … Is Truly a Bliss'.

A similar predicament extended to liberals' relationship to German Social Democracy, which, in light of its electoral success of February 1890 and the expiration of the *Sozialistengesetz* in October of that year, had attained a new political status in Imperial Germany. The new phase in the party's history was made official with its Erfurt Congress of October 1891 and rechristening as the Social Democratic Party of Germany or SPD [Sozialdemokratische Partei Deutschlands]. In Erfurt, Social Democrats could celebrate not only their successful resistance in the face of the exception law but also the fall of the figure behind the repressive measures, Otto von Bismarck.[71] Crucially, the congress also marked a transition away from the heritage of Lassalle and the open adoption of Marx's ideas as the central reference for the party's programme.[72]

The broad awareness around the up-and-coming, politically well-organised labour movement in Imperial Germany was, however, not simply a function of its internal developments. The final decades of the twentieth century coincide with a heightened international resonance of labour struggles and a growing global coordination of its main representatives in the political party sphere. German Social Democracy gave, for instance, strong coverage to the labour movement abroad, such as in the case of the 1 May 1886 Haymarket events in Chicago,[73] when a mass demonstration in defence of the eight-hour working day resulted in the trial and subsequent execution of its anarchist organisers – many of them German immigrants. As the biggest and most influential socialist party in Europe, German Social Democracy also played a key role in founding the Second International, which convened 'the socialist world' with its first congress of July 1889.[74] This international dynamic of feedback and coordination would not abate until the First World War.

The conjugation of the heightened international relevance of organised labour and the growth and electoral success of the SPD in Imperial Germany is also reflected in Weber's greater emphasis on the 'labour question' and on the role of Social Democrats in his running political analysis of the Reich in the early 1890s. The end of the *Sozialistengesetz* had meant, in the words of one historian, that 'the pathway for an open debate on Social Democracy

71 Liebknecht 1891, p. 324.
72 See Liebknecht 1891, p. 323 f.
73 Engelberg 1990, p. 534.
74 See Joll 1955, pp. 4–29.

was free after twelve years' in Imperial Germany. This was also true of Weber, who during the ensuing decade would make the question of how liberals should 'react politically to the labour movement' – as well as 'how much of a danger it posed for the *status quo*'[75] – a central part of his scholarly engagement.

The last relevant letter from Weber to his uncle Hermann Baumgarten dates from April 1892 and it makes direct reference to the SPD. Before discussing its contents, it is worth mentioning that the letter also marks a transition in the main sources for my analysis of Weber's relationship to Social Democracy. In early 1892, the first of Weber's writings to have an impact beyond a narrow academic environment were published;[76] compared to his two accomplished but dry academic qualification works of 1889 and 1891, respectively, they were consciously addressed to a broader readership of enlightened liberals and social reformers. In other words, his last Berlin years (1892–4) mark the moment that Weber began articulating his stance on workers, the labour movement and Social Democracy primarily *in the public sphere* (and not only as a scholar, but as a political actor). This was in stark contrast to the scattered, if significant remarks on labour and Social Democrats from his private letters of the 1880s, which I have systematically analysed in previous chapters. Hence, my main source material will in the chapters that follow accordingly shift from Weber's correspondence to his engaged writings and speeches of the early 1890s.

The April 1892 letter to Baumgarten is, in this sense, a fitting transition to Weber's new phase – and for Part 2 of this work – considering it boasts a frank assessment of the SPD's role in Imperial German politics. The letter is typical insofar as it contains Weber's thoughts on the latest ministerial intrigues and the legislative agenda as well as another stock-taking of the state of German liberalism. This time, however, 'any attempt to discuss the situation and prospects of our camp' was hampered by what Weber called an 'absolutely unpredictable' factor, i.e., 'the Kaiser'.[77] Two years into his post-Bismarckian reign and Wilhelm II had confirmed most of Weber's worst fears from previous letters. Weber recounts how the Kaiser's 'wilful ways' and 'uncanny power urge' had created 'unseen disorganisation in higher circles'. In this short time span, Wilhelm II had also managed to make a 'caricature' of Chancellor Caprivi, who Weber saw as a 'highly respectable' individual. His prospects looked dim, however, consid-

75 Kieseritzky 2002, pp. 377–8.

76 I am referring to his first essays on the 'rural labour question' (gathered in MWG I/4), which I analyze in detail in Part 2.

77 MWG II/2, p. 268.

ering the German Emperor had permanently compromised the authority of his government.[78] After lamenting that 'European politics are no longer made in Berlin', Max Weber then surprisingly adds that

> The existence of Social Democracy and of the fear it instils in all other parties is truly a bliss [*ein Glück*], for without them we would be assured of having the most desolate partisan conflicts. Likewise, the downright childish hatred of Bismarck ... also plays a role on the [liberal – V.S.] left. The terrible destruction of autonomous convictions, which Bismarck heralded amongst us, is obviously one of if not the main reason for all the misgivings of the current situation. But do we not carry at least the same amount of guilt as Bismarck himself?[79]

Weber returns here to common refrains from his previous few letters to Baumgarten: an ambiguous stance towards Bismarck, which, though critical, hints at some degree of appreciation – if not fascination – regarding his stature as a historical figure, as well as the notion that liberals were partially responsible for the Chancellor's excesses. The same view had already been advanced by Weber in a letter from 25 April 1887,[80] and a year later he had also expressed his low regard for the current party political landscape in Germany.[81] The critical stance towards Wilhelm II had also already surfaced in Weber's correspondence even before the former's ascent to the throne, as previous sections have shown. The truly new element here is the – ironic, indirect – praise of Social Democracy and the role it played in German party politics. If all other views mentioned above are compatible with the moderate National Liberalism represented by his father and uncle – and may or may not have been the result of their influence – this stance on Social Democrats clearly belongs to a liberal from another generation, one who has reacted to the tumultuous events of 1888–91 with the incorporation of a new set of values – amongst which are a greater concern for the 'social question' – and a reformed political agenda. In fact, the 1890s would see the young Weber leverage his insight into the 'rural labour question' in the German East, not only into a coherent new vantage point on Imperial German politics, but also on social life itself, as Part 2 will argue.

---

78 MWG II/2, pp. 268–9.
79 MWG II/2, p. 269.
80 See MWG II/2, pp. 69–74.
81 In a letter of 30 April 1888, MWG II/2, pp. 151–9.

Max Weber concludes the 1892 letter by saying the current situation could only be helped by a 'significant transformation of our party system', though he believed 'the political energy to do so was missing'.[82] That year, incidentally, marks the moment Weber started to contribute concretely to this transformation, primarily through his own scholarly engagement, but also through his own political activity, both of which he would conduct with tremendous intensity until the onset of his illness in 1898.

As the next chapters will show, Weber will attentively follow the internal developments of German Social Democracy and especially how its reformist wing fared. What the quote above clearly indicates, however, is that the SPD had a *legitimate*, if clearly circumscribed place in the transformed political landscape Weber envisioned for Imperial Germany. Weber's reservations regarding a mass politics 'from below' notwithstanding,[83] this stance marked a clear break with the views of two generations of German liberals regarding working-class politics, as Chapter 6 will discuss.

82 MWG II/2, p. 269.

83 See Part 3 of this work.

PART 2

Max Weber's Laboratory: The 'Rural Labour Question' and the Genesis of Weberian Social Thought (1892–4)

CHAPTER 6

Contextualising Max Weber's Dialogue with German Social Democracy: The Debate on the Worker as a Political Actor from the Pre-1848 Period to 1890s Imperial Germany

On February 1847, the Prussian monarch Friedrich Wilhelm IV summoned a long-awaited United Prussian Diet. His goal was securing the approval of a loan meant to finance a large railroad project in the Eastern reaches of the kingdom. Hopes that the United Diet would represent a step towards constitutional parliamentarisation in Prussia were quickly dispelled by the strictly estate-based nature of the assembly, which was dominated by the nobility and called into existence by a ruler lacking any constitutional inclinations.[1] Parallels with the convening of the Estates-General in France in 1789 were not lost on contemporaries, among them a young Friedrich Engels, who saw it as a prelude to revolution, just as its French equivalent had been.[2]

There was, however, one key difference between the assemblies gathered in 1789 in France and 1847 in Prussia-Germany. Namely, the fracture between the 'third' and 'fourth' estates in the latter case – i.e., between the various segments of the bourgeoisie and the working classes. This fracture had, in fact, been detected by political actors at the time, who tried to exploit it to the benefit of their respective camps. Most notably, segments of conservatism present at the Diet attempted to split liberals' ample base of support in the masses by introducing a provision that would extinguish indirect taxes on meat and cereal consumption weighing mainly on city dwellers. Conservatives also proposed replacing the lost revenue with an income tax, that is, to shift the burden to the propertied classes. They expected the latter to turn against the measure, thus drawing the ire from the working classes. The move, however, did not work as planned: the nobility refused to follow the government in approving the provision and liberals actually came to its defence.[3]

In this section, I aim to briefly situate Max Weber's stance on the working classes in the 1890s within an already long-running debate on their political

1 Wehler 1989, pp. 677–78.
2 See Mayer 1975 [1932], vol. 1, p. 263; MEW 4, pp. 30–6.
3 Valentin 1977 [1930], vol. 1, p. 77.

status in the German lands. I start with a reference to the United Diet episode, not only to stress that this debate was already raging in the 1840s, but because it led to an illustrative controversy opposing the conservative Hermann Wagener – a proponent of 'social monarchy' – and a young Karl Marx in 1847.

It began with an article published anonymously by Wagener in the conservative outlet the *Rheinische Beobachter*, in which he argued that the broad interests of the monarchy and of the lower strata of the population coincided. The true enemy of the people was, instead, the liberal bourgeoisie, whose concern with the 'social question' was only a matter of political expedience, a stance Wagener contrasted with the Prussian government's true commitment to its amelioration. His conclusion was that 'the people were simply cannon fodder for the [bourgeoisie's] great assault on governmental authority'.[4]

Marx sharply rejected these arguments in a September 1847 article titled 'The communism of the *Rheinische Beobachter*'. He began by arguing that while the critique of hypocrisy and opportunism on the part of the bourgeoisie was correct, the working class did not need conservatives to enlighten them in this regard, as it was a known fact. More importantly though, Marx believed at that stage that if the worker has to decide between the 'rule of bureaucracy', i.e., the current situation, and the 'rule of the bourgeoisie',

> He need only compare the political situation of the proletariat in England, France and America with its situation in Germany to see that the rule of the bourgeoisie not only provides him with entirely new weapons *against* the bourgeoisie, but also with a completely different status, the status of a recognized party.[5]

Marx saw the recognition of the working class as a legitimate political actor as the main stumbling block in a possible alliance with agrarian conservatives against their bourgeois 'common enemy'. What bourgeois rule *potentially* offered that feudal-aristocratic authority could not was, in his words, the acquisition of an entirely new *Stellung*, a new condition or status for workers in political struggle, i.e., that of a 'recognised' or legitimate party. While the bureaucracies of absolutist regimes might act 'in the name' of workers' well-being, they could not extend workers a political status that allowed them to voice their own interests.

---

4 As quoted by Marx *in* MEW 4, p. 193.

5 MEW 4, p. 193. In the original the last sentence reads: 'eine ganz andere Stellung, eine Stellung als anerkannte Partei'.

On the other hand, in extending such a status, bourgeois liberals only 'recognised' workers' particular interests, i.e., their economic or economic-corporative claims (to use Lenin's and Gramsci's later terminology, respectively).[6] In other words, this form of recognition only encompassed workers' immediate interests as subaltern segments of bourgeois society. That workers' interests could represent – and simultaneously shape and direct – those of the vast majority of society was a notion that *surpassed* the mere 'recognition' of their economic-corporative interests, because it put class rule into question and, hence, the bourgeois societal formation itself.

The inflection behind the emergence of socialist politics in the 1830s and 1840s consisted precisely in leveraging workers' standpoint and political praxis towards the revolutionary reorganisation of the ensemble of social relations in an emancipatory direction. The political current that represented this project of transformation would be known in the second half of the nineteenth century as *social democracy*.

What the controversy surrounding the United Diet of 1847 demonstrates is that, even before the status as a recognised party had been acquired by workers – and they would achieve it in Germany only after the Revolution of 1918 – the call for overcoming this condition in the name of a more fundamental transformation of social reality had *already been raised*. As the following chapters will examine in detail, this fundamental tension will also underscore Max Weber's relationship to German Social Democracy.

Struggles for the 'recognition' of labour and for its emancipation have historically not emerged as self-contained 'stages' or political projects. One evidence of their interrelationship is the fact that recognition has seldom, if ever, arisen as a one-sided act on the part of the propertied classes – Max Weber's particular case constituting no exception in this regard. In fact, already in the *Vormärz* (or pre-1848) period, the German lands would witness a number of outbursts of working-class revolt, most significantly the Silesian weaver uprisings of June 1844, which 'demonstrated', in the words of one contemporary historian, 'what the poorest of the poor were capable of when desperate'.[7] It is no surprise then that when the liberal Ludolf Camphausen expressed the need for this act of recognition at the 1847 United Diet, he did so by drawing a direct connection to forms of working-class politics:

6 On Lenin's use of and critique of 'economism', see Lih 2008, p. 220. For the definition of 'economic-corporative', see Giovanni Cospito's entry in the *Dizionario Gramsciano*, available at http://dizionario.gramsciproject.org/.

7 Wehler 1989, p. 671.

> As dark and deranged as the concepts behind the catchwords of our time may be – pauperism, proletariat, communism, socialism, organization of labour – no one will dispute that there lies a truth at the bottom of this billowy surface, namely, that all men who live have also the right to live, and that this right must be recognized by society to a broad extent.[8]

Yet, this gesture of recognition was abstract at best, in line with the timid – and ultimately hollow – constitutionalising efforts of 1847. Its limits become clear when Camphausen addresses the question of taxation at the centre of the debate between Hermann Wagener and Karl Marx:

> The government's draft of the law is welcome to us as an outflow of this idea, as an act of social progress. It achieves a greater dissemination of the *acknowledgment*, that the propertied have the duty to do much for the unpropertied, it confers the unpropertied *the greater recognition*, that the propertied are willing to sacrifice themselves for them.[9]

In other words, Camphausen's call for a measure of recognition of the 'unpropertied' is predicated on the notion that the duty to act – and the sacrifices this entails – fall exclusively on the shoulders of the propertied classes. This was a far cry from the effective status of a 'recognised party' for the working classes as articulated by Marx, i.e., the achievement of true political representation and a voice in public affairs in Prussia-Germany. And yet, not even Camphausen's moderate stance bore fruit. The defeat of the 1848 revolution in Germany and the reactionary 1850s would only cement workers' subaltern political role in a context of growing estrangement with the liberal camp in the lead-up to national unification.

The single greatest symbol of this estrangement is Ferdinand Lassalle, the political agitator whose hatred of liberals was born out as much by his experiences in 1848 as by his socialist convictions. Lassalle's trajectory is especially representative, because he would not only be responsible for the founding of the first autonomous working-class political party in the German lands since the defeat of the 1848 revolution – the General German Workers' Association (ADAV in German), founded in 1863 – but would also see his opposition to liberals go as far as proposing an alliance of workers with the Prussian state against

8 Cited in Valentin 1977 [1930], vol. 1, p. 77.

9 Ibid, my emphasis.

their common liberal enemy. In fact, in the debate between the conservative Wagener and Marx, Lassalle would take the stance of the former, much to the chagrin of the latter.[10]

Lassalle would also be a protagonist in the political struggles of the late 1850s and early 1860s known as the 'Constitutional Conflict', approached in the previous chapters primarily as the event that contributed to German liberalism's split and Bismarck's rise to prominence. Crucially, it also ultimately led to what Gustav Mayer called the 'separation of proletarian democracy from bourgeois democracy', that is, the 'breakaway of autonomous workers' parties from liberalism's democratic wing'[11] between 1863 and 1870, first in Prussia then extending to the entirety of what would become the unified Reich. The process of unification, which had raised the issue of the (lacking) recognition of workers' political status afresh, cemented the break of liberalism and working-class politics:

> In the interest of the only realistic solution to the national question, liberalism had to reject a national-democratic alternative and find an arrangement with the forces of the old regime; therefore, the existence of a liberal-democratic radicalism as liberalism's left-wing – as was the case elsewhere in Europe – was, at least since 1866, an impossibility. The perspective of attaining *equal political standing* under the aegis of liberalism did not appear viable to the radical representatives of workers. Thus, the politically self-conscious workers *took on an autonomous expression.*[12]

While the quote above is questionable in its eagerness to paint the *kleindeutsch* or 'lesser-German' solution to unification as the only historical possibility available,[13] it nevertheless makes clear that in the formative years of the Reich workers' status as political actors had still not evolved to correspond to the situation of a fully 'recognised party', which Marx had characterised as an important, but insufficient advance as early as 1847.

---

10 Friederici 1985, pp. 164–5.

11 Mayer 1969 [1912], p. 108.

12 Nipperdey 1993, p. 353, my emphasis.

13 By suggesting the inevitability of the 'peculiar' German pathway to modernity and nationhood, Nipperdey attempts to distance himself from scholarship painting this trajectory as fundamentally compromised or deviating – a stance that had been subject to a radical critique by David Blackbourn and Geoff Eley (1984) in the 'Sonderweg' controversy. Yet, as Stefan Berger (1997) has forcefully argued, it is equally problematic, as Nipperdey does in the quote above, to 'normalise' German history by portraying the authoritarian pathways taken at key historical crossroads as 'inevitable'.

In earlier chapters, I made reference to the marginal importance of the issue of workers' political and social rights to the generation of liberals of which Max Weber's father Max Sr. and uncle Hermann Baumgarten were leading representatives.[14] The young Weber would, nevertheless, become aware of the fractured relationship between bourgeois liberals and workers in the previous half-century of German history. This is confirmed by the recently-published materials from Weber's lessons on the 'labour question' and the labour movement of 1895 and 1898,[15] in which he locates the break between the communist and liberal-democratic camps in Germany as early as 1846, referencing, in the same breath, the Wagener-Marx controversy during the United Diet:

> 1846 communism breaks with democracy …
> The Prussian government and the absolutists (Hermann Wagener in the 'Rheinischen Beobachter') attempt to instrumentalize the communists against liberals.
> Against this: Marx and Engels from Brussels.[16]

The lessons on the 'labour question' – which I will approach in more detail in Part 3 – also show Weber was quite knowledgeable about the trajectory of Ferdinand Lassalle,[17] whose biography Gustav Schmoller actually invited him to write (Weber declined the offer).[18]

∴

Another controversy, this time from the early 1870s, shows how little the issue of the recognition of the working class as a legitimate political actor in Germany had advanced, despite the decisive shift brought about with the introduction of universal male suffrage for the Reichstag elections during the process of unification. While the solution of the 'national question' – coupled with the fresh memory of the Paris Commune – had by then brought the attention of an enlightened segment of liberals and conservatives to the 'social question', the early post-unification period shows how a gulf still separated the latter from workers' own initiatives to improve their situation. This cleavage translated

14 See Chapters 1 and 2.
15 MWG III/4.
16 MWG III/4, p. 170.
17 See MWG III/4, pp. 299–302.
18 See MWG II/3, pp. 582–3.

to an adherence of these sectors to separate organisations aimed at enacting social change (to different degrees); these were notably the Verein für Socialpolitik (founded in 1872–3) or 'Association for Social Reform', Imperial Germany's foremost organisation for moderate social reform, and the twin social-democratic parties – the Lassalle-founded ADAV and the Eisenach socialists, respectively – which had experienced their first significant electoral success in the January 1874 elections, before merging in Gotha the following year to form the SAP.

The controversy started when, in 1874, conservative professor Heinrich von Treitschke published a harsh rebuttal to an essay from Gustav Schmoller, a political economist and *Verein* co-founder, titled *The social question and the Prussian State*. Schmoller's main argument concerned the role of the state in the mitigation of social conflict and especially in the 'elevation of the lower classes'. He approached the matter historically, but especially in terms of how the recent spread of capitalism had noticeably widened the gulf between the classes. Significantly, Schmoller attempted to tie his call for state social policy with working-class struggles, praising the 'legitimate side of the current social movement',[19] which he opposed to a 'radical segment of socialism' whose objective was 'the complete annihilation of the established order'.[20]

Treitschke, in turn, sharply condemned Schmoller's considerations, arguing there was no difference between radical socialists and moderate social reformers, i.e., between 'socialism and its patrons' – which was also the title of his rebuttal.[21] Yet, what seemed to especially aggravate the conservative historian was Schmoller's partial recognition of workers' demands. The Verein co-founder had indeed made the argument that the 'enormous increase in wealth' of recent decades 'had to at least partially benefit the hitherto dispossessed classes', affording them a greater degree of 'participation in all the higher goods of culture, education and welfare'.[22] Most importantly, he added that

> it should be accepted that the lower classes will rightfully struggle for this, and that their unified striving for a better situation was a necessary and legitimate product of our free political life.[23]

19 Schmoller 1890 [1874], p. 54. 'Social movement' should be understood here in the original sense of the term, i.e., as defining the struggle of the working class as such.

20 Schmoller 1890 [1874], pp. 40–1.

21 See Treitschke 1875.

22 Schmoller 1890 [1874], p. 55.

23 Ibid.

Such statements did not mean Schmoller saw the activities of emerging German Social Democracy as 'necessary and legitimate'; he termed it, rather, a mere 'adolescent fever' of this 'great social movement'. Just like Chartism before it, Social Democracy's radical challenge to the established order was 'a passing phase' that would be followed by more mature – i.e., moderate – perspectives, as had been the case in England.[24] Schmoller's gesture of recognition was, therefore, 'incomplete' insofar as it did not extend to an autonomous organisation of labour with a socialist programme. Yet, to Treitschke, who naturalised social inequality and saw it as the source of – rather than a hindrance to – the development of culture, even a *conditional* recognition of workers as political actors was entirely unpalatable:

> And I ask: is this a party with which we can negotiate? ... We say to them, first recognize the sovereignty of the state, then we can seek an understanding on individual matters of dispute; but we must shout out even more decidedly to Social Democracy: first submit yourselves to the traditional order of society. This demand is obviously equivalent to saying: first become the opposite of what you have always been! Conditional recognition does not rectify fanaticism, it only feeds grist into its dirty mills.[25]

The Schmoller-Treitschke controversy had another participant, in a testament to the existence of a third camp that went beyond both 'conditional' recognition and outright rejection of working-class politics in Imperial Germany. It was articulated in a rebuttal to Treitschke – suggestively titled *Mr. von Treitschke, the socialist-killer, and the ultimate goals of liberalism: a socialist response* – and published anonymously on the grounds that it spoke for the 'thousands of socialist workers who could just as well have authored it'. Its author was a young Franz Mehring, still a liberal democrat, who systematically rejected Treitschke's vitriolic arguments, mostly based on Lassalle's ideas.[26] Mehring would, however, stop short of a full defence of the standpoint of the working class and the unqualified affirmation of its radical critique of the status quo. This was consistent with his belief at the time that Social Democracy was 'part of a left-wing spectrum led by liberal-democrats', rather than constituting *the* 'organization for the self-liberation of workers'[27]

24 Schmoller 1890 [1874], p. 53.
25 Treitschke 1875, p. 83.
26 See Mehring 1875.
27 See Kramme 2015, p. 44.

(a stance he would abandon in the late 1880s as a result of his own growing involvement with the SAP).[28]

Bismarck, whose social policy initiatives were in line with the programme of Schmoller's Verein für Socialpolitik, was, in turn, closer to Treitschke's hawkish stance when the question of workers' role as political actors was raised. According to one historian, the chancellor's inflexible repressive streak with regards to the labour movement was a rare blind spot in his otherwise cunning political realism.[29] Bismarck notoriously addressed his stance on workers in a speech on the 'social question' given after the two attempts on the Kaiser's life in 1878, i.e., shortly before the approval of the 'Law against the Socialists' (to which he already had a majority in place). In the speech, Bismarck describes Social Democracy as a sect dedicated to anarchy and subversion which should not be confused with other 'honest efforts at improving the situation of workers'.[30] With regards to what some called the 'social-democratic question', but which he preferred to term the 'social question', Bismarck maintained he had, in fact, 'a warm heart and an open ear'.[31]

This two-pronged approach was typical of a patriarchal stance towards workers, i.e., one that combined the enactment of measures *in their name* – with the expectation of gratefulness and obedience – while at the same time repressing (and delegitimising) any autonomous demands or acts of rebellion from below. This meant that, despite the introduction of universal male suffrage during the unification process (1866–1870/1) and of pioneering welfare measures in the 1880s – in both instances against the opposition of a majority of liberals – Bismarck and German conservatism in general still regarded the working class primarily as *recipients* of state policy. In other words, it was not as citizens of an equal legal standing that they were entitled to have a say in German politics and obtain access to a social safety net, but as the Emperor's subjects.

---

28 Mehring's trajectory is illustrative of the shifting relationship of intellectuals with German Social Democracy in unified Germany. In a symptomatic stance for the period of the *Sozialistengesetz*, Mehring distanced himself from Social Democracy altogether in the late 1870s and early 1880s, even publishing a hostile history of the movement in 1877. At that point, he would temporarily defend 'social reform from above', in line with Bismarck's proposals for state social policy. Mehring would eventually start collaborating with the social-democratic press in the mid-1880s, finally joining the SPD in 1891 and soon after becoming one of its most important intellectuals (see Kramme 2015, pp. 48–55).

29 Pöls 1960, p. 81.

30 Bismarck 1981 [1878], p. 170.

31 Bismarck 1981 [1878], p. 180.

This is the backdrop to Max Weber's own contribution to the debate on the 'social question' in Imperial Germany, which began with his participation in a Verein-commissioned study on the 'rural labour question' in early-1892. At this juncture, i.e., almost a half-century after the debates surrounding the United Prussian Diet in 1847, workers' political status in Imperial Germany still fell short of 'a recognised party'. The new factor, however, was how the 'social question' had been thrust to the centre of public debate and the political arena through the combined impact of the end of the *Sozialistengesetz*, Social Democrats' electoral success and Wilhelm II's early commitment to social policy. It did not take long for Max Weber to make his own stance on the matter known. In fact, he did so in his very first relevant intervention in the public sphere in April 1892. While I will examine the circumstances of this particular article later on,[32] one passage of Weber's intervention speaks directly to the overarching theme of the last few pages:

> The worker desires neither charity nor relief from charitable work to redress his economic hardship; he demands instead the *right* to a greater share in the goods of this world. He accepts health, accident, old-age and disability benefits because he believes himself entitled to them as rights; if they were charity he would reject them.[33]

With this statement Weber broke with the patriarchal stance of previous generations of bourgeois and aristocratic social reformers regarding workers. It also shows Weber's understanding of individual well-being as a function not merely of economic situation, but of access to the 'goods of this world', i.e., to tangible *and* intangible ('cultural') goods – a key point I will return to throughout this work. More importantly, however, is Weber's effort to engage workers' own standpoint. As he put it, *they* demand a decent standard of life and a social safety-net as rights and would refuse them if they were charity.

This refusal was, Weber added, primarily a consequence of workers' demanding of 'respect before [their] intellectual personality and moral capabilities' which could only be fulfilled through '*the positive and emphatic recognition of [their] intellectual autonomy and self-responsibility*'.[34] As the next chapter will examine in detail, this perspective on workers – anchored in the recognition of their autonomy and moral capacity – was not only relevant in terms of where

32 See Chapter 8.
33 MWG I/4, p. 114.
34 Ibid., my emphasis.

it put Weber within the long-standing debate on the legitimacy of working-class politics discussed above; it also had far-reaching implications for Weber's budding understanding of social life, whose peculiarity would lie precisely in the engagement with actors' subjective drivers and in the reconstruction of the value constellations that framed them.

In fact, it is precisely Max Weber's insight into worker subjectivity that allowed him to propose an alternative view of the transformative trends unsettling the agrarian social structure of Imperial Germany as a result of capitalist development. This argument forms the thread of Part 2 of this work.

CHAPTER 7

Social Science Takes On Social Conflict: The Stakes behind the Surveys on the 'Rural Labour Question' in 1890s Imperial Germany

1 Introduction

The aim of this chapter is to demonstrate how an insight into workers' ethical drivers was Max Weber's main takeaway from his research on agrarian relations in the German East in the early 1890s. This insight would play a decisive role in shaping the outlook on social life he would later become known for, with its emphasis on culture and values as the fundamental drivers of agency.

In this opening section I aim to provide evidence for this hypothesis in two ways; first, by demonstrating that Max Weber's stance towards the 'labour question' was shaped by his engagement with workers' own standpoint; second, that this perspective set Weber apart from most establishment social scientists and intellectuals at the time, who still largely held on to a 'patriarchal' view of workers. While an exhaustive survey on the relations of bourgeois intellectuals of various affiliations to the working class in Imperial Germany would be a research effort unto itself, ascertaining what set Max Weber's outlook apart from those views on workers prevalent in the circles of scholars he engaged with during the 1890s – mainly the Verein für Socialpolitik and the Protestant Social Congress – is a more reasonable goal. Contrary to the patronising attitude that cut across the various currents of social reformers active in the Verein and in the Lutheran Church, Weber was uniquely able to draw far-reaching conclusions from his insight into workers' point of view, including the role their subjective stances played in shaping broader societal processes.

The Verein für Socialpolitik (henceforth Verein) was the leading forum for social reform in Imperial Germany whose activities were largely tolerated by the establishment. It brought together a cross-section of reform-minded political economists, jurists as well as members of the state bureaucracy with a shared concern for the 'social question'. Having emerged soon after the foundation of the Kaiserreich, its members were split into two distinct currents – so-called 'state socialists' and 'free-marketers' – depending on the emphasis they placed on the state vis-à-vis market forces to appease social conflict. Despite this fundamental divide, one conviction was shared by its members, as Gustav Schmoller would state in the association's 1872 inaugural meeting in Eisenach, namely that 'that the future of Imperial Germany, and indeed the very future of our culture, will be crucially influenced by how our social conditions are shaped in the immediate future'.[1] Though Max Weber would start actively participating in the Verein only two decades after this remark was made, the concern with the 'social question' amongst the German upper classes had by then spread beyond specialised circles and those active in charitable initiatives to become the hallmark of the 'generation of 1890', to which Weber belonged.[2] Yet, if Schmoller and his cohort were concerned about how 'social conditions' would shape culture in its broadest sense, Weber inverted the terms and made culture the axis of his approach to social conflict in East Elbian Germany. Weber would come to the conclusion that the 'rural labour question', i.e., the issue of labour shortage, indiscipline and migration in the German East, was not a strictly economic problem to be corrected, but an upshot of significant transformations in how rural workers related both to work and social hierarchies, culminating in a discernible yearning for a greater measure of personal freedom. Weber saw this shift in workers' outlook as a decisive phenomenon in the changing German agrarian landscape; understanding its roots and broad ramifications became his main intellectual interest within the scope of the Verein's research effort into the 'rural labour question', a stance that put him at odds with the association's leadership and set him apart from the other political economists involved in the survey.

In this section my aim is precisely to tease out Max Weber's developing understanding of the role of culture in social life through an analysis of the materials from the Verein's 1891–2 survey on the situation of rural workers in Imperial Germany. As source material, the survey has the advantage of providing a manageable empirical basis to grasp what characterised Weber's particular stance as well as offering the first instance in which he would directly interact with members of German Social Democracy.

No less illuminating, however, is the juxtaposition of Weber's outlook with the views of other Verein members, considering that, despite their internal differences, this group of intellectuals converged on the notion that the 'social question' played a decisive role in the fate of the *Kaiserreich*.[3] The association was founded in 1872 with the goal of supporting authorities through empirically backed policy and reform proposals meant to ameliorate the situation of workers. Its goal was to aid in dampening social conflict, diagnosed as a threat

1 Schmoller 1890 [1872], p. 2.
2 See Introduction.
3 Bruch 1985, p. 82.

to Imperial Germany almost from the moment of unification.[4] The spectre of the Paris Commune – alongside its vocal domestic supporters in Social Democracy, such as August Bebel – would indeed haunt the newly-formed Kaiserreich. Within this context, the Verein staked a position between, on the one hand, so-called 'Manchester liberalism', which rejected the 'collective regulation of labour relations' and, on the other, radical socialism, which 'questioned private property itself'.[5] While these were fundamental coordinates for its self-identification, the 'spectrum of bourgeois social reform' encompassed by the Verein also aimed to constitute an alternative to 'parliamentary-bureaucratic' reaction backed by industrial and agrarian elites; it built, according to one historian, an ethically plural 'third way' between the latter's repressive stance and the revolutionary aims of organised labour. The search for this intermediate position and a moderate reformist stance did not, however, spare the Verein from accusations of socialist leanings, from which the byname 'Kathedersozialisten' or 'socialists of the lectern' emerged.[6]

Max Weber would first actively intervene in the Verein through his participation in its efforts to shed light on the so-called 'rural labour question' (*Landarbeiterfrage*) in Imperial Germany, culminating in his report on the *Situation of the Rural Workers in East Elbian Germany* (1892). The sprawling work was part of a general survey on rural workers in the whole of the Reich, leading to reports on its various agrarian regions. Max Weber did not take part in the survey's proposal or initial preparation; he was tasked, rather, with turning hundreds of reports and questionnaires filled out by large estate owners of East Elbian Germany into tables and providing a detailed and coherent analysis to accompany them. He would fulfil this task within six months, starting immediately after he was done with the formal proceedings of his *Habilitation* – i.e., the qualification that enabled him to teach at university – on Roman agrarian history in February 1892.

The challenge of working out what was particular about Weber's approach to the 'rural labour question' is how to achieve this without embarking on a lengthy comparison of his report on the German East with those on other regions of the *Kaiserreich*.[7] In fact, a more fundamental question pertains to

4 Bruch 1985 pp. 72–82.

5 Bruch 1985, p. 82.

6 See Bruch 1985, p. 122.

7 Outside of the introduction to the MWG's volumes containing Weber's writings on the 'rural labour question' (I/3, I/4), the only systematic attempt to contrast his report on East Elbian Germany to those on other regions of the Reich commissioned by the Verein is, to my knowledge, Dibble 1968.

just how much can be gleaned about Weber's perspective from a work that originated from an *external* demand and relied on empirical data *he did not collect.* Luckily, a clear basis of comparison exists, considering that the report for the Verein would not be Max Weber's only empirical engagement with the 'rural labour question' in the German East; he also took part in the elaboration of a supplementary survey – alongside Paul Göhre – in the immediate aftermath of the conclusion of his report for the Verein in late summer 1892. Indeed, the need to complement the Verein's survey with a follow-up study was already evident to Weber only weeks into the preparation of his report on East Elbian Germany. This led to a *second survey* on the 'rural labour question' – carried out under the auspices of the Protestant Social Congress [*Evangelisch-Sozialer Kongress*, henceforth ESK] – which sent questionnaires to ministers from rural parishes, as opposed to the exclusive focus on large landowners in the Verein's survey. While Weber would never produce a systematic analysis of the second survey's material, he interpreted it on a more general basis in several instances, eventually assigning the task of writing the reports to his doctoral students at the Universities of Freiburg i.B. and, subsequently, Heidelberg.[8] Thus, while Weber was only centrally occupied with the 'rural labour question' between 1892 and 1894, his engagement with the surveys would continue until his very last productive months before his breakdown in 1898–9, neatly framing his first period of scientific production. In fact, the very last output of significance in this phase was the revealing editorial preface Weber produced in February 1899 – i.e., immediately before the interruption of his scholarly activities for several years – for the publication of his students' reports on the survey of the Protestant Social Congress.[9]

The two surveys on the 'rural labour question' offer an ideal basis for comparison,[10] also to the extent that in the second inquiry Weber's task would be

8 See EB *in* MWG I/4, pp. 687–92.

9 The preface is an inexplicably overlooked milestone in Weber's trajectory. It contains a reflection on the second survey's methodological framework as well as on how it refracted the political and social issues gripping Imperial Germany in the 1890s, thus constituting a fundamental source on his output in this period. Indeed, it can be read as Weber's testimonial on the entire period of activity which had started eight years earlier with his engagement with the Verein (See MWG I/4, pp. 705–11). As Weber's last relevant publication before the onset of his illness the preface also shows signs of a transition to his later production. I will return to it in the epilogue to this work.

10 Interestingly, there were very few attempts at comparing both Verein and ESK surveys in the scholarship; two such efforts are found in Gorges 1980 and Oberschall 1965. For all their merits, both works are of a panoramic nature, i.e., they approach empirical research in Germany in the late nineteenth and early twentieth centuries as a field, rather than through any particular works or a focus on Max Weber's interventions.

precisely inverted. Contrary to his role as author of the Verein report with no bearing on the makeup of the initial inquiry, he both proposed and elaborated the ESK survey, yet would not write any of the reports on its findings himself. For this reason, rather than comparing the reports resulting from each of the surveys, I will systematically compare the questionnaires (alongside other methodological and conceptual elements) that underscored these research efforts. My goal is to tease out Weber's maturing viewpoint regarding rural labour in Imperial Germany and, especially, how this empirical research effort impacted his overall perspective on social life, culminating in his peculiar take on the role of culture in human agency.

2 Two Surveys on the 'Rural Labour Question': Establishing a Manageable Basis for Comparison

Both the Verein and the ESK surveys were ostensibly directed at the same goal, i.e., to understand the situation of rural workers in Imperial Germany in a time of major transformations in the productive structure and social relations of its hinterland. Gustav Schmoller went so far as to state that, in comparison with the 'industrial labour question', the so-called 'rural labour question', i.e., the combined issues of availability, discipline and migration patterns of rural workers, was just 'as important or even more so'.[11] A survey on the topic was first suggested in the decisive year of 1890 by Max Sering – an expert on agrarian political economy[12] – at a meeting of the executive committee of the Verein.[13] Its approval resulted in Sering being joined in the preparations by Hugo Thiel, an influential expert with the Prussian Ministry of Agriculture,[14] and Johannes Conrad, a professor of Political Economy at Halle; their task was suggesting the most adequate approach for the research undertaking. They settled on a questionnaire that would lead to detailed reports – rather than just the filling out of tables – by landowners throughout Imperial Germany. This procedure

11 Schmoller in Verein für Socialpolitik 1893, p. 2.

12 For a short biography of Max Sering and an illuminating account of the transnational roots of his views on the 'agrarian question' in the German East in his trips to North America, see Nelson 2010 and 2015.

13 EB *in* MWG I/3, p. 18.

14 For a short, but insightful biographical sketch of Hugo Thiel and his peculiar mix of practical knowledge in agriculture and training as an economist, as well as a reflection on his role as a mediator between the Verein – of which he was a long-standing member – and the Prussian bureaucracy, see Tennstedt 1988. Thiel played a decisive role in Max Sering's career and research pathways (Tennstedt 1988, pp. 535–36).

was approved and the two-part questionnaire was sent out in December of 1891 and mid-February 1892, respectively. As Martin Riesebrodt details,[15] these dates alone practically rule out Max Weber's participation in their elaboration as his *Habilitation* kept him busy until early February 1892. It's only in the direct aftermath of his oral examination that he accepts the task of writing the report on the rural labour question in the East-Elbian region. Further evidence of Weber's lack of participation before February 1892 are his remarks on the shortcomings of the Verein's questionnaire in the conclusion of his 1892 report: 'It is the destiny of all questionnaires, i.e., that those who have not formulated it would want to ask additional or different questions'.[16] Indeed, while he was still working on the report in the first semester of 1892, Weber already expressed the desire to organize a *new inquiry* that would fill the gaps left by the Verein's efforts.

The result was a second survey – approved as early as 22 June 1892,[17] i.e., when Weber had not yet delivered a finished manuscript of his report to the Verein – this time conducted by the Protestant Social Congress [ESK]. Max Weber and Paul Göhre were charged with elaborating a reworked questionnaire to be sent to a new respondent, namely, ministers from rural parishes.

While the ESK organised an 'action committee' to examine and ultimately approve the questionnaire, the sources make it clear that it stems largely from Weber and Göhre. A quote from Weber's presentation at the general assembly of the Verein on 20 March 1893 seems to indicate that the committee's impact was minimal:

> Together with my friend Göhre, I have elaborated a questionnaire which had to take a completely different form when compared to one fit to be sent to employers ....[18]

Even if on some occasions Weber and Göhre stressed that the work on the questionnaire was not theirs alone,[19] remarks such as the one above strongly point

15 EB *in* MWG I/3, p. 19.
16 MWG I/3, p. 887.
17 See MWG I/4, p. 126, n. 12.
18 MWG I/4, p. 166.
19 In his overview of the genesis and motivation behind the ESK survey printed in the *Christliche Welt* [Christian World] in June 1893, Weber mentions that Paul Göhre was responsible for the first draft of the questionnaire, a remark that Göhre himself felt did not give the full scope of Weber's contribution, as made clear in a footnote by the editors of the article at the time (See MWG I/4, p. 210, n. a.). Weber also mentions that this original version was evaluated across several sessions of critique and discussion by the ESK's 'action com-

to the authorship being essentially their own.[20] Moreover, it is not difficult to separate Weber's and Göhre's own priorities in the ESK survey, considering Weber had been vocal about the gaps and inadequacies of the Verein's questionnaire even before he started working with Göhre on a new one.

This means that the comparison of the two questionnaires – the Verein's, on which he had no bearing, and the ESK's, which he had a direct hand in – offers a unique window into Weber's own maturing perspective in this phase of his intellectual production, making it possible to closely chart his development as an empirical researcher. Indeed, the 'rural labour question' would constitute a veritable laboratory for Weber's approach to social life, as the following sections shall argue.

3 The Debate on the Need to Involve Workers Directly in the Surveys

The first major difference between both research efforts is, as mentioned above, those elected to fill out the ESK's questionnaires, i.e., Protestant ministers. This choice is the result of three sets of considerations I will examine more closely in this item. The first pertains to the inadequacies and constraints that resulted from the Verein's decision to address questionnaires on the situation of rural workers to their employers and masters; the second is the notion that Protestant ministers were relatively 'neutral parties' in the arena of social conflict, while at the same time reliable and knowledgeable observers; the third – shared by the organisers of both surveys – was the belief that it would be too onerous and perhaps undesirable (or even dangerous) to canvas workers themselves directly. This politically charged methodological issue deserves a closer look as it is also the first instance of a direct dialogue between Max Weber and Social Democrats.

At the beginning of a June 1893 article concerning the genesis and motivation behind the ESK survey, Weber attributes two reasons for the Verein's

mittee', in which the Free-Conservative politician and economist August Nobbe and the political economist Adolph Wagner were the most influential voices (see MWG I/4, p. 211).

20 One characteristic of the questionnaire that likely resulted from a suggestion from the 'action committee' is the fact that a single version was elaborated for the whole of the Reich. Weber reports being told that doing otherwise, i.e., restricting the survey to a specific region – his preference, as he had made clear with regards to the *Verein*'s questionnaire (MWG I/3, p. 888) – 'would have gone against the character of the [Protestant Social] Congress, and would have drawn ill will' (MWG I/4, p. 316).

decision to address landowners; they had followed the procedures of two previous works on the situation of rural workers (carried out in 1849 and 1873, respectively)[21] and, most significantly, their *resources* would not have sufficed for a direct interviewing 'of rural *workers* themselves'.[22] While such pragmatic or purely technical justifications were raised often by Weber and the survey's planners for not addressing workers directly, subsequent discussions would point to limited resources not being the only reason for the decision.

The key critical voice whose intervention helped bring the actual basis of this methodological decision to light came from outside the academic establishment and the bureaucracy altogether. As Weber reported, the lack of direct recourse to workers 'was heavily criticized by the socialist camp as unjustified one-sidedness'.[23] This critique can be traced back to Max Quarck (1860–1930),[24] a Social Democrat who was at home both in party politics and in circles of policy-oriented scholars like the Verein. He would express an interest in the Verein's survey and voice his criticism of it at every available opportunity during 1892/3, as the 'rural workers' question' was not only a burning issue in Imperial Germany generally, but also a matter of fierce debate within the SPD.[25] That Quarck had great interest in the matter is evident from the fact that he would start voicing his disquiet with the survey's shortcomings as early as 8 February 1892, i.e., shortly after the undertaking had been announced and the first set of questionnaires had been sent. His initial critique came, of course, long before any findings could be expected.[26] As Quarck himself argued, his misgivings were directed at methodological aspects of the survey and could thus be externalised before any concrete results were available. Above all, he criticised the lack of direct recourse to workers: 'In a scientific "portrayal" of labour rela-

21 See *Einleitung* in MWG I/3, pp. 5–6.

22 MWG I/4, p. 209.

23 Ibid.

24 For a biographical account of Quarck's trajectory, see Gniffke 1992.

25 From 1890 to 1895, as Social Democrats were able to resume their agitation openly and legally, the so-called 'agrarian question', i.e., how the party should position itself with regards to the rural working classes and the peasantry, was a central – and hotly contested – issue (See Lehmann 1970).

26 The journal in which Quarck printed his remarks was not an SPD outlet, but a weekly journal on social issues entitled the *Sozialpolitisches Centralblatt* or the 'Central Journal for Social Policy' – henceforth SpCb. It was published by Heinrich Braun, another Social Democrat who was able to traverse both the realm of working-class politics and circles of bourgeois intellectuals concerned with the 'social question'. Braun was, incidentally, also the editor of the *Archiv für soziale Gesetzgebung und Statistik*, the scholarly journal that would be acquired by Max Weber, Werner Sombart and Edgar Jaffé in 1904 and rechristened the *Archiv für Sozialwissenschaft und Sozialpolitik*.

tions, even one that only seeks to serve practical considerations, no one can nowadays bypass workers themselves'.[27]

Though Quarck did not ignore the constraints that made this a difficult proposition (like the short timespan given for the conclusion of the survey), he suggested that at least those responsible for the general reports – like Max Weber – 'could complement the one-sided information given by [rural] entrepreneurs through a personal survey as well as by interviewing a sample of workers'.[28] Quarck was also troubled by what he felt were key questions on workers' lives that were missing from the first (or 'specific')[29] questionnaire. He complained about the lack of questions on topics such as female and child labour, and felt the questions on housing and living conditions were generic and failed to encompass issues such as whether workers had proper heating, enough light or if their nutrition was adequate.[30]

The article caused enough of an impact that Gustav Schmoller, the Verein's chairperson, felt the need to publish a rebuttal in the same journal, two weeks later. While he mentioned that the second (or 'general') questionnaire addressed some of the missing issues Quarck complained about, Schmoller would either reject or ignore most of the Social Democrat's misgivings. The single most important grievance – the failure to interview workers directly – he did address, however, pointing to limited resources: 'the commission would have desired nothing less ... But we lack the money to do so, even if we might have found the personnel to carry it through'.[31] Quarck, in turn, published a reply in the same number of the journal stating that if a limited budget was an unavoidable issue, then the Verein should 'only take on things which it can thoroughly investigate', in other words, that it should tailor its scientific objectives to its resources, rather than employ procedures it knows to be inadequate.[32]

27 Quarck, Max, 'Eine "Aufnahme" der ländlichen Arbeiterverhältnisse' [A 'snapshot' of agrarian labour relations], *Socialpolitisches Centralblatt* [SpCb], I, 6 [08.02.1892], p. 78.

28 Ibid.

29 The 'specific questionnaire' (*in* MWG I/3, pp. 37–45) sent on December 1891 was centred on factual data such as the wages of different categories of workers, what crops were grown etc. A second 'general questionnaire' would follow in February, seeking a more 'coherent comment on the general labor conditions of each district' (see '*Begleitschreiben zum Fragebogen II*' in MWG I/3, p. 45). It contained questions that were more subjective in nature and touched on politically sensitive topics like the impact of migrant workers, issues of social provision and social-democratic agitation (see MWG I/3, pp. 46–7). As I will discuss in the next item, it is likely that Quarck's critique had an impact on the contents of the *Verein*'s second – 'general' – questionnaire.

30 Quarck, 'Eine "Aufnahme" ...', SpCb, I, 6 [08.02.1892], p. 78.

31 Schmoller in SpCb, I, 8 [22.02.1892], p. 105.

32 Quarck in SpCb, I, 8 [22.02.1892], p. 116.

Quarck had correctly inferred that financial constraints were not the primary reason for not turning to workers directly. What was truly at stake was rather the status of workers' standpoint, a matter on which Verein leadership and Social Democracy held opposite stances.

Max Weber, who no doubt was aware of Quarck's criticism,[33] seemed to be in search of an intermediary position in this debate, considering he agreed with the Social Democrat that relying on landowners was a key shortcoming of the Verein's survey, but still rejected the notion of interviewing workers directly. This mediating stance – which contained advances regarding the Verein's survey in terms of approaching workers' point of view, but still did not go far enough in truly contemplating workers' voices – would define the ESK's revised effort on the 'rural labour question' as well. Weber was open about the limitations of the Verein's decision to centre the survey on landowners:

> it is simply indisputable – and it was not disputed by anyone – that both the need for control of the information provided and even more so the often quite subjectively biased judgements of employers made it evident that interviewing other trustworthy sources was necessary.[34]

Weber turned, therefore, to Protestant ministers, whom he believed gathered several traits that made them superior sources with regards to large estate owners. More importantly, perhaps, interviewing ministers also meant avoiding the 'issues' supposedly attached to addressing workers directly. Foremost among them was, in Weber's words, the 'peculiar character of these workers' – i.e., those of the German East. He argued that interviewing these workers would have 'raised confusion', without generating 'any objective [*sachlich*] results'.[35] It was thus both political and methodological reservations – rather than a simple lack of resources – that led Weber to bypass workers and seek another mediator in his effort to portray their outlook more faithfully. Hence, what Max Quarck had first hinted at in his critique of the Verein's survey still applied to Weber's

33 As evidenced by a series of mostly indirect, yet clear references (see MWG I/3, p. 887 and MWG I/4, p. 165), which led Quarck to go as far as confronting Weber directly about not referring to him by name while still rejecting his criticism of the survey (See Quarck in Verein für Socialpolitik 1893, pp. 87–8). Weber's response and the question of whether Quarck's criticism impacted the questionnaire devised by Weber and Göhre will be addressed further on (see Chapter 9).

34 MWG I/4, p. 209.

35 MWG I/4, p. 210.

own refusal to address workers directly in the ESK inquiry, namely, that there was a fundamental reluctance to prompt workers to speak on their situation of oppression and exploitation; perhaps because of the fear that this might motivate them to act upon their grievances.

The issue of partisanship in scholarship – and its connection to class standpoints – was, in this sense, already a chief concern for Max Weber at this juncture, even if his well-known essay on the 'Objectivity of knowledge in the social sciences and social policy' would only be published over a decade later (1904). And while he did not accept Quarck's main rejoinder, a comparison of the questionnaires shows that Weber did attempt to address some of the gaps the Social Democrat had identified in the Verein's efforts. Crucially, while Verein survey organisers had demonstrated an awareness of how politically explosive the 'rural labour question' was, they framed this danger from a different vantage point than Weber's. The central concern for the Verein was not how to reach 'objective results' in confronting the highly charged 'rural labour question'; instead, what worried its promoters the most was the risk of providing 'ill-wishing parties' with empirical findings that could be used in workers' struggle against employers. Hugo Thiel made this explicit in a July 1891 letter to agrarian employers' organisations, intended to garner support for the Verein's undertaking:

> False descriptions, which depict conditions in an all too pessimistic or optimistic form, could in the present conjuncture – in which labour relations receive increasing attention from both well-meaning and ill-wishing parties – seriously damage the agrarian sector.[36]

In the organisers' attempt to argue the survey would not damage the interests of large estate owners – whose collaboration they obviously needed – they nevertheless took on a clearly partisan stance with regards to the 'rural labour question'. If the reference to supposedly 'ill-wishing parties' – i.e. Social Democrats – was not enough, Thiel provided further evidence to this effect by suggesting that an insight into labour relations in the countryside would be essential if landowners were to 'secure the labour force they needed' and successfully 'work against breaches of contract'.[37] *Kontraktbruch* or 'breach of contract' was a byword for any expression of worker dissatisfaction, from strikes and other organised forms of labour struggle, to workers simply leaving or migrating –

36 Hugo Thiel in MWG I/3, p. 34.
37 Ibid.

the latter constituting far more common occurrences in the countryside, where organised labour was mostly absent and Social Democracy had struggled to gain a foothold.

In his pitch to landowners, Thiel touched on the central contradiction arising from the impact of capitalist modernisation on the relations of production in the German East, i.e., that the same increased labour mobility that enabled estate owners to freely dispose of a seasonal wage-earning workforce was being used against them by workers tied to the estates; the latter were increasingly unwilling to accept the heightened exploitation that came with the partially unfree labour relations still widespread in the German countryside in the late nineteenth century, choosing to migrate to the cities or abroad in growing numbers instead.

The various segments of landless rural workers and domestic servants in East Elbian Germany remained subject to various *Gesindeordnungen* or 'Statutes of Laborers', ordinances that 'were firmly rooted in the paternal labour relations characteristic of early nineteenth century and earlier'.[38] In the words of Karl Kautsky, the *Gesindeordnungen* were rooted in the efforts of 'ruling classes to save as much of serfdom as they could, once the feudal-absolutist state had collapsed'.[39] In their most repressive aspects, these ordinances extended police powers to the landlord in his estate, allowed for employers to arrange workers' forced retrieval in the case of prolonged absence or departure and even foresaw the right to subject workers to corporal punishment.[40] Rural workers increasing willingness to depart from their places of work when conditions became too disadvantageous had, in effect, put a limit to landowners' legally sanctioned arbitrariness. Max Weber's stance in this matter is exemplary of the intermediate – or rather ambivalent – position he occupied in the debates surrounding the 'rural labour question'. The debate on the issue was polarised by figures like Hugo Thiel, who aimed to accommodate the desire of landowners to both profit from economic modernisation and retain their patriarchal privileges, and by Social Democrats, who demanded the immediate repeal of the various *Gesindeordnungen* as well as the extension of the right to collective bargaining to rural workers.[41] Max Weber was both ambivalent towards

38 Jones 2009, p. 61.

39 Kautsky 1899, pp. 340–1.

40 For a discussion of the complicated matter of the various *Gesindeordnungen* still in force throughout the countryside in Imperial Germany, see Jones 2009, pp. 59–67. Despite the role these ordinances played in the everyday lives of a large segment of the working population in the Kaiserreich, there are surprisingly few sources on the topic. For a discussion from the standpoint of legal history, see Vormbaum 2011, pp. 189–215.

41 As Kaustky put it in his classic treatment of the *Agrarfrage*: 'The right to collective bar-

these vestiges of patriarchal relations and sceptical that trade unions would be able to organise rural workers split into a complex set of subgroups with often opposing interests. Weber's framing of the question, instead, shows the tension inherent in attempting to account for the standpoint of workers, while not going as far as subjecting patriarchal relations in the countryside to a radical critique.

> The harsh patriarchal oversight used to be tolerated because it corresponded to the economic foundations of the relationship [of authority]. Scrutinising whether that's still the case today and if it will remain so in the future is one of the main tasks of the following study.[42]

In other words, Weber conceded that such authoritarian forms of labour control were 'tolerated' by workers within a mostly pre-capitalist social arrangement, but he left open the question of whether that was still the case with the growing economic modernisation of the German countryside in the late nineteenth century. Though cautious, this stance was nevertheless far more provocative to landowners than Hugo Thiel's.

The issue of partisanship and of the possible political repercussions of interviewing sources other than large landowners also figured in Weber's very first publication calling for an additional survey. It appeared in April 1892, when he was barely two months into his evaluation of the material from the Verein. Weber recounts how, for instance, the 'political press raised objections' to the involvement of Protestant ministers in the survey, a stance that had 'less to do with objective [*sachlicher*] reservations than with a concern with the endangerment of power interests of a political and economic nature'.[43] With this statement, Weber brushed aside criticism from the conservative press along the lines that a survey directed at ministers could be exploited by Social Democrats for propaganda reasons.[44]

Thus, while Weber did not seek to involve workers directly, he equally rejected siding with landowners in setting the goals and formatting the procedures of the survey. He searched, instead, for a methodological solution that would somehow render valid the findings of the ESK effort in spite of the conflicting standpoints surrounding the 'rural labour question'. Weber clearly believed

---

gaining and freedom of movement are the two most important means of the free activity and organisation for the rural as well as the industrial proletariat' (Kautsky 1899, p. 343).

42 MWG I/3, p. 80.

43 MWG I/4, p. 74.

44 See EB *in* MWG I/4, p. 71.

that interviewing workers entailed political risks, considering 'the misinterpretation and mistrust that such an attempt would encounter in light of the situation in the countryside today'.[45] Thus, though rejecting those who criticised the survey in the name of 'power interests', he still took such interests into consideration when shaping his research procedures. In fact, Weber seemed to dread the prospect of unwittingly raising rural workers' awareness of their own situation through their involvement in the research effort. In the third part of his series of articles on the need for a new survey, dating from July 1892, this emerges clearly:

> No expert would consider a written survey of rural workers themselves advisable. Such a survey could be utilized perhaps to suggest things to people in the name of party interests, but not to learn anything from them. In addition, on account of their temper alone, it would cause enormous confusion in the heads of rural folk.[46]

Weber thus did not disagree entirely with Hugo Thiel, who believed the mere inquiry on the issues surrounding the situation of rural workers could be politically volatile. Yet, Weber came early to the conclusion that, despite all the data it had generated, the Verein's survey had failed to deliver the necessary information for a faithful depiction of the conditions of rural workers. One central element was missing, i.e., *the portrayal of rural workers' awareness of their own situation*. In a way, Weber wanted to access workers' viewpoint without unwittingly fanning the flames of class struggle. If it was politically dangerous to inquire upon workers' perceptions directly – lest the awareness of their own misgivings be heightened – Weber nevertheless considered it imperative to obtain an account of their views through other means. This is where Protestant ministers came in. The Verein's survey, in turn, was hopelessly compromised in this regard as landowners were the sources least likely to accurately provide the information Weber needed.

At same time, Weber's solution and half-hearted search for objectivity made his own biases on the matter all the more evident. His reservations regarding the reliability of workers' unmediated voice (even when the goal was gaining an insight into their subjective outlook) shows a general scepticism towards workers' capacity for clarity and self-awareness as well as an underestimation of their intellectual capabilities. Yet, as the remainder of this chapter will show,

45 MWG I/4, p. 78.
46 MWG I/4, p. 101.

these biases did not prevent Weber from concluding that workers' standpoint was a central *causal factor* in the dynamics of the 'rural labour question' in the German East. This insight is where his stance departed the most from that of other Verein members and where the legacy of his research in the early 1890s for his later work is most clear. Reconstructing how Weber arrived at this key conclusion is the main goal of the sections that follow.

4 Subjectivity and Social Change: Weber's Call To Engage Workers' Standpoint (... Indirectly)

The missing consideration of the role of workers' subjectivity for the 'rural labour question', which Weber was intent on addressing, was not the only reason he organised a new survey. The Verein effort showed significant gaps in data as well, especially with regards to workers' budgets. As he put it, 'in the most important point, that which pertains to the *material* situation of workers, i.e., how the budget of the worker family ... is arranged, the material falls short in a comparatively high number of instances'.[47] Ascertaining the composition of a rural worker's household finances was no easy task; depending on the category of worker and local peculiarities, income was split between payment in kind and in cash in highly variable ways. A worker's income could be composed by a share in the landlord's harvest, by the produce obtained by the worker and his family from their own vegetable garden (or a section of the landowner's field assigned to them) and be supplemented by various forms of monetarily remunerated activities, from work during the harvest period to odd jobs and selling meat and produce on the market. The key recent phenomenon was how wage-labour was becoming ever more present, though usually mixed with other forms of income.

As Weber advanced in his evaluation of landowners' reports for the Verein, he became convinced that this budgetary dimension was central to the fate of the 'rural workers' question' in the German East.[48] First, because the advance of monetary remuneration was a key expression of the growing depersonalisation of the relationship between worker and landlord; second, because wage-labour – or even its precursor, i.e., payment in fixed amounts of goods [*Deputat*] – disturbed the previous 'community of interests' between workers and their employers; third, because workers' budgets could provide indications

47 MWG I/3, p. 63.
48 MWG I/4, p. 78.

as to the viability of small tenant properties or of small land-ownership in various regions and under distinct conditions.

Now, while ascertaining the composition of household budgets might at first seem an empirical task with no bearing on the issue of culture and the vantage point of workers, Weber connected these aspects through an analytical strategy that, already at this point in his trajectory, sought to combine both objective and subjective dimensions of social phenomena. Assessing workers' economic life meant to Weber considering not only how they ran their household, but also the subjective perceptions associated with bread-winning activities. As Weber put it, the analysis transpired 'less through the assertion of objective facts than through *subjective* opinions'.[49] Culture, in turn, emerges as the overall framework that both informs these subjective stances and shapes its feedback with economic life and social structures.

Weber made this insight clear in the introduction to his full-length study for the Verein by emphasising that understanding rural labour's 'condition' was less a question of unearthing the actual amount of workers' income than of ascertaining whether 'orderly economic conduct [*ordentliche Wirtschaftsführung*]' on their part 'was at all possible'.[50] That means that even if Weber had access to precise descriptions of working families' income and expenditures, it would still not deliver all the information he felt was necessary to form an adequate picture of the situation of rural workers. In fact, Weber understood the term 'situation' or *Lage* in a dynamic, rather than static sense, which means he aimed at a study of class relations and their 'developmental tendencies', rather than (merely) a snapshot of the material conditions of different segments of workers in the German East. In his approach to the *causal* role of subjective inclinations and attitudes in economic life, Weber went beyond what a study from the standpoint of political economy would strictly require:

> It is precisely these *subjective* views of workers that matter most. Not only with regards to the question of how workers are objectively and subjectively faring, but first and foremost, with respect to which developmental tendencies are decisive for the configuration of the relations observed.[51]

In other words, if access to workers' budgets would allow an objective estimation of whether their situation was economically sustainable in the long run, what remained to be established was whether '[the worker] and the employer

49 MWG I/4, p. 81.
50 MWG I/4, p. 64.
51 MWG I/4, p. 78.

would feel content or not in this situation in accordance to their – justified or unjustified – *subjective perspectives* and why'.[52] To Weber, workers' own views and opinions were the cornerstone of any adequate assessment of the overall situation of the German East. If the bias of landowners was one of the main drawbacks of relying on their accounts, i.e., a skewing of the data due to the (class-rooted) subjective tinge of their responses, it was the *lack* of an adequate portrayal of *workers' subjectivities*, their views and opinions, which constituted one of Weber's main motivations for undertaking a second survey. The latter would be aimed at determining 'which tendency underpins the *subjective* desires or interests of both parties, since it is *on this aspect* that the future direction of the development depends'.[53] This engagement with workers' subjective drivers and how they interacted with changing material conditions was the distinct trait of Weber's approach to the 'rural labour question'. It made 'local autoptic investigation' a necessity, even though Weber would never consider carrying out even a part of these observations himself, as Max Quarck had suggested.[54]

If the danger of raising workers' self-awareness and angering large estate owners were the arguments Weber raised for refusing to engage the unmediated voice of workers in the second survey, turning to ministers, as the next item will detail, actually bore a political intentionality on Weber's part. Weber extended a strategic role to Protestant clergy in managing social conflict in the German East, a role that participation in the ESK survey was meant to actively foster.

5 In Search Of Workers' 'Ethical-Ideal Drivers'

The choice of ministers as the privileged intermediary for the survey headed by the Evangelisch-Sozialer Kongress was not a fortuitous one. The idea of turning to the Protestant clergy is mentioned for the first time by Weber in April 1892, when he remarked that the trust enjoyed by ministers in their communities meant they 'would be fully able to establish the perspective of rural workers on their situation as well as the way the latter purposefully constitute their

52 MWG I/3, p. 64.

53 Ibid.

54 While Weber's visit to the East German province of Posen in 1888 likely contributed to his later interest in the matter and meant he had some first-hand knowledge of local realities, it hardly justifies his flat refusal to do field-work in his rural worker surveys.

budgets',[55] i.e., the two main aspects he had diagnosed as lacking in the first survey. By June 1892, as Weber was about to conclude his report for the Verein and a proposal for the second survey had already been formally submitted to the ESK,[56] he discussed the advantages – but also the risks – of engaging ministers as respondents. The survey would, for instance, benefit from the fact that there were questions '*only* they would be able to answer'; yet, Weber conceded that ministers also ran the risk of inadvertently politicising their interviewees, should they 'sharpen their awareness of class antagonisms through the unprejudiced [*vorurteilslos*] discussion of the economic situation of their flock during their pastoral duties'.[57] Two aspects of this quote are of interest. The first, Weber's reference to class consciousness and class antagonism, will be dealt with in a later chapter, where I approach how Weber will seek to reframe these Marxian concepts to a significant degree.[58] The second aspect relates to the issue of ministers' *own* partisanship as both respondents in the survey and in their pastoral activities. Though expressing concern for its political ramifications, Weber did not suggest Protestant clergy should simply steer clear from discussing economic issues. In fact, he sharply rejected the notion that conflicts regarding 'material interests' should be off-limits to pastors as if 'the concern for the outer aspects of everyday life' would supposedly 'cloud the perspective for that which alone is essential', i.e., spiritual salvation.[59] His view on the matter was clear: '*we* believe ... that a "neat division" of both spheres [i.e., material and spiritual-ethical – V.S.] is unfulfillable in practice' and that the only consequence of maintaining 'embarrassing distance' would be

> that in those broad areas of man's life where ethical and material interests are inseparably enmeshed together, they would lose terrain in terms of social-political importance in the eyes of the mass of the people to those caretakers of their physical welfare, i.e., physicians.[60]

55 MWG I/4, p. 78.

56 See MWG I/4, p. 100, n. 18.

57 MWG I/4, p. 101.

58 See chapter 10.

59 MWG I/4, p. 101.

60 MWG I/4, p. 102. Weber was asked by a physician why he had not turned to medical doctors in the countryside for the second survey (see EB *in* MWG I/4, p. 154). He replied in February 1893 that doctors would have been the fittest respondents regarding the 'hygienic (housing and nutritional) question', but that their scattered locations and sheer numbers would rule out such an undertaking on financial grounds alone. He also mentions that, by then, many replies from ministers had arrived and that their quality and number suggested this choice of respondent had been a fruitful one (MWG I/4, p. 156).

And quite possibly to Social Democrats as well … (though Weber did not openly state this). Pastors were the ideal subjects to counteract this danger, because of the guiding role they played in their local contexts and in workers' everyday lives. In this sense, Weber did not envision converting them into neutral observers; he aimed, rather, to stoke their awareness of 'material' questions through their role in the survey itself. Once conditioned to give proper attention to objective data, ministers' adeptness at assessing subjective perceptions would open up a window into aspects of workers' lives that went far beyond 'purely economic observation'.

The rural worker, Weber remarked, did not 'live from bread alone, nor did his material interests exclusively shape his being'. In this sense, workers' 'illusions', as 'one might call them from an economic-material standpoint', could play a far more significant role, he argued. If that was the case, then Protestant ministers would be uniquely positioned to identify what Weber called 'ethical-ideal drivers [*ethisch-ideelle Beweggründe*]':

> Interwoven with the countless peculiarities of popular mores, with personal idiosyncrasies, as well as all manner of petty or disagreeable facets of human weakness in all its forms, and often barely recognizable in their awkward appearance, there lie no doubt ethical-ideal drivers, which we must not only *take heed of*, due to their mere presence, but which can also demand to be *respected*.[61]

As the passage indicates, Weber argued that recognising workers' standpoint meant 'respecting' the key role played by their subjective inclinations in societal issues more broadly and, in the case at hand, in the fate or 'developmental tendencies' of the agrarian structure of the German East. Significantly, this attention to the ideal drivers of workers' agency is derived from what Weber describes as a legitimate demand for respect. In the quote above Weber gives an active voice to 'ethical-ideal drivers', i.e., he states that *they* (these drivers) 'demand' – rather than merely deserve – 'to be respected'.[62] This demand springs from workers' own attitudes, rather than from the stance of the condescending observer.

By framing the 'rural labour question' in these terms and attributing a central role to workers' own standpoint in the analytical effort, Weber deemphasised

---

61 MWG I/4, p. 102.

62 In the original, the passage reads '… liegen hier unzweifelhaft auch, oft kaum kenntlich … ethisch-ideelle Beweggründe, mit welchen wir nicht nur *rechnen* müssen, weil sie nun einmal da sind, sondern die auch *respektiert* zu werden, verlangen müssen'.

employers – the Verein's primary addressees – and their concerns; the fact that this gesture is tied to workers' autonomous activity is also significant, as it expresses a historical landscape where the agency (and rebelliousness) of workers emerged as a central factor, an agency of which Social Democracy was simply the most highly organised expression and self-conscious form.

Even if Weber introduces caveats to this autonomy – identifying workers with a low cultural status, i.e., 'human weakness in all its forms' – and ultimately sought to channel workers' subjective drivers into a new social arrangement where they would assume an improved but still subaltern status,[63] the impact of their self-affirmation was such that it broke through both Weber's intention to politically domesticate them as well as his prejudices regarding 'popular mores'. What Weber had grasped in his scholarly efforts was that workers' agency – in its various forms – had asserted itself as a decisive causal factor with regards to the transformations in the social structure of the German East, and, given the strategic importance of the region, of Imperial Germany as a whole.

6 The Methodological (and Political) Implications of Protestant Ministers as Sources

A final note on the motivation behind the new survey must be made before we proceed to a closer comparison of the questionnaires themselves. As mentioned previously, it was not only due to their privileged insight into workers' subjectivities that Max Weber chose to engage ministers in the new survey, but to impact ministers themselves:

> the questionnaires do not by any stretch seek merely to bring forth more observational material; at least as important was the aim of giving rural ministers, in their own interest, an incentive to undertake systematic observation of the economic conditions of their communities.[64]

This passage epitomises a dual break with the procedures adopted in the Verein's survey. Not only was a greater consideration of workers' subjectivities expected in the reports, but the respondents themselves were meant to be lastingly shaped and influenced – 'in their own interest' – by undertaking their

63 See Part 3.
64 MWG I/4, p. 212.

observations in a systematic manner. The attempt to furnish ministers with an alternative standpoint on their communities did come under criticism, especially from liberals, who Weber claimed spread 'the well-known prophecy of doom [*Unkenruf*]' that the survey's questions would in and of themselves 'spread social-political dilettantism among ministers'. Indeed, Weber had no qualms in conceding that the new survey aimed precisely to sharpen pastors' perspectives with regards to 'social-political'[65] issues:

> We have developed the questionnaire above all with a view to nurturing the social-political thought of respondents, and thus to help them become accustomed to differentiating between that which is important and that which is fleeting or unimportant for social development out of the abundance of phenomena that life confronts them with every day.[66]

Weber clearly thought the changes in the economic landscape and social relations in the German East demanded a new vantage point to be adequately understood, i.e., what he termed a 'socio-political' perspective. This meant not only a raised awareness of economic factors, but of social stratification and social conflict. The perspective of political economy was no doubt a key ingredient of this stance, but, as Weber himself remarked, it was also insufficient when it came to grasping workers' subjectivities, that is, the way they *autonomously* reacted to economic and social change.

And here is where the issues of partisanship and scholarship become increasingly interwoven; by providing ministers with the analytical tools necessary for gaining a better grasp of the transformations in the German countryside, to what extent do Weber and Göhre also seek to actively politicise them? If interviewing workers directly was a dangerous proposition, how could

---

65 The meaning of the adjective *sozialpolitisch* as used by Weber should not be confused with matters strictly related to social policy as such, in the sense of state interventions vis-à-vis the refractions of the 'social question' (e.g., as in the pioneering measures of social reform introduced in Imperial Germany in the 1880s). When referring to the latter Weber will always use the term 'staatliche Sozialpolitik' or 'state social policy'. With the adjective 'sozialpolitisch', on the other hand, Weber pointed to a matter related to the broader issues of class relations and social conflict, in line with the meaning that 'social/sozial' had taken on in the German language from the 1830s through to the late nineteenth century. 'Social-political' questions were, in this sense, those that pertained to the dynamics of modern social structure, social conflict and social change, with the word 'social' here bearing a close relationship to that which relates to the working class and the labour movement, as opposed to 'society' in its entirety (see Pankoke 1970 and Strazzeri 2014).

66 MWG I/4, p. 315.

Weber justify that ministers should, in a way, change their stance on workers by taking part in the survey? As mentioned previously, at the heart of the new outlook ministers were to incorporate was an awareness of how workers' subjectivities interacted with (and influenced) economic transformations. Given their daily contact with workers in their communities and the fact that taking heed of subjective perceptions formed a key part of their pastoral activities, ministers would seem the ideal segment to target with this goal in mind. Nevertheless, what Weber and Göhre aimed at was a significant change in their outlook, i.e., the recognition, up to a certain degree, of the existence of social conflict – what Weber would later call the 'legalisation' of class struggle.[67] This, in turn, entailed some recognition of the legitimate character of workers' demands.

Weber and Göhre's attempt to assign Protestant clergy a broader societal role was in line with debates of the time. The atmosphere of the early 1890s in Imperial Germany had spurred even the arch-conservative and monarchically oriented highest organ of the Lutheran Church – the Protestant High Church Council – to take a clearer stance regarding the 'social question'. In line with the Kaiser's 'February Decrees', this translated to a loose commitment to 'recognize the justified social needs of workers'; though even this gesture was framed as a measure to 'further combat Social Democracy'.[68]

Such anti-socialist rhetoric was essential in a context where the fair consideration of workers' demands was close enough to social-democratic agitation to warrant suspicion from the establishment and even, it seems, from workers themselves. We learn this from Weber, who, by the time he held his talk at the Verein's convention on its original 'rural labour' survey in March 1893, could already report on the first returns from ESK questionnaires that

> … the attempt by ministers to approach workers has led to an extraordinary degree of mistrust on the part of the latter. We have reports from many districts stating that these clergymen have henceforth been regarded as 'Social Democrats'.[69]

In the following years Weber would learn just how narrow the political space between Social Democrats and social conservatives was; in fact, the mere attempt to give greater recognition to workers' views was enough to put one squarely in the socialist camp in the eyes of many segments of German society,

67 MWG I/4, p. 329.
68 Aldenhoff-Hübinger 1988, p. 286.
69 MWG I/4, p. 167.

not least of Imperial authorities. This was the main contradiction of the so-called 'New Course', which marked the beginning of Wilhelm II's reign; it was an attempt to give greater heed to the 'social question' and workers' demands that was, nevertheless, propped up by a patriarchal view that, in the same breath, denied their autonomy and their legitimate claim to political participation and collective bargaining rights. From this standpoint, German Social Democracy constituted a subversive force, rather than an integral part of the political landscape of the *Kaiserreich*.

7 The *Verein* Questionnaires under Social Democrat Scrutiny

Interestingly, Weber follows the quote above by casually mentioning how 'others that have attempted to reach rural workers directly, have had similar experiences'. This was a reference to Social Democrats, whose long-time leader, August Bebel, he had apparently corresponded with:

> … at least that's what *Herr* Bebel openly admitted, when he wrote me that the difficulty of reaching these workers should not be ignored, also for his party – which has had considerable first-hand experiences in the countryside.[70]

While this letter from Bebel has not survived in Weber's papers, we know that he did send a copy of his volume of the Verein's survey to Georg von Vollmar,[71] the main figure of the moderate wing of the SPD in the early 1890s. The initiative to contact Bebel was, however, highly symbolic. It gives further confirmation that, at least in Weber's case, there was a growing acceptance of Social Democracy's place in the political and social debate in the *Kaiserreich*, even if this stance fell well short of adhesion to its goals.

Hence, despite its episodic character, Weber's interaction with Bebel and Vollmar, two of the most prominent figures of German Social Democracy at the time, is significant to the extent that it indicates a willingness to openly engage with Social Democrats when facing the 'labour question' in Imperial Germany. His interaction with the SPD was, however, not restricted to these brief exchanges with high-profile members. In the early 1890s, he had much more intensive contact with lesser known Social Democrats such as Bruno

70 MWG I/4, p. 167.
71 See *Einleitung* in MWG I/3, pp. 16–17.

Schoenlank and Max Quarck, party publicists who often interacted with intellectual circles closer to the German establishment.

Max Quarck was, in fact, the key mediator in Weber's first attempts at a direct dialogue with Social Democracy. Despite criticism of the 'rural labour survey' coming from across the political spectrum, the evidence points to Quarck's comments having elicited the clearest response by both Verein survey organisers and Max Weber. Quarck's challenge must have carried special significance in that, in his capacity as an SPD member and spokesperson, he could claim to uncompromisingly represent the point of view of workers themselves.

His critique of the first questionnaire sent out by the Verein in December of 1891 singled out the fact, as mentioned above, that it would bring back little or no data on workers' own views as well as on their actual living and labouring conditions. His critical piece was published in the *Socialpolitisches Centralblatt* on 8 February 1892, i.e., a week or so before the second or 'general' questionnaire was sent to landowners.[72] Is it possible that in this short window the organisers of the Verein introduced changes to the new questionnaire, despite Gustav Schmoller's harsh rebuttal of Quarck's critique? A contrast of the two questionnaires points to this having plausibly been the case.

The first or 'specific' Verein questionnaire was relatively straightforward: it asked which crops were cultivated, the size of the properties and, especially, how many workers there were from each of four major categories, i.e., 1) unfree servants [*Gesinde*], 2) free wage-earning laborers, 3) workers bound by contract and who resided on the property [*Instleute*] and, finally, 4) migrant workers. The questions mostly address the issue of the availability of workers and whether retaining them – or hiring them at opportune times – presented a challenge. The content of the questionnaire strongly overlapped with landowners' own concerns and, indeed, addressed the 'labour question' as *they* defined it, that is, in terms of the increasing difficulty of securing labour power when they needed it. This standpoint and intellectual focus partly explains why the only questions on female and child labour in the first questionnaire address their availability as workers and the extent of their working day, but ignore the issue of the conditions they toiled under. Beyond the availability of labour power, the questionnaire only significantly addressed attempts at parcelling larger estates into smaller plots and the existence of social provision and insurance for workers of all categories (except migrants). The only questions addressing more subjective elements of workers' daily lives pertain to their reading habits.[73]

72 See EB *in* MWG I/3, p. 21.

73 See EB *in* MWG I/3, pp. 37–45.

The first or 'special' questionnaire was, furthermore, accompanied by a note from Hugo Thiel assuring landowners that the information provided would primarily serve their own interests – which included 'successfully contesting unjustified demands' from workers[74] – and would not be utilised in any way that could damage the 'agrarian sector'.[75]

The second or 'general' questionnaire sent by the Verein was, in turn, accompanied by the request that a 'broader picture of the current general situation of labour relations in one's district' be given.[76] The landowner is asked to inform 'his view of the situation of labour relations in his district', but, more significantly, to 'illuminate this issue from both the standpoint of employers and workers'.[77] Thus, if Quarck's desire to see workers' themselves be interviewed would not be fulfilled, at least now the need to integrate workers' standpoints got some mention, even if the prospects of achieving this through a questionnaire addressed to landowners were remote at best. Quarck's impact on the second questionnaire becomes more plausible due to the additional aspects of workers' lives it encompassed. Landowners are asked to assess improvements in workers' situations both in 'material' (housing, diet) as well as 'ideal' terms (education, 'morality'); it inquires, for instance, if there was 'overexertion' on the part of female and child workers and whether the *Gesindeordnung* seemed in need of reform,[78] a key demand of Social Democrats.

The impact of Quarck's critique notwithstanding, the patent incompatibility between the patriarchal stance on workers of survey organisers and the notion of a fair consideration of their standpoint is undeniable. The second Verein questionnaire also asks, for instance, if 'patriarchal relations – in the best sense of the word – still existed', and if 'discipline was faltering', that is, if there were 'breaches of contract'.[79] Surprisingly, it follows up these questions with the first attempt to truly account for workers' point of view:

> Do landowners take the heightened self-consciousness of workers into account, or do they often neglect using the right tone in their dealings with them?[80]

74 Thiel *in* MWG I/3, p. 36.
75 Thiel *in* MWG I/3, p. 34.
76 See EB *in* MWG I/3, p. 45.
77 See MWG I/3, p. 46.
78 See MWG I/3, p. 47.
79 Ibid.
80 Ibid.

Hence, even for the patriarchally-inclined organisers of the Verein survey, workers' heightened self-consciousness was a phenomenon to be taken into account. Not least because of its political ramifications; the quote above is, non-coincidentally, followed by questions addressing workers' attempts at securing their economic and political interests. The questionnaire inquires, specifically, whether 'any associations concerned with the improvement of rural workers' economic situation' exist and, in its conspicuous final item, it asks about the 'dissemination and success of social-democratic agitation'.[81] The second questionnaire, therefore, not only reveals a direct response to Quarck's critique, but also the existence of a tension within the association between those proposing a greater consideration of workers' standpoints and those more worried about maintaining the patriarchal *status quo* in the German countryside, a split that would become visible in the Verein's general assembly of 1893.[82]

Max Weber was no doubt aware of Quarck's critique of the Verein survey. In the conclusion of his 1892 report, he remarks on how 'easy it is to roll out an extensive list of missing questions on numerous – and in themselves very important and highly interesting – aspects of labour relations, which the survey does not ask',[83] a thinly veiled reference to the Social Democrat's criticism. But how did Weber's own questionnaire for the ESK measure up against the ones sent out by the Verein – and to what extent did they incorporate Quarck's critique? The answers to these questions, and how they illuminate Weber's own peculiar stance on the 'rural labour question', are the topics of the next chapter.

81 Ibid.

82 See chapter 9.

83 MWG I/3, p. 887.

CHAPTER 8

Social Research, Agrarian Change, and the Question of Workers' Vantage Point: The Genesis of Max Weber's Social Theory in His Engagement with the 'Rural Labour Question'

1 Max Weber and Paul Göhre: The Issue of Workers' 'Rightful' Claim to Recognition and the Spectre of Social Democracy.

Max Weber's critique of the Verein für Socialpolitik's survey indicated that the distinctive element of his approach to the 'rural labour question' was a more significant engagement with workers' standpoint. To the contemporary reader it may seem like no great feat of Weber's to have acknowledged workers' own views in a study explicitly fashioned to shed light on their situation. Yet, in the early 1890s, most members of the propertied and ruling classes of Imperial Germany had little knowledge of the realities of working-class life and much less of workers' views and values. From the large landowner of the Prussian East, who oversaw various segments of rural workers from a place of unchallenged authority, to the enlightened member of the bourgeoisie, whose contact with the working class was reduced to instances of charitable engagement, a profound lack of awareness as to the livelihood and thought-world of the toiling masses emerges. Finally, any attempt at somehow bridging such class divides suggested social-democratic leanings.

Interestingly, this assessment on class relations does not stem from historical scholarship on the period, but from Max Weber's own writings on the issue from the 1890s. If my effort to tease out Weber's views on and relationship to the working class during his student and legal clerkship years demanded a wide array of sources, ranging from his letters and readings to his experiences in Berlin's urban canvas, starting in 1892 – i.e., with his intensive confrontation with the 'rural workers' question' – his writings provide ample data.

Weber's earliest contribution of significance in this context, a short piece in the Protestant outlet *Christliche Welt* [Christian World] entitled 'In defence of Göhre',[1] deserves closer attention not only because it is his first political inter-

1 MWG I/4, pp. 108–19.

vention in the public sphere, but also for the insight it offers into how polarising the 'labour question' was at the time. 'In defence …' is a rebuke directed at influential theologian Hermann Cremer, who had criticised Weber's fellow participant in the Protestant Social Congress (and subsequent survey collaborator), Paul Göhre. The dispute with Cremer is rooted in the controversy surrounding Göhre's book *Three Months as a Factory Worker and Craftsman Apprentice*. As the title indicates, the young theologian had spent three months living as an industrial worker in the city of Chemnitz in 1890 and published an account of his experience – including his earnest views on workers' daily lives, the 'labour question' and Social Democracy – in mid-1891, causing a sensation.[2]

Göhre dedicated an entire chapter to 'social-democratic agitation'[3] which, aside from the usual warnings regarding the threat these activities represented to 'morality' and religion, included some perceptive observations. Göhre cleverly points out, for instance, that no party whose 'exclusive conscious goal was the irruption of a bloody revolution' would be able to produce such good satirical newspapers as the SPD did.[4] Indeed, a lot of attention is given to the labour press and to cultural activities promoted by the party. This led Göhre to conclude that 'a great deal of healthy strength and fresh blood pulsates' in the SPD, 'despite all that is morally reproachable … and the grave and perilous combustive material that unquestionably lies within it'. In fact, Göhre would go as far as saying that 'given the right handling and influence, it [Social Democracy – V.S.] too could be shaped into a divinely welcome and blessed factor in the cultural development of humanity'.[5]

In addressing culture in a passage on Social Democracy the book touched upon a key blind spot of the propertied classes of Imperial Germany with regards to workers. In this sense, Göhre's account not only ran counter to the commonly held notion that the lower strata of German society had no attachment to culture and no cultural expressions of their own, he argued that the activities of Social Democracy played a key role in *fostering* them. This notion was arguably just as taboo for the Kaiserreich ruling elites as considering the SPD a legitimate political actor. Indeed, both stances went hand in hand: the SPD was a threat to 'culture' *and* to the established political and social order.

---

2 For a concise account of Göhre's portrayal and an analysis of his peculiar, religiously informed ethnographic perspective, see Poore 2000, pp. 29–34. For a summary of the book's reception and the controversy it generated, see Poore 2000, pp. 34–8.

3 Göhre 1891, pp. 88–108.

4 Göhre 1891, p. 96.

5 Ibid.

Göhre's unexpectedly provocative account did not go unnoticed. In his suggestively titled article 'The preaching task of our Church in the face of Social Democracy', Cremer not only criticised Göhre's immaturity and overly forthcoming attitude towards the SPD, but dismissed the entire premise of the work; *Three Months* ... was the work of a naive preacher-to-be that added 'nothing new' to the discussion.[6] Ultimately, Göhre's effort at giving an accurate account of the material situation and aspirations of ordinary workers was, according to Cremer, redundant for members of the Protestant clergy, whom he argued already had plentiful insight into workers' lives. In his defence of Göhre, Weber sharply rejected this claim, alluding to the sheer variety of the regionally diverse and stratified working classes on German soil,[7] which no single minister would become acquainted with just through their pastoral activities. This remark was consistent with his efforts to utilise the new rural worker survey as a tool to raise ministers' awareness of social and economic issues. Yet the brunt of Weber's critical response addressed the notion that the book had nothing to offer to its readers in the upper classes (and the bourgeoisie in particular).

Weber caustically remarks that for those who held the 'philistine notion that dark and mysterious forces are at work in the working class' and came to Göhre's work in search of vindication for such views, there was indeed 'nothing new' on offer.[8] The unintended achievement of the book was, inversely, to lay bare the fundamental *likeness* between those it portrayed, on the one hand, and its readers, beyond class boundaries. In Weber's words, the (upper-class) reader was left with the impression

> ... that regarding *this* category of worker, they were dealing with individuals of their own flesh and blood, with essentially the same intellectual (*geistigen*) and spiritual (*gemütigen*) needs; individuals who pursued their material as well as internal interests – as ascribed to them by the organisation of human society – with roughly the same degree of understanding and foolishness as themselves and their peers.[9]

Ultimately, to 'get to know individuals such as these', readers in the cultivated strata 'need not go amongst workers'. While the caveat to this sweeping state-

6 See EB *in* MWG I/4, pp. 106–7.
7 MWG I/4, p. 110.
8 Ibid.
9 Ibid.

ment is that it was valid only for *this kind* of (highly-skilled) worker, i.e., '*this* singularly important category of the future industrial "middle strata"' – a provision Weber would repeatedly emphasise and which I will delve into later on[10] – it is no less significant. Acknowledging this fundamental equality – or refusing to do so – had, in Weber's own words, a direct bearing on how a member of the ruling classes stood on the 'labour question':

> Those who would believe this fact is universally recognized, i.e., that the essential equality of intellectual and spiritual interests between these workers ... and a broad bourgeois segment of the propertied and ruling classes builds the fundamental basis upon which the 'labour question' is evaluated, need only consider the realm of assumptions [*Vorstellungskreis*] from which the minister draws his perceptions on worker's spiritual interests.[11]

As the passage indicates, Weber draws a direct connection between how workers are regarded as subjects, especially in terms of their intellectual standing, on the one hand, with how social struggle is approached, on the other.[12] In this sense, the significance of Göhre's book lay in presenting workers as familiar, rather than exotic or peculiar, i.e., as individuals with traits and inclinations readers themselves possessed.[13] This bestowed on the book what Weber termed a 'practical social-political' value, i.e., it became a part of the effort to bridge the divide between the educated bourgeois and the (skilled) proletarian.

10 See Part 3.

11 MWG I/4, pp. 110–1.

12 Weber had made a similar connection between a critique of workers' autonomy and a certain class perspective a few years earlier during the Ruhr miners' strike. In a letter from 14.07.1889, Weber tells of his disagreement with the daughter of a mine owner who thought the strikers' most reproachable deed had been the 'breach of contract' with their employers. 'That was surprising to me especially coming from a young woman and it made me think once more just how dependent we are on the social circles [*Lebenskreisen*] we originate from in terms of the direction our moral judgement takes and what it draws on' (MWG II/2, p. 193).

13 MWG I/4, pp. 110–1. According to the social-democratic reviewer of *Three Months ...*, Max Schippel, the work showed how commonplace and prosaic most elements of working-class everyday life were, something he considered a major achievement. He specifically mentions – in similar terms to Weber's – how workers' free-time activities, though subject to the limits of their material condition, were 'no better or worse than the amusements of other segments of the population' (Schippel 1891b, p. 499).

> … it is under this guise that the book must be judged, that is, whether it brought closer the class of people which it portrays and that which it was written for. *That is undoubtedly the case.*[14]

Cremer had disputed this notion, arguing that elementary schools and military service presented enough opportunities for members of the upper classes to gain an insight into the views of workers.[15] Weber, whose first real contact with working people was indeed during his own time in the military, rejected this argument while at the same time criticising Cremer's likening of workers' intellectual capacities to those of children. It was typical of a 'patriarchal point of view', Weber remarked, to hold that experiences accrued in elementary school and military service would be sufficient to form an accurate picture of worker mentality; for this was equivalent to supposing that workers remained stuck in a 'lifelong stage of intellectual infancy or [at most] at the stage of development of a twenty-year old'.[16]

Weber also charged Cremer with denying workers autonomy as subjects, pointing out how he 'apparently regarded [workers] first and foremost as *objects* of pastoral activity'.[17] In dismissing this claim, Weber crucially does not position himself as the defender of the helpless underdog. His recognition of workers' autonomy extends to the awareness of their own capacity to demand respect, in other words, *to socially and concretely enforce it*. This break with a patriarchal perspective on the 'labour question' is hard to conceive without the presence of the SPD as an instrument of social change and a living embodiment of working-class politics in Imperial Germany, even if Weber's references to the labour movement are mostly indirect. He disputes, for instance, Cremer's claim that Göhre belittled workers by making them sources for his study based on the fact that the labour movement press showed no misgivings in this regard.[18] The same begrudging awareness of social-democratic activism informs Göhre's own enlightened stance towards workers. As *Three Months*' social-democratic reviewer Max Schippel framed it, Social Democracy is a permanent if spectre-like presence throughout the book:

> Social-democratic propaganda is something Göhre cannot quite catch, but which he perceives in every moment and every situation for the entire

14 MWG I/4, p. 111.
15 MWG I/4, p. 112.
16 Ibid.
17 MWG I/4, 113.
18 MWG I/4, 116. In a likely reference to Max Schippel's two-part review of *Three Months …* in Social Democracy's theoretical journal, *Die neue Zeit*.

> three months: for when two or three workers are gathered in the name of large industry, Social Democracy is among them.[19]

In Weber's case, this awareness of Social Democracy emerges not only through his clear interest in workers' perceptions and everyday lives, but especially in the fact that he emphasises their *active role* in demanding respect and recognition. In key passages of his 1892 article, Weber's critique of Cremer takes the form of workers' own arguments against the latter's patriarchal stance, with Social Democrats figuring as particularly conscious, but by no means as the only outspoken members of the working class:

> It is highly doubtful whether workers – and not only the Social Democrats among them – would find in [Cremer's] stance towards them the measure of respect with regards to their intellectual needs that they demand from all other classes and of those exercising spiritual ministry; a measure of respect which, from their point of view, they *must* demand.[20]

In pointing out that workers demand respect above all for their intellectual needs, Weber does not deny the importance of material demands addressed to the state, i.e., the need for social policy. Yet, because his recognition of workers' standpoint is anchored on the acknowledgment of the 'moral' aspects of their personalities, instead of on a gesture of empathy towards their hardship, a new perspective on agency and personality is at play. As Weber himself framed it, there is a crucial difference between merely showing understanding and being indulgent towards workers, on the one hand, and a stance of consideration and justified recognition, on the other.[21] In his words:

> The worker desires neither charity nor relief from beneficent work to redress his economic hardship; he demands instead the *right* to a greater share in the goods of this world. He accepts health, accident, old-age and disability benefits because he believes himself entitled to them as rights; if they were charity he would reject them. He thus confronts those guardians of the moral qualities of the people [i.e., the clergy – V.S.] with the demand that they show respect before his intellectual

19 Schippel 1891b, p. 501. Schippel is, of course, parodying Matthew 18:20 ('For where two or three are gathered in my name, there am I among them').

20 MWG I/4, p. 112.

21 Weber's words in the German original are: 'Nicht nur *verstehen* und nachsichtig beurteilen, sondern *berücksichtigen* und als berechtigt anerkennen …' (MWG I/4, p. 114).

> personality and moral capabilities – also visible in the worker's pursuit of rational knowledge – demanding they take heed of these capabilities, not through 'indulgent' toleration of given facts, but through *the positive and emphatic recognition of his intellectual autonomy and self-responsibility*.[22]

In emphasising workers' *right* to recognition, Weber breaks with the perspective of conservative proponents of social policy who understood the introduction of protective legislation in the 1880s mainly as a realisation of Christian values. Framed in this manner, social policy emerges as an act of goodwill towards the masses on the part of the state, with the added benefit of pacifying social conflict and binding workers to established authorities (driving them away from Social Democrats in the process).[23] Weber subverts this conservative stance by establishing workers' autonomous demands as the basis for a fairer distribution of social and cultural goods. In fact, Weber seems eager to show what he believes is the radical distinction between both stances. Shortly after the passage quoted above, he again stresses that workers – or, as he constantly reminds the reader, *the category of (skilled) workers* depicted by Göhre – strove for something '*essentially* different' than simply being 'indulgently tolerated or understood'.[24] Instead, '... what they demand is the *recognition of their right* to think of those matters, which the "cultivated strata" think about and in the way the latter think about them'.[25]

Workers' demand to *think* about matters usually reserved for the contemplation of the propertied classes was, therefore, a central part of their claim to a greater share in 'the goods of this world'. This is consistent with Göhre's portrayal, which went beyond the description of living conditions and economic aspects of worker existence and focused instead on their perceptions and thought-world. Along the same lines, Göhre claimed Social Democracy represented 'not only a new political party or new economic system ... but at the same time a new view upon life and the world, i.e., the worldview of consequential materialism'.[26] What really seemed to fascinate Göhre, in

22 MWG I/4, p. 114, my emphasis.

23 See Müller 1971, p. 73.

24 MWG I/4, p. 114.

25 MWG I/4, p. 115. Weber was not only aware of workers' thirst for knowledge, he knew that, at that point, German Social Democracy was its main purveyor amongst working people. As such, worker cultivation was embedded within a universalist view of culture, an internationalist perspective on social struggle and possessed a revolutionary edge, all of which gave Weber reason for concern (See sections 9.5 and 9.6 below).

26 Göhre 1891, p. 106.

line with Weber's stance, was *working-class culture* as expressed by workers' impressive intellectual and rhetorical abilities. Commenting on a bi-weekly meeting of the local SPD electoral association where 'whomever had something in their hearts spoke out, both old and young, without distinction', he first refers to the 'appalling mix of knowledge and ignorance' that was often on display. Yet, that was not the most enduring impression left by these meetings:

> There were, however, among us also a number of speakers so adept, so quick-witted, so penetrating and practical in their judgements that I concluded in silent admiration and shame that only a small number of those averagely cultivated among us could equal these humble weavers, metalworkers and craftsmen in their eloquence and self-assurance in thought and demeanour.[27]

More than his forthcoming views towards rank-and-file Social Democrats, it was the portrayal of workers as thoughtful individuals with sharp judgement and a sense of humour that made Göhre's portrayal so compelling (and controversial).[28] The chief merit of *Three Months* ... was, in this sense, to have offered a glimpse into a dimension of workers' lives that was impervious to statistical analysis and to prevailing methods in the field of political economy. The book's portrayal of the cultural – rather than strictly economic – ramifications of Imperial Germany's feverish industrialisation also drew praise from its social-democratic reviewer, Max Schippel:

> A young political economist ... would have surely brought better and richer material about work times, wages, the price of food and housing ... To the theologian, 'grub and wage issues' are all secondary; what he is inclined to depict ... is rather the great economic, spiritual and moral transformation, which the relentless development of large industry has brought forth everywhere.[29]

27 Göhre 1891, p. 90.

28 Max Schippel also drew attention to this feature of the book: 'Our theologian depicts the workers from Chemnitz in essence as individuals who displayed a self-conscious facade, but amongst themselves were mild-mannered and jovial ... all manner of well-meaning teasing and wittiness, which helped one shorten the long workday, was most welcome' (Schippel 1891b, p. 499).

29 Schippel 1891a, p. 469.

Just as Schippel, Max Weber saw in Göhre's *Three Months* a less accurate and empirically well-founded account than one a political economist could deliver, yet one that illuminated a dimension of social relationships no purely economic standpoint could shed light on. According to Weber, a 'decisive feature' is often missing from the 'picture' that is produced through 'the naked figures of statistics in conjunction with other first-rate general research methods', that is:

> ... the temperamental reflex [*Stimmungsreflex*] in individuals' bosoms, a reflex that can be colossally different under absolutely identical economic circumstances. This *psychological factor* is palpably conveyed by no explanation, no matter how meticulously didactic; only the epic nature of a portrayal like the one Göhre has managed to deliver can render it palpable to those whom – if I understand him correctly – it was written for.[30]

Weber introduced the notion of the 'psychological factor' in his writings on the 'rural labour question' of 1892–3 precisely to highlight the limits of an analysis of social conflict based exclusively on the economic drivers of human agency. With the concept, Weber attempted to address the 'culture' gap in political economy; for both the empiricist 'historical' school, with its panoramic portrayals of economic development, and the more theoretical neoclassical school, which based its analysis on the profit-maximising choices of the abstract individual, overlooked the role of 'ideals' in individual agency and how they fed into larger processes of social change.

To Max Schippel, an SPD intellectual and member of the middle strata, the value of Göhre's book equally resided in its depiction of the more subjective dimensions of class struggle. It showed, for instance, how workers cultivated bonds of solidarity and mutual support to resist a punitive and patriarchal factory regime.[31] Weber termed such phenomena 'the numerous and highly significant "imponderables" of the labour question', which only 'local autoptic investigation' could reveal.[32] One of these 'imponderables' was workers' thirst for knowledge, which Göhre traced back to a 'crisis' that took hold precisely of the 'most gifted and motivated' amongst them, arising 'without significant influence or pressure from others ... just through their own perception of contradictions .... their own autonomous reflection about the people and things

30 MWG I/4, p. 111 – my emphasis.
31 Schippel 1891a, pp. 471–2.
32 MWG I/4, p. 111.

that surrounded them'.[33] Joining Social Democracy was, in this sense, a consequence and prolongation – rather than a cause – of this autonomy and self-consciousness, something Weber would also recognise in a later essay.[34]

Max Schippel ends his review by commending Göhre's commitment to truthfulness and attributing his misrepresentations rather to 'common prejudices of the bourgeoisie' than to individual faults of the author. Yet, he finishes on a slightly despondent note, coming to the conclusion that if, despite his best efforts, Göhre 'did not always succeed in accurately depicting workers' living conditions and thought-world, then this is only further proof of how far apart classes were nowadays'.[35] He closes the article not with his own words, but with those of the book's reviewer in the *Kreuzzeitung*, a conservative outlet:

> We are aware … that Göhre's book will offer to many a glimpse into an entirely unknown world. The fact that such a book could be written so naively is more worrying to us than what it contains. Consider this: in Imperial Germany there is a class of people which is so far apart from its compatriots in every aspect of its life and activities, thought and ideas, that it takes an adventurous expedition, as if into the heart of Africa, and a great work of 'travel writing' so that they might learn something about them.[36]

Revealing just how deep the distance between workers and the German propertied classes had become and attempting, perhaps unsuccessfully, to bridge this divide was thus the main achievement – and most provocative aspect – of Göhre's *Three Months as a Factory Worker and Craftsman's Apprentice*. Weber no doubt took away important impulses from it for his own investigations into the 'rural workers' question', which culminated in a new methodological standpoint also meant to overcome one-sided class perspectives.

The presence of Social Democracy made this an urgent task in Imperial Germany, something the reviewer from the *Kreuzzeitung* – who does not refer directly to the SPD in the passage – seemed to suggest. He would finish his review by pointing out that the same state of 'mutual estrangement' and the

---

33 Göhre cited in Schippel 1891b, p. 501.

34 '… only after a certain level in the standard of life is reached, does a capacity for political judgement begin, that is reflected in the conscious affiliation to a party. Only after a certain level does affiliation to Social Democracy begin' (MWG I/4, p. 739).

35 Schippel 1891b, p. 506.

36 Neue Preußische Zeitung [*Kreuzzeitung*] – 19.06.1891 – cited in Schippel 1891, p. 506.

'same inability to understand one another' had characterised France in the eighteenth century: 'That's what made the irruption of the revolution such a surprise'.[37]

The threat of revolution cast its shadow throughout Göhre's portrayal. Despite his sympathetic take on workers and insistence that only a lack of reforms and consideration of their demands drove them to the Social Democrats, he does remind the reader that he 'never for a moment denied the danger of revolution'.[38] The underlying cause of this threat was the 'opposition of interests' between worker and employer. Yet, this factor alone did not raise the prospect of major social upheaval; it was workers' growing *awareness* of how their interests clashed with those of factory owners that made this cleavage politically combustible:

> The Chemnitz factory laborers I worked with do everything in their power to distance themselves from the idea of a bloody revolution. Nevertheless, they know quite well that a sweeping change in their situation – which all of them desire, strive for and await – is impossible without struggle. They have *seen and experienced* the nowadays unbridgeable opposition of interests between themselves and the entrepreneurial class too often to think otherwise.[39]

An opposition of interests on the economic plane became an acute political issue because of workers' first-hand experience of the irreconcilable nature of this social division; crucially, this growing awareness that struggle was a necessary step to transform their situation found in Social Democracy and its affiliate union movement the political instruments for its organisation and unified expression on a much broader scale. If the same situation crystallised in the German countryside – where a much larger proportion of Imperial Germany's lower strata resided – than revolution became a palpable prospect indeed. Social Democrats knew this and would spend the 1890s debating how they could expand their influence beyond urban and industrial centres. German elites were equally cognisant of this mounting danger and the Verein survey would constitute the main scholarly effort commissioned to shed light on it.

These were the stakes behind the 'rural labour question' which Max Weber would dedicate his first major work to and which would occupy the better part of his research efforts throughout the 1890s. Far from a commissioned project

37 Ibid.
38 Göhre 1891, p. 128.
39 Ibid. – my emphasis.

keeping him from his actual interests, Weber would put all his energy into deciphering the drivers of social change in the German East. As he quickly became aware that available methods in political economy were insufficient in this regard, Weber made the 'rural labour question' in East-Elbian Germany a veritable laboratory and proving ground for his emerging analytical perspective. As the next section will argue, the methodological key to forging a new science of social life was drawn from an engagement with the point of view of the lowly rural worker. The pathway to Weber's social theory, therefore, passed through his confrontation with the 'social question'.

2 The Breakdown of 'Patriarchal Relations' in the German Countryside and the Changing Makeup of Its Rural Working Class

It did not take long for Max Weber to realise that the social fabric of the rural German East was subject to many of the same tensions as highly industrialised Chemnitz, the site of Paul Göhre's ethnographic study. As capitalist relations of production advanced into Imperial Germany's countryside, the same 'opposition of interests' between employer and worker Göhre had witnessed in an urban setting began to upend the 'patriarchal structure' of the German East, in place since the incomplete emancipation of the peasantry in the aftermath of the Napoleonic Wars.[40]

Weber's analysis of the 'rural labour question' in East-Elbian Germany was, at bottom, an attempt to explain the breakdown of these 'patriarchal' bonds in agrarian estates. Put differently, his chief goal was understanding what had led the interests of different sectors of the rural working class to be starkly at odds with those of their employers and 'masters'. Weber's hypothesis was that the main factor behind this bourgeoning conflict was the switch from non-monetary duties and allowances between landowners and workers to either fixed forms of remuneration (partially or fully in kind) or to purely monetary compensation. The change was felt particularly by the *Instleute* – partially dependent rural worker families – who went from earning a share of the harvest in grain, to a fixed amount of either grain, potatoes or cash. This shift had vast ramifications as the worker no longer partook in the risks inherent in the overall agricultural enterprise of the estate or, if paid in cash, became interested in the lowest possible grain prices in the market, i.e., the exact opposite

40 See Wehler 1989, pp. 162–73.

of landowners' interests.[41] The phasing out of grain as a means of remuneration also undermined what Weber describes as the centrepiece of the partially dependent rural workers' economic existence, namely, cow husbandry. The breakdown in milk and fertiliser production this entailed made workers more dependent on wages – since they were less able to produce their own food or a surplus they could sell – in other words, essentially *proletarianising* them:

> Cow husbandry ... lay at the centre of the worker's economic life. The situation of an *Instmann* who only raises goats or receives a periodic allowance of milk, regardless of how he sees that, is fundamentally different in social terms and indeed closer to that of the proletariat.[42]

Central to Weber's analysis on the situation of rural workers was his attempt to find the proper equivalence between the world of industrial work and the social structure that was emerging as a result of the irruption of capitalist relations into the German countryside. This included the question of what set apart the rural proletariat from the lower strata of the peasantry. Weber soon realised that the situation of wage-labourers had certain advantages over that of impoverished tenant farmers and small landowners because, despite having access to land, many of the latter could not cover their basic needs solely through work on their plots; contrary to rural proletarians, however, they were not mobile and, therefore, were unable to migrate in search of better wages or living conditions.

This assessment led Weber to a more significant discovery, namely that 'the relatively superior condition of the [rural] proletarian vis-à-vis the small [agrarian] enterprise ... was not the most decisive factor for class stratification'.[43] Hence, it was not economic data in the strict sense (wage levels and living standards), but the degree of personal freedom each segment of rural worker enjoyed that constituted the decisive factor in determining their overall 'situation'. Crucially, this meant taking into account both actual freedom of movement, but also *freedom in the more subjective sense* of a yearning for self-determination. What weighed the most on impoverished farmers – whether tenants or owners of land – was, therefore, a lack of mobility that restricted their possibilities of diversifying their income; tied to their plots, these farmers were at the mercy of landowners offering employment nearby or, in the

41 See, for instance, MWG I/3, p. 738.
42 MWG I/3, p. 84.
43 MWG I/4, p. 241.

case of the partially dependent *Instleute*, of what their landlords offered. If this situation became generalised, then what Weber considered 'the most dreadful of all dreads' would materialise, i.e., 'a proletariat of landowners; individuals whose inherited plots become a terrible burden'.[44]

Fundamentally, what led Weber to realise that the 'rural labour question' was not reducible to either a problem of 'labour availability' for landowners nor simply of economic hardship for labourers, was the fact that even those partially dependent workers enjoying relatively favourable and secure arrangements were reportedly becoming unruly and prone to abandon their estates in increasing numbers. Thus, just as in Göhre's account, a purely economic consideration did not suffice to give the true picture of the patterns of change in the social constitution of the German East, i.e., what Weber called its 'developmental tendencies'.[45] This meant that ascertaining workers' own awareness of the growing opposition of interests with employers as well as, more generally, understanding their views, aims and desires were to Weber key stepping stones in the proper assessment of the 'rural labour question'.

The fact that the provinces Weber was charged with analysing were in the Empire's Prussian Eastern frontier, only made this task more difficult. For starters, landowners in much of this area – so-called *Junkers* – provided a disproportionate share of the Reich's political, military and bureaucratic elites, which made any findings potentially combustible (political) material. The biggest challenge was, however, the enormous diversity in the labour relations in the region. Though Weber would often stress that the urban working class was not a homogenous entity, rural workers in Imperial Germany were an even more varied social segment. While forms of wage-labour made inroads into the countryside, they existed alongside partially unfree labour, often in the same district or even within a single estate.

Navigating the diversity of the rural working class in the German East meant, therefore, taking several variables into consideration; 1) the degree of remaining dependence in the relationship with landowners; 2) how workers were remunerated or otherwise provided for (i.e., whether in kind or in wages, if they received land and housing and so on); 3) the degree of freedom to seek out other employment; 4) how subject they were to the landowner's authority; and 5) how mobile they were.

According to these criteria, rural workers were usually split into *four major categories*. The first, the *Gesinde*, were usually young unmarried servants tied

44 MWG I/4, p. 84.
45 MWG I/4, p. 78.

to the landowner's household, who – in exchange for room and board – were at their employers' service around the clock and had limited possibilities to opt out of their contractual bond (most commonly doing so through marriage). They were contractually subject to the patriarchal authority of the landowner, who could even administer corporal punishment on certain occasions;[46] their urban equivalent were domestic workers.[47] The *Gesinde* provided the clearest example of how the most economically secure situation for a worker in the German countryside carried the highest price in terms of personal freedom. In the conclusion to his 1892 report, Weber points out how this trade-off was responsible for a drop in the number of *Gesinde*, despite 'advantageous salaries'. Thus, rather than economic drivers,

> It is without a doubt fundamental psychological factors [*Momente*] which are at play here, since the material situation of the *Gesinde* – specially with regards to diet – can definitely be regarded as the best amongst all workers.[48]

The second type of worker – the one Weber considered 'by far the socially and economically most interesting category of rural worker in the East'[49] – was that of *Instleute*. They comprised those married workers who, in exchange for the provision of land and housing (as well as the use of the estate's mill and oven) and other minor monetary payments, made their – in the harvest season, also their family members' – labour power available for the estate. Though these workers were tenants in the landowner's property, they were not part of the rural proletariat. *Instleute* were, namely, required to possess their own furniture, tools and seeds, and at least a cow and/or some goats (i.e., the means to produce their own fertiliser).[50]

The last categories comprise two kinds of 'free' (or non-contractual) day-labourers, who earned wages and were not tied to any one property. In Weber's study – as with the Verein and ESK surveys in general – this type of worker is split into two categories comprising 'native' and 'foreign' migrant labourers, respectively. Though both were basically equal in the *form* by which they were remunerated and in the work they performed, there were significant dif-

46 Wehler 1995, p. 186.

47 MWG I/3, p. 69.

48 MWG I/3, p. 899.

49 MWG I/3, p. 71.

50 Weber describes at length the many variations in the situation of the *Instleute* in the introduction to his 1892 report for the *Verein* (See MWG I/3, pp. 71–82).

ferences in how much they earned and, for instance, in the overall conditions of housing provided to them. Thus, the fact that one was a domestic migrant and the other a foreign one (usually from Austrian or Russian Poland) determined their separation into two distinct categories – a topic I will return to below.

This picture of the social stratification of labour had been in place for most of the nineteenth century in the German East. By the 1890s, however, the spread of capitalist relations and its accompanying technical advances had altered the balance between the four categories, and were reconfiguring the class structure of rural Germany as a whole. The advance of rural capitalism manifested itself in the switch by many large landowners from the production of grain to more profitable cash crops, such as sugar beet or potato, and by the mechanisation of threshing; this meant that a task that lasted until winter was now usually restricted to the summer months. This transformation had dramatically increased the – already existing – seasonality of labour, as the imbalance between demand for hands in the harvest season and in the rest of the year was now even greater. Crucially, this had made workers with year-round availability, like the *Instleute*, mostly superfluous.[51]

3 'The Heavens and the World Market': Agrarian Capitalism and the Growing Social Divisions in the German East.

Given the increasingly world-spanning nature of the capitalist system in the late nineteenth century, these changes were, of course, not only a function of the German context; this period saw global markets for foodstuffs become more and more integrated, changing the demand for certain crops and putting producers of different regions in the world in direct competition.[52] East German grain had now to contend with Russian, North-American and Argentine grain. This also extended to agro-industrial export products:

> The intensively cultivated large enterprise has no doubt been the carrier of technical culture. Only that its future is problematic. It is economically identical with the question of which place German spirits and German sugar will take in the world market.[53]

51 MWG I/4, pp. 172–3.

52 See Hobsbawn 1987, pp. 56–73, Torp 2005, pp. 28–36.

53 MWG I/3, p. 922.

Weber clearly understood the entanglement between the spread of capitalist relations in the German countryside, the introduction of technical advances to rural production and the pressures of the world market. The key question was

> ... whether the in some places uninterrupted expansion of distilleries and of sugar beet cultivation (which is identical with the tendency for land concentration) is rational from a national and world economic standpoint [*volks- und weltwirtschaftlich rationell*]; and, finally, whether the cultivation of grain for the market will be profitable in the East once again.[54]

Crucially, advances in machinery, transportation and in the integration of markets did not give the full story of capitalist modernisation and 'globalization' in the late nineteenth century. Labour had equally become more mobile and workers were increasingly in the position to choose between staying in the countryside, moving to industrial districts or migrating oversees – especially to the Americas and Australia.[55] This global context was the fundamental backdrop to the 'rural labour question' and Weber duly reflected it in his approach to the issue (as I address in more detail in Part 3). Tackling the 'rural labour question' thus meant addressing developments with far-ranging social and political ramifications for Imperial Germany; above all, the fact that, a mere two decades after national unification, the Reich's rural backwater and fortress of conservatism, the German East, had become just as vulnerable to developments in the world market (and potentially just as prone to social upheaval) as its urban and industrial centres. Though geographically peripheral and economically backward, as the seat of Junker aristocracy, East-Elbian German had direct ties to key power centres of the Empire: the Crown, the military and the bureaucracy.[56] The ramifications of national unification, in which Junkers had played a prominent part, were transforming the rural social structure that had underscored their traditional role as the political and military backbone of the Kingdom of Prussia. Junkers were becoming agrarian capitalists, the proportion of 'settled' rural workers was diminishing, remaining labourers were more and more akin to proletarians and there was an increasing inflow of Polish migrant workers. This scenario helps explain why the future

54 Ibid.

55 See, for instance, MWG I/3, pp. 362–3.

56 MWG I/3, p. 927.

of 'Deutschtum' or 'Germanness' was such a central preoccupation for Weber throughout his engagement with the 'rural labour question' and why it intertwined with his considerations on culture and worker agency, as later chapters will explore.[57]

What I want to emphasise at this point, however, is that the prism through which Weber chose to assess the long-term impact of these developments to social and political life in Imperial Germany was understanding how they affected the lives of rural workers. A case in point was his approach to the issue of the breakdown in the bonds and duties between different categories of workers and large landowners. Weber believed that the economic basis for the patriarchal relations once predominant in the German East had been the high degree of shared interests between landowners and partially dependent workers. This applied to *Gesinde*, but especially to the *Instmann*, who – along with their families – had served the function of providing a stable reservoir of labour power to the estates; in exchange, they were granted access to enough land and idle time to be able to not only provide for themselves, but to generate a small surplus they could sell on the market.

With the fate of agrarian enterprise increasingly determined not only by the climate and crop yields, but by market forces – the 'heavens and the world market', as Weber put it[58] – this was key. While the *Instleute* received compensation through a share of the harvest, they partook in the risks and the profits of agrarian production alongside the landowner. Within this arrangement, the *Instleute* desired high grain prices as much as their employers, considering they could go to market to sell their surplus or use it to feed animal stock – which they could equally sell for a profit.

As mentioned in the previous section, this relationship started to break down as a result of the greater seasonality of labour resulting from shifts in agrarian production (the introduction of cash crops, mechanisation etc.). This did not only increase the presence of wage-labourers on the estates, who became more attractive to the landowner since they could be employed for a few short months and generated no further costs or commitments in the rest of the year, but also had a bearing on how the remaining *Instleute* were compensated. From a share in the crop – which either no longer comprised grain or was entirely sold off by landowners – the *Instleute* began receiving a *fixed* allowance of grain (or, more likely, potatoes); finally, instead of pasture for their own cows, they were assigned set quantities of milk. With *Instleute* forced

57 See section 9.6 and Chapter 10.

58 MWG I/4, p. 80.

to buy food and other necessary goods on the marketplace, their interests no longer coincided with those of landowners.

The biggest change in the situation of the large landowner, in turn, was the growing insecurity in terms of the availability of workers in the labour-intensive season from year to year. The reliance on wage-labourers and migrant workers meant employers had difficulty ensuring there would be the necessary number of workers at any given time, considering they were now in competition for these workers with other properties and regions – and especially with industry. Finally, there was the matter of the loss of disciplinary control and authority over these workers, especially when the relationship was both precarious and temporary and given on a purely monetary basis. The result was both a growing reliance on cheap migrant labour from abroad and the decline in the more stable *Instleute* posts, leading to an overall increase in the proletarianised segments of the rural working class.

The ultimate question, also because of the obvious political ramifications, was whether the social landscape of the German East would come to resemble that of large cities and industrial districts with a reduced number of large landowners-turned-entrepreneurs opposed by a mass rural proletariat, with an ever-dwindling middle-strata of peasants and tenants in between.

Similarly to Eduard Bernstein's considerations to this effect from the late 1890s, Weber both accepted the general trend of proletarianisation, but did not believe intermediary social segments would necessarily disappear as a result. If Bernstein pointed this out in the urban landscape, Weber would seek to do so in the agrarian context, where he believed small peasants and tenant farmers could coexist with large estates and even thrive, if proper policy measures were put in place to protect these segments. Bernstein would, along similar lines, argue that Marx's diagnosis of a trend towards social polarisation and proletarisation in the capitalist mode of production 'was correct above all if taken as a tendency', and that, in Marx's portrayal, 'the social effects of antagonisms appear much stronger and immediate than they are in reality'.[59] This is precisely what Weber intended to prove with his analysis of the effects of the spread of capitalist relations into the German East. Yet, the truly novel aspect of his approach was, as the next section will discuss, the notion that assessing the viability of middle-strata in the countryside required not only the consideration of strictly economic criteria, but also of rural workers' *desires and aspirations*.

59 Bernstein 1899, p. 47.

4 The 'Psychological Factor': Max Weber's Early Conceptualisation of the Immanent Logic of Social Processes

The key methodological innovation that resulted from Max Weber's research into the 'rural labour question' was his emphasis on the 'ideal' drivers of individual agency. Faced with macro-scale issues such as the possible long-term consequences of the German East's capitalist modernisation, Weber productively centred his approach on the question of how workers were subjectively impacted by this transformation and, at the same time, contributed to driving it further. To this end, his analytical task was asserting to what extent 'psychological factors' came to bear on the ongoing economic and social changes in the German countryside:

> The material and economic grounds for this development are to a large extent known to us. Conversely, it will necessarily be the task of local individual surveys to determine the *psychological* factors, which emerge partly as contributing causes and partly as accompanying occurrences or as effects of this transformation. *Only* local investigations can achieve this goal, and their task is all the more relevant considering these *subjective* phenomena are the most decisive element ... for the question concerning *which development of the labour constitution is probable in the future, which is desirable and which is possible.*[60]

As the passage indicates, Weber conceptualised workers' subjective stances not only as effects of the economic transformations in the German countryside, but as contributing causal factors for subsequent developments. In attributing central importance to the subjective response of workers, i.e., to how they apprehended and reacted not only to the advance of capitalist relations, but also to landowners' patriarchal stance and the introduction of state social policy, Weber displays an early iteration of the analytical perspective on causation in social life he would later become known for. In other words, the pathway to Weber's conceptualisation of the role of religion in the origins of modern capitalism and, more fundamentally, of the centrality of culture for human agency,[61] began through his discovery that the segment of the population most

---

60 MWG I/4, pp. 89–90.

61 In another intervention of the early 1890s that evokes the already central role of culture in Weber's understanding of agency, he remarks how 'objectively quite identical situations' can originate 'entirely distinct and equally unwarranted conceptions of their own situations on the part of those involved'. These different conceptions were, nevertheless, 'more

subject to economic pressures in the German East – proletarianised workers – often acted according to purely 'psychological' or 'ideal' drivers, rather than merely economic ones. Weber's inquiry into rural workers' agency was thus one of the first building blocks for an analytical perspective he would later generalise to the study of the entire cosmos of social action in modern society.[62]

Crucially, this theoretical synthesis was only possible as a result of Weber's empirical social research into the 'rural labour question'. His insight was that, when 'apparently quite insignificant elements [*Momente*]', which in and of themselves lack any decisive importance, 'emerge as hundreds of thousands of mutations', they make up a 'phenomenon that, taken in its entirety, represents an aspect of vast *social-political* importance'.[63] In other words, Weber drew a causal connection between the mass of molecular changes in workers' individual consciousness and the large-scale 'social-political' transformations in Imperial Germany, i.e., those relative to its class relations and social structure.

He arrived at this conclusion by focussing on the situation of one specific category of rural worker in the German East, i.e., the *Instleute*. As mentioned previously, *Instleute* occupied an intermediary position in the social structure of the German countryside; contractually bound and partially dependent, they nevertheless enjoyed greater freedom and a higher social standing than domestic workers (*Gesinde*); on the other hand, they were not as autonomous as tenant farmers – who were free from feudal duties – or the entirely proletarianised (and mobile) rural workers. The *Instleute* were, in this sense, an embodiment of the compromise between feudal past and modern agricultural relations in the social structure of the German lands. That is also how Karl Kautsky defined *Instleute* in his classic treatment of the agrarian question (*Die Agrarfrage* – 1899): 'The *Instmann* is a half-way thing [*Mittelding*] between the serf and the tenant farmer, he is usually submitted to the *Gesindeordnung* and constitutes

---

important than the [material – V.S.] situation in itself' in terms of setting 'the wider trend of development' (MWG I/4, p. 102).

62 This does not mean that a reference to the role of 'psychological factors' in economic life was entirely new; indeed, it was a feature of the writings of the previous generation of German political economists, such as Wilhelm Roscher and Gustav Schmoller (see Riesebrodt 1986). What made Weber's perspective unique was the fact that this insight structured his entire approach to the 'rural labour question'. Weber would in fact debate the issue with Schmoller and other economists at the Verein's 1893 conference. As Chapter 9 will detail, their contrasting views on the role of workers in the social transformation of the German East are illustrative of the qualitative leap inherent in Weber's approach.

63 MWG I/4, p. 81, my emphasis.

a remnant from feudal times'.[64] Incidentally, this passage came after a quote from Max Weber's 1892 report. The peculiar status of the *Instleute* survived into the late nineteenth century, because while capitalist relations had already been introduced to the German countryside – to different degrees depending on the region – since the Stein and Hardenberg decrees of the early 1800s,[65] agrarian capitalism was only truly unleashed in Germany by the combination of national unification and an ever more integrated world market.

It is no accident that the most important early work on the capitalist transformation of agriculture from a leading intellectual of German Social Democracy took precisely this aspect of the young Weber's work into account. Because of their peculiar standing as neither feudal nor modern, Weber saw in *Instleute* an ideal barometer to assess the pace and direction of transformations in the German East. The burning question was whether this type of partially dependent labourer would disappear and give way to a purely wage-earning landless proletariat. Weber quickly realised that answering this question meant raising another, namely, 'how workers regarded each form of remuneration', especially because 'landowners claim that *it is they* [the workers – V.S.] who desire and push for the aforementioned change',[66] i.e., for a switch to a 'freer' but more precarious wage-labour relation.

Despite its inherent insecurity, Weber realised workers saw wage-labour as a 'successive alleviation'. This assessment was 'to some extent correct', he argued, 'as the heavens and the world market had a significantly smaller influence on the amount of their gross income' as a result.[67] Put differently, as wage labourers, workers earned their pay regardless of crop yield and the price it fetched on the market. The task was, therefore, 'to investigate the psychological consequences of this transformation', which implied 'firstly, asserting how the actual standard of life was affected and whether the impression of improving one's situation was not partially based on an *illusion*'.[68] Weber used the term 'illusion' to stress that, even though certain perceptions lacked an objective basis, they could still prove consequential in social life if individuals saw fit to act upon them. This could only be determined by asserting the extent to which theses 'illusions' effectively shaped workers' outlook and decisions.

64 Kautsky 1899, p. 158.
65 See MWG III/5, p. 362 f. and Wehler 1987, pp. 409–27.
66 MWG I/4, p. 81 – my emphasis.
67 MWG I/4, p. 80.
68 Ibid. – my emphasis.

> The rural worker does not live from bread alone and his being is not shaped solely by his material interests, but to a large extent by illusions – as could be said from a material-economic standpoint – or rather by factors, whose psychological underpinnings may be problematic to us, but which are mostly inaccessible to purely economic observation.[69]

Once more, Weber contrasted his consideration of agents' subjectivity – and the 'illusions' that propelled them – with an analysis based purely on economic factors (which he *did not exclude* entirely). Assessing the mindset of rural workers provided an ideal opportunity to test out this analytical premise, considering that they seemed to be acting either in disregard of or in direct opposition to their immediate economic interests. Weber raised three hypotheses to explain this phenomenon, taking workers' growing preference for 'free' wage-labour, despite its higher insecurity, as his measuring stick. The first hypothesis was that 'workers might find the allocated land and share in the harvest', i.e., the main forms of remuneration of *Instleute*, 'inadequate', i.e., materially disadvantageous; the second was that there might be a reluctance on workers' part to enter into a 'community of interests' with the landowner due to the situation of 'partial dependence' this implied – in spite of obtaining greater material security in return; in other words, because relations of dependence had become intolerable to workers. Weber was confident this was the most relevant factor. As he put it, the labour-relation that underscored the situation of *Instleute* was 'no longer sustainable'; this was '*not* due to material reasons', but to workers' 'reluctance to be tied to the estate through bonds of dependence for a lifetime'.[70]

The third hypothesis Weber raised was workers' possible unwillingness to face the 'inconvenience and the risk of independent economic conduct' [*Wirtschaftsführung*].[71] With this hypothesis, Weber addressed the only prospect available for *Instleute* to leave their dependent status and achieve upper social mobility, namely, amassing enough savings for the acquisition of a small plot of land and a transition to an independent peasant existence (or that of an independent tenant-farmer). Under favourable conditions, *Instleute* were able to accumulate enough of a surplus from their family income to purchase (or lease) land, something that was anyhow out of reach for most wage-labourers.[72]

69 MWG I/4, p. 102.
70 MWG I/4, p. 98.
71 MWG I/4, p. 81.
72 MWG I/3, p. 97.

Regardless of its purely economic viability, Weber found the discipline necessary to amass these savings over several years required a specific attitude not found in all *Instleute*.

Crucially, however, Weber did not argue that workers' 'thriftiness' was the only factor in play in their social mobility; the effective likelihood that their efforts would culminate in the acquisition of a new social status was key as well. In other words, the actual *possibility* of upward social mobility was a decisive factor for whether a new segment of small peasants and tenant farmers could emerge in the German East:

> We will need to eliminate precisely these barriers [the *Instmann*'s low ceiling of mobility – V.S.] to make space upwards, by giving estate-bound workers the possibility to leave their dependent situations and move to an independent small peasant existence.[73]

Yet, if the prospect of becoming a peasant or tenant-farmer was perceived as either too difficult or as riddled with obvious disadvantages – because plots had poor soil quality or were too small to guarantee a family's livelihood – then this would, in Weber's view, tip the balance in most workers' minds towards migration to the cities or abroad, as opposed to a continued existence under the patriarchal rule of the landowner. 'It is the self-conscious workers who prefer to migrate', Weber emphasised.[74]

In this sense, while Weber held that economic factors were not the exclusive drivers of agency, he did not underestimate their relevance. The question of whether a small plot was economically viable no doubt played a role in workers' intention to acquire or lease one. Nevertheless, Weber realised that this did not suffice to spur the change to a more self-reliant economic existence; this demanded 'a yearning for independence' on workers' part, 'even if in detriment of their material situation'.[75] The reason only a few workers were willing to make the sacrifices necessary to acquire or lease a small plot of land, Weber argued, 'almost surely did not reside in the material sphere'; it was, at least in part, 'the ideal reflection [*Reflex*] of *social* relations of stratification on the individual' that was at play.[76]

Thus, according to Weber, it was one thing to simply leave the situation of partial dependence that characterised the *Gesinde* or *Instleute* through flight

73 MWG I/4, p. 98.
74 MWG I/3, p. 743.
75 MWG I/3, p. 270.
76 MWG I/4, p. 85.

or migration; another thing entirely was having the will power and foresight required for the transition to a peasant existence. Again, this was not just a matter of thrift vs. profligacy on workers' part, but of a specific desire to achieve the independent economic existence *and* social status of the small proprietor (regardless of actual improvement in living standards). Weber viewed this as the most important question raised by his study in terms of the fate of the social structure of the German East: Would a middle strata of tenant-farmers and small proprietors emerge as a result of workers' desire for greater freedom? Or, rather, would this yearning – in the absence of a culture of abnegation and a drive to ascend socially – culminate in an ever-larger mass of rural and urban proletarians, whose drive for freedom only went as far as escaping the patriarchal rule of landowners? Along these lines, Weber argued that life in the large estates did not foster the attitude needed to awaken workers' desire to move up into the rural middle strata:

> The profoundly dispiriting notion that there will only be 'masters and servants' on this Earth for all eternity is not a burden for the rural worker who witnesses first-hand the difficult struggle for survival of the peasant landowner who, just as himself, physically puts in the work; the worker of the large estate is, in turn, incapable of not apprehending the economic underpinnings of an enterprise in which he is but a subordinate component.[77]

In other words, the large gap separating landowner and workers at the large estate sharpened the latter's awareness of social inequality in the German East, along with the rigid property relations that perpetuated it, yet made no contribution to their entrepreneurial education. This situation made any effort to be more productive or to amass savings on workers' part seem futile. On the other hand, the dependent *Gesinde* who 'ate at the peasant's table', as was the case in the peasant properties in the South and West of Imperial Germany, was likely to be more convinced of the existence of common interests with their master and to aspire to reach the same social rank.[78] The large estates East of the river Elbe represented, in this sense, a not at all virtuous combination of feudal hierarchies and an ever-more intensive and efficient exploitation of resources and labour power as per the modern capitalist enterprise.

77 MWG I/4, p. 85.
78 Ibid.

This was the paradox of modernisation that Weber's study diagnosed, namely that, despite having become in effect rural capitalists, favouring a cheap disposable workforce to which they owed no duties, large landowners of the German East still clung to their prerogatives of patriarchal authority when it came to addressing and disciplining workers. In East-Prussia, for instance, morale had reached a low point, with workers feeling like 'mere machines' in the eyes of employers lacking any concern for their 'overall well-being and woes'. In a manner reminiscent of Marx's definition of capitalist exploitation as a process through which workers are reduced to the status of mere 'things', rural labourers reported feeling that, if they received heating material from landowners at all, it was 'only so they apply their bodily warmth and energy to the latter's advantage'.[79]

The frequent complaints about landowners using the 'wrong tone' when handling their workers were, in turn, another symptom that social tensions had reached a tipping point. Reports detailed how workers would express their displeasure with the traditional patronising language of their patriarchal masters and how in some areas 'the heightened self-awareness of workers' was responsible for the effective elimination of the traditional enforcement of 'fatherly' discipline. 'The willing obedience of past times has ... disappeared anyhow'.[80] To Weber, once the patriarchal basis of the agricultural enterprise – and the underlying 'community of interests' between dependent worker and landlord – had vanished, the patriarchal form of running the estate had also run its course.[81] Furthermore, as these estates became fully capitalist enterprises subject to the world market, the balance of strength between landowner and the increasingly proletarianised workers also shifted to reflect a typically industrial condition of class strife:

> Between natural economic opponents there can only be struggle, and it is a smug delusion to believe that the strengthening of the economic power of one party will benefit the social standing of the other.[82]

A case in point was the province of Silesia, where the entanglement between industry and agriculture was at its most intense[83] and where capitalist entrepreneurs were acquiring estates and sweeping away the remnants of the old

79 MWG I/3, p. 267.
80 MWG I/3, p. 265.
81 MWG I/3, pp. 741–2.
82 MWG I/3, p. 903.
83 See MWG I/3, p. 594.

'patriarchal' rural economy. Weber saw Silesia as a possible – indeed an ominous – snapshot of the future of the German East. In his initial appraisal of social conditions in the province, Weber likens its rural labour relations to a veritable 'field of rubble' as a result of the 'transformation of the patriarchal organization into a capitalist one'.[84] Nevertheless, even in cases less dramatic than Silesia, individual landowners could do little to stop this dynamic. The clearest sign that the patriarchally-administered estate had become unsustainable was workers' refusal to play their (passive) part in it. Commenting on his report for the 1893 general assembly of the Verein, Weber highlighted this point:

> I have not argued that the unsettling of labour relations [*Arbeitsverfassung*] in large estates is the 'fault' of the individual large landowners. On the contrary, workers also do not want its continuation ... *Nothing* bespeaks a more annihilating verdict for the future of *Inst*-relations than this aspect. The patriarchal control that the master has over the fate of the worker, as is the case with the old *Inst*-arrangement, is precisely what people are no longer willing to endure. It is these psychological factors of overwhelming power which not only bring about migration to the cities, but also the unsettling of the constitution of labour [*Arbeitsverfassung*].[85]

Despite Weber's dramatic tone, there was nothing fatalistic about his outlook on the fate of social structure in the German East. Indeed, the attribution of a central role to workers' subjective stances is what allowed him to put forth a non-deterministic perspective on how developments *might* unfold. While the trend for modernisation in the countryside could hardly be reversed, Weber stressed that surrendering to the blind action of market forces and calling for state action aligned exclusively with landowners' interests were not the only policy options at hand; there was, namely, the possibility of engaging with workers' ideal drivers:

> The transformations in the psychological needs of individuals are almost greater than the reshaping of material life-conditions, and it would be scientifically inadmissible to ignore them. All purely economic consider-

84 MWG I/3, p. 735.

85 MWG I/4, p. 174. The term *Arbeitsverfassung*, which translates literally to 'constitution of labour' is, according to Lawrence Scaff, 'the key theoretical term in Weber's major writings from 1892 to 1894'. It 'resists precise translation' and 'was common among political economists, Weber included, as a shorthand way of characterizing the historically-given "constitution", "condition" or "organization" of labour, or labour-relations' (Scaff 1984, p. 200).

> ations, especially with regards to agrarian organisation, would be unrealistic; and yet, precisely in the agrarian realm and precisely at this moment there are *several* possibilities for further developments according to *purely* economic perspectives.[86]

The question was thus how to channel workers' heightened self-awareness and desire for freedom to reshape the economic foundations of the German East. Weber reports these 'psychological factors' did not only lead to workers' yearning for a more autonomous existence and to their refusal to be treated as either children or machines; crucially, it also increased workers' productivity, or at least, their *potential* for greater productivity. Weber quotes in this regard a landowner who had become convinced that 'heightened intelligence and better intellectual education enables workers to better execute their tasks'.[87] This is precisely the insight that allowed Weber's critique of the patriarchal standpoint on workers to become the basis for his own 'proto-Fordist' hegemonic project, i.e., for his proposal of a rearrangement of class relations in Imperial Germany that incorporated skilled workers into a new power bloc led by the more dynamic sectors of the German bourgeoisie.[88]

Thus, the same 'individualistic streak' that led rural workers to reject personal relations of domination was also at work when they acquired land at exorbitant prices and high interest rates in the name of achieving 'the "autonomy" they longed for'.[89] The question, therefore, was not only whether a wide enough segment of partially dependent workers would be able to acquire a plot of land; just as crucial, in Weber's perspective, was whether they would also adhere to the specific 'status honour [*Standesehre*] of agricultural enterprise'.[90] Both an appropriate economic conduct and a yearning for social prestige were, therefore, essential for the viability of the small rural property, as much so, in fact, as soil quality and the size of the plot. Weber believed this was largely predicated on large landowners' ability to act as role models, rather than mere superiors, inspiring the drive for social ascension in their own workers.

But there was an issue here. Even in the presence of such suitable role models of agrarian entrepreneurship, rural workers might still converge towards an altogether different standpoint and set of ideals, i.e., proletarian class con-

86 MWG I/3, pp. 920–1.
87 MWG I/3, p. 266.
88 For Weber's early projection of a Fordist class constellation as the basis for a reformed Imperial Germany, see Rehmann 2015.
89 MWG I/3, pp. 919–20.
90 MWG I/3, p. 97.

sciousness. Max Weber was not blind to the fact that the expansion of capitalist relations had produced a response on the level of conscience (or culture) that claimed to be an alternative to both patriarchal subjection and bourgeois individualism. The 'material interests' of rural wage-labourers predisposed them, as Weber put it, not only to 'seek upward mobility … by joining the industrial working-class', but also to 'let themselves be captured by the grandiose development of class consciousness of the modern proletariat in the cities and the countryside'.[91]

Weber understood class consciousness, therefore, as another form of collective self-awareness by workers. Already at a very initial phase of his research on the 'rural labour question' (c. March 1892), Weber raised the question of whether the phenomenon of class consciousness could unite different segments of the rural working class, such as dependent workers and 'free' wage-laborers, or if a higher-standing segment of workers would detach itself from the remaining working masses. In Weber's own terms, the key question was whether 'modern labour's specific urge towards autonomy' could be channelled into entrepreneurship through the ascension of a segment of relatively well-off industrial and rural workers.[92] In an alternative scenario, clogged pathways of social mobility and a shared experience of oppression would drive workers *en bloc* into the arms of the SPD and culminate in the revolutionary unification of both skilled and unskilled segments of the working class against the status quo.

Max Weber saw the 'rural labour question' as a decisive element with regards to which of these scenarios was likelier to materialise. As Weber stressed in the conclusion of his report for the Verein (mid-1892), however, rural social struggle had clear specificities, such as the fact that, in contrast to its industrial counterpart, it was fundamentally a '*land* question'. In this sense, its resolution hinged on whether 'ascension to an autonomous existence' was possible for a relevant share of workers, that is, if land ownership in conditions that went beyond those of a 'landowning proletariat' was viable. With this premise in mind, Weber concluded that the 'main trait' of the *rural* 'labour question' was the fact that its solution took an *individualist* rather than a 'socialist' form.[93] Weber thought it essential, therefore, to take the aspirations of workers themselves into account – at least, that is, of a 'higher-standing' segment among them.

There were also political dividends to be reaped from this effort at engaging workers' standpoint; if an 'individualist' solution to the 'rural labour question'

91 MWG I/3, pp. 97–8.
92 MWG I/4, p. 83.
93 MWG I/3, p. 921.

could be found, it would equally neutralise or at least marginalise the threat of a socialist alternative, i.e., the expropriation and collectivisation of large estates. Here was a clear normative aspect in Weber's early conceptualisation of the role of culture in agency. As Weber himself put it, the goal of the inquiry into the 'rural labour question' was not only to ascertain 'which development of the labour constitution [was] probable in the future', but also which was '*desirable*' and which was 'possible'.[94]

As Part 3 will discuss in detail, Weber's defence of the small peasant and tenant farmer – and of a 'labour aristocracy' in the case of industry – were openly articulated as counterweights to the levelling and socialist tendencies of a growing rural proletariat.[95] Understanding that the working class was a stratified entity whose different segments possessed diverging, even opposing, mentalities, Weber posited that 'higher-standing' workers should be engaged with and fostered purposefully for political ends.

Thus, if Weber's analytical breakthrough regarding the role of 'ideals' in human agency came embedded in a highly politicised issue that made unbiased stances difficult to articulate, his efforts at objectivity at this point unapologetically coincided with taking a stance for the bourgeois-individualist solution to the so-called 'rural labour question'.

5 Conclusion: Workers' Standpoint and the Genesis of Weber's Social Theory

A clear example of how Weber's engagement of worker subjectivity went beyond an analysis of developmental tendencies in the German countryside and fed directly into his budding social theory is his discussion of the piece wage [*Akkordlohn*]. The term refers to the practice of paying workers with reference to how much they produce in a given timespan as opposed to a fixed wage. Landowners reported having attempted to introduce this (more precarious and exploitative) form of remuneration, especially during the harvest; the result, however, was a pushback by workers who dreaded and/or actively resisted its adoption.[96] Employers attributed this to workers' 'laziness', a view Max Weber did not share.[97] He saw in this resistance, instead, a symptom of the growing rejection of relations of dependence and the corresponding

94 MWG I/4, p. 89.
95 See MWG I/3, p. 742.
96 See MWG I/3, p. 270.
97 MWG I/4, p. 86.

lure of wage-labour and migration to the cities. In his own words, the introduction of the 'piece-wage system' resulted in

> the mobilization of workers … whose thoughts of a change of trade become only logical, considering [the piece wage] eliminates the factor of (apparent) wage stability, the only true advantage for the worker paid in cash in comparison to the thresher [who earns a share of the crop – V.S.].[98]

According to Weber, what lay at the bottom of the rejection – and overall inadequacy – of this form of remuneration was the fact that it impacted the 'orderliness of economic conduct' [*Planmäßigkeit der Wirtschaftsführung*] as a consequence of the 'inferior calculability of the piece-wage system'.[99] That's why, in a passage of his 1892 report, Weber calls the introduction of piece wages the 'beginning of the end of the productivity of *permanent* workers, since it fundamentally ignores the ethical dimensions of the human drive to work' [*die ethische Momente des menschlichen Arbeitstriebes*].[100]

Here a central theme of Weber's later writings, i.e., the ethical drivers of labour and economic activity, emerge in embryonic, but clear form. In fact, Weber seemed aware he had made an important theoretical breakthrough in his studies on the 'rural labour question'. After pointing out how the 'individualistic streak' embodied in a desire for autonomy was present in all segments of the rural working class, he described the 'grandiose and pure psychological magic of "freedom"' as a phenomenon with a much broader significance:

> This trait of the modern world is the product of a psychological development of universal character and we ourselves experience its effect …; we too strive for the daily bread achieved through our own efforts, away from the table of the parental home and the circle of our own.[101]

Highlighting this passage does not mean arguing that Weber's conceptualisation of the 'capitalist spirit' was fully developed at this stage, nor that he saw the expressions of this 'trait of the modern world' in the working class alone (his reference to 'ourselves' clearly indicates a cross-class phenomenon). The quote shows, rather, that it was at least partly through an insight into *worker* subjectiv-

---

98 MWG I/4, p. 86.
99 MWG I/3, p. 86.
100 MWG I/3, p. 882.
101 MWG I/3, p. 920.

ity that Weber was able to develop the basis for his mature conceptualisation of social action. The discovery of how workers' ethical drivers impacted the social transformation of the German East is, in this sense, a little-recognised, yet fundamental piece of the analytical puzzle behind Weber's later scholarly accomplishments, most notably, his argument for the centrality of ascetic Protestantism to the rise of modern capitalism's work-ethic. Weber will, in fact, return to these reflections on the 'piece-wage' in *The Protestant Ethic and the Spirit of Capitalism*, more specifically to demonstrate how workers' attitude towards this form of remuneration serve as a benchmark for their 'traditionalism'.[102]

The rural labour question was, in this sense, the ideal laboratory for Weber's social theory inasmuch as it provided empirical evidence to the two-way or reflexive nature of the economic modernisation process: not only did the introduction of capitalist relations impact workers' agency, but their own perception of these changes and subsequent reaction to them built a part of the overall development. If in the previous generation of political economists there were those who, like Gustav Schmoller, had already pointed to the role of 'ideal factors' in economic life – as I will approach below – it was the manner in which Weber articulated the reciprocal interrelation of 'material' and 'psychological' factors that prefigured his subsequent development of a novel perspective on social life.

The fundamental dissonance between Max Weber's views and those held by the previous generation of German political economists came to a head in the Verein für Socialpolitik's conference of March 1893. As the results of the 'rural labour survey' across the Reich were expounded during the proceedings, the contrast between Weber's peculiar perspective and that of the representatives of 'patriarchalism', on one side, but also of Social Democracy, on the other, took on the form of a lively debate, as I will examine next.

102 See MWG I/18, pp. 176–80. On this point, see also my Epilogue below.

CHAPTER 9

The Standpoint of 'State Reason' vs. the Standpoint of the Working Class: Max Weber's Squares Off with Social Democrats on the 'Rural Labour Question'

1 Introduction

In March 1893, the Verein für Socialpolitik hosted a general conference in Berlin to debate the results of its survey on the 'rural labour question'. Three aspects of the conference are of interest; first, the fact that Max Weber's report and views set the tone for the whole gathering;[1] second, and more importantly, the question of the adequate *standpoint* on the 'rural labour question' shaped discussions throughout the event. A third relevant factor is the presence and active participation of two Social Democrats, Max Quarck and Bruno Schönlank – then an editor of the SPD's daily newspaper *Vorwärts* – at the proceedings. The conference provides, in many ways, a microcosm for the issues raised in Part 2 of this work and a testing ground for the theses it raises. During the proceedings, the qualitative leap of Weber's approach to the 'rural labour question' was recognised and openly discussed with intellectuals of the previous generation; there were also direct exchanges between Weber and social-democratic intellectuals on the conference's topic, allowing for a shorter analytic route to compare their respective views.

That Max Weber's report on East-Elbian Germany far outweighed reports on other regions in importance and analytical value in the eyes of organisers and attendees alike is beyond question. Weber was the only author of a report to give a lecture at the conference. Moreover, participants with outlooks as distinct as Georg Friedrich Knapp,[2] a long-standing authority on agrarian history and policy, and the Social Democrat Max Quarck[3] explicitly highlighted the

1 A record of the conference's lectures and debates is available in Verein für Socialpolitik 1893. For a summary of the conference, see Mommsen and Aldenhoff [*Editorischer Bericht*] *in* MWG I/4, pp. 157–64. In this section I will focus on the first day of proceedings, dedicated to the 'rural labour question'; the second day – which centred on the issue of land distribution and protection of small properties – does not have relevant discussions for my efforts, apart from Weber's intervention in the debate that concluded it (MWG I/4, p. 162).

2 See Verein für Socialpolitik 1893, pp. 6–7.

3 See Quarck, SpCb II, 28 [10.04.1893], p. 330.

value of Weber's contribution out of all others. Indeed, even if not every participant left convinced by Weber's arguments – and especially the social and political conclusions he drew from his study – all attendants had to somehow contend with his stance on the 'rural labour question'. This overwhelming consensus as to the quality of Weber's contribution elicited, in fact, a series of tensions and controversies, which were themselves magnified by the diversity of social and political backgrounds of conference participants. Consequently, the Verein conference provided a unique sounding-board not only for Weber's emerging stance on social life, but more generally for his take on the issue of class relations in Imperial Germany and their recent, capitalism-fuelled transformations.

2 Two Generations of Political Economists Take On the 'Labour Question'

One of the tensions that came to a head in the conference corresponded to the relatively clear-cut generational cleavage amongst its attendees/speakers. After two decades of existence, the Verein für Socialpolitik was now incorporating a new cohort of political economists who had been socialised in post-unification Germany. Max Weber, at 28 years of age, was among the youngest participants. He would, in fact, address the broader implications of the generational gap explicitly. Towards the end of a lecture that contained his main conclusions on the 'rural labour question', Weber took a more personal and reflexive tone suggesting his audience had probably detected 'an element of resignation' weighing over his words:

> The reason for it – and I have here the honour of addressing predominantly older and more experienced gentlemen than myself – is the difference in the situation of the older generation regarding the tasks they faced in their time and the situation in which we from the younger generation now find ourselves. I do not know whether all my contemporaries experience it as starkly as I do at this moment: the severe curse of the epigone that burdens the nation from its broader strata up to its highest echelons.[4]

---

4 MWG I/4, p. 195.

Weber would go on to say that his generation not only had different tasks than the previous one, it also lacked the illusions of their forefathers.[5] Weber's reference to a generational divide made sense; there was a clear two-decade gap between academic and political doyens in their fifties – G. Schmoller (b. 1838), G.F. Knapp (b. 1842), Adolph Wagner (b. 1835), Hugo Thiel (b. 1839) – and those scholars under 35 years of age and on the very beginning of their professional trajectories such as Karl Kärger (b. 1858) and Max Weber (b. 1864), in addition to the Social Democrats Max Quarck (b. 1860) and Bruno Schönlank (b. 1859).[6] Nevertheless, the younger cohort was able to influence both the scholarly aspects of the discussion and the dynamics of debates. An oft-quoted statement by a representative of the older generation about Max Weber shows that the former were somehow aware of this. In his lecture dedicated to giving an overview of the survey's results, G.F. Knapp remarked how Weber's report, above all others, 'has given me the impression that our expertise is no longer up to par' and that 'we have to start anew'.[7] The use of the first person plural indicates Knapp was addressing his contemporaries as a group; Weber, in his reply to the comment, again spoke in generational terms, acknowledging Knapp's friendly and generous stance 'towards us in the younger generation as well as young academics'.[8] More than simply an exchange of pleasantries between two conference participants, this recurring adage pointed to an actual tension along generational lines. This was especially visible in the diverging relationship these cohorts had to working-class politics.

∴

In the conference's opening lecture, Gustav Schmoller did not directly address the generation issue. He did look back at two decades of Verein activities, stressing how it 'had always remained true to itself and its program of advoc-

5 What tasks and illusions Weber had in mind will be the object of this chapter's concluding section, 9.5.

6 Both SPD representatives had also had a fairly typical middle-class education, going from the Gymnasium to degrees in law (Quarck) and political economy/philosophy (Schönlank), having both written doctorates in their respective fields in the early 1880s before encountering the typical barriers for social-democratic students – especially in the years of the *Sozialistengesetz* – and, finally, turning to journalistic work for the party. For biographical treatments of Schönlank's and Quarck's trajectories see (Mayer 1972) and (Gniffke 1992), respectively.

7 Knapp in Verein für Socialpolitik [Verein] 1893, p. 7.

8 MWG I/4, p. 165.

ating the elevation of the working class'.[9] Crucially, in restating this goal and the fact that empirical research and influencing public opinion remained the association's preferred levers to realise it, Schmoller discretely adjusted the Verein's foundational credo so as to adapt it to the changed circumstances of the 1890s. Considering the rise of Social Democracy and the spectacular rekindling of the labour movement in previous years it is no coincidence that the issue of what constituted an adequate – as opposed to a 'partisan' – standpoint regarding said 'elevation of the working classes' emerged as his main concern.

The conference's focus on the 'labour question' was, in fact, especially evocative of the ambiguities that had been inscribed in the programme of the Verein since its inception. Schmoller crystallised them in referring to the association's goal of 'advocating for the elevation of the lower classes' by means of 'seeking out a truth that could be of use to both practical life and the fatherland', yet 'stood above parties and classes'. Schmoller forcefully argued that this emphasis on 'scientific knowledge' to improve the situation of the 'lower classes' was precisely what had allowed the Verein to gain acceptance amongst the 'propertied and cultured' segments of German society.[10]

This statement was very much in line with Schmoller's inaugural address at the Verein's 1872 founding conference in Eisenach; yet there was one notable change of focus or, rather, of interlocutor in his March 1893 lecture. If, in 1872, Schmoller stressed how the profound change in political circumstances brought forth by national unification meant earlier reservations against state intervention had to be reconsidered – along with the orthodox 'free market' views of the 'Manchester school'[11] – he now drew attention to the political and methodological consequences of another political shift, i.e., the rise of a self-conscious working class embodied in German Social Democracy. A brief comparison of Schmoller's lectures set two decades apart can provide a useful contextualization of the peculiar circumstances in which Max Weber addressed the Verein.

In the association's inaugural address of 1872, Schmoller directed his critical remarks against those political economists who denied the existence of the 'labour question' entirely, like the free-marketer John Prince-Smith; Schmoller argued such a stance was tantamount to converting liberalism from a universalistic defence of economic liberty and human rights into a bulwark for the

9 Schmoller in Verein 1893, p. 3.
10 Ibid.
11 Schmoller [1872] 1890, pp. 5–6.

'one-sided class standpoint of entrepreneurs'.[12] Schmoller argued, instead, for a standpoint that went *beyond* class and that, like state authorities (as he framed them), 'stood above selfish class interests, legislated and conducted administrative affairs in a just manner, protected the weak and elevated the lower classes'.[13]

Schmoller maintained this outlook in 1893 insofar as he restated that the Verein's task was to 'stay above these [political and class] antagonisms'.[14] Yet, a key change had occurred in how he framed the working class in his discourse. If in 1872 he had recognised the existence of class struggle and the threat of social revolution,[15] he ascribed a fundamentally passive role to the 'lower classes' in the improvement of their own situation. Schmoller did raise concerns about workers' increasingly 'crude and intemperate' behaviour at the time,[16] but argued this unrest was a sign that, while economic progress might have led to material improvements in their situation, it had not yet had the same effect on their moral qualities. His call for the 'elevation' of the lower strata was, along the same lines, aimed primarily at what he termed 'psychological conditions', i.e., at fostering 'diligence, thrift, respectability and family life' as necessary complements to their economic advancement. To Schmoller, then, the 'social question' carried primarily moral repercussions and perils. The 'most dangerous gap' between workers and the 'propertied and cultured classes' was, in this sense, not in their respective economic standing, but in 'morals, education, perceptions and ideals'.[17] Hence the Verein's moderate reformist goal to

> … elevate, educate and reconcile the lower classes to the point that they would be able to incorporate themselves in peace and harmony into the organism of society.[18]

By 1893, this underlying objective remained, but it was now threatened by socialist workers rather than dogmatic free-market economists (in spite of a revival of free-trade policies under Chancellor Caprivi).[19] Which is why, instead of merely distancing himself from the 'standpoint of entrepreneurs', Schmoller

12 Schmoller [1872] 1890, p. 7.
13 Schmoller [1872] 1890, p. 9.
14 Schmoller [1872] 1890, p. 2.
15 Schmoller [1872] 1890, p. 5.
16 Schmoller [1872] 1890, pp. 9–10.
17 Schmoller [1872] 1890, pp. 10–11.
18 Schmoller [1872] 1890, p. 11.
19 Wehler 1995, pp. 1005–6.

now centred his efforts at clarifying the Verein's stance regarding the standpoint of workers themselves. If the 'elevation of the lower classes' had been a goal of the Verein since the beginning,

> [w]e could obviously not, to that effect, simply identify ourselves with working people's class interests, much less with their one-sided ideals and theories; but we have always stood for their justified demands.[20]

Schmoller's remarks on the Verein's relationship to workers' interests were just the first salvo in a debate on the legitimacy of different standpoints on the 'labour question' that would last the entire conference. But, his opening words attended to other concerns as well. The triumph of Social Democracy over repression and the new emphasis on social policy brought on by the 'New Course' meant both greater exposure for the Verein as an organisation committed to social reform, but also the need to ward off accusations of social-democratic leanings. On the one hand, the new political juncture offered a chance for the Verein to go back to playing a more active role in governmental policy, as had been its original goal;[21] yet, ever since the Ruhr miners' strike of 1889, the organisation had also been 'the object of open attacks on the part of entrepreneurs'.[22] The rising tide of social struggle since the late 1880s had lifted all actors engaged in social reform, from associations of scholars and officials like the Verein to German Social Democracy. Indeed, to one historian, 'Social Democrats and social reformers had a narrow – even if indirect – bond: the more the membership of Social Democracy grew, the more indirect influence the Verein für Socialpolitik won in internal Imperial politics'.[23] Conversely, this made it even more vulnerable to the accusation that it was nothing more than a social-democratic organisation with a more reputable façade, as had already been the case in the 1870s.[24] This ambiguous situation of both profiting from the changes brought with the rise of Social Democracy and coming under criticism for a supposed kinship to it, explain Schmoller's repeated exhortations that the Verein should resist the urge to 'one-sidedly inflate this or that class interest'.[25] The novelty consisted in the fact that workers' interests were now articulated with enough clarity and political weight in Imperial Germany that

20 Schmoller [1872] 1890, p. 3.
21 See *Einleitung* in MWG I/3, pp. 1–3.
22 Plessen 1975, p. 48.
23 Plessen 1975, p. 60.
24 See Schmoller's debate with Treitschke in 1874–5, portrayed in Chapter 6 above.
25 Schmoller in Verein 1893, p. 2.

the Verein chairman felt the need to openly clarify the association's relationship to it. The manner in which Schmoller went about this shows just how much his previous image of the worker – depicted alternately as a passive object of social policy and a dangerous revolutionary – had become untenable and how the tension between top-down efforts to 'ameliorate' workers' situation vis-à-vis their autonomous struggle for their own interests had now risen to the status of an unavoidable contradiction in German political life.

In a poignant passage of his opening lecture, Schmoller remarked how most, if not all those gathered at the conference 'did not see the contemporary labour movement, including Social Democracy, as a misfortune or inconvenience, as something that needs to be combated'. Instead, he estimated that they saw it as 'a necessary historical consequence of our cultural and economic development'. Schmoller believed universal schooling, the press and the 'democratic hue of current state structures', on the one hand, and 'the wonders of modern technical advance and transportation', on the other, had '*awoken the lower classes from the slumber of mindless stupor*'.[26] The political consequences of this shift were clear.

> [the lower classes] have awoken, they demand the right to a certain degree of political influence, of consideration of their interests, of a greater share in the economic and intellectual goods of our culture. They demand – and in certain senses rightfully so – to partake as equals through their self-conscious activity in state and economic life.[27]

Schmoller believed this constituted no less than an 'epochal shift, the beginning of a new great age in world history'. Beyond its hyperbolic status, however, what is notable in the statement above is how Schmoller articulated workers' demands in the active voice ('*they* demand ... to partake as equals'). This was a subtle indication of how a perception of workers as passive objects of patriarchal care was becoming untenable against the backdrop of twenty years of working-class struggle and mobilisation since the foundation of the Verein. This gesture of recognition of workers' standpoint nevertheless demanded clear qualifications and had strict limitations; in this sense, Schmoller would warn that all 'extreme forms of democracy have quickly led to the political and economic decadence of the states in question' and that 'social democracy would achieve the same result'.[28]

26 Schmoller in Verein 1893, p. 4.
27 Ibid.
28 Ibid.

How then, could Schmoller call for workers to have a greater share of 'cultural' and 'economic' goods while at the same time pleading that the 'great tradition of our monarchy, our patriotic state life' be retained? His answer again reflects the specific context of 1890s Imperial Germany. Instead of emphasising the issue of the 'organic' integration of the working class *within* the Reich's social structure, as he had in 1872, in order to stabilise it, the focus was now on the need for an outward projection of the nation's power – of which workers would allegedly also profit:

> In the struggle of nations – which though dampened, cannot yet be eliminated – the lower classes only have any prospect of elevation and improvement where a solid state authority is present that assures and expands the nation's reputation and power, assuring its maximum economic expansion and the external markets it needs, protecting them from any blowback.[29]

Support to imperialism was, therefore, the condition of a partial recognition of workers' demands and of the improvement of their material situation in the absence of deeper transformations of German political and social reality. Securing the nation's place in the world was a task which the worker presumably both benefited from and needed to contribute to in their putative new role as legitimate member of the national community. Weber will also espouse these views, as I will show in detail below, but he would strip them of any patriarchal sentimentality and illusions of 'class harmony'.[30] What Schmoller's intervention ultimately illuminates – and this tension marks the central problem of this section – is the fact that this recognition of workers' standpoint culminated not in their expanded citizenship and an overarching democratisation of German society, but rather in the *reconfiguration* of their subaltern status, whereby a larger political role is combined with the integration into a project of imperial expansion, entailing a clear rejection of the emancipatory horizon and the internationalism of the SPD's working-class politics.

∴

If Gustav Schmoller gave an updated view of the Verein's role in light of increased public attention to the 'social question' and, especially, the rise of Social

29 Ibid.

30 See Chapter 11 below.

Democracy in Imperial Germany, G.F. Knapp's intervention demonstrated that this new context equally shaped the Verein's analytical effort with regards to assessing the 'rural labour question'. Charged with giving an overview of the results of the survey on the topic, Knapp's intervention also makes plain how the new standpoint introduced by the Verein's younger members impacted his own comprehension of social change in the German countryside. Knapp's statement that his generation had to 'start anew' very likely referred to two specific aspects from the reports written by his younger peers, especially those of Max Weber and Karl Kaerger. The first is the centrality given to the issue of migration. The backdrop to the pre-eminence of the topic was, on the one hand, the fact that migration to Germany had overtaken migration overseas on the part of Germans in the 1890s.[31] What is key, however, is not simply that the younger cohort of researchers had brought migration – especially by Poles from neighbouring Russia and Galicia (so-called *Sachsengängerei*) – to the attention of the older generation as a crucial aspect of the 'rural labour question' in the German East; more significant was the fact that this intergenerational dialogue transpired under the specific *framing* Weber and Kaerger had given to the issue. As this chapter will discuss in detail, both young scholars had approached the phenomenon through the lenses of race and cultural difference.[32] Knapp termed it, for instance, an especially alarming prospect if 'a situation such as the one in Galicia or Ireland, where there is a national difference between landlords and their workers' materialised in Imperial Germany, 'including in what used to be fully German districts'.[33] These remarks and especially Kaerger's intervention in the debate would eventually lead to a discussion – conducted in undeniably racist terms – on what ethnicity of worker was better suited to fulfil the seasonal scarcity of labour in the German countryside, whether 'Slavic', 'Chinese' or 'negro'.[34]

The second aspect of Knapp's general summary that, with a fair amount of certainty, can be traced back specifically to how Weber framed the 'rural labour question' in the German East was the attribution of a decisive role to worker subjectivity. Knapp will remark, for instance, that the social structure of the German countryside was 'no longer regarded with the dull sense of the natural individual as something simply given'.[35] Indeed, its reform by means of internal colonisation would be predicated on what, according to Knapp, were a series

31 See Wehler 1995, pp. 545–6.
32 On this aspect of the conference, see Zimmerman 2012, pp. 80–95 and pp. 99–105.
33 Knapp in Verein 1893, p. 18.
34 See Verein 1893, pp. 99–100 and *passim*; Zimmerman 2012, pp. 104–5.
35 Knapp in Verein 1893, p. 19.

of positive developments, like the preservation of the 'political role of the landlord', the conversion of peasants into 'modern agrarian producers' and, finally, the existence of 'rural workers, who are no longer scum [*Auswurf*]'.

In a clear indication he had appropriated Max Weber's central argument, Knapp tied his greater consideration of rural workers – his disparaging tone towards them notwithstanding – with their emerging self-consciousness. In his appraisal of the possibility of introducing tenancy forms typical of rural Western Germany (such as the '*Heuerling*') to the Empire's East, Knapp remarked that it was not enough to reproduce the legal form of the labour relation in a new context, i.e., give the dependent *Instleute* families more land, as 'the question was not merely filling stomachs'. In this sense, the weakness of the *West*-German tenant farmer was that 'he [had] a soul, and because his soul finds nourishment, the Westphalian *Heuerling*, feels content'.[36] Again, in direct reference to Weber, Knapp mentions the case of the province of Mecklenburg as one of the few exceptions where a relatively well-off segment of tenant farmers – or 'Häusler' – was able to subsist and thrive in the East. But the proximity to peasant properties, and most of all to 'peasant mores',[37] is considered decisive, since the *Häusler* 'also have souls',[38] i.e., an ethical drive to cultivate their property *and* seek temporary work in the harvest season. In the absence of thrifty and diligent peasants as role models, this would fatally give way to the desire to work as little as possible.

This appropriation of aspects of Weber's perspective on the 'rural labour question' by an established expert of a previous generation is another indication of the novel character – and fruitfulness – of the analytical perspective that informed his report for the Verein, and whose main features I approached in Chapter 8; Weber's suggestion that workers' own subjective drivers were a key variable in the dynamics of the 'rural labour question' proved especially impacting to the Verein's agrarian experts, breaking through their scholarly conventions (and prejudices). Thus, if Weber had critically appropriated specific elements from the writings of Schmoller, Knapp and others and integrated them into a new outlook, this intergenerational dialogue showed a clear flow of ideas and perspectives in the opposite direction as well, that is, from the budding scholar Weber to his established peers. Weber had, in this sense, already begun to break new analytical ground in 1892–3, long before his studies on the relationship of ascetic Protestantism and the rise of capitalism would emerge.

36 Knapp in Verein 1893, p. 16.
37 Ibid.
38 Knapp in Verein 1893, p. 18.

As the next section will discuss, the generational cleavage was not the only fault line in the Verein's conference. The different class standpoints on the 'rural labour question' personified by Max Weber, Karl Kaerger and not least by the Social Democrats present at the proceedings would also lead to a fierce but revealing debate, with both political and analytical ramifications that I will approach in the sections that follow.

3 Max Weber Debates Karl Kaerger on the Role of Worker Subjectivity in the 'Rural Labour Question'

> It is evident that the same material evokes different impressions in different heads. It obviously depends on *the standpoint which one adopts*, from which one confronts the material; and thus it has transpired that Dr. Weber and I have arrived at totally different results.
>
> KARL KAERGER, speaking at the Verein conference of 1893 (my emphasis)

Weber's intervention in the conference was conceived, as he put it, 'as a bridge to the debate'.[39] The talk indeed mostly summarised the main insights and conclusions from his report for the Verein on the 'rural labour question' in the German East, to which he added some remarks on the politically sensitive subject of the past importance and possible future role of Prussian landowners. The key to his intervention was how he articulated the *social standpoint*, underscoring his approach to 'the rural labour question', as this was the issue which – alongside race and migration – permeated the entire debate on the survey's findings.

The lecture also features Max Weber's most precise definition of what constituted the 'rural labour question', i.e., the existence of 'a socially separate, self-reproducing rural worker segment'.[40] As such, Weber claimed it was fundamentally absent from the Reich's Western and Southern countryside. There were, of course, rural workers in these regions; these were mostly small proprietors or tenants, who sought work in the larger properties of peasant landowners because they were not able to live off their land alone. Yet, they didn't fulfil

39 MWG I/4, p. 165.
40 MWG I/4, p. 167.

Weber's criteria for the rural proletariat; first, because, in the West, rural workers were socially *integrated*, meaning there was very little separation between worker and employer in material and 'moral' terms; second, because rural workers in the West and South tended to be a product of the fragmentation of inherited peasant property, which, from sustaining one family plentifully, did not cover the needs of the families that resulted from its subsequent parcelling out. Crucially, there was a possibility of rising back to peasant status by progressively accumulating more land. Thus, in the German West and South there wasn't a stable, 'self-reproducing' segment of rural workers, i.e., a rural proletariat invariably dependent on wage-labour – even in the case that they owned some land.

If a 'land-owning' proletariat seems anathema to the classic definition of a class that owns nothing but its labour power, it is important to highlight that Weber saw the absence of land ownership as having secondary importance in the characterisation of a rural proletarian. One of the key conclusions of Weber's report had been, after all, that providing small plots of land to 'settle' workers *would not necessarily raise them above the proletarian condition.* This was at the root of his criticism of the policy of 'internal colonisation' which, since 1886, had been acquiring and parcelling out large estates in the German East. If plots were too small, they would not create a sustainable segment of tenant farmers, but rather an impoverished rural working class with the added *disadvantage* of being tied to the land (i.e., unable to migrate in search of more favourable employment conditions in other regions).

Such insights indicate the extent to which Weber's consideration of worker subjectivity had changed the terms of the discussion of social stratification in the German countryside. Observed in isolation and from a purely economic standpoint, the small *landowning* rural worker of the German East and West were highly similar. The differences between them only became legible if the relationship of workers and their employers was taken into account in each region, not only in terms of the objective degree of inequality between them, but in the 'psychological' ramifications of each particular hierarchical relationship and, above all, how such perceptions shaped individual workers' stance towards their own labour activity. Thus, it was the absence of significant social differentiation between rural worker and peasant employer in the West that explained, for instance, why 'the worker demand[ed] to be treated as an equitable party, through the stripping away of all indicators [that a] relationship of rulership' was in effect.[41] This led Weber to the conclusion that, in the 'thought-

41 MWG I/4, p. 168.

world' [*Gedankenleben*] of this member of the rural working class, 'the concept of work was totally divorced from the concept of duty'; in other words, this worker will perform work 'because he must, yet thinking it is because it pleases him'.[42]

Weber explicitly qualifies this statement as an 'exaggeration of a typical aspect', through which a clearer differentiation of rural workers in the German East and West can be reached. The assessment of workers' perceptions and desires plays a central role in this ideal-typical analysis *avant la lettre*, considering that the main question it raises is *what drives individuals to work*. In this sense, Weber argued the '*rural* labour question' was peculiar for three distinct reasons; 1) rural workers were not necessarily proletarians in the sense of lacking all property except over their own labour power; 2) because the demand *for* labour power – and the need to sell it – was highly seasonable in the countryside; 3) because there was a 'way out' of the condition of rural worker through migration to the cities or abroad. These elements combined made individuals' subjective willingness to work a central variant in the policy effort to constitute a stable supply of workers for agrarian production. Conversely, two factors explained why there was no scarcity of rural workers in the Western countryside of Imperial Germany, despite what Weber describes as the 'individualistic', 'non-organic' character of its social stratification – epitomised by the landowning worker's self-serving nature. First, the absence of great differentiation between employer and worker meant the latter's sense of self-worth was not offended by the employment relationship – and the subjugation it necessarily implied; second, the prospects of rising to the status of a peasant motivated workers to labour beyond what was needed to cover their basic necessities. Both conditions were absent in the East, where small landowners and estate tenants – such as the *Instleute* – felt disrespected and degraded in their relationship to employers whose wealth and attitudes were nothing like their own and, at the same time, saw no prospect of rising to an independent peasant-status.

Thus, if on the surface a policy of 'internal colonisation' in the German East was introducing a strata of landowning workers akin to the one existing – and well-established – in the West, they would lack the 'drive' and the long-term aims required to fulfil the role of a stable source of labour power to large properties in the region. The wholesale break-up of the larger estates in the German East would, in turn, be equally problematic, considering the region's small-scale peasants would not be numerous enough to employ the resulting

42 Ibid.

'land-owning working class', meaning the latter would either fall into destitution or migrate, thus reinforcing – rather than counteracting – the existing 'rural labour question'.

Weber's policy proposals not only took these issues into account, but merged them with the consideration of what he termed those 'issues of high politics' [*hochpolitische Fragen*][43] that the fate of the East's social structure raised for Imperial Germany. By this he meant the 'defence' of the Reich's Eastern border from both a 'national' and military standpoints. As I will approach in the final item of this chapter,[44] Weber's insight into the interaction of economic change and worker subjectivity in East-Elbian Germany led him to draw *broad social and political conclusions* from the 'rural labour question'; these went beyond its more immediate refractions in the economic landscape of the German countryside (labour shortage, declining discipline on the part of workers etc.), i.e., the main issues the Verein had initially sought to shed light on through its survey. This stance raised the stakes of the ensuing debate and, in another foreshadowing of a central topic of Weber's later work, highlighted in particular the question of the objectivity of the Verein's research effort. What was the adequate standpoint on the 'rural labour question'?

∴

Karl Kaerger's intervention constituted the most consistent attempt to provide a different interpretation to Weber's insights on the 'rural labour question'. The divergence in approached boiled down, in Kaerger's own words, to the question of what social standpoint should underscore the definition of the phenomenon:

> ... in all of Germany – and especially in the East – there is a labour question, but only from the standpoint of employers. The labour question does not consist in how the material situation of workers is to be improved.[45]

At this point, Kaerger's provocative intervention was interrupted by protests from the audience – perhaps from the Social Democrats present at the proceedings – and he attempted to justify his statement.

---

43 MWG I/4, p. 165.
44 See 9.5 below.
45 Kaerger in Verein 1893, p. 96.

> Yes, gentlemen, that [improvement] cannot be decided in absolute terms, for it depends entirely on how good one believes the material situation of workers needs to be. And no one will be able to agree on this point.[46]

To Kaerger, who argued that the survey pointed to an actual improvement in the situation of workers, the 'rural labour question' was fundamentally a question of scarcity of labourers. Contrary to how the labour question manifested itself in an industrial context, where 'crises in production' led to the formation of a labour 'reserve army' which, in turn, allowed employers to 'one-sidedly determine labour conditions to the detriment of workers', Kaerger maintained that the challenge in the countryside was to 'find those individuals that have any desire at all to work on the estates'.[47]

Kaerger was far from the most one-sided representative of landowners' interests present at the Verein's conference. That post belonged to survey organiser – and Agricultural Ministry official – Hugo Thiel, who had a much narrower focus on the 'labour question' as an issue of labour scarcity for the large estates. Indeed, Kaerger would go on to explain that arguing that 'a labour question exists significantly only from the standpoint of employers', was different from believing it 'should also be *solved* from the standpoint of employers'. Any solution, he added, should 'indeed be pursued with full consideration of the interests of workers as well'.[48]

But there was a qualitative difference between Kaerger's 'sympathy' for workers, and Weber's clear understanding that any policy for the German countryside would *need to engage* workers' standpoint. In his intervention, Kaerger mentions high salaries did not prevent workers from migrating and that the expansion of land-tenancy Weber proposed was not enough to keep workers tied to the land, as they could still leave after their contracts expired. For these reasons, his solution was either the expansion of small land-ownership – more effectively tying workers to a certain district and forcing them to work because of the impossibility to survive on the yield of their lands alone, or, more controversially, to directly 'procure' workers from Germany's colonies, more specifically 'negroes', who 'worked quite well' and eliminated the risk of the increasing settlement of Polish workers in the German countryside, considering African laborers would only be employed for a few years before being shipped back to the colonies.[49]

---

46 Ibid.

47 Kaerger in Verein 1893, p. 99.

48 Kaerger in Verein 1893, p. 96.

49 Kaerger in Verein 1893, p. 99. For a critical analysis and contextualization of Kaerger's proposal and his background, see Zimmermann 2012, pp. 91–3; 104–5.

Weber rejected Kaerger's proposals, because he saw the depopulation of the countryside as the more fundamental problem. Intervening at the level of the subjective drivers of worker migration to the cities or overseas was, therefore, his preferred strategy for tackling the 'rural labour question'. This emphasis on the ethical drivers of agency did not prevent him, however, from calling for a ban on Polish migrant workers, who he claimed were pushing down native workers' 'standard of life'. On the contrary, both proposals were based on the same understanding of culture – rather than on kneejerk national sentiment or 'prejudices' on Weber's part – a hypothesis I will approach in Chapter 10. What I want to stress at this point is that, though the racialisation of subjects played a role in both Weber's and Kaerger's outlook on migrant labour, there was nevertheless a fundamental difference in their respective understanding of workers' agency. While Kaerger's solutions to the 'rural labour question' favoured naked coercion and barely took worker subjectivity into account, that was the central variable in Weber's approach.

In this sense, Weber sharply rejected the notion that impoverished small landowners could provide a steady supply of labour for large estates and he never considered the recourse to patriarchal authority or the direct use of violence as valid instruments to address the 'rural labour question' – in contrast to Kaerger's call for the German state to 'procure' African colonial subjects as seasonal workers. During the debate, Weber in fact made a direct connection between Kaerger's colonialist approach to the 'rural labour question' and the old patriarchal standpoint. Even if the colonial option was a 'new' proposal – it was, in Weber's words, a '*ballon d'essai*' or a mere hypothesis – it shared patriarchalism's authoritarian component:

> It is our consistent standpoint, that [Kaerger] is intoxicated with the idea of a relationship of lordship over men [*eines Herrschaftsverhältniss über Menschen*], conceived in the manner that a vigorous rural patriarch handles his workers – and that's likely the reason he used negroes as examples – 'not as men, not as cattle, but as servants [*Kerl*]'; I quote from his book on East Africa.[50]

Weber traced Kaerger's far-fetched plan to bring over workers from the colonies back to the old patriarchal instincts still found in many large landowners in the German East. Weber's insight into workers' subjectivity meant he rejected

50 MWG I/4, p. 202.

such an outlook.[51] That did not mean, however, that he necessarily *identified* with workers' subjective leanings. Young workers' decision to migrate to the cities were, in Weber's words, often 'incredibly unplanned, lacking in objectives or any inkling of the consequences', with an actual improvement to their situation a highly unlikely outcome.[52] Despite this estrangement, Weber once more drew the line at the open use of violence: even if there were ways to stop or reverse migration to the cities by force, he 'would certainly take exception with a violation of the supposedly universal human right of free disposal over oneself'.[53] He emphasised, instead, the need to persuade workers, considering that, when it came to the 'rural labour question', 'it wasn't the worsened situation of workers, but their transformation into proletarians that was decisive'.[54]

For this reason, in a summary of his findings published shortly before the Verein conference, Weber had argued that it was not enough to call for the material improvement of workers' situation. What was necessary, instead, was 'to awaken the *notion* that it was possible to be independent in one's native land'. In other words, if there was a credible chance for *Instleute* to reach peasant status, they would no longer leave the countryside as promptly. This is what was driving workers to the cities, i.e., the notion that there was a chance that 'the independence one dreamed of' was achievable. The question was, therefore, *how to channel this drive* into an individualistic and 'orderly economic conduct' and away from the collectivist and internationalist alternatives embodied in the programme of German Social Democracy. Weber's description of the reward mechanism that would allow a channelling of workers' aspirations is revealing of how he articulated the role of subjectivity and class consciousness in broader social processes:

> Illusions belong to men's daily bread and the question here is not to awaken unfulfillable hopes or to consciously mislead the tremendous desire of rural workers to be free and earn their own living; rather, it consists in the notion that if a part of them – not even a sizeable one –

51 Though not imperial expansion, see Part 3.

52 MWG I/4, pp. 184–5.

53 MWG I/4, p. 185. This timid and sceptical acknowledgment of a human right found its limits when it came to the freedom of movement of Polish migrants. In this inconsistency, Weber was strictly in line with a central contradiction of the liberal tradition, namely, that 'liberalism finds its boundaries in boundaries' – as the title of a contribution on the topic accurately and poignantly summarises. See Falk 2011.

54 MWG I/4, p. 203.

> effectively reaches this independence, then the entire class [*Stand*] will be elevated in its own eyes as well as in those of the agrarian propertied classes, growing more attached to the native land [*Heimat*].[55]

The passage highlights the political stakes behind Weber's engagement with worker subjectivity and associated understanding of culture. He derived from it a call for an improvement in workers' economic situation, but only in terms of creating the possibility for a small segment of the working class to ascend, thus functioning as a model for the remaining majority of workers, whose livelihoods would remain largely unaltered (at least in economic terms) in the process. Those that did experience an improvement and detached themselves from the rest of the class, rising to the status of small proprietors, would see an increase in their sense of self-worth and earn, in the same breath, a new status in the face of propertied classes; finally, upward mobility would trigger sentiments of national belonging in a class that, to Weber and German elites more generally, was dangerously short on them.

4 'Let's Leave That for *Workers Themselves* to Sort Out!': Social Democrats' Critical Approach to the 'Rural Labour Question'

Max Weber's policy proposal regarding the 'rural labour question' in the German East consisted in a state-led effort to foster a sustainable middle-stratum of tenant farmers and a gradual expansion of the peasantry, mainly in those areas where large entrepreneurial estates were not viable. At the Verein conference, Weber promoted these measures as the most effective means to integrate rural workers into Imperial Germany's social hierarchy, not only counteracting proletarianisation and depopulation in the countryside, but also sustaining the Reich's agrarian economy – he did not ignore the issue of labour-power scarcity – and serving its strategic interests (the 'defence of the Eastern border', manpower for imperial expansion etc.).

In previous sections, I argued that Weber was only able to articulate this particular alternative to the ongoing process of social change in Imperial Germany because of his insight into workers' own standpoint and his consideration of their drivers and aspirations. This had meant a break not only with the patriarchal views of earlier generations of social scientists like Gustav Schmoller and G.F. Knapp, but also a rebuff to alternatives

55 MWG I/4, p. 152.

to the 'labour question' centred in the use of coercion and unfree labour, as was the case of Karl Kaerger.

Nevertheless, the enthusiasts of patriarchal perspectives – old and new – were not Weber's only interlocutors in his engagement with the 'rural labour question'. The presence of Social Democrats at the conference was a stark reminder that there were other actors, organised in a mass party no less, claiming to articulate workers' true interests. Weber's early efforts at fashioning a new standpoint on modern social life emerged, therefore, from the crucible of a two-front contest with the still prevalent patriarchal outlook of the German upper classes, on one side, and the radical emancipatory horizons arising from the labour movement, on the other.

The Verein conference provides a microcosm of this dynamic to the extent that representatives of both class standpoints Weber sought to overcome were gathered at the proceedings. The presence of Social Democrats is itself revealing of the peculiar situation of party in the early 1890s, when the undeniable rise of the labour movement led to tentative initiatives by establishment intellectuals to engage with its organisations in spheres they had no access to before. This gesture by the Verein was not without consequence for the tenor of discussions, considering the question of the standpoint of workers themselves with regards to the 'rural labour question' – raised during the survey's preparation, but never adequately accommodated into its procedures – necessarily returned to the foreground (alongside its political ramifications).

It was not a surprise, then, that Max Quarck, the survey's earliest and most consistent critic, was the first to ask to comment on the initial round of debates. In a lengthy intervention, he brought up old misgivings as well as new issues based on the survey's results. Quarck was convinced that his warnings regarding the bias of employers had been confirmed. Hence his sardonic remark that, instead of 'Based on the surveys organized by the *Verein für Socialpolitik*', the subheading of the published volumes on *The situation of rural workers* ... should read 'Based on employers' assertions',[56] which drew (derisive?) laughter from the audience. Quarck argued no clear picture of rural workers' situation emerged because precise data on workers' living conditions was lacking; equally absent was an assessment of how recent economic and social transformations had impacted their livelihoods. Finally, old mechanisms of oppression – like the *Gesindeordnung*[57] – which dated back 'almost a century' to a

56 Quarck in Verein 1893, p. 90.

57 *Gesindeordnungen* were ordinances governing unfree rural labour that were still in force in late nineteenth-century Germany. They are dealt with in more detail in section 7.3 above.

time 'with completely different viewpoints' and 'contained a series of rigors that heavily affect the worker', were only 'very seldom mentioned in the Verein's employer survey'.[58]

Quarck also accused the authors responsible for the general reports of a biased analysis. He cited two examples which, though not applicable to Weber's report, are nevertheless revealing. The first directly addressed the status of Social Democracy:

> In his opening statement earlier today, Professor Schmoller expounded in both a rather objective and ideal form, that the stance of the Verein with regards to Social Democracy is not a trivial one; he does not simply condemn this movement but understands it as a historical necessity. Very well, gentlemen, yet in the survey reports you will find in every page the most egregious slanders on the part of entrepreneurs against the social-democratic movement in the countryside.[59]

Schmoller's words on Social Democracy clashed, in Quarck's view, with a survey that characterised the party's agitation in the countryside as a danger to landowners' interests and its press as 'subversive' and 'disgraceful'.[60] In his second example, Quarck singled out a scornful reaction to workers' 'heightened self-awareness', quoted in one of the reports (not Weber's). In the words of one employer, whereas addressing old workers was not a problem, he took care to address younger ones as 'Mr. knucklehead' instead of 'you knucklehead'.[61] Again the audience laughed, but this time Quarck was sharp in his rebuff: 'As a bad joke this may be fitting for the bar bench, but it certainly has no place in a sober survey, even one elaborated from the standpoint of employers'.[62]

The 33-year old Quarck closed his intervention addressing, as Max Weber had done earlier, the generational cleavage amongst conference participants. Quarck mentioned being in the unusual position of pleading with his more

58 See Quarck in Verein 1893, pp. 88–92.

59 Quarck in Verein 1893, p. 92.

60 Ibid.

61 In the original: *'Du Schafskopf/Sie Schafskopf'*. Weber mentions at several points of his report (for instance, MWG I/3, p. 741) that one of the ways rural workers expressed their heightened self-awareness was through the desire to be addressed with the formal 'Sie' instead of the customary 'du'. The use of 'du' by landowners – who demanded to be addressed as *gnädiger Herr* ('gracious Mr.') – reproduced the asymmetry between an adult, addressed as 'sir', and a child, referred to as 'you'.

62 Quarck in Verein 1893, p. 93.

senior listeners to avoid 'hasty conclusions' based on the survey's problematic data, whereas this would usually be the role of experienced researchers with regards to their younger peers. On the grounds of this data alone, Quarck argued, no proper assessment of the 'rural labour question' was possible. That included drawing 'social-political' conclusions from it 'in the manner that Dr. Weber' had done, i.e. 'with a great deal of national vigour, but perhaps with insufficient footing [mit *mangelhafte Unterlage*]'.[63]

Max Weber took exception to this comment because he understood Quarck was accusing him of insufficient knowledge of the social and political dimensions of the survey effort, a sensitive point for a legal scholar on his very first work of social research. Quarck clarified he had meant the source material was inadequate, not Weber's expertise (prompting the latter to apologise for his mistaken reaction as well). More significant is the fact that Quarck addressed Weber in his closing statement precisely on the matter of engaging workers' standpoint. The Social Democrat articulated the gulf separating the latter's conditional engagement with workers' standpoint and his own adoption of this vantage point, bringing out its fundamental consequences:

> Dr. Max Weber said earlier that we in the younger generation lack many illusions. Well I would very much like to identify as *an ideal* ... that which is yet to be achieved here. The ideal that we of the younger generation pursue consists in achieving the most thorough immersion [*Durchdringung*] in the worker's being, down to its tiniest elements and roots. Based on this immersion – which has yet to be achieved – one would come to entirely different results than could ever be achieved based on this one-sided, scientifically inadequate survey. My verdict regarding it can only be: *non liquet* [inconclusive].[64]

With these remarks, Quarck did not aim to simply oppose one partisan view, that of employers, with another; the Social Democrat expounded, rather, a different *basis* for an objective standpoint on social life. The immersion in workers' very being was the gesture that, at bottom, made objectivity possible. The fact that Quarck describes this gesture as an aim, rather than a readily accessible vantage point, highlights the role of praxis, of the actual exchange between intellectuals and workers; his use of 'we', in turn, suggest the party as an instance that enables this exchange. The thorough permeation into workers'

63 Quarck in Verein 1893, p. 94.
64 Quarck in Verein 1893, p. 94.

livelihood and thought-world emerges as Social Democracy's ultimate ideal. As such, the approach to the 'situation' of the working class changes from that which is to be assessed to that which is to be transformed. The revolutionary political ramifications of adopting the workers' standpoint were, however, more clearly drawn in another social-democratic intervention at the conference.

∵

Quarck was not the only Social Democrat on hand. Bruno Schönlank, then an editor of Social Democracy's main outlet *Vorwärts*, also intervened in the debate. Contrary to Quarck, who sought to legitimise his presence and standpoint through a methodological critique of the survey and its one-sided reliance on employers' standpoint, Schönlank aimed to stress the point of view of the working class on the 'rural labour question' in a more immediate sense. Put differently, whereas Quarck cast doubt on the Verein survey by claiming a higher degree of objectivity would be reached via a thorough 'immersion' in workers' point of view, Schönlank chose to highlight the *partisan* aspect of social standpoints. Although Weber subsequently rejected Schönlank's manner of critique, he clearly saw him as a more compelling debate partner than Quarck, whom he charged with clinging to trivialities.[65]

Schönlank started his intervention by wryly pointing out that, 'paradoxical as it may appear', he was 'extraordinarily pleased' with the survey's results. Not because it portrayed 'the actual situation which rural workers objectively find themselves in ... Dr. Weber himself said this was not to be expected from the survey'.[66] He welcomed, instead, 'the confessions of beautiful employer souls' it had brought to light. The Social Democrat was surprised by how naively forthright landowners had been in their accounts, despite having come to the survey in 'full dress and buckled shoes'.[67] Irony aside, Schönlank made the point that despite clearly constituting a one-sided portrayal, the survey had still conveyed enough of the plight of rural workers that it could not be considered a failure:

65 Another reason Weber appreciated Schönlank's intervention more than that of Quarck's was, perhaps, the fact that the editor of *Vorwärts* equally believed that it was in the interest of German workers to restrict Polish migration (See Schönlank in Verein 1893, p. 111).

66 Schönlank in Verein 1893, p. 111.

67 Ibid.

> Even though the state of affairs was portrayed somewhat too rosily, the sheer length of the list of ills and misgivings the survey brings to light is such that I can only be satisfied with its results.[68]

If he believed more attention to the 'principles of social methodology' might have delivered better results, Schönlank conceded – contrary to Quarck – that interviewing all parties would have been a task that only Reich authorities (or at least the Prussian government) could have fulfilled.

After these brief appeasing words, Schönlank switched to a sharp attack on the survey's problematic underpinnings. The issue of standpoint – and how it related to objectivity – was at the heart of his critique. This is evident in his rebuff of Karl Kaerger, who had argued in his intervention that if one took landowners to be witnesses to a certain situation, than the recurrent similarities in their testimonies must count for some level of truthfulness: 'But Dr. Kaerger forgets', Schönlank replied, 'that the testimonies do not come from witnesses, but from parties. It would therefore be necessary to hear the other party, i.e., the workers'.[69] The brunt of Schönlank's attack was directed at those Verein members who, like Kaerger, saw the 'rural labour question' fundamentally as a problem of 'scarcity of labour power', but made token calls for the need 'to hear workers' side'.

Framing workers' and employers' standpoint as partisan was also consistent with Schönlank's subsequent assertion that workers could very well take the improvement of their situation into their own hands. If the dire conditions of rural workers had emerged even in the survey's employer-written reports, then Schönlank's conclusion was that change should be expected, if not by means of the state, then surely by 'popular will'.[70] It would be, therefore, 'through the efforts of rural workers themselves' that archaic forms of subjecting labour, such as the *Gesindeordnung*, would be overcome.[71] Regarding the extension of collective bargaining rights to rural workers, a measure dismissed by social-reformers – including Max Weber – with the argument that the various segments of the rural working class would be unable to 'take more than three steps together without seeing their interests collide', Schönlank replied: 'Very well, but let's leave that for *workers themselves* to sort out!'[72]

---

68 Ibid.
69 Ibid.
70 Ibid.
71 Schönlank in Verein 1893, p. 112.
72 Schönlank in Verein 1893, p. 113.

The Social Democrat concluded his intervention by pointing out the universal character of the social and political achievements of modern democracy, which he connected to worker emancipation. Taking aim at the *Gesindeordnung*, Schönlank contended that there was no place for it in the age of universal military service, universal education and universal suffrage. He closed with the typical historical optimism that characterised German Social Democracy in the period between the end of the *Sozialistengesetz* and the start of the First World War. Referring to the need to afford rural workers the same legal status as their counterparts in industry, i.e., eliminating all traces of unfree labour that remained in place in Imperial Germany, Schönlank remarked:

> You would reply that it won't happen. It will happen, gentleman, as surely as industrial worker protection has prevailed and will prevail in all civilized nations (*Kulturstaaten*), so will every social reform prevail through the will of the people.[73]

5 The 'Standpoint of State Reason' as the Young Max Weber's Compromise between Partisanship and Objectivity

Max Weber acknowledged Social Democrats as interlocutors at several points of his interventions during the Verein conference. He openly raised, for instance, the question of whether the time had arrived for the urban proletariat to aid in the resolution of the 'social tasks' of the nation. While he 'did not believe that was the case', Weber refused 'to rail against socialism in the usual manner, i.e., *in contumaciam*', a legal term designating the trial of an absent party. He hoped, instead, that socialism's representatives would make their voices heard during the proceedings, after which he would gladly debate them.[74] That is precisely what occurred, with Weber spending most of his reply-time addressing the interventions of both Quarck and Schönlank, adding that it had been a pleasure to 'cross swords with gentlemen of [Quarck's] political-economical orientation'.[75]

This willingness to engage with Social Democrats did have clear boundaries, however. These came to light, not surprisingly, on account of Schönlank's

73 Schönlank in Verein 1893, p. 114.
74 MWG I/4, pp. 196–7.
75 MWG I/4, p. 200.

unrestricted affirmation of workers' standpoint. In rejecting this stance, Weber remarked that he welcomed 'adversaries', but only if they were ready to take 'equal ground in the form of the debate'. Whereas there was no expectation that a *Vorwärts* article would constitute a 'scientific product' on account of its 'agitational purposes', a discussion on a scientific setting should be conducted on a 'factual' [*sachlich*] basis, not through 'personal' altercations.[76]

Weber was clearly struggling with the questions of partisanship and objectivity in social research himself and, at this point in his trajectory, his solution involved taking on what he called the 'standpoint of state reason'. Crucially, this vantage point did not attempt to exclude a class-based outlook entirely. In calling for Social Democrats to abide by a more scientific form of debate, he remarked that this 'might appear ... a matter of "class habits" on our side. Even if that is the case, taking them into account would be suitable, or at least harmless'.[77]

This suggested that rather than transcending class standpoints altogether, Weber was in search of a particular standpoint that enabled a *generally valid outlook* on social life, i.e., one that could be legitimately universalised. His solution, then, was to 'consider the "rural labour question" ... exclusively from the standpoint of *state reason*'.[78] In his subsequent clarification, Weber sought to dissociate this horizon from attempts to generalise the standpoint of employers and the proletariat, respectively:

> The interest of the state and nation can differ from the interest of specific strata, not only from that of large landowners, which is forgotten at times, but also from the proletariat, which *lately* has been forgotten just as often.[79]

For Weber, these class standpoints were formally equivalent, whereas taking the vantage point of the state meant accessing a *higher order of generalisation*. It was, therefore, from the imperative of advancing the interests of 'state and nation' that Weber drew his call for a direct intervention on the 'social organisation' of the countryside. Weber qualified such an intervention as a form of state 'social policy', i.e., the conscious attempt on the part of authorities to influence the social makeup of the Reich in the name of its strategic interests. This pecu-

76 MWG I/4, pp. 206–7.
77 MWG I/4, p. 207.
78 MWG I/4, p. 180.
79 MWG I/4, pp. 180–1 – my emphasis.

liar understanding of social policy emerges clearly in Weber's closing words to the conference's first day of activities:

> Again, gentlemen, we do not know where the shaping [*Gestaltung*] of the East is likely headed in the coming centuries, nor how future generations will proceed in this regard; we do not know if the organizational patterns we create today will crumble once more in the future. That is true, but we do not need to know this ... we believe the only realistic social policy is the one that attempts to inject fresh blood into the arteries of a social body; it must, however, be left up to the body itself, if it will learn to engage in economics [*Ökonomie zu treiben*] with these fresh fluids and become stronger for it.[80]

As Weber framed it, such a notion of social policy could claim to go beyond a one-sided class standpoint because its aim was to reshape the 'social body' in its entirety, not address particular social ills. Along the same lines, Weber would remark later in the 1890s that the 'social question' was not reducible to the 'labour question'.[81] With this distinction he meant that an improvement in the economic situation of workers – which he equated with addressing the 'labour question' – was not an end in itself, but was subject, rather, to the goals of 'social policy'. The latter pertained, as previously discussed, to a higher order of interests, those governing the nation-state. 'Social policy' was hence the conscious attempt to rearrange the social makeup of the nation to serve its (political and economic) standing on the world stage. Weber's 'social policy' is more akin, therefore, to a concerted effort of 'social engineering' by a country's political leadership, as opposed to the implementation of a set of welfare measures by its state apparatus.

Max Weber's 'social policy' proposals were derived, in turn, from the 'standpoint of state reason'. The claim for the objectivity of this vantage point hinged on the notion that it overcame *particular* class interests. Not in the sense that Schmoller and the Verein construed the role of the state, i.e., as that of a neutral instance hovering above class strife. Weber's 'standpoint of state reason' was an outlook articulating, in Jan Rehmann's terms, the interests of a 'class *constellation*',[82] i.e., a cross-class alliance. In other others, *the apparently formal-objective vantage point Weber articulated had concrete class content*. The

80 MWG I/4, p. 205.
81 MWG I/4, p. 476.
82 Rehmann 2015, p. 57, my emphasis.

transformations and reforms Weber advocated for the German East confronted, in this sense, a range of 'opposing interests', starting with those of large landowners themselves, whose dominant role in the German East would be challenged as a result of 'internal colonisation' – i.e. the parcelling of unprofitable large properties – and the fostering of a mostly autonomous middle strata.

German unification had also been the product of a 'class constellation', one led by the power of landed aristocracy and the liberal bourgeoisie. Weber believed this alliance had run its course, but there were lessons to be learned from its role in the events of 1870/71. Especially in terms of where Junkers, and by extension the Prussian state, drew their power from. As Weber framed it, Prussian aristocracy had succeeded in forging a 'social organisation'[83] and 'a consequential organisation of labour'[84] that the state was subsequently able to leverage towards achieving the task of unification. Its basis had been the 'community of interests' between landowner and partially unfree worker and the fact it was now in decline, meant not only that Junkers' power basis was itself dwindling, but also that they would tend to prioritise their particular (or narrow) class interests rather than the resolution of the 'most important political tasks of the state'.[85] A new hegemonic class constellation was, therefore, a precondition for elevating the internal cohesion and propelling the outward projection of the Reich in what Jan Rehmann called 'the programme of the Freiburg Inaugural Address'. It consisted in the formation of a 'Fordist bloc of modern entrepreneurs and workers' which would

> free the bourgeoisie from its 'Caesaristically' mediated alliance with the agrarian class, providing it with a class self-consciousness of its own [and enabling it to] win [over] the 'higher strata' of the working class.[86]

Incorporating the role of harbinger, Weber argued the moment had arrived for the 'Prussian state to recognise its social calling in a timely manner' and intervene 'in the spokes of the wheel of social development'. He hoped to look back at a Prussian leadership that not only acted in this manner 'out of its own initiative', but also 'dared, for the first time, to do so *at the right time*'.[87]

---

83 MWG I/4, p. 181.
84 MWG I/4, p. 199.
85 MWG I/4, p. 182.
86 Rehmann 2015, p. 57.
87 MWG I/4, pp. 197–8.

6 Conclusion: The Imperative to Defend German *Kultur*: Max Weber between Worker Self-Consciousness and the Legacy of 'Prussianism'

Max Weber's Junker readership did not immediately grasp the ultimate ramifications of his report for the Verein. In essence, he expected Prussian aristocrats to voluntarily abdicate their power position in favour of membership in a new hegemonic constellation that, at best, reserved a peripheral role for them. Did Weber's veritable ode to this aristocratic lineage in the final pages of his report perhaps eschew its initial reception?

> The dynasty of Prussian kings is not destined to rule over a mass of nomadic Slavs and rural proletarians with no fatherland, alongside Polish small farmers and depopulated large properties, [a situation that] the current development of the East, if it is allowed to run its course, will likely bring forth. Rather, [they are destined to rule over] German peasants alongside a landowner segment whose workers carry within them the awareness that their future lies in the fatherland and the ascension to an independent existence.[88]

Upon its publications, the report was actually quoted favourably by both a National Liberal paper and a conservative outlet, each of which argued Weber's conclusions supported their respective stances on trade and agrarian policy.[89] In subsequent interventions from 1893–5, however, Weber became increasingly outspoken in terms of his antagonism to Prussian dominance in the Reich, leading the German East's large landowners to see the young political economist for the adversary that he was. Weber's antagonism first emerged in his lecture at the Verein conference, where he sought to clear up the press debate on his report by spelling out its (anti-conservative) conclusions.

Weber articulated his stance clearly: because the 'social organisation' which had bred Junker power and leadership qualities in the past was now in a 'process of chronic decay', the large landowners of the East were no longer in a position to solve the 'most important tasks of the state', which to Weber constituted no less than 'the safeguarding of German culture in the East, the defence of the Eastern borders and of German nationality, even in peacetime'.[90] Beyond the problematic tenor of these goals – which I will approach below – the

88 MWG I/3, pp. 928–9.

89 See MWG I/4, p. 181, n. 32.

90 MWG I/4, p. 182.

fact that Prussian aristocracy was not able to pursue them signalled to Weber that Junker tutelage over the modern economic and political development of Imperial Germany had outlived its purpose.

But had it ever been beneficial? Weber seemed to think so and, despite his sharp criticism of Prussian aristocracy in the 1890s, he still maintained that their pre-eminent role in German political and culture life had been a necessary (and even welcome) development in decades prior, and that it should not be 'radically done away with'.[91] Above all, Weber felt it was necessary to preserve that 'characteristic Prussian concept of the "damn duty and obligation"', i.e., the 'perception of duty' as an imperative 'in and of itself';[92] it had not only presided over Junkers' strict harnessing of the labour power under their control, but had crucially also fostered the 'political organisation' and fashioned the 'political instinct' which culminated in 'the unification of the Empire'.[93]

Such remarks indicate that while Weber had broken with Prussian aristocrats politically, his relationship to the legacy of 'Prussianism' [*Preußentum*] as a *cultural* phenomenon was more complicated.[94] In the words of Leo Kofler, the social and political pre-eminence of Prussian landed aristocracy in the German lands had allowed it 'to enter into every pore of society and to organize and rear it intellectually as well as morally' in its own image.[95] This means Imperial Germany not only projected the vectors of militarism, bureaucratic formalism, conservative Lutheranism and monarchism that had characterised the Prussian state and their East-Elbian aristocratic carriers over a larger continental canvas, it amplified their cultural imprint as well.

While the Reich was far from a monolith – the entire premise of this work is that democratic and emancipatory trends were just as integral to German society as its more oppressive and regressive facets – the fact that Max Weber grew up in an Imperial Germany whose dominant cultural values, political institutions and ruling classes all paid tribute to 'Prussianism' no doubt shaped his personality and thought at a fundamental level; while Weber was no enthusiast of the willing subjection to authority, the alternating mix of brutality and patriarchal condescension in dealings with workers and women, and not least the open hostility to democracy as a 'foreign element', notions that were deeply rooted in German culture and society in the late nineteenth century, he was

91 MWG I/4, p. 169.
92 MWG I/4, p. 168.
93 MWG I/4, pp. 168–9.
94 See Georg Lukács' essay *Über Preußentum* or 'On Prussianism' (1967 [1943], pp. 330–53), which informs this concluding section.
95 Kofler 1966, p. 281.

not immune to them. The same was true of the 'formalist stressing of duty', which Weber had so much praise for; it bred, in Kofler's words, 'a concept of honour that was misguided because it was in permanent and tragic conflict with life ...'.[96] Would this not be a constant thread in Weber's own trajectory?

As he made his entry into public debate with the 'rural workers' inquiry' in the 1890s, Max Weber was clearly struggling with this peculiar legacy; moreover, the fact that his report encompassed East-Elbian Germany meant a reckoning with Prussianism was unavoidable. As I explored in an earlier chapter,[97] his uncle Hermann Baumgarten had dealt with a similar dilemma in the context of unification, ultimately helping to pave the way for an alliance between liberals and Prussian aristocracy. Baumgarten's chief justification at the time was the nobleman's greater 'vocation for rulership' when compared to the 'practical' bourgeois, regardless of national setting. In the 1880s, he would distance himself from this pro-Prussian stance in a bitter dispute – on objectivity in scholarship no less – with the most notorious defender of Prussianism in the German intelligentsia, i.e., Heinrich von Treitschke.[98] Like many of the societal trends of Imperial Germany discussed so far, the legacy of the Prussianisation of Germany was entangled with Max Weber's family history.

Contrary to his uncle's stance in 1866, however, Weber underscored a specific 'debt' of the German nation to its East-Elbian gentry. The latter's supposedly selfless commitment to the interests of the Prussian-German state was, in his words, 'not typical for an aristocracy'.[99] Weber also de-emphasised the merits of individual Prussian aristocrats such as Bismarck or Moltke in the process of unification, stressing rather 'the social organisation' – or class constellation – that these figures 'were a product of'.[100] While this social organisation was fast becoming unsustainable for both economic and cultural reasons, Weber argued forcefully that it needed new foundations so as to continue to fulfil its role as a breeding ground of the Reich's political elites:

> ... we neither can nor desire to eliminate the large rural properties of the East. There is no reason to destroy them, there is an interest, in fact, in pre-

96 Kofler 1966, pp. 290–1.

97 See Chapter 2.

98 See 2.4 above.

99 MWG I/4, p. 181.

100 MWG I/4, p. 181. In the closing words of his report for the Verein, Weber asserts that even the 'brilliant traits' (and 'deep shadows') of Bismarck's towering personality were 'incomprehensible' outside the framework of the 'soil out of which they sprang' and the 'inborn art of ruling over land and men' that it reared (MWG I/3, p. 928).

> serving these economic and, above all, societal intelligence centres in the countryside, precisely so this intellectual capital [*geistiges Kapital*] is not monopolized by the cities and becomes exclusive property of the urban bourgeoise.[101]

Weber seemed intent in avoiding a scenario in which this valuable reservoir of 'political intelligence' would emigrate from the countryside to the cities, following in the footsteps of disgruntled rural workers.[102] If, therefore, the hegemonic class constellation Weber projected for a reformed Imperial Germany assigned a place for skilled labour alongside the bourgeoisie, these passages from his Verein lecture make it clear that, especially in terms of political culture, he still saw the large landowner of the East as the main ally of the urban upper strata he identified himself with. Workers simply lacked the necessary political maturity to perform anything more than a subaltern role in the new power configuration Weber envisioned:

> And we turn now finally to the proletariat; yes, the time is still far off when in seeking the solution to social tasks we will be able to show an outstretched hand to the proletariat of the cities. I hope that this time will come; but, in my opinion, it has not arrived yet.[103]

The passage captures both Weber's willingness to engage with workers' point of view and the clear limits of this gesture, especially when the question of an autonomous politics of the working class is raised. While it was through the consideration of workers' vantage point that Weber arrived at one of his chief insights into the 'rural labour question', namely that as a result of workers' growing self-consciousness, large landowners would no longer be able to oversee (and exploit) their labour force in the old authoritarian way, he refused to draw the far-reaching political conclusions this implied. In other words, instead of opposing the increasingly hollow and self-serving 'rigid ethics of duty' of Prussian landowners with a programme of agrarian reform anchored in the interests of a mass of landless rural workers and small proprietors, Weber was intent on breathing new life into the large estates of the German East so that the old aristocratic lineage they sustained did not disappear. As he saw it, there was no reason to break up those large properties that were competitive in the world market; his proposed policy of state support for the establishment of

101 MWG I/4, p. 192.
102 MWG I/4, p. 192.
103 MWG I/4, p. 196.

a 'middle strata' of tenant farmers and small landowners was, after all, also meant to provide a steady reservoir of labour power to these 'modernised' large estates.

Thus, despite declaring that the 'patriarchal system [had] no future from the standpoint of popular psychology [*völkerpsychologisch aussichtslos*]',[104] by which he meant that workers would no longer be willing to submit to it, when it came to the system's most egregious remnant, the feudal-like practices of labour subjection inscribed in the *Gesindeordnungen*, Weber symptomatically took a conciliatory stance. He called for an end to its application to 'anyone who does not belong to the household servants' segment' – as was the case of the *Insleute* of East and West-Prussia. Yet, because 'no sharp limits could be set on the grounds of prevailing law', it was at most a question of 'establishing an equitable application' across the German East.[105] Weber retreated here to the standpoint of formal law, overlooking the ongoing scandal of legalised corporal punishment and 'forced retrieval' of 'escaped' domestic servants by authorities that the *Gesindeordnungen* foresaw. Weber's consideration of workers' standpoint was *overridden* in this case, not only by his consideration of a supposedly higher order of interests, but also by the lowly position of domestic workers in the social hierarchy; in a similar vein, Weber's adoption of the 'standpoint of state reason' justified an approach to the 'rural labour question' that consciously ignored the issue of whether 'workers were doing well or badly, and if they [could] be helped somehow'.[106] Here was a double capitulation to Prussianism; on the one hand, in the refusal to address its social roots, i.e., the persistence of unfree labour and the concentration of land and political power in the hands of Junker aristocracy; on the other, in the unwillingness to break with the deep-seated observation of hierarchy and social rank that Imperial Germany had – at least in part – taken on from its Prussian founders.

Max Weber's ambiguous relationship to Prussianism and its *Junker* carriers highlights, in turn, the fundamental disconnect that underscored his relationship to the working class. To be sure, he never conceived of his engagement with workers' point of view as a platform to rethink – and reform – German society 'from below'. In fact, Weber did not believe it was even possible to articulate a universalising viewpoint on society (and a political programme for its transformation) on the basis of the standpoint and interests of the working

104 MWG I/3, p. 928.
105 MWG I/4, pp. 186–7.
106 MWG I/4, p. 180.

class. As a result, there was a missing democratic component in his projection of a reformed Imperial Germany. Later on in the 1890s, when Junker hostility to his proposals and an overall scenario of conservative retrenchment had made it clear that Prussian aristocracy would not willingly cede the power and influence it still yielded to self-professed 'ascending classes', Weber stated that 'any emerging political party would stand before the choice' of

> ... electing which of the antagonistic interests of the current leading classes it wanted to support: bourgeois or agrarian-feudal. A political intervention that does not take this into account is a utopia ... Even when [political actors] refuse to do so and believe theirs is a third pathway, a politics of the fourth estate, everything they achieve will exclusively and always result in the advancement of either of these two interests.[107]

Weber reverts here to the old liberal stance of the pre-1848 period, which reserved a structurally subaltern role for the working class in a political arena occupied, on one side, by the bourgeois forces of progress and, on the other, by the agrarian-feudal forces of reaction.[108] Such an emphatic denial of the possibility of an autonomous *politics* of the 'fourth estate' evokes, in turn, his stance on the question of the possibility of a distinct working-class *culture*. As Part 3 will approach in detail, Weber will attribute both an economic and a cultural dimension to worker ascension, the former embodied by an increase in forward-looking activity and self-reliance, the latter by greater individual autonomy and access to the 'goods of *Kultur*'. In economic terms, the process is underscored by the status of the small proprietor – or the drive to become one; cultural elevation, in turn, is fundamentally understood as bourgeois cultivation and individuation. In other words, Weber was just as sceptical of the existence of an autonomous working-class culture as he was of working-class politics. Working-class 'elevation' proceeded to Weber along a predetermined (and narrow) road to the 'cultured' middle strata that was not accessible to just any worker. Understood in these terms, Weber's call to 'eliminate barriers' for workers' social mobility and 'make space upwards'[109] easily coexisted with the overt disparagement of so-called 'low-standing' workers in general, but espe-

---

107 MWG I/4, p. 621.
108 See Chapter 6.
109 MWG I/4, p. 98.

cially of *foreign migrant workers*, who put the upward-striving elements of the 'native' working class at risk by 'debasing' theirs and the nation's overall 'level of culture'.

Though I will unpack these claims systematically in the next chapters, I feel a preview of Weber's peculiar understanding of the relationship between labour, culture and ethnicity is necessary to properly frame his clearest policy recommendation with regards to the 'rural labour question', one that doubles as the most controversial – and little understood – aspect of his writings on the topic. Put briefly, Weber considered the '*absolute exclusion* of Russian-Polish workers from the German East'[110] as the only way to avoid continuous downward pressure on salaries of native workers, but especially *on the cultural level and the standing of the German nationality* in the region.

Far from an isolated outburst of nationalism or bigotry, the fact that Weber saw the closing of the borders to migrant workers as the 'most important demand on this terrain at the present juncture' epitomises the paradox (or main contradiction) of his approach to the 'rural labour question'. For if Weber's main methodological advance in his writings on the topic was his engagement with workers' standpoint, his chief conclusion was predicated on ignoring the perspective of entire segments of labourers, namely, Polish migrants and, to a lesser extent, 'low-standing' German proletarians. Accused of proposing 'a nationality policy for the East out of "chauvinism"', Weber replied that his critics 'either cannot or do not want to understand what it was really about', namely:

> That it is not possible for our workers to compete with Polish workers. German workers would have to climb down a cultural level [*Kulturstufe*] in their needs in order to do so; it is very much the same with our agricultural enterprises which are noncompetitive because they would have to climb down a cultural level in order to compete with those of Russia, Argentina and America.[111]

'Chauvinism' (and racism) no doubt informed Weber's perspective on migration, despite his protests to the contrary; it is, for instance, in this context that he made the infamous statement that Germans and Poles had 'distinct bodily constitutions … differently constructed stomachs, to be very concrete'. Yet there was a clear reason behind his posturing as the 'adult in the room' when

110 MWG I/4, p. 182.
111 MWG I/4, pp. 182–3.

it came to cross-border migration. Weber saw his policy proposals on the issue as imperatives set by the realities of fierce competition in the world market. In other terms, the single most important phenomenon that not only shaped his vision for a reformed German East, but also his understanding of labour and culture was the *pervasiveness of imperialism* in the increasingly interconnected (and unequal) world of the late nineteenth century.

If imperialism organised the world economy along a hierarchy of profiteering metropolises and subjected colonial states, much in the way society was stratified by ruling classes and subaltern ones, then Weber felt he had an objective basis to claim German workers were superior to Poles, with the caveat that 'higher-standing' Germans were more demanding and, therefore, more expensive and less competitive in the market for labour power. A culturally elevated, highly skilled working class was, however, a valuable asset to the nation-state in terms of productivity and technical knowledge, which is why Weber asserted that it should be 'defended' from what he considered to be unfair 'foreign competition' and rewarded with access to a higher standard of life.

Once again, imperialism emerges as the enabling factor; as the British precedent had shown, those branches of industry that can sustain a well-paid, unionised 'labour aristocracy' – a term Weber appropriated from Friedrich Engels long before Lenin popularised it[112] – were dependent on the foreign markets and monopoly position that only imperialist expansion could secure. Not surprisingly, Weber expected workers to rally behind the nations' flag as it embarked on projects of overseas conquest. In short, Weber's formula for tackling the 'rural labour question' and reforming the Reich boiled down to 'social imperialism'.

While Weber did not employ the term, his proposals articulated it precisely in what Geoff Eley has called its 'original stress', i.e., as a strategy to foster 'working class quiescence'; in other words, Weber understood that 'higher wages, improved social conditions, the provision of welfare' and *not least* 'ideologies of racial superiority' were instrumental in 'transmitting the benefits of empire to the masses'.[113] Crucially, such ideologies did not apply only to Imperial Germany's colonial subjects, but also to neighbouring Poles (and German ethnic-Poles) dictating Weber's 'closed-border policy' in the German East. But was Weber's stress on cultural difference (rather than 'biological race') in his disparaging remarks on Poles not simply a case of nationalist clouding of a framework

112 See Chapter 11.
113 Eley 1976, p. 73.

otherwise open to diversity in social life? While I will systematically flesh out the extent to which imperialism *structured* Weber's understanding of culture, labour and race as overlapping dimensions of social life in the next chapter, two factors that dispel attempts to relativise the racism inherent in his stance on Polish migrant workers are worth mentioning here. The first is the 'stomach' comparison quoted above, which shows that the limits between cultural and biological racism in late nineteenth-century thought were, at the very least, porous. The second, Weber's rejection of liberal reservations to a migrant ban in the East, recovers the thread of this concluding section, namely, his relationship to the legacy of 'Prussianism'.

∴

Max Weber was clearly aware that his call to put a radical stop to labour migration carried coercive implications. He anticipated having to push through such measures against 'the instincts of a part of the population oriented to free-market ideas', because the latter 'will see them as exception measures and fear they could be extended to other spheres'.[114] In his willingness to transgress what he termed the 'supposed human right of free disposition over oneself',[115] Weber appears at his most brutal, calling for the Imperial German state to unleash yet another wave of exception measures, following the repression of religious freedom embodied in the *Kulturkampf* and of civil and workers' rights in the *Sozialistengesetz*. As I discussed above, while the young Weber had shown reservations in both instances, he never fundamentally rejected the persecution of Catholics and of the socialist labour movement, respectively.[116] Now he stood firmly behind the mass exclusion and deportation of migrant workers, minimising liberal concerns that this could push the political culture of Imperial Germany in an authoritarian direction and, perhaps, open the door to further repressive measures against its own citizens.

Weber's willingness to bypass basic rights under the pretext of preventing unfair economic competition amongst workers and 'defending German culture and nationality' was in stark contrast to his formal-legal refusal to call for the abrogation of the *Gesindeordnungen* because the latter were anchored in the Reich's legal framework. The brutality of his remarks on Polish migrant workers, in turn, ran counter to a consideration of rural workers' point of view that, in some cases, reached the point of direct self-identification with their yearnings.

---

114 MWG I/4, p. 196.

115 MWG I/4, p. 185.

116 See sections 1.1 and 4.2, respectively.

Was this a case of Prussian-German repressiveness and liberal enlightenment views coinhabiting the same individual, with the former explaining his conservative, the latter his more progressive stances?

A range of factors expose this kind of reasoning as a flawed oversimplification. While the authoritarian streak and sacralisation of social hierarchies legated by 'Prussianism' no doubt shaped Weber's perspective to some degree, his 'social imperialism' (and proto-Fordism) were fundamentally novel configurations that allowed the aforementioned contradictions in his views to be harmonised into a coherent, if no less problematic, whole. Hence the mistake of identifying social imperialism 'solely with *conservative* policies to the explicit exclusion of *reformist* ones'.[117] In this sense, instead of offering a programme of democratic change to overcome Junker tutelage of Imperial German society, Max Weber proposed a conservative alternative to it that, while pledging new life to Prussian aristocracy, was fundamentally concerned with driving forward bourgeois modernisation. This programme was built upon the insight that Imperial Germany's growing embeddedness in the world market had a direct bearing on its domestic political landscape. As such, Weber's project of 'social imperialism' spoke not to a specific party, but to what Geoff Eley termed the new 'determinate *context* in which all politicians had to work', articulating a platform able to respond to 'the changing *forms* of state power and the pressures which affected *all* politics, whether conservative, liberal or socialist'.[118] On the other hand, despite constituting a reformist stance anchored in a clear-eyed assessment of current realities, Weber's alternative was far from a progressive one, its programme of change invested fundamentally in entrenching existing class divisions, even if it allowed for greater social mobility; along the same lines, the only answer Weber found conceivable to the heightened nation-state competition of his already 'globalised' time were strict migration controls and a concerted social and political effort to advance the colonialist projection of the Prussian-German state.

He would not, therefore, be 'joining the underdogs' anytime soon, to quote the title of an essay by Wolfgang J. Mommsen on Weber's relationship to the SPD. 'It was above all the lack of any sense of power which', according to Mommsen, 'he considered the most critical deficiency of the German working class'. The SPD-held notions that class power from below could be affirmed to establish an egalitarian society or that internationalist solidarity should be the answer to the competition of workers from different nationalities in the world-

117 Eley 1976, p. 73.
118 Eley 1976, pp. 73–4.

market were, in turn, dismissed by Weber as 'merely radical rhetoric devoid of any rational assessment of social reality'. This was, as Mommsen stresses, in stark contrast to the 'support given to British imperialism by important sections of the British working class, who allegedly fully understood the need for empirical [?] and power politics'. The problem with their 'German counterparts' was that they 'excelled in a doctrinaire anti-colonialism'.[119]

∵

Adolph Wagner, who was clearly on the conservative end of the Verein conference's participants, concurred with the connection Weber drew between the 'standpoint of state reason' and the imperative to ban Polish migrant workers. 'State reason has to decide in these matters', said Wagner during the debate, in acknowledgment of Weber's articulation of this vantage point. 'State reason', Wagner added, 'unquestionably called for the competitive economic struggles in German soil to be fought out between Germans on both sides'. In its present configuration, this struggle was being fought out between German employers and 'members of a foreign race which thereby contributed to push down the *standard of life* of our workers'.[120] Though it could be argued Wagner's association with the anti-Semite Adolph Stoecker[121] had made him receptive to anti-Polish discourse, his emulation not only of Max Weber's main conclusion, but of his particular framing of the 'rural labour question' shows how the 'social imperialist' alternative proposed by the young liberal could win over an elder conservative.

Did the same apply to Weber's contemporaries, the combative Social Democrats present at the proceedings? At one point in his intervention Weber made an explicit effort to point out his proposals also contemplated the interests of organised labour:

> I believe that, through the defence of our nationality in the East, we do socialism a favour, even if against its will; for if at least some of its pos-

119 Mommsen 1989, p. 76. Despite his clear association of Weber with imperialist positions, Mommsen seems nevertheless inclined to take his understanding of what is a 'realist' stance at face value. For an argument on why Weber's narrow understanding of what constituted a 'rational assessment' of reality made him an anti-utopian, rather than a realist, and the implications of this for the overall makeup of his thought, see the epilogue to this work.

120 Wagner in VfS 1893, p. 128. The expression 'standard of life' appears in English in the source material.

121 Wehler 1995, p. 922.

> tulates are to be realised, [socialism] needs to strive for a culturally very high-standing worker population – and its preservation is only possible in our concrete case on the basis of nationality. We therefore foster interests whose promotion should not be regarded by [socialism] as acts of hostility against its goals.[122]

Surprisingly, it was Bruno Schönlank, the same outspoken SPD representative who had prophesised that 'popular will' and worker self-organisation would inexorably bring about all the universal achievements Germany still lacked, that declared that he *personally* believed Weber's call for a 'Polish ban' [*Polensperre*] was 'worth considering' by his party; just as, he added, the 'Chinese ban' had not only been considered 'in America', but 'fought for and voted for in tremendous fashion by its organised workers'.[123]

Though such views were not predominant amongst Social Democrats, they were obviously not immune to anti-Polish discourse and xenophobia. As Ralf Hoffrogge has argued, while the old 1848ers Bebel and Liebknecht 'still advocated a radical-democratic concept of nation, parts of the young generation [of Social Democrats] had already transitioned to the essentialist-*völkisch* nation idea, which had asserted itself after 1871'. Crucially, the novel (but by no means progressive) nationalism it bred came 'mixed in with cultural-racist and colonial arguments'. Nevertheless, to the SPD's and its associated union movement's credit, they did ultimately settle on a strategy to 'win over Polish and Italian workers', converging on the idea that 'common labour struggles' – as opposed to border closures – 'were the best means to combat competition over wages due to labour migration'.[124]

As for colonialism, the SPD's record was beyond reproach, especially if compared to other German political forces of the time, to which 'colonial propaganda and nationalism' were a common trait of varying intensity.[125] Indeed, outside of its 'revisionist' wing and isolated 'pragmatic' figures like Gustav Noske, 'support to colonialism constituted a taboo' in the SPD.[126] Just as significant, Hoffrogge concludes, is the fact that the 'mere existence of a socialist international constituted a permanent provocation' to the nationalist and colonialist status quo:

122 MWG I/4, p. 197.
123 Schönlank *in* VfS 1893, p. 113.
124 Hoffrogge 2017, pp. 172–3.
125 Hoffrogge 2017, p. 176.
126 Hoffrogge 2017, p. 174.

> Socialism with its idea of a world-proletariat beyond nations was the political force that, in spite of all its weaknesses, raised most consistently the demand of a humanist politics directed at the equality of all people.[127]

This core agenda also explains why the SPD was the force that most clearly broke with the legacy of 'Prussianism' in Imperial Germany. Max Weber's 'realism' meant that an alliance with Social Democrats on the basis of the humanist ideals described above bordered on the unthinkable. Indeed, his interest in the party followed a different strategic outlook altogether; he hoped to win over its 'revisionist' wing and skilled worker base to social imperialism and, by extension, to the select membership in the new hegemonic configuration he envisioned for Imperial Germany. Weber's plan would, however, fall short in this regard, as Social Democracy neither gravitated to a mature 'reformist' stance, nor split along the 'cultural' fault lines he believed cut through the party. Though the SPD struggled over the question of labour migration and counted supporters of imperial conquest amongst its vast membership, the party's anticolonialism and internationalism ultimately made it an unreliable partner in Weber's political strategising. This historical fact provides, in turn, the best argument against the notion that Weber's stance on Polish labour migration was rooted in commonly held 'prejudices of the age'; the existence of militant alternatives to such views in Imperial Germany, of which the SPD was the clearest embodiment, dispels such analytical shortcuts. In Part 3, I will argue Weber's stance on labour was, in fact, indissociable from his understanding of culture and its imperial frame. Instead of a side-issue or a case of 'youthful excess', his remarks on Polish workers emerge, in this light, as a key indicator of the intricate nexus of class, culture and race in his early thought.

127 Hoffrogge 2017, p. 176.

PART 3

Imperialism and the Nexus of Class, Race and Culture in Max Weber's Early Thought (1894–8)

CHAPTER 10

Between a Global Standpoint and a Normative Concept of Culture: Max Weber on Labour, 'Cultural Difference' and the World Market

1 The World Market as an Inescapable Reality

From his very first interventions as a scholar, Max Weber approached class conflict and the relationship between labour and culture through a global horizon, i.e., with an analytical scope that went beyond the confines of the nation-state. This section aims to show not only that the fundamental reference point of Weber's views on labour was the increasingly globalised world of the late nineteenth century, but also to closely examine the mix of insight and obfuscation he drew from this vantage point. If my emphasis on this particular aspect of Weber's outlook signals an adherence to recent trends in German historiography, which contend that 'the constitution and transformation of the German nation need to be articulated with the imperial and global contexts in which it evolved',[1] it is just as much a result of the general thrust of Weber's early writings. In them, Weber will continuously evoke a global vantage point, even when dealing with seemingly remote phenomena of the German countryside. In this sense, he was a typical example of what Sebastian Conrad termed those 'astute intellectuals in the Kaiserreich who likewise saw the nation transformed fundamentally by the new global structures'.[2]

Another early purveyor of a global standpoint on German history was, without a doubt, Friedrich Engels. Writing in February of 1870, that is, before the irruption of the Franco-Prussian War, but already in the context of the formation of the North-German Confederation, he remarked:

> Much more important than the actions taken by the state and its leadership in 1866 is the upsurge of industry and commerce, and the emergence of the telegraph and of the oceanic steamship in Germany since 1848. Even if the progress in these fields is still behind those made in the same period in England and even in France, for Germany it is unprecedented

1 Conrad 2013, p. 547.
2 Ibid.

> and has brought forth more in twenty years than had been achieved in entire centuries. Germany has at last been drawn, truly and irrevocably, into *world trade*.[3]

Shifting the focus from the seismic political shifts occurring in the German lands in the 1860s, Engels suggests that, even before the 'national question' had reached its Prussian-led solution through the foundation of the Kaiserreich in 1870/71, the increasingly globalised nature of capitalism already had a strong bearing on German economic life. As a result, by the time unification laid the basis for another round of economic expansion on German soil, it was already subject to the forces of the world market and to the dynamics of cross-border and transatlantic migration, among other transnational trends. This was the world Max Weber was born into and would experience first-hand, from his contact with National Liberal debates on protectionist trade tariffs and colonialism in the late-1870s and mid-1880s, respectively, through to his engagement with the Verein für Socialpolitik's 'rural labour' survey during the early 1890s, in which the question of cross-border migration played a central role.

Indeed, Max Weber's report for the Verein demonstrates his keen awareness of Imperial Germany's global embeddedness. His understanding of the social consequences of unification was, therefore, not all that different from the assessment Engels had made two decades before: 'With the unity of the Reich, industrial and large-urban development received an enormous upsurge', wrote Weber in the closing chapter of his report. This meant, he added, that one of the protagonists in the process of unification, the landed aristocracy of the German East, would also be the main bearer not only of the military but also of the 'economic costs of Prussian hegemony'.[4] Though it might at first seem that Weber was referring to a strictly internal process in his analysis of the rearrangement of class relations on German soil after unification, the broader context of this shift is clear in an ensuing passage:

> The South and the West, with their overpowering capital, force the East to absorb their industrial products, but reject the bread that Eastern agriculture onerously and expensively wrests from the native soil.[5]

The new balance of social forces in Germany was not only the result of industrial development, but of increasing imports of grain that, in turn, constituted

3 MEW 16, p. 396.
4 MWG I/3, p. 927.
5 MWG I/3, p. 928.

just one facet of the insertion of German agriculture into a truly global market for foodstuffs. Trade in agricultural commodities had been propelled since the 1870s by falling transportation costs and the exponential increase in the areas of cultivation in countries like Argentina, Canada, Australia and especially the USA.[6] In Weber's portrayal of this process, Imperial Germany's industrial sector was literally bleeding its rural counterpart dry:

> Just as the East primarily provided the manpower which laid the military foundation for the political greatness of the nation, now it provides Western industry with the labour power that lays the foundation for Germany's economic power position; as a result of the splendid development of German industry and large cities, its very lifeblood – new cohorts of workers – is sucked from its veins.[7]

In this passage, Weber paints the economic competition between nations as the direct successor to the great power politics which the Kaiserreich had emerged from. After unification, economic power had taken over the projection of military might as the primary expression of the nation's standing in the international arena. This new context also brought with it a shift from the European setting of Prussia-Germany's wars up to 1870/71 to the global expanses of colonialism and the world market. As accurately portrayed in the Engels quote above, this introduced a driver of social transformation of an entirely new order of magnitude into the German lands, one that was to a certain extent more menacing than the intra-European rivalries of old, though geopolitical tensions remained in play after unification and were in fact accentuated by the new global stakes of nation-state competition. This context helps explain why, in spite of the undeniable nationalist thrust of Weber's writings in this period – and especially of his inaugural lecture of 1895 – his was a standpoint that embedded the nation-state into a wider, global frame.

The papers Weber elaborated for his courses on political economy taught from 1894 to 1898 in Freiburg and Heidelberg[8] make clear that he saw insertion in the world market as a fundamental condition of modern economies. In his only recently published materials on the *Conceptual Foundations of Political Economy*,[9] for instance, Weber not only remarks that 'in no modern nation is the fulfilment of needs even approximately based on domestic trade alone',

6 Wehler 1995, pp. 688–9.

7 MWG I/3, p. 928.

8 See *Einleitung* in MWG III/1, pp. 8–21.

9 MWG III/1, pp. 122–54.

but that a key element in the definition of a modern national economy [*Volkswirtschaft*] is the 'possibility and presence of a state economic policy domestically and a state-based representation of interests abroad (e.g. through trade policy)'.[10] Thus, while it has been correctly pointed out that Max Weber's early work theorised the transition from 'patriarchalism to capitalism',[11] Weber's 'patriarchal society' was not necessarily a pre-capitalist one. To Weber, modern capitalist enterprise as he understood it – i.e., companies with limited liability and double-entry bookkeeping – had arisen in the middle-ages[12] and the patriarchal agrarian economy of the German East was already a market economy; it had been one since the aftermath of the liberation of the serfs in the early nineteenth century.[13] Already at this juncture, the 'patriarchal' landlord produced grain for the market – including the foreign market – and while most of his workers were, to different degrees, in a situation of dependency, serfdom was no longer the basis of the relations of production in the estate. The 'patriarchal' estate analysed by Weber was already a capitalist enterprise,[14] the key question being whether its remaining pre-capitalist features – partially unfree labour, remuneration in kind, etc. – would be necessarily shed en route to a fully modernised operation where an agrarian capitalist would be opposed by a mass of proletarianised rural labourers.

Yet, in addressing this question, Weber did not merely take the advance of capitalist relations *within* Imperial Germany as a decisive factor; he realised that the degree of global insertion of German agrarian production also had a key bearing on its ongoing process of transformation and would continue to play a central role in its future makeup.[15] Thus, the key phenomenon of social and economic change that Weber witnessed and devoted the most scholarly attention to in the 1890s was not the shift from feudalism to capitalism. Rather, it was the transition from an initial phase of competitive capitalism, where England was practically the sole industrial nation, to the 'age of empire',[16] characterised by the expansion and technical development of industrialisation in

---

10 MWG III/1, p. 136.

11 See Mommsen 2004, pp. 22–36 and Riesebrodt 1986.

12 MWG III/1, p. 101.

13 cf. MWG III/5, p. 149.

14 For Weber's take on the Stein-Hardenberg reforms and their ambiguous consequences for German agrarian social structure, cf. MWG I/4, p. 321.

15 See, for example, MWG I/4, pp. 372–3.

16 According to Eric Hobsbawn's definition, the age of empire emerged from a 'world economy whose pace was set by its developed or developing capitalist core', in which, furthermore, 'the "advanced" dominated the "backward"' (Hobsbawn 1989, p. 56). The relevance of this framing to the development of Weber's thought is hinted at by Hobsbawn himself,

the capitalist core, the rise in global competition and in the power of finance and, no less significantly, the vast spread of colonialism, in whose wake 'most of the world outside Europe and the Americas was formally partitioned into territories under the formal rule or informal political domination of one or other of a handful of states'.[17] It is, therefore, a crucial factor that when Weber embarked on an analysis of capitalism, he did so in the 'age of empire' and from the vantage point of one of its emerging (if 'late-arriving') powers. Weber's awareness of living in a new age in the global development of capitalism is signalled by the last item of a periodisation under the rubric 'The historical foundations of the modern economy'.[18] It reads: '6. The emerging world economy and the seeds of its regression'.[19] With the last term, Weber did not suggest there was a way back from the globalised nature of capitalism, but that, through policy measures, the nation-state need not necessarily be at the complete mercy of the forces of the world market; in fact, it could, to an extent, channel those vectors that were advantageous to its global projection and contain those that were seen as damaging in terms of the strict geopolitical hierarchy that was characteristic of the period. Nevertheless, no nation-state would be able to freely shape or fully counteract the impacts of globalised capitalism in its domestic social life, which is why, despite Weber's emphasis on the mediating role of policy, he would make the horizon of his 'standpoint of state reason' *global* in reach.

2 Max Weber's Global Standpoint on Social Conflict and Two-Pronged Understanding of Culture in the 1890s

Weber's awareness of the embeddedness of national economies in the world market meant that he placed social conflict within the nation-state in a relationship of interdependency with the forces of the world economy. As a result, the critique of particular class outlooks that followed from Weber's 'standpoint of state reason' necessarily took into account how the situation of a given class or social segment interacted with transnational trends. Thus, if in a passage

whose chapter entitled 'Age of Empire' starts with a quote from Max Weber's intervention at the Fifth Protestant Social Congress from 1894 (which I examine in the next section).

17 Hobsbawn 1989, p. 57.

18 MWG III/1, pp. 96–105.

19 MWG III/1, p. 105. In a passage from another manuscript on political economy, Weber alludes to the progressive change in the geographical scope of economies based on trade, pointing to the 'world economy' as the final stage in a development that starts with the 'village economy', and proceeds through the stages of the 'city economy' and the 'national economy', but was not impervious to partial reversals (MWG III/1, pp. 135–6).

quoted above Weber was critical of the industrial bourgeoisie for turning to cheap foreign grain to the detriment of Prussian agriculture, he would also criticise Junkers for lobbying for protectionist tariffs for grain while, at the same time, favouring a policy of free movement of labour so they could continue to employ seasonal migrant labourers to the detriment of native rural workers.[20] Finally, this also applied to Weber's perspective on the working class. The imperatives of global competition were among the elements that Weber believed had driven a wedge between the 'shared interests' of large landowners and their dependent workers. When *Instleute* were still mainly remunerated in kind through a share of the crop, 'sun and rain, frost and hail, cattle diseases and *the price pressures brought on by economic crises and foreign competition* impacted [their] economic situation in the same way as that of the landlord's'.[21] Yet, with the advent of a 'planned "entanglement into the world economy"', also described by Weber as the 'subordination to the imperatives of the international division of production',[22] it became disadvantageous (in economic terms) to remunerate workers in kind. The turn to wage-labour that ensued was not only the clearest expression of the proletarianisation of rural workers, but also meant their interest was now in low food prices, the opposite of what the landlord would benefit from.[23] The break up of the 'community of interests' between landlord and worker corresponded, therefore, to a twofold transformation as the proletarianisation of rural workers put them at odds with landowners not only in terms of their immediate class interests (higher wages, better working conditions etc.), but also in terms of the type of trade policy that would directly benefit them (i.e., free-trade, which would bring down food prices). For this reason, in an 1894 essay Weber described unchecked migration literally as a tool of class struggle for landlords, who could pressure the wages of (native) workers downwards through the employment of migrants. To Weber, class struggle played itself out in a transnational arena:

> It is not those workers with the highest standard of life [*Lebenshaltung*] that are favoured [by the landlord], but those with the lowest possible *Lebenshaltung* that come to predominate; indeed, it is not only the entrepreneur's purely economic interest that is decisive in this matter, but also his power interest, even if it is only indirectly tied to the former. The enlist-

20 MWG I/4, p. 180.
21 MWG I/3, p. 77 – my emphasis.
22 MWG I/4, p. 399.
23 See, for instance, MWG I/3, p. 738 and Chapter 8 of this work.

> ing of the Poles is, in the clearest sense, a weapon in the anticipated class struggle against the growing self-consciousness of workers.[24]

A striking aspect of the interplay between Weber's global outlook and his stance on labour is precisely this argument, i.e., that the working class had a stake in the closing of the borders for migrant workers since only by restricting the competition with foreign labourers would German workers supposedly be able to improve their standing within the nation-state. That this was not only a matter of *economic* competition is clear from Weber's reference to the level of consciousness of German workers (as opposed to wage levels alone); in fact, behind Weber's rejection of Polish migrants is a normative concept of culture which placed ethnic groups in a hierarchal relationship to each other, as the next section (10.3) will address. What is worth mentioning at this point is the fact that putting a stop to Polish migration was not the only policy Weber derived from his globalised view of the relationship between labour, social conflict and the nation-state. In the second half of the 1890s, Weber would place growing emphasis on imperial expansion, whose pursuit he claimed was in the interest of both the state and the higher strata of the working class.[25]

Before approaching Weber's brand of 'social imperialism',[26] it is necessary, however, to tease out the central elements of his concept of culture, as it provided the framework informing his outlook on the world economy and Imperial Germany's place within it. As I argued in Part 2, Weber's insight into the role of culture in social life was rooted in his engagement with the vantage point of 'higher-standing' workers. Weber's proposal to foster this social segment in the countryside, in turn, equally involved a consideration of how the global economy impacted domestic class relations. His call for expanding the amount of relatively self-sufficient tenant and small peasant properties was predicated on their being '*relatively* independent from the price variations of the world market'.[27] These were rural strata who, as he put it in another passage,

> … deliver their products primarily to the place where the price formation in the world market makes the least difference, i.e., to their own stomachs.[28]

24 MWG I/4, pp. 416–18.
25 cf. MWG I/4, pp. 609–11.
26 See Section 9.6 above for the definition of the concept.
27 MWG I/4, p. 94.
28 MWG I/4, p. 191.

Weber's call for state subvention of a social segment that was less subject to globalised economic forces again points to the fact that, despite holding the world market to be an inescapable reality, he still believed that there were solutions on the level of policy that dampened what he considered its more disruptive tendencies. Indeed, the importance Weber attributed to the state in actively managing the global and transnational tendencies that put pressure on national economies cannot be understated. It illuminates, for instance, why it is precisely in 'state reason' that Weber found the springboard for a universalised perspective which aimed to rise above narrow class interests. It also helps to explain why the 'nation' seldom appears disconnected from the state in his considerations in this period.[29]

The role Weber extended to the state and economic policy is, moreover, what he believed separated his stance from competing perspectives at opposite ends of the political spectrum. He openly stated that his call for the advancement of small tenant-properties 'went against the conceptions of both extreme free-trade [*manchesterlich*] and extreme socialist currents regarding the influence of the world market and the future [predominance] of large enterprises'.[30] Weber criticised both socialists and free-trade proponents due to what he considered a shared 'dogmatic belief' in economic laws and, especially, their convergence on the need for a stronger integration of the national economy into the world market (to Weber, the culmination not only of free-trade policy, but also of worker internationalist solidarity).

Ironically, Weber gathered both adversarial currents under the common denomination of 'internationalism'[31] and criticised them due to an insufficient consideration of the harmful consequences that an unmediated integration into the world economy could unleash. Thus, it wasn't enough to consider if a certain form of production was the most efficient in terms of output and the most advanced in technical terms; Weber had no doubt that the 'intensive large enterprise' was 'the carrier of technical culture'; yet this in itself did not justify the need for the state to promote it.

The basis for this argument is found in Weber's peculiar conceptualisation of culture [*Kultur*] in his writings of the 1890s, namely in the fact that it bears two

29 It is illustrative that the *Antrittsrede* or 'Inaugural Lecture' was published as *Der Nationalstaat und die Volkswirtschaftspolitik* [The nation-state and economic policy] instead of bearing its original title of *Die Nationalität in der Volkswirtschaft* [Nationality in political economy], which evoked the charges of chauvinism Weber was already confronted with in this period (see EB in MWG I/4, p. 537).

30 MWG I/4, p. 94.

31 MWG I/4, p. 302.

separate meanings: 'intensive culture' or 'technical culture' is clearly tied to capitalist, rationally-planned economic activity, i.e., *Kultur* in the sense of 'material' production; besides this use, however, there is a notion of culture with a subjective core, whose main variables are the degree of individual autonomy and the intensity of needs [*Bedürfnisse*] on the part of individuals (in addition to their productivity, as I will examine below). For reasons of clarity, I will refer to this second, more subject-centred meaning in the German original: *Kultur*. It is worth highlighting that the concept of rationality underscoring Weber's understanding of technical culture is purely instrumental and is modelled on profit-maximisation, while his notion of *Kultur* has a clear bourgeois-individualist tinge.[32] In other words, whereas this two-pronged conceptualisation of culture might at first seem purely formal in nature – stressing technical rationality and autonomous subjectivity, respectively – upon closer inspection it betrays both a normative aspect and a specific class content.

The fundamental insight Weber drew from this dual understanding of culture was that the advance in the number of enterprises employing intensive culture, i.e., managed under rational principles and based on modern relations of production, was not necessarily accompanied by the promotion of an equally high level of *Kultur* in the sense of enhancing individuals' autonomy etc. According to Weber, this was predicated on how the benefits accrued by technical advancement impacted the situation of the various social classes within a given nation-state. This meant considering economic activity from two distinct points of view. On the one hand, Weber held the question of whether large modernised agrarian enterprises served the interests of 'state reason' to be 'identical in economic terms with the question of what *position German spirits and German sugar can take up in the world market in the future*'.[33] In other words, this meant asking if sugar and spirit production in the German East was 'rational in a national and a world-economic sense [*volks-und*

32 In Weber's writings of the 1890s, *rationality* and *irrationality* are explicitly tied to economic activity and therefore, to culture in the 'material' sense. The reduction in the availability of land, for example, is mentioned by Weber as an incentive to operate 'rationally' in economic terms (MWG I/4, p. 129), i.e., through the calculation of the most efficient exploitation of labour power and resources etc. On the other hand, *Kultur* is not *directly* tied to rationality in this instrumental sense, but rather to an individual capacity for autonomy and a forward-looking ponderation of means and ends – a more subject-centred brand of rationality. Finally, Weber also remarked on occasion that there was an 'irrational' component to *Kultur* (cf. MWG I/4, p. 340), in terms of the unrestricted affirmation of an ideal. I will approach this 'irrational' dimension of culture in Weber's conceptualisation below (See 11.4).

33 MWG I/3, p. 922.

weltwirtschaftlich rationell]'. Put briefly, from a strictly economic point of view, the criteria for evaluating a certain field of economic activity was its degree of competitiveness in the world market. Crucially, Weber argued that the desirability of a given entrepreneurial activity for the nation-state should also obey a different criterion, that of its impact on the country's 'level of *Kultur*'.

Weber held that if success against foreign competitors in the world market required a 'debasement' in the realm of *Kultur*, this counteracted any economic benefits that might be accrued by entering global trade. In the concrete case of the German East, Weber believed that the viability of modernised agricultural enterprise had come at too great a 'cultural' cost, since it was synonymous with the disappearance of rural middle-strata as well as with a drop in German workers' standard of life, which Weber attributed to the competition of Polish migrants. In other terms, in the case of the German East, a higher level of technical culture was equivalent to a debasement of *Kultur*:

> It is not possible for our workers to compete with Polish workers. German workers would have to climb down a cultural level [*Kulturstufe*] in their needs in order to do so; it is very much the same with our agricultural enterprises which are noncompetitive because they would have to climb down a cultural level in order to compete with those of Russia, Argentina and America. There is a certain situation in capitalistically disorganized national economies, according to which the higher culture not only is not superior in the struggle for existence, but is, in fact, weaker vis-à-vis a culture with a lower standing.[34]

Despite the obvious nationalist connotations of extending a higher cultural status to German workers with regards to Polish ones, Max Weber's nationalism does not surface in his writings in the period merely in terms of his attributing an inherently superior value to his *own* 'national community'; if this is all nationalism represented in Weber's work – and it certainly possessed this dimension – it would be tempting to dismiss it as a kind of unreflected bias on his part, an 'unconscious' contamination by the prejudices of his time (though the tendency to naturalise historical actors' biases is still a highly problematic analytical blind spot). What must be stressed, however, is 1) the underlying concept of culture in which Weber's notion of *Deutschtum* – translatable as 'Germanness' – was embedded; this meant Weber was less concerned with affirming the superiority of the *German* nation than with stressing its worthy

34 MWG I/4, pp. 182–3.

standing alongside other (so-called) 'higher cultures'; 2) Weber developed a systematic conceptualisation for what he claimed influenced the 'cultural standing' of a given nationality/ethnic group, i.e., it was far from a case of 'Eurocentrism by default'. Weber's 'nationalism' was the result of both a typically imperialist, yet also uniquely intricate and thought-out perspective on *Kultur*. As Manuela Boatcă has argued:

> Inherent in Weber's defence of the 'standpoint of Germanism' in the 1890s is therefore a roundabout theory of ethnicity premised on the inequality of the cultural levels and the attitudes towards work of different 'nationalities' that both reflects the views of his time and goes beyond them.[35]

Weber's normative conceptualisation of *Kultur* as a theory of ethnicity has two key traits. First, it is *hierarchical*, as Weber clearly believed there were unequal levels of culture from one 'nationality' – understood as ethnicity, not as citizenship in a nation-state – to another in global terms. Second, because the 'cultural level' of various 'nationalities' was *not fixed*, neither was Weber's global hierarchy of culture. Considering each 'nation' was subject to internal as well as external economic developments as well as by the status they had in the pecking order of colonialism and imperialism, its cultural standing was liable to change. The resulting perspective posits a global sliding-scale of culture for the 'age of empire', according to which nation-states competed not only in terms of productivity and technical advance, but also in a kind of race to the bottom in the realm of *Kultur* (considering the direct bearing of 'cultural level' on the costs of labour power and its reproduction).

Nowhere is Max Weber's understanding of *Kultur* – and its relationship to culture in the 'technical' sense – more clearly articulated in his early thought[36] than in his short essay on 'Argentine settler-economy', from early 1894. In it, Weber sets out to contest the claim made by free-trade advocates that the lack of competitiveness in German agriculture was the fault of the 'backward enterprise forms' of Junker landowners, who were supposedly holding back the 'cultural progress' of the German countryside.[37] Weber will cast doubt on this notion through a detailed analysis of a single Argentinean agricultural property producing grain for export, claiming it contained 'certain typical traits in

35 Boatcă 2013, p. 69.

36 On the question of survival of a normative understanding of culture in Weber's 'mature', i.e., post-1903 work, see Farris 2013 and the epilogue to this work.

37 MWG I/4, p. 286.

its economic activity which appeared *mutatis mutandis* in the productive conditions of [Germany's] effective competitors' abroad.[38]

Weber would define the form of export agriculture conducted in Argentina as 'pillage agriculture' [*Raubbau*] as it relied on an otherwise unsustainable drainage of the soil as well as of material and human resources which were only viable in a colonial – or, in the case of Argentina, postcolonial – context with plentiful land and cheap, disposable labour, financed by a steady provision of credit from speculators.[39] Weber will characterise the migrant workers of the Argentine plains in terms similar to those he had used to refer to Poles – 'swarms of nomads',[40] 'nomadic barbarians'[41] etc. – indicating, once again, that national distinctions played less of a role in these comparisons than the supposed shared 'level of *Kultur*' attributed by Weber to both Polish migrants workers and Argentinean Gauchos.[42] Both nationalities were racialised by Weber and, as a result, united in a condition of inferiority with regards to an 'old sedentary *Kultur* people [*Kulturvolk*] with a complex and distinctive social organization and typical cultural needs',[43] as was the case of Germans (and other so-called '*Kulturvölker*'). Thus, at the equally 'low level' of *Kultur* that both Argentines and Poles were at, the differentiation that emerges in higher cultures was simply not present, making them effectively interchangeable in Weber's global tapestry of *Kultur*.

As with his rejection of the economic benefits of Polish migration into the German East, Weber argued that it would be impossible for German agrarian producers to compete with Argentine agriculture without '*debasing* our social structure and our level of *Kultur*'.[44] In his application of the adjective 'old' to German culture and likening of Germany to 'a grown man' as compared to

---

38 Ibid.

39 See MWG I/4, pp. 287–91.

40 MWG I/4, p. 292.

41 MWG I/4, p. 298.

42 As Manuela Boatcă has pointed out, in excluding Poles from the realm of *Kultur*, to Weber, the 'modern, the civilized and the rational are thereby confined to an even more exclusive space within the European continent, which the imperial imaginary conceives as ending at Germany's eastern border' (2013, p. 69). Yet, 'barbarism' was no exclusive trait of Eastern Europe and South America. Peoples of Northern Europe were also liable to be outside the frontiers of *Kultur* as Weber perceived them. In his trip to Ireland and Scotland, for instance, Weber will make constant reference to 'barbarians' from the Scottish Highlands and equate the Irish to the Poles. See my extended review of the correspondence volume where Weber chronicles this trip (Strazzeri 2017).

43 MWG I/4, p. 299.

44 MWG I/4, p. 297.

Argentina (a 'pubescent street youth'),[45] Weber in fact reverted to some of the same derogatory terminology for characterising 'lower cultures' that the German ruling classes employed to dismiss workers as dependent subjects lacking in self-responsibility. As I will discuss below, this similarity in how both racialised groups/nationalities and the working classes were disparaged is not coincidental, pointing instead to the similarly – 'low' – status they were perceived to possess in the eyes of elites.

Again, such remarks should not be understood as mere prejudices. Weber's references to his sliding-scale of *Kultur* built the core of his argument in the essay on Argentina; it was the centre-piece of his reply to the critics of the 'backwardness' of the German East, considering that despite being 'specifically capitalist' in how it organised production, Argentina nevertheless remained at a lower level of *Kultur*. Thus, landowners' 'fabulous profits' were made at the cost of all other social segments with the exception of financial speculators.[46]

The importance of this short essay, however, goes beyond his use of Argentine agriculture as the negative projection – or inverted image – of how German agrarian production should be organised and integrated into the world economy. In it, Weber gives the clearest expression to the underpinnings of his globalised view of culture and its *structurally* hierarchical nature. Weber believed both internationalist socialists and free-trade proponents foolishly ignored this, which, as mentioned previously, is why he would assert that '[t]he enemy is internationalism in all its forms'.[47] By internationalism, Weber meant 'the fundamental opposition to the *national* underpinnings of modern economies [*Volkswirtschaften*]'. Both currents set out from what Weber described as the 'completely unreal premise of an international *cultural equality* [*Kulturgleichheit*]'.[48] What they failed to realise, however, was that '[w]ithout a world-state and full equality in humanity's level of *Kultur*, the world economy of the free-trade doctrine is, ultimately, an utopia; the road to it is long'.[49] Again, Weber's normative conceptualisation of culture does not exclude a contingent aspect – i.e., *Kultur* is not a static property of some nations, much less the German nation – and it even allows, as the last remark suggests, for an eventual levelling of the degree of *Kultur* across mankind in some far-away future. This separates Weber, to some extent, from the strictly determinist – and therefore more virulent – biological racists, yet it does not exempt him from *racialising*

45 MWG I/4, p. 299.
46 MWG I/4, pp. 300–1.
47 MWG I/4, p. 303, n. 4.
48 MWG I/4, p. 302.
49 MWG I/4, p. 303.

ethnic groups precisely *through* his understanding of cultural difference. This element of his viewpoint combined with a default understanding of rationality as instrumental and of subjective autonomy as bourgeois and individualist starkly counteracted the analytic possibilities opened up by his early perspectivism, i.e., the insight into the plurality of subjective outlooks he arrived at through his confrontation with the 'rural labour question'.

In the closing words to the essay on Argentina, Weber will explore the possibility of a universal cultural levelling of humanity while also making it clear that he believed the convergence towards equality was not yet the order of the day. His use of a metaphor from the natural world shows just how porous the borders between racialisation on the basis of culture and on the basis of 'biology' actually were (and continue to be):

> As long as we are still in the beginning of this process, as is the case in the present, we act in the best interest of its advancement if we do not all too hurriedly fall the old trunks – the historically constituted national economic entities – from which perhaps future lineages [*Geschlechter*] shall manage to carve out the fabric of the economic and cultural community of mankind, nor try to trim them for future edifices, but preserve and nurture them in their naturally-given growth.[50]

3 The Labour-Culture Nexus in Max Weber's Early Thought

In this chapter, I have so far examined two ways in which Weber's global perspective had a bearing on his stance towards labour. The first pertained to the intricate relationship of the nation-state – and its social classes – to the world market; the second to Weber's claim that capitalism underlined and functionalised the 'unequal' cultural status of 'national' (ethnic-racial) groups. Both are interrelated and help illuminate elements of Weber's early work that have either been overlooked or have not been properly understood in the scholarship. It is through this framing, for instance, that Weber's stated goal in the opening words of his *Inaugural Lecture* of 1895 emerges as a coherent expression of his overarching research interests, namely, 'to illustrate the role of physical and psychological racial differences between nationalities in the economic struggle for existence'.[51] Weber quite explicitly mentions 'physical' racial differ-

50 Ibid.
51 MWG I/4, p. 545.

ences here, which goes to show that they played a part in his framework for understanding (and naturalising) inequality; at this point, however, I will focus on his intricate theory of cultural difference.

Crucially, while Weber's *articulation* of this fundamental research interest is at its clearest in the *Antrittsrede*, he was already operating under this framework from the time of his very first writings on the 'rural labour question'. The latter effectively constituted the testing ground for his attempt to centre the analysis of economic life on the notion of 'cultural difference'. Thus, it was the 'lower cultural status' of Polish and Argentinian workers that put them at an 'advantage' in the world market. Despite being individually less productive than workers with a 'higher' cultural status, as a cheap and disposable workforce they were more suited for a purely commercial and export-oriented form of agricultural production. German workers were, according to Weber, verifiably more productive, *provided* their material and psychological needs were met, yet this made them more costly to employ and harder to exploit.[52]

Weber's global perspective on labour was, however, not limited to statements on how workers with varying 'levels of *Kultur*' compete in a world grown interconnected through the spread of capitalism. This insight presupposes a theory of 1) what made a particular 'nationality' a carrier of a higher or lower degree of *Kultur* and 2) of how this translated to economic activity and/or performance. What is at stake here are the foundations of what Angela Zimmerman termed Weber's 'political economy of cultural difference', that is,

> a generalized theory of the empire presupposed by colonial-imperialism and revealed most directly in the phenomena of migration and internal minorities rather than in foreign conquest.[53]

The *political economy of cultural difference* was the broader prism through which Weber understood the 'labour question' and, indeed, the ramifications of capitalist development for a given nation-state. In this sense, it built the global and cultural complement to the proto-Fordist understanding of modern social structure that underpinned Weber's 'standpoint of state reason'; the latter, therefore, raised a dual imperative of integrating higher-standing workers into a power bloc led by the bourgeoisie at home and projecting the nation's power abroad.

---

52 See, for instance, MWG I/4, p. 205.

53 Zimmerman 2006, p. 54.

Weber's political economy of cultural difference rests on the premise that culture was an essential factor in understanding individuals' relationship to work. This insight was significant, because it represented a break with political economy's prevailing framing of labour and economic activity from the standpoint of the profit-seeking individual that maximises advantages to serve narrowly defined needs. In a passage addressing the East German district of Posen, for instance, Weber points to how needs are culturally variable and that it is they that determine the material standard of workers and not the other way around:

> [T]here is no doubt that within the province [of Posen], neither the fertility of the soil, nor the intensity of its cultivation determine the level of nutrition of the population; the contributing influence of these factors notwithstanding, it is rather the intensity of Germanness [*Intensität des Deutschtums*] that is to an overwhelming degree decisive for the average level of nutritional need and, therefore, of the material culture within the labouring population.[54]

It is important to point out that in assessing the predominant role of 'national' characteristics in the 'material' situation of the working class – considering that ethnic traits form the basis of his understanding of cultural difference – Weber is referring to a specific region and a specific segment of workers, which indicates that not necessarily *all German workers* have in his eyes the same 'level of culture'. This contrasts to a kneejerk and unreflected brand of nationalism in the sense that, while not any less chauvinistic, it has particular analytical as well as political ramifications that merit closer examination. The use of the word 'intensity', for instance, signals that Weber understands 'cultural difference' as a sliding scale rather than an intrinsic property and that it is, therefore, highly variable *even within members of the same national community*. If the comparatively low standard of life of German workers in Posen could be traced back – in Weber's *Kultur*-paradigm – to the strong Polish component of the district's population, in the case of Silesia the low degree of *Kultur* was attributed to aspects of social stratification that were not primarily tied to migration, but to the fully capitalist nature of agrarian enterprise in the region. This also means that Weber's refusal to engage with the subjective drivers of those ethnic communities he racialised through 'cultural difference' equally extended to segments of the *German* working class with a supposedly low level of *Kul-*

54 MWG I/3, p. 585.

tur. Weber's understanding of hierarchies of class and culture were, therefore, deeply intertwined and followed a similar logic.

Before I address this point, it is necessary to stress two other traits that Weber understood to be predicated on 'cultural status' – i.e., besides the level of nutrition/material needs, referred to in the passage above. The first is the *degree of individual autonomy and responsibility* which Weber gathered under the notion of 'self-consciousness': 'The level of nutrition and the self-consciousness of the rural working-class is, in the East, quite simply identical with [their] Germanness'.[55] This assertion from Weber is directly related to his 'discovery' of the lure of 'freedom' to rural workers, who preferred to be worse off in material terms if this afforded the possibility to enjoy a higher level of personal freedom. Weber also attributed workers' preference for wage-labour – rather than payment in kind – to the intensified striving for autonomy that accompanied a 'heightened' cultural status.[56] Finally, this sense of individual autonomy was also the driver behind the desire of (German) workers to migrate to the cities or abroad: 'The self-conscious prefer to migrate'.[57]

A second aspect came to bear on the labour-culture nexus of Max Weber's analytical outlook, namely, his direct association of productivity with 'cultural standing'. To prove the causal relationship between these two factors 'it was enough', Weber asserted, 'to compare the daily piece-loan' of a 'German worker' (6–8 Marks) to that of a 'native Polish worker' (2.50–3.50 Marks) and a 'Russian-Polish worker' (1.50–2 Marks).[58] Thus, with regards to productivity, i.e., a factor where culture and labour were in direct connection, Weber believed he had clear evidence for his sliding scale of 'cultural difference' and the causal role of the so-called 'intensity of Germanness' in economic life. For there wasn't only a difference in productivity between Germans and Poles, but an equally noticeable drop-off in output between *German-born* ethnic Poles and foreign-born Poles. This 'extraordinary difference', which Weber is careful to say 'does not appear to this degree and with this clarity anywhere else', was in part the product of Germans' 'higher wage requirements', i.e., of their greater self-consciousness, but was 'predominantly' due to the 'higher productivity of German workers'. This, in turn, was explained by Weber on the basis of the notion that, 'especially for the cultivation of grain, the interest of the worker himself as well as his cultural level also had economic significance'.[59]

55 MWG I/3, p. 915.
56 See MWG I/3, p. 903.
57 MWG I/3, p. 743.
58 MWG I/3, p. 585.
59 MWG I/3, p. 585.

The reasons that still made it advantageous to employ Polish workers, despite their lower productivity, were the lower wages they commanded and the fact that they could be employed only when needed, i.e., during the harvest season, instead of having to be kept at the estate year-round. The 'level of culture' was, in Weber's eyes, the predominant element at play here, even when purely economic considerations such as wage-levels tipped the balance towards the choice of Polish migrant laborers, rather than more productive German workers.

4 Culture, Race and Labour: The Genesis of Weber's Cultural Approach to Economic Activity and Its Contradictions.

The characterisation of Weber's perspective in this period as simply an offshoot of 'nationalist' bias,[60] though not entirely incorrect, misses the role of the labour-culture nexus in his analyses not only of the 'rural labour question' in the German East, but of global inequalities in general (as is evident from the essay on Argentine agriculture).[61] Weber's attempts at grasping the interplay between economic and cultural drivers in individual agency in his writings of the 1890s are, in fact, no less sophisticated than similar efforts in his later work, if less methodologically refined. In this sense, attributing the narrowness of Weber's standpoint to 'bias' alone is both misleading and a critical misfire; Weber's understanding of the relationship between 'nationalities' and affirmation of 'Western' and by extension German superiority was a function of his attempt to frame both social *and* ethnic-racial inequality through the prism of a normative concept of *Kultur*. This culminated in a highly contradictory stance towards workers:

> The question of wage-levels in the countryside is, within certain – yet widely drawn – limits, a simple *power question*; the outraged complaints of employers that the elevation of workers' living conditions has led to ever higher demands on their part is directed against the self-evident fact

60 An example is Kaesler 2014, p. 409.

61 For an examination and critical take on the connection between Weber's perspective on culture and modernity and his understanding of global inequalities, see Boatcă 2015. As Boatcă argues, 'Weber's views on inequality and stratification are intimately tied to his larger theory of the rise of the modern world', i.e., a broader frame than the one-sided affirmation of the 'nation'. For this reason, understanding Weber's 'theory of modernity is an indispensable prerequisite for any analysis of this approach to social inequality' (Boatcă 2015, p. 21).

> that only after reaching a certain level in their standard of life are workers bestowed with the physical and psychological energy necessary to succeed in the struggle for a measure of participation in the goods of this Earth.[62]

In this passage, Weber casts doubt on a narrow economic view of how wage-levels are determined by extending a central role to social conflict and therefore emphasising agency, i.e., denaturalising workers' subaltern status. He does so, however, while in the same breath positing a *deeper* cleavage, drawn not between ascendant workers and employers, but between those workers able to identify and struggle for their own interests and those 'physically' (again a reference to biology) or 'psychologically' – i.e., culturally – unable to do so.

In other terms, with one gesture Weber articulates a complex, non-deterministic view of economic phenomena that rejects employers' desire to undercut workers' demands by maintaining them at a position of deprivation, only to immediately negate it by setting a minimum cultural threshold before workers can even begin to vie for a greater share in worldly goods, that is, in the tangible as well as intangible goods of *Kultur*. In doing so, Weber draws a normative line between, on the one hand, inherently passive workers and, on the other, a self-conscious segment of the working class; this divide, in turn, is very much akin to the one Weber draws between 'lower-standing' and 'higher-standing' cultures on a global scale.

This hints at the fact that, in Weber's framework, both the low-skilled worker of the 'peoples of *Kultur*' and non-Western subjects in general share a similarly low status. The analytical construct Weber elicited in the passage above as an indicator for subjects' putative 'degree of culture' is their 'standard of life' or *Lebenshaltung*, i.e., their level of material and spiritual needs.[63] Weber uses the same construct to draw the global divides of *Kultur*. Thus, if Weber's critical stance regarding the inflow of Polish migrant workers into the German East was predicated on the supposed disparity between their 'standard of life' and that of 'native' workers, culminating in what he saw as unfair economic competition and a general debasement of *Kultur*, the quote above suggests that be believed this divide also existed *within* the same 'nationality' or ethnic-racial group.

62 MWG I/3, p. 913.

63 In the German original, Weber will at times use the English expression 'standard of life' as a byword for *Lebenshaltung*, suggesting their equivalence.

The fundamental cleavage in Weber's globalised understanding of inequality is, thus, given less along strict 'national' lines than along supranational – and, therefore, more porous and less fixed, though no less problematic – 'cultural' ones. This is what allowed Weber to group Poles, Argentines *and low-standing German workers* under the same broad notion of a low level of *Kultur* and, correspondingly, to extend to German and other Western elites, but also *higher-standing* workers, a superior cultural status. This does not mean that the race-like underpinnings of Weber's notion of 'cultural difference' are somehow diluted when he addresses the 'lower cultural status' of certain German workers. On the contrary, the way Weber frames culture means it operates analogously to race, in the sense that the latter is, in the words of Angela Zimmerman, 'totally imaginary' and a 'hallucination', but one that 'organized populations transnationally, much as national identity organized the inhabitants of a territory ruled by a single state'.[64] As such, Weber's understanding of culture displays what has been a consistent trait of racist outlooks, i.e., to deny membership to the 'superior' group – whether it be to 'whiteness', 'Germanness' etc. – to poor and working-class whites or, in this case, Germans. This did not mean, necessarily, that the social cleavage was more decisive than the ethnic-racial one, but rather that racist worldviews have historically been interconnected with the aggressive reaffirmation of class hierarchies. This is a crucial insight to understand the problems of Weber's sliding-scale of culture which, despite being less fixed and deterministic than (purely) biological understandings of race, converges with them in the end-result of naturalising global and social hierarchies:

> Individuals defined themselves as white in relation, primarily, to blacks, but also to a whole gradation of people of colour and of white people perceived as not fully white, groups such as Poles that we would today call ethnicities, as well as whites who, because of their poverty, did not exhibit all the traits that white elites liked to attribute to their own 'race'.[65]

I highlight this aspect of Weber's outlook, because it is decisive in explaining why his consideration of the standpoint of workers entirely excluded *both* Polish workers and unskilled German workers. In the case of the two latter groups, Weber forfeited any engagement with subjectivity and 'psychological' drivers and treated social phenomena involving their agency as purely 'object-

64 Zimmerman 2012, p. 14.
65 Ibid.

ive' occurrences. Though this emerges more clearly in the case of Weber's views on Polish cross-border migration, it is the same fundamental framework that drew him to consider the subjective drivers of *some* German workers while, at the same time, framing 'lower-standing' ones as a muddled and subdued mass.

The relevance of this understanding of the labour-culture nexus to Weber's later works – and especially to the *Protestant Ethic* – becomes evident in a passage from his materials on political economy from the 1890s. In it, Weber not only reaffirms the shared exclusion from *Kultur* of both the lowest segment of workers of a given national community and non-Western subjects in general, but also provides an early take on the ethical underpinnings of modern capitalism:

> Economic activity [*Das Wirtschaften*] is instilled into human beings through a process of adaptation lasting millennia. The magnitude of planned economic activity in the modern sense was and is historically very different according to race and – also within modern occidental culture – according to profession, education, intellect and character of individuals, though its development is, without exception, incomplete; accordingly, the margin that purely economic motives occupy within the realm of the driving forces that define the action of a particular person is highly variable in historical and individual terms.[66]

In this passage, which is well worth unpacking due to its significance, Weber first sets a culturally-based 'racial' divide in assessing the degree of forward-looking, rational activity of a given individual, suggesting certain 'races' have become more adept at performing 'planned economic activity' than others. The extent to which Weber's understanding of race also rested on 'biological' determinants is unclear from this passage, but his constant pairing of 'physiological' with 'psychological' when characterising the factors behind difference between human groups, as shown in various quotes in previous sections, indicates that he was at the very least 'agnostic' in this regard. In other words, he did not deny physiology could play a role in establishing patterns of inequality; isolating it as the decisive causal factor was the issue. Another passage from Weber's materials for his courses on political economy expresses this 'agnostic' position on race clearly:

66 MWG III/1, p. 122.

> That *innate* differences of disposition in race characteristics exist between *individuals*, without question
>
> Also uncontested, that they exist *typically* between human *groups* (races)
>
> The *consequence* of innate race characteristics for human economic and social order greatly contested.
>
> ⟨That they *exist*, beyond all doubt⟩
>
> Scientific observation a[nd] *differentiation* of their *effects* on the realm of *human* life, almost impossible, – secular intervals of time necessary.
>
> Human beings due to the influence of life circumstances so *variable*, that in any event highly questionable, ⟨what effect of race is⟩ what derives from 'disposition'.
>
> This above all in the psychological realm.[67]

Even if in the quote before this one Weber argues that economic activity is 'instilled' across 'millennia', i.e., suggesting a framing of race that is primarily cultural, rather than static-biological, the resulting *naturalisation* of global and social inequalities is no less problematic. Economic performance is depicted as akin to a skill which individuals and cultures acquire with a greater or lesser degree of success. Through this framing, Weber erases the historical peculiarity and violent genesis of capitalist entrepreneurship and renders it equivalent to 'planned economic activity' as such. The apparently formal concept – '*das Wirtschaften*' – hides a normative bourgeois core, meaning it both eternalises modern-individual economic agency and obfuscates its actual historical roots in mass exploitation and dispossession (whether as a result of colonialist conquest or the confiscation of the 'commons' that underscores primitive accumulation).

Weber then states that a hierarchy of '*Wirtschaften*' exists not only across different cultures but also *within them*; he then proceeds to stratify members of 'occidental culture' according to how well they perform 'planned eco-

67 MWG III/1, p. 347. 'Daß *angeborene* Differenzen der Veranlagung ⟨Rassen-Eigenarten⟩ zwischen *Individuen* existieren, zweifellos/Ebenso nicht bestritten, daß sie *typisch* zwischen Menschen*gruppen* (Rassen) existieren/Die *Tragweite* der angeborenen Rassen-Eigenarten für die menschliche Wirtschafts- u. Gesellschaftsordung überaus bestritten. /⟨Daß solche *vorhanden*, außer allem Zweifel⟩/Wissenschaftliche Beobachtung u. *Abgrenzung*: ihrer *Wirkungen* auf dem Gebiet des *Menschen*lebens fast unmöglich, – dazu säculare Zeiträume nötig./Der Mensch unter dem Einfluß der Lebensverhältnisse so *variabel*, daß in jedem Fall höchst zweifelhaft, ⟨was Wirkung der Rasse ist⟩ was auf „*Anlage*" beruht./Dies besonders auf *psychischem* Gebiet'.

nomic activity' – again hinting at the common status of its lowest representatives and non-Western subjects in general. Beyond individual traits – 'intellect and character' – Weber points to two clearly social criteria as being decisive for this ability: profession and education. '*Wirtschaften*' for Weber is therefore a function of cultural status – determined by race/ethnicity – *and* of class.

As mentioned previously, it is not only the capacity for forward-looking or planned agency along bourgeois-individual lines that indicates the influence of *Kultur* in economic life in Weber's framework. An individual's degree of needs is the other key variable in this regard. Weber's constant mention of workers' varying nutritional and living standards as proxies for their level of *Kultur* in his studies on the 'rural labour question' clearly suggest as much. In Weber's materials on the conceptual foundations of political economy this insight receives a theoretical grounding. Weber frames the pondering of 'current' vs. 'future' needs as a function of both a class gradient as well as a cultural one:

> Future needs are normally perceived as less urgent with regards to current needs of a similar kind; their urgency rises:
> α) *with* rising *satisfaction* of current needs – it is therefore, for instance, *socially* variable,
> β) *with rising economic education* (education to *foresight*) altogether – therefore generally with rising culture [*Cultur*].[68]

The level of *Kultur* is framed here as a function of the ability to engage in forward-looking activity, which is tied directly to 'rising economic education'. This ability, in turn, has its own prerequisite, namely, a minimal degree of satisfaction of current needs, which Weber attributes to social status. Again Weber elicits a two-pronged minimum threshold, analogous to the 'physical and psychological energy' he claimed was required before workers could vie for a greater share in the goods of *Kultur*. Thus, in the case of the consideration of needs, a certain level of destituteness leads to an emphasis on *current* necessities by the lowest segments of the working class, despite the fact that the 'higher' cultural status of certain nations is accompanied by a superior degree of 'education to *foresight*'. Thus, in Weber's perspective, both 'material' and 'cultural' factors prevent workers and non-modern, non-Occidental peoples from full integration into the world of *Kultur*.

68 MWG III/1, p. 124.

Here was the central contradiction of Weber's path-breaking, but also incomplete engagement with workers' standpoint; it did not extend to the agency of all workers, as not all were seen as equal bearers of *Kultur*. This explains why his stance towards Polish migrant workers, non-Western subjects and low-skilled German workers alike was at odds with his insightful consideration of the subjective drivers of the upper strata of the working class. The implications of this contradictory vantage point for his overall perspective on workers and Social Democracy will be examined next.

5 Class and Cultural Difference in Weber's Engagement with Workers' Standpoint

The more overtly political conclusions that Max Weber drew from his analysis of the 'rural labour question' in the German East met with criticism within both the Verein für Socialpolitik and the Protestant Social Congress. Karl Kaerger, for instance, accused Weber of being a 'reactionary'[69] due to the latter's reservations regarding the unfettered expansion of capitalist relations in the countryside. Weber's response to this critique is equally his clearest articulation yet of the insight that the 'material' or purely 'technical' advances brought forth by modern economic relations did not necessarily coincide with a general rise in *Kultur* for a given nation-state.

He countered Kaerger's accusation of *Kulturfeindschaft* or 'antagonism towards culture' on his part by arguing that, though he set off from the premise that a more intensive cultivation of the soil would lead to a rise in workers' standard of life, his study of agrarian relations in the German East had shown this was not necessarily the case. Thus, if the 'interest of *Kultur*' was the central concern, the imperatives were to intervene in the realm of social stratification[70] and to drive Polish workers out.[71]

In other words, while the onset of the 'rule of capital'[72] was an indispensable condition for raising the 'technical' culture of a nation-state, it did not necessarily elevate the standing of its people – understood in ethnic-racial terms – in the global hierarchy of *Kultur*. Weber would illustrate the double-edged nature of technical progress from the standpoint of 'cultural level' in a lecture given in May 1895:

69 MWG I/4, p. 319.
70 See chapter 11.
71 MWG I/4, p. 414.
72 MWG I/4, p. 327.

> On the one hand, Indians and Blacks retreat when faced with the more highly cultivated Whites; yet, as in the German East, the opposite is the case and the lower culture displaces the higher one.[73]

This was a fundamental conclusion in terms of Weber's stance towards workers, since it both framed how he understood their place within the nation and established the contradictory nature of his engagement with their standpoint. Inscribed in Weber's rejection of the mechanical equivalence between modernisation and cultural progress, which he translated into a call for imperial expansion and the expulsion of migrants, was a gesture of (partial) integration of workers' demands that was, nevertheless, predicated on the *reaffirmation of their subaltern character* – as a cog in the imperial project – and which, furthermore, only extended to the highest strata of workers.

In this sense, every gesture of recognition towards the working class on Weber's part was qualified and implied the simultaneous exclusion of 'lower-standing' workers from consideration; be it in terms of their role in political life, as bearers of their own cultural values, or even in their status as subjects. A reconstruction of Weber's engagement of workers that does not take into account the equally central moment of *refusal* it contains would necessarily be one-sided and incomplete. From his first and most committed call to engage with workers' standpoint in his defence of Paul Göhre in 1892,[74] he had already introduced a clear caveat as to the *category of worker* he was contemplating. Addressing the impression left by Göhre's *Three Months as a Factory Worker*, Weber remarked that '... the reader is left with the impression that, with *this* category of worker [Weber's emphasis – V.S.], he is dealing with his own flesh and blood ...'.[75] In the same page he would again emphasise that it was, 'mind you, not the worker in general, but indeed *this* extraordinarily great and important category of the future industrial "middle class" [*Mittelstand*]' he was referring to when he spoke of their 'essential equality of spiritual and intellectual interests' with regards to 'those of a broad bourgeois segment of the propertied and governing classes'.[76] It is no coincidence then that in specifying which segment of workers he was addressing, Weber tied them to a future membership in the 'middle class', i.e., to their eventual *detachment* from the working class proper – a point I will return to in Chapter 11.

73 MWG I/4, p. 726.
74 See 8.1.
75 MWG I/4, p. 110.
76 Ibid.

The specific class content of Weber's apparently formal concept of culture becomes evident when he designates a convergence with the 'intellectual interests' of the bourgeoisie on the part of higher-standing workers as a key indicator of their cultural status; the normative and Eurocentric thrust of the concept emerges, in turn, when he stresses how *these* workers had 'emancipated their intellects from the bondage of tradition' and, as a consequence, had a legitimate claim to consideration.[77] If the subjective drivers of workers *fell short* of such an emancipated status, as was the case of those Weber depicted as living in a state of 'dull resignation',[78] they did not merit his analytical interest or consideration.

This pattern is visible when Weber articulated the fundamental discovery of his investigation of the 'rural labour question', i.e., the notion that, rather than an improvement in workers' livelihoods, 'intensive cultivation' had brought forth a major 'cultural achievement' [*Kulturerfolg*] in the German East: the fact that rural workers had become acquainted with *freedom*, which they came to value more highly than their material wellbeing.[79] Weber even expressed his personal identification with this 'trait of the modern world', when he attributed the drive of rural workers to be 'the architects of their own fortune – or misfortune', to 'a psychological development of general character' which 'we experience ourselves'.[80] Yet, when it came to the consideration of the agency of Polish – or, for that matter, Argentinian – workers, his attitude and analytical standpoint were reversed as the consideration of subjective drivers was replaced by the external observation of social trends as given facts. Commenting on the survey he and Göhre had proposed, Weber argued that even if 'the assessment of *subjective* factors [was] in the foreground' of their analysis, there was 'another phenomenon', 'this time pertaining to the *objective* situation' that needed to be considered, i.e., 'the situation of migrant workers'.[81] In other words, the migration of Polish seasonal workers figured as a purely objective factor in Weber's approach to the 'rural labour question' in the German East.

In what is at once a striking yet entirely coherent consequence of his normative understanding of *Kultur*, when it came to assessing the drivers of migration of *German* rural workers – either to the big cities or overseas – Weber emphasised their desire for autonomy, freedom and upward social mobility. This because, as he often pointed out, it was the rural workers 'who have it best

77 MWG I/4, p. 114.
78 See, for instance, MWG I/4, p. 374.
79 MWG I/4, p. 422.
80 MWG I/3, p. 920.
81 MWG I/4, p. 86.

and who have the highest social standing' that most often chose to leave the German countryside.[82] Hence the need to consider their ideal drivers.

The same dynamic of shaping the analytical approach in accordance with subjects' perceived level of culture emerges in the case of the (socially) lower-standing *German* labourers migrating *within* their native countryside. These workers, who also fit the denomination of *Sachsengänger*[83] or seasonal migrant laborers, were similar to Polish migrant workers in every respect with the exception of their ethnicity. Weber was challenged to provide an explanation of why these poor German workers migrated, considering the wages in their districts of origin were not necessarily lower than where they sought seasonal work. He concluded that two factors were in play, namely, a subjective desire to earn a living – even if temporarily – outside of the grip of their patriarchal masters, and the greater sums they were able to accumulate in the months they worked away from their homes. This was due, according to Weber, to the temporary lowering of their 'material and social-ethical level', which their families would never accept in the long term. Yet, when considering the parallel phenomenon of Polish migration, Weber abandoned this weighing of subjective and objective factors, since 'Russians and upper-Silesian Poles' did not temporarily lower their standard of life, but rather 'brought the lower cultural level of their native land to the districts they worked in'.[84]

Indeed, even if Weber applied a sliding – and therefore contingent – scale when considering the relative 'cultural status' of both classes as well as 'nationalities', when referring to Polish migrants he used language that suggested a much more static or intrinsic basis for their 'lower cultural standing':

> Gentleman, whoever wants to believe that we conduct national policy in the East due to 'chauvinist' grounds, cannot or does not want to understand what it is about. It is not possible to allow two nationalities with distinct bodily constitutions – differently constructed stomachs, to be very concrete – freely compete with each other as workers in the same area.[85]

Max Weber seemed surprised by the charge of 'chauvinism' that his attitude elicited when he addressed the Protestant Social Congress.[86] Though later in the

---

82 MWG I/4, p. 170.
83 See Zimmerman 2012, p. 188.
84 MWG I/4, p. 88.
85 MWG I/4, p. 182.
86 Ibid.

same intervention he would allude to the metaphorical aspect of the stomach comparison,[87] the passage above indicates (once more) that Weber was open to the idea that his political economy of cultural difference rested, to some extent, on a physiological basis.

If Weber was agnostic in this regard, when it came to the role of culture in economic life he claimed to have found two instances of hard empirical evidence; 1) the greater labour productivity and higher remuneration demands of ethnic German vis-à-vis Polish workers and 2) Germans' higher level of needs, which he believed could be demonstrated empirically by comparing their diets (based on grain, dairy and some meat) to that of Poles (mainly potatoes).[88]

Contrary to a strictly biological racism, Weber's sliding-scale of *Kultur* implied some mobility, i.e., it was not based on an entirely static hierarchy of supposed 'national/racial traits'; he thus allowed for the possibility 'to elevate the domestic [i.e., German-born – V.S.] Polish proletariat to the level of German *Kultur*'.[89] The condition to achieve this, however, was stopping the 'continued incursion of Eastern nomadic hordes, which undid this labour of *Kultur* and turned it into its opposite'.[90] This reasoning is what is behind Weber's frantic agitation against cross-border labour migration in his interventions on the 'rural labour question'.

In this sense, despite not being grounded *primarily* on perceived biological traits or on the innate superiority of certain ethnic groups over others, Max Weber's perspective at this juncture still rested on a hierarchisation of different peoples, cultures and groups that is akin to racist views. Angela Zimmerman has argued this hierarchic element qualifies Weber's thought as *de facto* racist, because it establishes 'a system of cultural differences that functions as effectively as race as a means of underwriting political and economic inequality'.[91] Weber's infamous remark that Germans had raised Poles 'from beasts to men'[92] demonstrates how his hierarchical concept of culture could constitute simply

87 MWG I/4, p. 191.

88 MWG I/3, pp. 898–9. Weber's recurrent reference to diet as an indicator of *Kultur* not only in his writings on the labor question, but also in his travels are of great analytical interest. Weber linked Polish migration and the expansion of capitalist agrarian enterprise in the countryside directly to the formation of a landowning proletariat living solely from 'potato and milk' (MWG I/3, p. 591). These and other considerations on the changes brought by capitalism to workers' diet and relation to food are revealing and have yet to be explored in the scholarship.

89 MWG I/4, p. 183.

90 Ibid.

91 Zimmerman 2006, p. 53.

92 MWG I/4, p. 622.

another mode of naturalising social inequality that is analogous in its effects, if not identical in its premises, to biological racism. Fundamentally, both forms of racism, cultural and biological, contribute to justify the oppression of a people, ethnic group or segment of the population by means of their exclusion from equal status as subjects.

That said, the fact that Weber's thinking along racial lines was *not* strictly biological did have important consequences. Foremost among them was the fact that it was also applicable – and had the same ideological effects – to the comparison of members of the same ethnic background, as in the case of Weber's attribution of varying levels of autonomy and self-consciousness to different segments of the *German* working class. Just as a German worker was above a German-born Pole, who, in turn, was above a Polish migrant in terms of *Kultur*,

> The amount of subjective feeling of contentment [*subjektiven Glückgefühls*] is greater in intellectually lower, lethargically resigned segments of the population than in any of you gentlemen here [Weber is addressing the Protestant Social Congress in 1894 – V.S.]; it's greater in the *Instmann* than in the peasant, greater in the lethargically subdued workers of the East than in the urban proletariat, greater in the beast than in man.[93]

The contrast of different segments of the German working classes along a sliding scale that goes from ignorant contentment to sober rationality in this passage closely mirrors Weber's global hierarchisation of ethnically distinct groups in terms of their 'level of *Kultur*'. The conceptual peculiarity of Weber's comparison of German workers from different regions – in contrast to when Germans and Poles were compared – resided in his emphasis on how 'relations of social stratification' in each area of the countryside 'ultimately played the decisive role in their [the workers' – V.S.] material situation'.[94] In other words, structures of social stratification were understood by Weber to play the central role in terms of the level of *Kultur* when he contrasted members of the same ethnicity.

This key building block of Weber's insight into the role of 'cultural difference' in economic life was also based on a finding from his study of East-Elbian workers. Weber realised that the way the rural working class was structured in a

93 MWG I/4, p. 339.
94 MWG I/4, p. 406.

given region, i.e., whether a middle-strata of workers was able to establish itself or whether proletarianisation had fully taken hold, was a key determinant for wage-levels and, beyond those, for 'the entire economic situation' of workers.[95] In a later intervention, Weber termed this decisive variable as the 'historically grounded cultural level of the working class'.[96]

It was Weber's comparison of the agrarian social structure in the provinces of Mecklenburg and Silesia in particular that provided the basis for this finding. Their contrast revealed a disparity in 'standard of life' that was just as significant as the difference in 'cultural level' between German rural workers and Polish migrants:

> It is exclusively or at least predominantly the terrible dietary customs and low standard of life of Silesian and Polish workers which led to the wages in the fertile districts of Mid-Silesia and Posen – despite higher grain prices – to be behind those of the scant Pommeranian areas; it is only or quite predominantly the high standard of life of the inhabitants of Mecklenburg, which has sustained high wage-levels there.[97]

Weber attributed the relatively prosperous situation of Mecklenburg's rural working class to the presence of a 'materially well-off, sedentary worker that is, nevertheless, not tied to the land and mostly originates from the peasantry, whose peculiar customs he tenaciously clings to'. Furthermore, the fact that the small properties of rural workers 'amounted to 30% of households' in Mecklenburg assured them a degree of independence from local landlords that 'eluded the potato-eating, small landowning proletariat of Silesia'.[98]

One historical factor that Weber understood to be at the root of Mecklenburg's peculiarity is highly revealing of his stance towards workers. Mecklenburg was what came closest to the ideal social structure Weber envisioned for the whole of the German Eastern countryside, as he would constantly point out. As it happens, rural workers in the region had successfully imposed limits to the exploitation by large landowners, first, because they had a sufficient amount of land to live from; second and most significantly, however, because they stopped the complete loss of common grazing lands and woodland – unlike in the rest of the German East – in a struggle Weber traced back to 'the

95 MWG I/3, p. 319.
96 MWG I/4, p. 401.
97 MWG I/3, p. 913.
98 Ibid.

year of 1848'.[99] In the case of Mecklenburg, therefore, some of the positive features of agrarian social structure were directly related to achievements of the rural labour movement in the revolutionary period of 1848/9, when workers managed to secure, among other things, a court of arbitration for disputes with landlords.[100]

Yet, it seemed difficult for Weber to accept that a movement from the lowest stratum of workers in that region had secured, by means of autonomous struggle, improvements to their conditions that still remained in place – and in the memories of these workers, as Weber would admit[101] – a half-century later. Weber thus added a stratifying rejoinder to this history of social strife, centred on these workers' particular ethics and sense of status. He remarked, namely, that the stance of Mecklenburg's rural workers was analogous to that of a 'peasantry threatened with dispossession by landlords', whilst the rest of the German East's rural proletariat 'remained relatively indolent at the time'.[102] Hence, despite referencing the legacy of 1848 in the region, Weber seemed to attribute the higher 'standard of life' of rural workers in Mecklenburg mainly to the survival of patriarchal relations with landlords. This was, in turn, 'without a doubt' rooted in 'the even more intensive German character of the rural workers of Mecklenburg', as he put it.[103]

The only form of social struggle Weber recognised in the countryside of his time was the 'latent' one between rural workers and landlord, with migration as the weapon of the former and the 'import' of foreign migrant workers as the instrument of the latter.[104] The lowering of *Kultur* that resulted from this form of class strife meant Weber saw it as a hopeless proposition for both sides: 'Class struggle in Eastern agriculture would be to wrestle on a sinking boat. Both sides would perish'.[105] Weber disputed the notion that the struggle from below on the part of rural workers could take a unified conscious form, considering how disparate he thought the interests of the different segments of the rural working class were. Thus, to Weber, only workers' actual displacement was in play in the German East, not a political *labour movement*; Weber's references to the rural labour movement during the revolution of 1848 notwithstanding, he saw no lessons to be drawn for the present situation. This was a telling example of

99 Ibid.
100 See MWG I/3, pp. 882–3, MWG I/4, p. 185.
101 MWG I/3, p. 882.
102 Ibid.
103 MWG I/3, p. 881.
104 MWG I/4, p. 419.
105 Ibid.

Weber's scepticism with regards to political action from below – a topic I will return to in Chapter 11. There was, however, a notable exception that deserves mention.

6 Conclusion: Xenophobia as Legitimate Class Consciousness? Weber's Critique Of Social Democrats' 'Dream of Racial and Cultural Equality'

One form of collective action by workers that Weber approved of were the outbursts of xenophobia on the part of 'higher-standing' German workers against migrant labourers. Weber's interest in *this* particular mode of labour mobilisation was clear as early as mid-1892, when he argued that the second survey on the situation of rural workers had to contemplate the 'stance of native workers towards imported [sic] foreign labourers'.[106] He was already convinced at that point that the absence of a 'more forceful expression' of the 'ill will' that 'no doubt existed' on the part of native workers towards migrants could only be due to a lack of 'organisation on the part of rural workers'.[107] Weber attributed, in fact, a central role to organised labour in counteracting the migration of foreign workers, as I will explore below. What I want to highlight at this point, however, is that his consideration of the interplay of labour struggle and 'cultural difference' went much deeper. It wasn't enough to establish the existence of 'ill will' towards migrant workers:

> It is [yet] unclear and [therefore] highly relevant to inquire how this ill will – assuming it is present – expresses itself psychologically, that is, whether, in reaction to the introduction of foreign labourers with a lower standard of life, a class consciousness – on a national basis or on the basis of cultural difference – asserts itself within native workers or if it is met merely with dull indolence.[108]

Weber seems to suggest that class consciousness need not have a purely social basis, as was the case in struggles against landlords; it could also have either 'national' *or* 'cultural' underpinnings, which means that he saw xenophobia on the basis of nationality as related, but not identical to one based on 'cul-

106 MWG I/4, pp. 88–9.
107 MWG I/4, p. 89.
108 Ibid.

tural difference'. This particular expression of class consciousness was rooted in the disparity in the 'standard of life' between migrants and native workers. It emerged where the better-off segments of the rural working class were predominant, as in the case of Mecklenburg. There,

> native workers dutifully cut themselves off from their [i.e., migrants' – V.S.] influence; they look down with contempt at the low standard of life of the *Sachsengänger*. Further East, where this element is absent and there is a danger of assimilation, there the truly grave danger posed by migrant workers begins.[109]

The *shared* cultural status Weber attributed to the lower-standing German rural proletarian and the Polish migrant worker, respectively, is reflected in his fear of their 'assimilation' and the consequent debasement of German *Kultur*.[110] The fact that Weber found that the fully dispossessed rural proletarian also showed a tendency to sympathise with Social Democracy – whereas the *landowning* worker was closer to bourgeois democracy[111] – provided yet another reason for his rejection of the wholesale transformation of agriculture into a capitalist enterprise, as was well underway in Silesia.

The interrelated dangers of a widespread proletarianisation of the rural working class in the German East and of their 'assimilation' with Polish migrant workers explain why the internationalist component of Social Democracy's programme was particularly unsettling for Weber. As the next chapter will explore in detail, if Weber was ready to accept that a segment of highly-skilled workers be granted the right to collective bargaining to 'sort out their [economic] interests' and even earn 'a share of political power', this was predicated on a combination of imperialism (thus assuring markets and cheap raw materials) and of a relative stabilisation in the status of labourers (i.e., with their ascension into the middle class). The latter was to be achieved by limiting the expansion of the 'industrial reserve army'[112] in the cities and blocking foreign migration into the countryside. Social Democracy's internationalism was a clear impediment to these attempts to control the supply of labour power; most of all, however, it stood in the way of the development of a brand of collective consciousness rooted in 'cultural difference', one that affirmed the

---

109 MWG I/4, p. 172.

110 See MWG I/4, p. 727. Weber's use of the notion of 'assimilation' again points to the porous limits between cultural and biological naturalisations of human difference.

111 See MWG I/3, p. 742.

112 MWG I/4, p. 82.

superiority of 'higher-standing' workers' not only with regards to Polish migrants, but also to colonial subjects.

From Weber's perspective, fanning popular chauvinism was instrumental to gaining the support of workers for a programme of imperial expansion. Which is why Social Democracy's internationalist critique of imperialism was particularly aggravating to him. As Weber put it in a public lecture of 1895: 'This failure to recognize the national importance, the power of one's own state by German workers is even more dangerous than their social theories'. In the talk, he also denounced Social Democracy's rejection of national borders, whose economic importance, he argued, had been proven by the historic use of tariffs to protect early industry and, more recently, agriculture from foreign competition. Rejecting the existence of borders was, as Weber put it, tantamount to ignoring their 'natural' basis, i.e., 'racial difference', and, consequently, to overlooking the dangers of a debasement of *Kultur*. '*The ones with the most at stake here, German workers, are not yet aware of this*'. There were, however, precedents of workers acting upon their 'national interests': 'In Australia, the immigration of Chinese workers was prohibited by workers who came to power in some states'.[113] Alas, 'in its dream of racial and cultural equality', as Weber termed it, 'international Social Democracy overlooks this to its own detriment'.[114] Only with the development of a national outlook in the context of imperial expansion would the German working class have in his view both a safeguard against competition from foreign workers and a legitimate claim to a greater say in the political affairs of the nation:

> Will international Social Democracy be coherent and also fraternise with blacks and Chinese? English workers owe their political successes to the power position of England. As long as *power* is decisive [in the struggle] between nations, the modern economy will rest on *national* foundations. Workers must obviously have a share in political power and, through the establishment of collective bargaining, be put in the position to settle their own affairs.[115]

Hence, two decades before the debate on imperialism reached its maturity within the Second International,[116] Max Weber already understood that imper-

113 MWG I/4, pp. 726–7.
114 MWG I/4, p. 724.
115 Ibid.
116 As Day and Gaido (2011, p. 1) remark, the theory of imperialism 'originated during the Spanish-American and Boer Wars (1898–1902) and reached maturity with World War I, a

ial expansion was the necessary foreign policy counterpart to the proto-Fordist arrangement he proposed on the domestic front.[117] According to the newspaper reports on this lecture, a Social Democrat in the audience sharply criticised Weber's intervention, though we do not learn what his precise words were. Only Weber's rebuttal with 'fine humour' is mentioned, more specifically how he recounted that at a recent international conference of miners the theories of German Social Democrats elicited the laughter of a delegation of practical English workers.[118]

decade and a half marked by the accelerated arms-race and mounting apprehension of disaster'.

117 For a discussion of the relationship between Fordism and imperialism, which Max Weber presciently identified, see Lipietz 1982.

118 MWG I/4, p. 728.

CHAPTER 11

Breaking the 'Solidarity of All the Ruled': Culture and Imperialism in Max Weber's Solution to the 'Labour Question'

1 Introduction: Max Weber between the Liberal Brentano and the Socialist Engels

> Genius fashions itself through another great genius, less by assimilation than by friction.[1]
>
> HEINRICH HEINE 1834

In an essay published in 1885 in the scientific journal of German Social Democracy, *Die neue Zeit*, Friedrich Engels took stock of the changes in the situation of the working class in England in the four decades since the publication of his path-breaking study on the topic. Notably, Engels remarked how two 'protected' segments of the working class had experienced lasting improvements in their condition during that time. The first were factory hands who, thanks to labour regulations introduced by Parliament, now had a shorter working day and no longer experienced the most extreme forms of exploitation in the workplace. The second was comprised by large trade unions:

> They are the organisations of those trades in which the labour of *adult men* predominates, or is alone applicable. Here the competition neither of women and children nor of machinery has so far weakened their organised strength. The engineers, the carpenters and joiners, the bricklayers, are each of them a power ... They form an aristocracy among the working class; they have succeeded in enforcing for themselves a relatively comfortable position, and they accept it as final.[2]

1 'Genius bildet sich durch einen andern großen Genius, weniger durch Assimilierung als durch Reibung', HSA 8, p. 168.

2 MEW 21, p. 194. For the quotes from Engels in this chapter I will continue to refer to the volume

The 'labour aristocracy' was, Engels added, 'the model working-men … for any sensible capitalist' and – as he would amend in the preface to the 1892 German reissue of *The Situation of the Working Class in England* – 'of the philistine Mr. Brentano as well'.[3] Lujo Brentano (1844–1931) had built his career as a political economist in large part through his efforts at comparing state responses to social conflict in Germany and Britain. In his 1871/72 work on English trade unions, *The Worker Guilds of the Present*, he argued that the solution to the 'labour question' consisted not in a 'People's state' [*Volksstaat*] ruled by workers, as Social Democrats proposed, but in the establishment by ruling authorities of an 'institutional framework' that satisfies 'workers' needs' by recognising 'their interests and circumstances'. While the introduction of universal suffrage had contemplated German workers' *political* demands, Brentano argued, their economic and cultural needs remained unfulfilled.[4] Factory regulations, the legalisation of collective bargaining and the establishment of arbitration courts for labour disputes were the three sets of measures Brentano advocated to address those needs, with trade unions playing a central role by both limiting competition between workers[5] and serving as the main self-help organisations of the working class.[6] But their relevance went further: Brentano saw in trade unions fundamentally conservative organisations, which reinforced property relations, in contrast to the 'Social Democrat-like Chartists', with their unpatriotic and levelling demands.[7] Brentano was convinced, in fact, that the presence of strong trade unions had been key for the peaceful thwarting of the Chartist challenge to the established order in England in the 1830s and 1840s, a considerable feat in a period marked by uprisings and revolutions in Continental Europe.

As Brentano published his study in 1871/72, internationalist socialism and German Social Democracy were emerging as threats to the status quo; their parallels with Chartism suggested that the same stabilising force within the labour movement that had counteracted the latter could once again play this role:

---

and page number from the *Marx-Engels Werke* edition, but will be exceptionally using the English translations (with small corrections) from the volume *Marx and Engels on Britain* (Moscow: Progress Publishers, 1953) available at *marxists.org*.

3 MEW 2, p. 645.

4 See Brentano 1872, pp. 318–20.

5 This included preventing the wages of skilled workers from falling to a level in which, according to Brentano, only an Irish worker's needs would be fulfilled (1872, p. 331). Thus, just as Weber would do two decades later, Brentano framed trade unions as instrumental in rearing an *ethnically homogenous* higher segment of the working class.

6 Brentano 1872, pp. 325–8.

7 Brentano 1872, pp. 332–3.

> It is notable how, by pointing to the attachment to the established order as that which is most in line with their needs, the practical good sense of the mass of skilled workers showed its superiority to the spirit of theoreticians; it will also lastingly keep trade unions free from theories directed at the subversion of property, marriage and of society as a whole.[8]

With Social Democracy and the Second International having achieved a prominent political role in the 1890s, Brentano's comparison was taken up by a new generation of political economists with a concern for the 'labour question'. A young Werner Sombart, for instance, called Chartism the very 'first organised proletarian movement'.[9] In his lessons on *The Labour Question and the Labour Movement* of 1895 and 1898, Max Weber also referenced an article by Brentano characterising Chartism as 'the first social-democratic movement of the nineteenth century'.[10] The basis for the parallel with the SPD was the fact that Chartism had been a 'political' labour movement, i.e., one that went beyond strictly economic-corporative demands, and eventually stressed the conflict of capital and labour. Following in the footsteps of Brentano, both Sombart and Weber would converge on the hypothesis that fostering a moderate trade union-led labour movement was the best means to channel class strife into a legal and organised form and, above all, to lend more weight to demands that did not call the economic, social and gender order into question.

As I will argue in this chapter, what distinguished Max Weber's contribution to this debate was his emphasis on the need for policies that *actively fostered* the social bearers of the moderate workers' movement, i.e., skilled labour. With England as his reference point, Brentano – who had argued that 'the solution to the social question of today would be pursued by the better-off, skilled workers'[11] – was no doubt a key source for his considerations.[12]

An examination of Weber's recently-published materials from the 1890s[13] shows, however, that he had another central interlocutor when it came to drawing lessons from England, namely, Friedrich Engels. This connection has, not surprisingly, been mostly ignored in the scholarship so far.[14] Weber's intellec-

8 Brentano 1872, p. 332.
9 Sombart 1896, pp. 34–5.
10 MWG III/4, p. 281.
11 Brentano 1872, p. 328.
12 See *Einleitung* in MWG III/4, p. 31 and Rehmann 2015, p. 65.
13 Especially his teaching materials gathered in section III of the MWG.
14 A notable exception is Rehmann 2015, pp. 139–43.

tual kinship with the social-liberal Brentano is, for one, much easier to fathom. Yet, while both men were united by a 'common bourgeois identity' which was also at 'the root of a political affinity',[15] the common ground between them had clear limits.[16] Brentano's Kantian brand of humanism,[17] for instance, was entirely foreign to the Nietzsche-inspired Max Weber;[18] moreover, Weber did not share Brentano's rather idealised image of British politics, which guided the latter's lifelong, ultimately failed attempts at rekindling liberalism in Germany.[19] In this regard – and despite all that separated him from revolutionary socialism – Weber found in Friedrich Engels's work a more thorough and nuanced account of social conflict in England. The main lesson he drew from Engels pertained to how the establishment and preservation of a higher-standing segment of workers was instrumental in the consolidation of bourgeois hegemony, both in terms of breaking the power of agrarian conservatism and in counteracting challenges to it from below. As Engels put it:

> From the opposition of Chartists, not against free-trade, but against the transformation of free-trade into the only decisive question for the nation, manufactures had learned – and they learn more with each day – that the bourgeoisie can never attain full social and political rule over the nation, except with the help of the working class.[20]

Engels's insight that it was the congealment of a class *constellation* that was at the basis of the bourgeoisie's pre-eminence in England – as opposed to Brentano's focus on the role of institutional and legal frameworks – clearly had an impact on Max Weber. In his Freiburg inaugural lecture of 1895, Weber remarked that the function of social policy was not 'bringing delight to the world', but fostering a new class arrangement that would bring about the 'unification of the nation' and 'propel modern economic development' in Imperial Germany. The emergence of a 'labour aristocracy' – the very concept Engels had fashioned – was a decisive component of this social and political transformation. In Weber's words:

15 Ghosh 2009, p. 65.
16 Ghosh 2009, pp. 63–6.
17 See Lehnert 2012, p. 121.
18 See Majul 2018.
19 For a critical account of the trajectory of Lujo Brentano that has still not been outdone in its depth of scholarly treatment and historical perspective, see Sheehan 1966.
20 MEW 21, p. 191.

> If [social policy] were in fact able to create a 'labour aristocracy', which would deliver the bearer of political judgement we miss today in the labour movement, only then may the spear, which the arm of the bourgeoisie still does not appear strong enough to carry, be placed on those broad shoulders. The road to this seems long.[21]

Thus, whereas Brentano advocated a 'liberalism reoriented to social policy and anchored in the middle classes'[22] as a compromise between free-marketers and Social Democracy, Weber called for a more fundamental shift in the configuration of class power within the nation, one which involved an important, if subordinate role for the working class.[23] As this final chapter will examine, Weber embedded this claim in the defence of a larger role for Imperial Germany on the world stage (11.2) and of the German state in reshaping class relations domestically (11.3); finally, he extended a central role to culture in shoring up this new class arrangement at the level of subjectivity – and not least in the minds of workers (11.4). Thus, what set Max Weber apart as an intellectual was the fact that, beyond a mere political commentator or social-policy expert, he was, in the words of Jan Rehmann, 'an ethico-political reformer', who strove 'to modernise German capitalism according to a Puritan-Americanist model'.[24] Though this 'Puritan' component was still undeveloped in the writings of the 1890s, it is Weber's insights on class, culture and imperialism from this decade that informed the – mostly overlooked – political dimensions of his seminal work of 1904–5, *The Protestant Ethic and the 'Spirit' of Capitalism*.[25] I will approach these insights systematically in the sections that follow.

2 Imperialism and the Labour Aristocracy: Looking towards Britain with Engels as Mediator

The fact that Max Weber shaped his outlook on social struggle in part through a selective appropriation of Friedrich Engels's views on England deserves closer examination. It is another window into the peculiar dialectic that governed

21 MWG I/4, p. 572.
22 Lehnert 2012, p. 122.
23 See Rehmann 2015, pp. 51–8.
24 Rehmann 2015, p. 384.
25 On the question of the continuities and ruptures in Max Weber's thought between a supposedly youthful phase in the 1890s and a 'mature' period starting in the 1900s, see the Epilogue below.

Max Weber's relationship to the German labour movement and its intellectuals. Two separate but interrelated dimensions of this relationship are in play here; first, the fact that the rise of German Social Democracy had impressed upon Weber and a few other members of his generation the need to account for working-class politics as a key factor in modern social struggle; second, the imperative of counteracting the revolutionary ideology which ballasted Social Democracy's worldview. Hence, Weber's project of political and social modernisation of Imperial Germany neither ignored workers' demands nor simply aimed to repress their organisations; rather, its goal was to win over and integrate the upper segments of the working class into a new hegemonic configuration that simultaneously shored up bourgeois rule and diffused the revolutionary threat from below. Weber's reading of Engels is of particular interest because it shows that the former's proposed strategy of integration and neutralisation of the labour movement in the political and economic spheres had an equivalent at the ideological plane, namely, the selective appropriation of concepts from historical materialism. In other words, Weber did not denounce or demonise Friedrich Engels and his revolutionary worldview; rather, he teased out the elements he found useful from his own social and political standpoint whilst rejecting Engels's fundamental critique of bourgeois society and internationalism.

This is evident in Weber's fairly well-known use – and reframing – of core Marxist concepts such as 'class struggle' and 'class consciousness', the first instances of which I will examine in detail below. Yet, it is Weber's pioneering adoption of the notion of 'labour aristocracy', coined by Engels to shed light on an emerging cleavage within the English working class, that is most revealing of this dynamic of selective appropriation.

The late Engels's conceptualisation of the emergence of a new fraction of workers in the decades since the publication of his 1845 work was part of his two-pronged effort to explain why revolutionary socialism had had so little success in England since the defeat of Chartism and what would be necessary for its re-emergence. Engels drew a connection between the rise of the 'labour aristocracy' and the expansion of British imperialism:

> The truth is this: during the period of England's industrial monopoly the English working class have, to a certain extent, shared in its benefits. These benefits were very unequally parcelled out amongst them; a privileged minority pocketed most, but even the great mass obtained at least a temporary share now and then.[26]

---

26 MEW 21, p. 197.

Crucially, Engels did not believe this monopoly position was sustainable in the long-term and argued – presciently – that the organisation of the sectors of the English working class that did not benefit from it would eventually bring back the struggle for socialism to its shores.[27] That was, however, not yet clear as Weber picked up on Engels's concept of the labour aristocracy and its connection to imperialism, insights that were absent in more apologetic accounts of British history such as that of Lujo Brentano.

Weber's appropriation of Engels's conceptualisation is noteworthy, because it constitutes a striking act of political reframing. It is from the vantage point of its role in *diffusing* social strife on English soil that Weber raised the question of how to foster a 'labour aristocracy' in Imperial Germany.[28] As Jan Rehmann has argued, '[w]hat was formulated as a critique in Engels now becomes the economic justification for a "proletarian" imperialism'.[29] Yet, Weber did not simply seek to mechanically transpose elements of British social and political reality to Imperial Germany – as was the case with many of Brentano's proposals. Instead, he took into account two key disparities between both contexts; first, the fact that the Kaiserreich had not yet established a foothold in world politics in any way comparable to that of the British Empire[30] (whose pre-eminence it would, therefore, need to break); second, the presence of a labour movement that was not only rising in strength but was spearheaded by German Social Democracy. This modern-day Chartism presented a much more fundamental challenge to the established order than its British predecessor had had; German Social Democracy was not only much larger and better-organised than its British forerunners of the 1830s and 1840s; at the core of its programme was also a more sophisticated and consistent critique of the capitalist system and

27 Ibid.

28 On the concept of 'labour aristocracy', see Hans Willi Weinzen, 'Arbeiteraristokratie', HKWM 1, 1994, 422–9. While there is mention of the 'best paid segment of the working class, i.e., its aristocracy' in Marx's *Capital* (MEW 23, p. 697), Engels was primarily responsible for the development of the concept. It would, however, only take on greater importance within Marxist debate through its use by Lenin in his critique of the parties of the Second International after 1914. It is interesting to note that Weber's suggestion that the rise of a 'labour aristocracy' would be synonymous with the moderation of Social Democracy rests on the same insight as Lenin's, even if their stances on reformist currents in the labour movement were diametrically opposed. The fact that Weber came to this insight – even if by way of Engels – *two decades before* Lenin is all the more remarkable and shows just how attuned he was to developments in the labour movement internationally.

29 Rehmann 2015, p. 139.

30 Which does not mean arguing that Imperial Germany's colonial endeavours in the late nineteenth century were negligible or inconsequential both in domestic and geopolitical terms and not least for the peoples under its yoke (see Conrad 2013).

of state power. Crucially, this critique of the status quo also included a decided rejection of colonialism and Empire-building.[31]

Weber's glowing stance on imperialism and Engels's critique of it are, in this sense, like mirror images that their antagonistic political polarity has inverted:

> The interest in the power of the national state is greater to no one than to the proletarian, if he extends his reflection beyond the coming day. The highest-standing groups of workers in England would not be able to maintain their standard of life for a single day – in spite of all trade unions – if their empire's international power position came to decline.[32]

If, in the passage above, Weber initially addresses 'the proletariat', i.e., the class in its entirety, the reference to England adds the caveat that only a privileged segment of workers, i.e., the 'labour aristocracy', are 'benefactors' of the British Empire. Hence, relying on Engels's pioneering analysis, Max Weber showed the pathway for the integration of a strategic fraction of workers into the established order in Imperial Germany.

This economically more advantageous position required, however, a greater level of *Kultur*, as indicated by Weber's reference to the need for workers to look 'beyond the coming day', i.e. beyond their immediate needs. Indeed, Weber will almost always follow up his remarks on a possible improvement of workers' economic, but above all, political standing with admonitions regarding the need for them to break with what he considered a narrow class standpoint:

> That we do not yet have an ambitious [*großdenkend*] proletariat is something I have already mentioned; yet whoever has given up hope that we may acquire one in the form of a class-conscious, but far-seeing labour aristocracy, has given up hope on the political future of the fatherland.[33]

In other words, Weber was convinced that the higher-standing segments of the working class had a key role to play in the political future of the Kaiserreich, but that role was contingent on the acquisition of a new form of subjectivity that placed *Kultur* before mere economic demands and, to that effect, the

31 As forcefully argued by Guettel: 'Despite numerous statements to the contrary in recent scholarship, until 1914 the SPD's fundamental objections against colonialism held firm' even if 'they were not shared by all of its members' (2012, p. 478). Also in this direction, see Short 2012.

32 MWG I/4, p. 341.

33 MWG I/4, p. 344.

interests of the nation before those of class.[34] As with all of Weber's considerations on inequality, whether global or domestic, a 'higher' cultural status is framed as the subjective core of the superior economic situation of the 'labour aristocracy' vis-à-vis other workers. Along these lines, at the Verein conference of 1893, Weber had suggested to Social Democrats that if socialism was to fulfil even a part of its goals it would need a 'culturally very high-standing worker population'.[35]

Weber remained coherent with this position on the relationship of working-class politics and culture a few years later, as what he hoped would become a 'national party of bourgeois freedom', Friedrich Naumann's *National-Social Association*, was launched. During the debates on the new party's program in 1896, Weber stood for the inclusion of 'all ascending segments of the people' in its ranks, including 'all *ascending segments* in the working class',[36] with upward mobility here referring as much to 'cultural level' as to economic situation.

Weber painted the preconditions for the detachment of an 'ascending' segment of workers from the rest of the working class in the clearest terms; a 'labour aristocracy' emerged when workers join up in a coalition 'with the goal of taking up the power struggle with capital in an organised fashion'. This reframes their dealings with employers along the lines of a 'compromise between force and force'[37] – a remark reminiscent of a passage from the chapter on the working day in Marx's *Capital*: 'Between equal rights, force decides'.[38] Crucially, however, Marx is not referring to the struggle of a privileged sector, but of the whole working class against a 'general capitalist' (i.e., capitalists taken as a collective entity catalysing the capital valorisation process). Not because he argued these classes faced each other as two monoliths in the political arena, but because he was addressing the ultimate social and historical stakes of the struggle for the reduction of the working day. In *Capital*, this achievement is highlighted precisely because Marx understood it as a victory of and for the entire working class. Rather than a contingent arrangement of a sector of workers with specific employers, it impacted the elementary condition of the worker as a seller of labour power, hence the fundamental significance of this struggle.

Max Weber, on the other hand, was interested in how a higher-standing segment of workers with better wages and working conditions had emerged

34 See section 11.3 below.
35 MWG I/4, p. 197.
36 MWG I/4, p. 620 – my emphasis.
37 MWG III/4, p. 195.
38 MEW 23, p. 249.

in England. Rather than unity, the precondition was, precisely, a break in the 'solidarity of *all* the oppressed'.[39] Crucially, this would only be sustainable within the framework of an imperial power. Here was a key point of disagreement with Brentano, who, in light of the strongly imperialist content of the National-Social Association's programme, criticised Friedrich Naumann as a 'colonial fanatic', despite his affinities with the latter's social-liberal positions.[40] This critique no doubt extended to Max Weber, who was adamant that German workers depended upon imperial expansion for the improvement of their economic situation, as he clearly articulated in 1896:

> it is a vital question for us, that the broad masses of our people become aware that only the outward projection of Germany's power position can afford them lasting employment [*Erwerb*] domestically and the possibility to ascend. It is they, the progeny from below, whose fate is, above all, inseparably tied to the rise of Germany to a political and economic world power, to the power and the greatness of the fatherland.[41]

The fact that German imperial expansion was the central precondition for any lasting improvement in the situation of workers in a reformed Reich makes it plain that the new status Weber extended to workers within the latter was synonymous with their continued political and ideological subjection. Weber's recognition of the legitimacy of workers' political engagement was, in other words, framed in such a way as to exclude emancipatory (and internationalist) perspectives. This was, in turn, coherent with his argument that only a higher-standing segment of workers was in the position to fulfil a greater political role in the life of the nation.

More significantly, Max Weber did not only frame worker support for imperialism in terms of a utilitarian logic or 'quid pro quo' with the capitalist class, i.e., as a sacrifice of principles in exchange for economic advantages, but as a stance consciously grounded on a notion of cultural superiority and rejection of cross-border solidarity. Indeed, Weber understood nationalism and 'chauvinism' as the logical complements to a position of economic advantage derived from bolstering imperialism. This gave Weber's gesture of outreach towards workers as political actors a clearly conservative edge, considering the economic and political advantages they acquired within this framework bore a heavy price in terms of class autonomy. Referring to Friedrich Naumann's then analogous

---

39 MWG III/4, p. 195.

40 See Lehnert 2012, p. 120.

41 MWG I/4, pp. 610–11.

brand of 'social imperialism', Asaf Kedar has stressed the profoundly ambiguous character of the promise to afford (a segment of) workers 'a greater role in steering the national ship as well as a higher material standard of living' within the framework of imperialism; such an offer was predicated on 'domesticating the workers, excluding them from the domain of internationalist politics, neutering their revolutionary energies, and casting their subjectivity into a German national mould'.[42] Moreover, Weber was clearly aware that the formation of a 'labour aristocracy' was synonymous with relegating unqualified workers to the same degree of exploitation and to the same dire living conditions prevalent since the period of early industrialisation,[43] as well as with an acquiescence to the deportation of Polish migrant workers and, not least, the oppression of other peoples abroad. Max Weber had no illusions as to what his support for the outward projection of German power meant in terms of militarism and violence, remarking in 1896 that 'a dozen warships on the East-Asian coast are at times more valuable than a dozen rescindable trade-agreements'.[44] Weber knew all of this was contingent on whether the 'labour aristocracy' would place their upward mobility before solidarity with the rest of workers, i.e., if a class consciousness based on unitary struggle and internationalism would retreat before a more individualistic form of self-awareness and notions of superiority anchored on 'national' and 'cultural' difference.[45]

∴

One essential condition for Weber's programme of proto-Fordist bourgeois modernisation to come to fruition, was, of course, that its own main benefactors, the strategic segments of Imperial Germany's industrial and financial bourgeoisie, would adhere to it themselves and place their political influence behind the reforms – and reconfiguration of class relations – it presupposed. This wager began to seem far-fetched when the political situation in Imperial Germany took a conservative turn starting in late-1894 with the dismissal of Chancellor Caprivi and the end of the 'New Course'. As Geoff Eley has argued, in Germany

> the different fractions of the bourgeoisie each had their own reasons for doubting the advantages of democratic change, but their common

42 Kedar 2010, p. 72.
43 See 11.3 below.
44 MWG I/4, p. 610.
45 See 11.4 below.

> and justified assumption was that greater parliamentary powers would redound to the benefit of the SPD, by that time [1893] the largest single party.[46]

The same rationale extended to state social policy, which was not only deemed ineffective in the fight against Social Democracy, but very much to its advantage, as Saarland industrialist Stumm-Halberg polemically stated in a January 1895 speech. His call for a renewed crackdown on the labour movement and blanket condemnation of social policy advocates lent this phase of Imperial German history his name (die 'Era Stumm').[47] In another key development that hampered Weber's anticipation of a 'constructive' and 'ambitious' role for organised labour, moderate elements within Social Democracy had failed to gain the upper hand within the party. Crucially, their defence of an agrarian programme anchored on the expansion of small tenant and peasant properties – i.e., one analogous to Weber's own proposals – was defeated in the SPD's congresses of 1894 and 1895 in favour of a policy of collectivisation of large properties that aimed to establish worker cooperatives in the countryside.[48]

In other words, political developments indicated that, beyond the reactionary Kaiser Wilhelm II and Prussian agrarians, key components of Imperial Germany's urban ruling classes did not favour Weber's proposals of bourgeois modernisation as a response to the decline of liberalism and the threat of Social Democracy. On the other hand, the SPD's reformist wing led by Georg von Vollmar and, later in the decade, Eduard Bernstein, would fail to gain the upper hand within the party.

Weber's reaction in the second half of the 1890s was to make his arguments ever more forcefully, but from an increasingly isolated position. This became patent, for instance, during the debate on the programme of Friedrich Naumann's *National-Social Association* in late 1896. Naumann's aim was to establish a party of social and political reform uniting enlightened members of the capitalist elites, liberals disgruntled with the existing party landscape and labour movement moderates. The framework for this constellation was a nationalist and openly imperialist platform that did not denounce Germany's monarchical constitution, aiming rather to give it a social content. The result was an ambiguous formation that did not conform to Weber's favoured political strategy. The party's lack of a decisive positioning in the political spectrum was especially ominous to Max Weber:

46 Eley 1984, p. 122.

47 See Kott 2014, pp. 53–4.

48 See Lehmann 1970, pp. 191–201.

> Do have clarity on this. You have today the one and only choice of which of the antagonistic interests of the current leading classes you want to support: bourgeois or agrarian-feudal. A political engagement that does not take this into consideration is utopia. All aspiring new parties stand before the choice of whether they want to foster bourgeois development or unwittingly support feudal reaction. Even if you do not want to, and believe you can take a third route and conduct a politics of the fourth estate [i.e., of the working class – V.S.], what you will actually achieve is always and exclusively the support of one of these two interests. Between them you must choose ....[49]

The passage sees Max Weber revert to the old adage that any fracture in the 'modernising' opposition to conservatism, i.e., any detachment of a socialist element from within the liberal-led bloc, is necessarily and in all circumstances, 'grist for the mill' of feudal reaction. This harkened back to German liberalism's stance in the debates of the 1840s,[50] more specifically to its emphatic rejection of autonomous working-class politics. Within this frame, any political project from below aiming to set an alternative pathway of social transformation vis-à-vis Weber's proto-Fordist bourgeois modernisation is dismissed as 'utopian' and, at bottom, functional to conservative rule.

In terms of assessing the stakes of Weber's appropriation of socialist thought and especially the work of Friedrich Engels, this stance is revealing. Weber's engagement with workers' standpoint, while constituting a break with long-standing patriarchal stances of the German upper classes towards lower strata, ultimately denied their effective political and intellectual autonomy by 1) assigning them a structurally subaltern role in a reformed Imperial Germany and 2) by framing a combination of bourgeois individualism and popular chauvinism as a superior form of class consciousness vis-à-vis revolutionary socialism and internationalist solidarity. Conversely, Friedrich Engels was convinced as early as 1845 that English workers 'who can barely read and much less write, nevertheless know very well what *their interest is* and what *the interest of the nation as a whole is*'.[51]

The central contradiction of Weber's outlook in the 1890s consists precisely in his simultaneous *consideration* of workers' drivers, culminating in the central role he attributed to their longing for freedom, and *flat out refusal* of the notion that workers' interests could anchor those of the entire nation. This insight was

49 MWG I/4, p. 621.
50 See Chapter 6.
51 MEW 2, p. 342, my highlights.

precisely what the young Friedrich Engels's study of the working class in England had converged on; he saw workers as constituting more than simply 'a distinctive class with distinctive interests and principles and with a distinctive perspective vis-à-vis all propertied classes'. It was in these individuals 'as Working Men', Engels argued, that 'the strength and possibilities of development of the nation rested'.[52]

This antagonism at the level of political horizon is decisive to understand not only the specific intellectual relationship Weber established with Engels, but also the former's general stance towards working-class politics, with its combined gestures of engagement and subjection. As such, it is also a case study for the enlightened German bourgeoisie's troubled relationship to labour in Imperial Germany.

3 Fordism as Fate? Weber's Two-Staged Understanding of Social Conflict in the 'Factory System'

It is not only the concept of 'labour aristocracy' – and the insight of its connection to imperialism – that can be traced back to an appropriation of Friedrich Engels's work on Max Weber's part. The notion of 'objective class hatred',[53] which Weber used to describe the antagonism between workers and employers under a system of impersonal subjection to capital,[54] and his use of the Chartist expression 'knife and fork questions'[55] – meaning fundamental material interests – are both traceable to Engels's *The Situation of the Working Class in England*.[56] The same is true of the concept of 'industrial reserve army', which Weber will turn to on occasion to stress the pressures that mass migration from the countryside exerted on the urban proletariat.[57] Indeed, Weber openly

52 MEW 2, p. 455.

53 MWG I/4, p. 328, p. 330.

54 See MWG III/4, p. 265.

55 MWG I/4, p. 340.

56 See MEW 2, p. 343, p. 446.

57 See MWG I/4, p. 755, p. 790. Though it would be further developed by Marx, the concept of a 'reserve of labour', i.e., a population 'surplus' generated by the process of capital accumulation and functional to it, first appeared in Engels's *The Situation of the Working Class in England* in 1845 (See Cyrus Bina, 'industrielle Reservearmee', HKWM 6/II, 2004, 1003–4). Weber was also aware of Marx's further development of the concept in *Capital* (See MWG III/4, p. 214, p. 228). It delivered a key justification for Weber's call for 'internal colonisation', since he used it to base his claim that the corresponding decrease in migration to the cities would benefit industrial workers, who would face less competition (See MWG I/4, p. 787, p. 790).

stated his esteem for the young Engels's writings,[58] in which he found 'entirely new points of view of high scientific value'.[59] This admiration even extended to Engels's 'modest, selfless' personality.[60] He was, in turn, much less amicable towards Marx, whom he described in his course notes as a

> Domineering character with boundless personal ambition
> Without emotional dispositions
> Belief in his mission to rule over all intellects
> *This*, and not his rulership over the masses, in fact his goal.
> *Disdain* for his collaborators and the masses.[61]

His divergent esteem for both men aside, perhaps the most relevant product of Weber's enthusiastic reading of the young Engels – and of Marx's *Capital*, which he does not acknowledge as openly – was his two-stage framework for understanding social conflict in industrial contexts, which he explicitly based on 'the results of [Engels's] valuable research effort'.[62] This framework, derived from an analysis of developments in England, was meant to provide a clear conceptual basis for Weber's appraisal of the labour movement's prospects in Imperial Germany.

Weber expounds it in his aforementioned lessons on the 'labour question' and the labour movement, which he taught in 1895 in Freiburg and – with small modifications – in 1898 in Heidelberg.[63] In a key passage of these lessons, Weber argues that the nature of work shifted with the establishment of what he called the nineteenth-century 'factory system'; the key change was the fact that personal bonds between master and workers ceased to play a decisive role in relations of production. This was due to the fact that the 'remuneration the worker receives for his commodity of labour power' – another direct reference

58 In the notes to his lessons on the 'labour question' and the labour movement, Weber characterises Engels's study from 1845 as a 'standard work' of 'high scientific value' (MWG III/4, p. 171).

59 MWG III/4, p. 288. In another passage of the notes from the same lessons, Weber called Engels's *The Origin of the Family, Private Property and the State* of 1884 an 'achievement'; his *Anti-Dühring* of 1878, in turn, was 'scientifically valuable and measured' (MWG III/4, p. 172).

60 MWG III/4, p. 172.

61 MWG III/4, p. 174.

62 MWG III/4, p. 267.

63 Weber's personal lecture notes and a students' reproduction of the course's contents – clearly matching the former – were published in MWG III/4. The course was called 'The German labour question in the city and the countryside' in Freiburg and 'The labour question and the labour movement' in its Heidelberg iteration.

to Marxian concepts – became a function of 'the general tendencies of price formation, over which the master who acquires his labour [sic] has no influence'. As a result of the 'interchangeable' character of workers, 'the personal interest of the master over them is lowered to a minimum'. Finally, in light of the same reciprocally-determined process of depersonalisation and class formation, employers also become interchangeable in the eyes of workers.[64]

There can be no doubt that Karl Marx's characterisation of the 'impersonal power of money', as opposed to the 'power of landed property based on personal relations of servitude and rule'[65] is a key source – if not the sole basis – for Max Weber's stress on the impersonal 'rule of capital'.[66] Weber's references to this phenomenon in a review of Friedrich Naumann's work *Was heißt Christlich-Sozial?* [What does Christian-Social mean?], for instance, show great similarities with a passage from Marx's *Capital*, where the latter describes how, to workers, the interrelation between their collective labour appears 'ideally as a plan, and practically as the authority of the capitalists, as the power of an external will, which subjugates their agency to its aim'.[67] Weber, in turn, speaks of how 'modern development puts the *impersonal*, purely business-like [*geschäftlich*] rule of the *class* of proprietors, in the place of personal relations, [its] tributes paid to an unknown, invisible and impalpable power …'.[68] Which is not to say that Weber's particular emphasis on the enterprise form in his understanding of capitalism lacks originality, but simply that Marx is a relevant, if overlooked, source in this regard.[69]

It is in this framework that Weber raises the question of the impacts of the 'factory system' on the situation of the working class, explaining that it develops along 'two stages'. The first 'lasted until about the middle of this [the nineteenth – V.S.] century in England'; as for Germany, Weber only remarks that it had 'endured until recent times'. It isn't clear, however, whether he believed Germany had already made the transition from the 'first stage' or was simply on the cusp of doing so, since in his description of the 'second stage' he only reaffirms that 'it has existed in England approximately since the middle of the century'.[70]

---

64 MWG III/4, p. 265.

65 MEW 23, p. 161, n. 1.

66 MWG I/4, p. 327.

67 MEW 23, p. 351.

68 MWG I/4, p. 357.

69 Peter Ghosh (2014, pp. 65–6) inexplicably (and erroneously) dismisses Weber's appropriation of Marx's insights into the impersonal rule of capital, tracing this particular aspect of Weber's perspective exclusively to the formalism of his legal education.

70 MWG III/4, p. 266.

The fundamental trait of the 'first stage' was the 'tremendous superiority in the power of the capitalist'. Accordingly, the 'individual worker stands in an isolated position with regards to the employer and is at the mercy of his unchecked exploitation'.[71] Coupled with the introduction of machinery, this situation leads to the greatest possible expansion of the workday and the attempt to keep workers' 'wages and standard of life [*Lebenshaltung*]' at a minimum. This is not only pursued in order to keep production costs down, but also 'to repress [workers'] consciousness of their own desolate situation'.[72]

Two elements of this characterisation are noteworthy here. First, how in Weber's narrative the entire dynamic of the relationship between workers and employers is set by the latter, who seem the only active party; second, the fact that he claims it is the low standard of life of these workers that explains their limited degree of awareness of their own situation and, consequently, their low capacity to resist. Weber follows up these considerations by enumerating several social and political consequences of this initial regime of industrial labour, which he claims to be basing on Engels's *The Situation of the Working Class in England*.[73] His portrayal closely mirrors a specific chapter of this work titled 'Labour movements'.[74] Weber will utilise it first and foremost as an empirical source, introducing subtle changes to the original account so that it can fit better into his own conception of how social conflict developed. This effort at reframing is not accidental; the chapter in question is not only a portrayal of workers' first elemental attempts at resistance and organising – both in terms of trade-unions and political parties – but is also an account of the gradual separation of workers' socialism from bourgeois democratic radicalism. The chapter closes, in fact, with the affirmation of worker autonomy on the level of both consciousness and organisation. Because Weber saw the rise of the 'labour aristocracy' (and evidently not of a revolutionary workers' movement) as the culmination of the initial experiences of worker resistance depicted by Engels, his is ultimately a stark reinterpretation of the latter's account.

In his reading of Engels, Weber picks up especially on those passages where the interaction of culture, labour and political consciousness are approached. He comments, for instance, on how the conversion of women to the 'economic backbone of the family', coupled with child labour and the general poverty

71 Ibid.
72 MWG III/4, p. 267.
73 Ibid.
74 MEW 2, pp. 430–55.

of workers' existence, leads to a 'loss of forward-looking consideration for the offspring' and to the 'destruction of paternal authority' in the household.[75] Another key societal consequence of the 'first stage' of the 'factory system' was, in turn,

> [The] complete detachment of the factory worker from the political interests of the nation. A racial difference [*Rassendifferenz*] starts to assert itself. The propertied and the unpropertied no longer understand each other, they face each other as two nations, whilst between the unpropertied across national boundaries there reigns equal living conditions. 'Class hatred' arises at first out of purely negative elements, who sporadically stand in furious opposition to all forms of domination.[76]

Max Weber picks up on the metaphor Engels used to drive home the point that, in the context of modern industry, a situation akin to that of quarrelling nations and 'races' emerges within a single national space.[77] Yet, while Engels stresses the gradual loss of meaning of national and 'racial' differences for the working class, Weber seems to dread the fact that workers' interests become gradually – and dangerously – detached from those of 'the nation', i.e., that with their national identity they lose the one bridging element with their respective bourgeoisie. The levelling of the conditions of workers from different nationalities has the opposite effect; it sets the basis for international solidarity among the 'unpropertied'. Weber could well be referring here to how, in Friedrich Engels's account, English and migrant Irish workers, despite initial tensions due to being made to compete with one another, eventually find common ground in the struggle against exploitation and a shared capitalist antagonist, also by virtue of their 'complementary temperaments' – which Engels paints as sober and fiery, respectively.[78] This was obviously in stark contrast to Weber's view of the relations between Polish migrants and German rural workers.[79] Engels's dramatic

---

75 MWG III/4, pp. 267–8.

76 MWG III/4, p. 268.

77 MEW 2, p. 351.

78 Ibid.

79 Weber saw a clear analogy between the role of Irish migrant workers in England and of Polish migrants in the German East. As he remarked in a trip to Ireland in the summer of 1895: 'The only pleasant feature [the Irish] have is the [beautiful red – V.S.] hair. There is hardly a race as dreadful as this anywhere else. The Poles are infinitely to my preference' (MWG II/3, p. 136). Weber does, however, denounce the oppression of the Irish peasantry by English landlords (MWG II/3, p. 135).

conclusion, namely that the 'English nationality is annihilated in the worker',[80] was interpreted as fundamentally negative by Max Weber.

In fact, Weber frames his entire description of the 'first stage' of industrial conflict as a phase that is destined to be overcome as economic conditions improve and both employers and the working class reach greater maturity and willingness to compromise in their dealings with each other. Thus, the first 'primitive positive demands' that joblessness brings:

> ... can be summarized by the two postulates of the right to work and the transfer of the means of production from the property of the capitalists to that of the workers. These two demands belong to the pre-socialist early period of the labour movement.[81]

Weber frames, therefore, not only the 'furious opposition to all forms of domination', but both the demand for socialisation of the means of production – a clear reference to Marx and Engels – and the right to work – likely a nod to Louis Blanc and the French context – as belonging to an *early stage* in the development of modern social conflict. Harsh conditions of exploitation coupled with workers' 'low standard of life' lead to outbursts of unrest and to demands that are as radical as they are utopian and primitive. These are to Weber the excesses of the early labour movement which, once the 'second stage' in industrial class relations is reached, are duly abandoned by a more 'mature' iteration of organised labour.[82]

Yet, the element to signal the emergence of the 'second stage' does not rest in workers' agency, but in the fact that 'the limits of the superior economic power of factory owners start to appear'. This trait of the 'second stage' was rooted in the same factor that had previously allowed the bourgeoisie to massively expand exploitation, i.e., 'capital ownership'. The greater investment in factory facilities and machines – i.e., what Marx characterised as the rise in the organic composition of capital – meant that capitalists now had 'an interest in the stability and quality of the workforce'.[83] It was, therefore, as a consequence of the 'sophistication of machinery', that 'a segment of skilled

80 MEW 2, p. 431.

81 MWG III/4, p. 268.

82 Weber's characterisation of this early phase of the labour movement as 'pre-socialist' is also worthy of mention. It suggests Weber identified the denomination 'socialist', with a more integrated and reformist labour movement. A 'socialist' labour movement was, in this sense, a further development of the 'communist' currents of the 1830s and 1840s in France and Germany and of Chartism in Britain.

83 MWG III/4, p. 268.

workers developed'.[84] This had two central consequences, which Weber (symptomatically) approached with reference to the work of Brentano; first, that the employer now had 'an interest in a higher standard of life for workers' and, as a result, needed to set limits to the workday and to the downward pressure on wages;[85] second, that a 'market organisation of the working class' could emerge. In other words, once the segmentation of the class between skilled and unskilled workers took place, 'the old journeymen union [*Gesellenordnung*] returns in a new form, namely, in trade unions'. Weber characterised them as market organisations, because he believed their power rested on the capacity to regulate the supply of labour in a given branch. The result was a relative 'equalisation in the power struggle between worker and employer',[86] as the emergence of trade unions afforded skilled workers the 'possibility of an autonomous ordering of their economic means of existence'.[87]

Weber's analysis of social conflict in the countryside followed a similar framework, i.e., it equally de-emphasised worker agency in favour of a focus on processes of segmentation within the working class that produce a 'high-standing' segment. Even in his model case of Mecklenburg, where it was hard to overlook the fact that the workers' movement had 'wrestled' a series of concessions from landlords in 1848,[88] it was ultimately workers' higher standard of life and higher 'intensity of Germanness', Weber argued, that had led to their prosperity.[89] Weber interpreted the fate of social conflict in England in a similar key; the rise of Chartism and other episodes of revolt were offshoots of a primitive phase of industrialisation which, in his account, played no role whatsoever in the shift to the following stage, one marked by a relative improvement in the situation of workers.

∴

The parallels between Weber's accounts of social conflict in rural Mecklenburg and in a rapidly-industrialising England again raise the issue of the contradictory nature of his engagement with workers' standpoint. While Weber does not ignore expressions of worker resistance in his account of developments in

84 MWG III/4, p. 269.
85 Ibid.
86 Ibid.
87 In the original, 'Die Möglichkeit autonomer Regelung ihrer ökonomischen Existenzgrundlage'. MWG III/4, p. 269.
88 MWG I/4, pp. 321–2.
89 See MWG I/3, pp. 880–2.

England, tracing back labour revolts to the harsh working conditions of early industry, he outright rejects the notion that these struggles could have sprung from an autonomous and emancipatory point of view on social life, one of Engels's main conclusion. The radical critique of private property and of 'all forms of domination' inscribed in revolutionary action were to Weber primitive expressions of revolt, which disappeared when an improvement in living conditions – brought forth partly by technical advances, partly by employers' interest in fostering them – allowed workers to take on a more ordered form of representation of their (economic) interests. As Jan Rehmann has pointed out, here was another 'major difference between Weber and Brentano', namely that

> Brentano had proposed a principle of organisation that encompassed all workers, the ones organised in trade unions and unorganised ones, with the workers' elected representatives settling disputes with the representatives of the employers under the chairmanship of a non-partisan third party .... [For Weber, on the other hand], [t]he question of going on strike or not must not be decided according to party-political considerations; only economic considerations should play a role.[90]

While not inexorable, Weber framed the transition to this later stage of modern social conflict as equivalent to nothing less than the 'solution' of the 'labour question':

> In purely theoretical terms, this is the optimistic perspective of how, through labour organisation, the 'labour question' resolves itself. The consequence of such labour organisations, it must be said, is primarily the fact that the solidarity of workers is suppressed [*aufgehoben*] and a labour aristocracy emerges.[91]

It is understandable that Weber painted this scenario as optimistic. German developments had demonstrated that achieving the pacification of social strife in the actual historical process was a complicated matter. This caveat was likely a veiled criticism of Brentano, who underestimated the inexorable element of antagonism inscribed in modern social struggle; above all, however, it showed Weber's apprehension in relation to one clear by-product of the crystallisation of a 'labour aristocracy':

90 Rehmann 2015, p. 146.
91 MWG III/4, p. 270.

> The consequence of this development consists necessarily in the fact that a lower segment of excluded workers emerges. The question of what proportion of workers are liable to be organised in relation to the proletariat does not yet have a statistical answer. In virtue of this fact, the aforementioned optimism must be tempered somewhat.[92]

Crucially, though a general improvement in the situation of workers did not seem to figure prominently in the aims of Weber's social reformism, its goals on the terrain of hegemony and political strategy could be compromised if the weight of the labour aristocracy was negligible with regards to the overall composition of the working class (the 'proletariat' represents low-standing workers in the passage quoted above). This would mean that the threat of hostile proletarian masses remained in play. While Weber believed this was an issue even in the prototypical English case, it was especially relevant for Imperial Germany, whose transition to the 'second stage' of class relations in an industrial context seemed as yet undecided. As Weber put it in a lecture titled 'The meaning of luxury' in October 1895:

> It is not clear whether the aristocratic development within the working class – as is taking place in England – will not find very narrow boundaries in our case. In Germany one deals with the very unfortunate fact that a detachment of this labour aristocracy – of skilled workers from unskilled – has in no way established itself as a lasting phenomenon.[93]

In essence, Imperial Germany's inability to transcend the first phase of English industrial development meant that it would continue to boast a labour movement with a much more fundamental – to Weber, 'primitive' – critique of the *status quo*, the modern equivalent of English Chartism, i.e., German Social Democracy. That was in many ways Weber's central question with regards to the fate of social conflict in Germany, i.e., whether the tendency towards a unified class consciousness on the part of workers was a mere transitional phenomenon that would disappear as soon as the general tendency of proletarisation was partially reversed or, rather, if it constituted a sustainable phenomenon.

Here Weber's central concern with the development of *Kultur* intersects with his considerations on politics and class: did a higher level of culture mean

92 Ibid.
93 MWG I/4, p. 740.

a convergence towards a bourgeois-individualist ethic, a liberal political stance and, not least, a greater perception of national belonging? Weber raised this question – which was directly tied to the prospects of Social Democracy – from the very beginning of his inquiry into the 'rural labour question'. In fact, among the issues he argued the second survey should address was to 'what extent the existing conflict of interest between contractually bound and free workers came to their consciousness subjectively'.[94] For, if the rupture in the 'community of interest' between employer and worker was the *leitmotif* of Weber's examination of class relations in the German East, there was another set of potentially opposing viewpoints, this time *within* the rural working class, that was almost as relevant. It referred to the fact that for the *Instmann* to overcome his status as a dependent small agrarian producer, i.e., for him to rise to the situation of an independent small farmer or tenant, there would have to be a partial reversal of the purely export-oriented mode of agriculture that was expanding in the German East. This model clearly favoured seasonal wage-labour. Would rural wage-labourers – the 'benefactors' of the export economy – go along with this change? Despite the economic insecurity they faced, free rural workers had the advantage of neither being tied to an employer nor to a piece of land. Would they surrender this freedom in exchange for a different form of independence, namely that of the small rural proprietor – and, to a lesser degree, the tenant farmer – who strove for a peasant existence? Weber made a direct association between this question and the issue of a potential extension of proletarian class consciousness into the countryside, i.e.,

> if namely, as is no doubt already the case here and there, free workers are already generally imbued with the *collective* class consciousness of the modern proletariat, currently in tremendous development, and which aims to encompass both city and countryside; or, whether its precursor, the specific urge towards autonomy of modern labour, is developed.[95]

Here was Weber's main dilemma regarding the development of the 'labour question', i.e., if the proletarian class consciousness typical of a situation of impersonal subjection and dispossession would spread to large swaths of the working class or if a more individualistic form of self-awareness – more akin to a bourgeois concept of personal autonomy – would prevail. Put differently, would a social and collective understanding of freedom and of political agency

94 MWG I/4, p. 83.
95 MWG I/4, p. 83.

triumph over a more typically bourgeois identification of autonomy with property, individual liberty and upward mobility? This question was all the more significant, considering Weber's assertion that the prevalence of one or the other form of consciousness was also expressed 'in typical divergences in political standpoint'. For, while in East-Prussia the partially unfree *Instmann* generally adhered to the political preference of his landlord – conservative or liberal – in the more thoroughly capitalistic Silesia a gap emerged between the 'landowning worker, who ... aspired to rise to the middle class' and the 'landless rural proletariat'. While 'the political affiliation to bourgeois democracy was natural' to the former, the latter 'already showed socialist tendencies'.[96] This made the creation of middle strata in the countryside Weber's paragon solution for Imperial Germany as a whole. The question remained, therefore, whether 'through labour organisation, a *labour aristocracy* would emerge [in Germany], as we find it in some of the large English industries'. There, Weber added, 'full proletarianisation' had been *a phase*, i.e., it had 'constituted precisely the point of transition for an ascending movement of the highest segments of the working class'.[97]

This assessment led, in turn, to the question of whether a segment analogous to the 'labour aristocracy' would also emerge in the capital-intensive large estates of the German East, potentially raising the standard of life of workers in general and even of migrant laborers.[98] Weber's answer is a resounding 'no'. Firstly, due to the tendency of fully-capitalist agriculture to decrease the proportion of permanent workers with regard to seasonal ones. This meant that even if the former were able to secure a higher living standard due to greater yields and mechanisation, this could not be generalised to a large enough segment of the class to matter in the overall picture. Secondly, because any attempt to limit or regulate the 'supply' of seasonal labourers through rural trade unions could be undermined by the introduction of foreign migrant workers.[99] That's why Weber believed that, in the case of the countryside, internal colonisation – and especially land-tenancy within state-owned large estates – was the only solution to establish an intermediary sector between peasants and the rural proletariat in the countryside.[100]

This was, of course, also a crucial issue for German Social Democracy, which in the mid-1890s had raised with urgency the question of how the party and

96 MWG I/3, p. 742.
97 MWG I/4, p. 393, p. 444.
98 MWG I/4, p. 400.
99 MWG I/4, pp. 412–19.
100 MWG I/4, pp. 461–2.

its associated unions could win over an expanding rural proletariat that was numerically far superior to its urban counterpart.[101] Interestingly, while Weber conceded there was an ever greater transformation of the rural working class of the German East into 'a class of proletarian mould that is *unified* in its essential living conditions', thus validating the notion of a socialist peril in the countryside, he also believed the inherent spatial fragmentation and sheer diversity of contexts rural workers faced made 'the unification of their interests … an impossibility for the time being'.[102]

Finally, the absence of middle strata in the countryside meant another of Weber's strategic political goals could not be fulfilled, that is, *changing Social Democracy from within*. Weber was not frightened by the growing success of the SPD in the polls in Mecklenburg, for instance, where the 'socialist day-labourers' built its electorate. The question to Weber was only *how long* this and other 'popular segments gripped by socialism' would be 'digestible' for the party. With the 'rising self-consciousness' of these rural workers, Weber believed the 'unbridgeable nature of the city-countryside contradiction' would make its presence felt. By this rise Weber meant the awakening of the 'individualist "land-hunger"', which would make the 'grip' of socialism in the countryside an 'unnecessary' transitional stage to a 'more mature' form of social conflict. Would the same process hold true for the social-democratic proletariat in the cities? Would economic progress and cultural ascension mean a party base less ready to embrace radical socialist ideas and more open to bourgeois individualism and a liberal-democratic political horizon?

4 Conclusion: A Matter of (Worker) Conscience: The Role of Ideals and *Kultur* in Facing the Challenge of Social Democracy

The two-staged understanding of modern social conflict Weber gleaned from English developments in the nineteenth century helps explain why his proposed response to the rise of Social Democracy in Imperial Germany consisted in fostering both rural and urban middle strata. The solution was, in other words, to partially reverse the general tendency of proletarianisation of the working population. Crucially, however, Weber never understood upward mobility under capitalism as a purely economic process; it possessed a 'cultural' dimension as well. This is especially relevant in the case of the rise of

101 See Kautsky 1899.
102 MWG I/4, p. 419.

workers into the 'labour aristocracy' or land-ownership/tenancy, considering Weber saw in this process a parallel rise in terms of *Kultur*. Upward mobility in the economic sphere was not necessarily pegged to cultural ascension, as they did not always overlap in Weber's account; yet, there is no doubt that Weber understood the two factors as being closely intertwined. Thus, it was only after a certain baseline of economic well-being was surpassed – a process the spread of capitalism can either foster or undermine – that an individual became a bearer of *Kultur*. Between the resigned worker under relations of dependence and the freedom-seeking proletarian there was one such jump. It was with their access to the better-off tiers of the working class, however, that Weber started to perceive workers as 'cultural' equals with regards to members of the propertied classes. This ascension, in turn, signalled that a political alliance between bourgeois and worker had become purposeful. But where was German Social Democracy within this tiered understanding of cultural status? Was culture a relevant aspect of Weber's consideration of the main representative of working-class politics in Imperial Germany? A series of passages from his interventions in the 1890s indicated this was decidedly the case. In his lecture on 'The Meaning of Luxury' (1895), for instance, Weber clearly states that

> *From a political standpoint*, it can be said based on previous experience that only after a certain level in the standard of life is reached, does a capacity for political judgement begin, that is reflected in the conscious affiliation to a party. Only after a certain level does affiliation to Social Democracy begin.[103]

If party membership was, therefore, an indicator that a certain level of individual cultural achievement had been reached, the fact that Weber's understanding of *Kultur* was not only hierarchical, but relational, raises the question of what Weber's point of reference for this assessment of the SPD's cultural role was. For even if adherence to Social Democracy appeared as an indicator of a certain level of cultural achievement, this did not necessarily make it a fixture in Max Weber's firmament of modern *Kultur*. Weber's brief engagement in the founding of a new party (the National-Social Association) in 1896 shows he ultimately did not believe the SPD of the mid-1890s was a suitable political representative for 'culture-bearing' ascending workers. What follows is a close examination of how Weber understood the *cultural meaning* of Social

103 MWG I/4, p. 739.

Democracy; this will build the final element in my analysis of his contradictory relationship to working-class politics in the Imperial Germany of his youth and maturing years.

∴

The most important source here is Weber's address to the Fifth Protestant Social Congress in May 1894, in which he and Paul Göhre gave a first assessment of the results of the second survey on the 'rural labour question'.[104] As examined in detail in Part 2 above, Weber's main insight in this regard was that a subjective drive towards freedom had been a central factor for migration away from the countryside. Hence his conclusion that a 'deep idealistic urge, which asserts itself in the thirst for intellectual *Kultur*, also lies dormant in rural workers'.[105] Accommodating this thirst consisted in 'the most important tasks that the Protestant clergy would have to face in the near future'. It was also an urgent matter, considering that

> these intellectual needs will be attended to, you can all be sure of that, if not by you [clergymen], than by others and by means of other points of view. Never again shall this field of intellectual work be relinquished to Social Democracy.[106]

The same cultural component Weber saw as an integral part of upward social mobility in modern life emerges now in his *political* analysis. That workers were seeking Social Democracy as a mediator to fulfil their cultural needs was clearly a problem for Weber. The reason for this assessment has to do with the peculiarities of his concept of culture at this time and how it was, on the one hand, tied to 'national' or 'racial' traits and, on the other, to social stratification. Crucially, when referring to workers' search for cultural elevation, Weber at no point suggests this might be satisfied through forms of cultural expression that are connected to the working-class experience. Cultural elevation was equivalent to access to bourgeois culture or a culture of the German elites, which he associated with a bourgeois economic ethic and individualistic attitude. Thus, even though Weber speaks of the 'cultural and moral goods of humanity' as forming part of the aims of workers' thirst for cultiv-

104 MWG I/4, pp. 313–45.
105 MWG I/4, p. 333.
106 Ibid.

ation,[107] his *is not a universalist notion of culture*, at least in the sense of a concept which embraces cultural practices as a fundamental human experience. Weber's *Kultur* possessed, rather, a normative makeup and a clear class content; it was equivalent to a state of heightened individual self-awareness, embodied in a forward-looking stance and the pre-eminence of ideals over immediate material needs; as such, it was distributed unequally along both 'national' (or 'ethnic-racial') as well as social lines, in the sense that it was an achievement *primarily* of the 'modern Occident' and, within it, of the propertied classes.

According to this perspective, *Kultur* is something the worker does not possess and cannot pursue or foster within the confines of his or her own particular class experience and outlook; in Weber's portrayal, the more workers rise in their cultural status, the more they individuate themselves, eventually detaching from both their class origins and the majority of working people. Weber saw the onset of modern economic development as a trigger for this process; hence, when the spread of capitalist relations in the countryside broke the landlord's 'personal bond of responsibility' over his dependent workers, the 'natural psychological consequence' was greater individual autonomy:

> The old constitution of labour [*Arbeitsverfassung*] ... with its overpowering status for the ruler, also carried with it the psychological requirements for the submission of the ruled, as in every labour relation.[108]

Weber believed that the old patriarchal order in the countryside had rested on a state of 'dull resignation' on the part of rural workers. With the gradual decline of this mode of rulership and its transition to the 'rule of capital', 'the resignation of the subjected masses disappeared'. As a result, the latent conflict between dependent worker and individual landowner transformed into the impersonal conflict or '"objective hatred" ... of class against class', a 'well-known socialist technical expression'.[109] It is important to stress that, as this process advanced, it merely afforded the *possibility* of cultural elevation for a no longer dependent, but increasingly proletarianised working class. As mentioned previously, Weber believed capitalism carried its own 'perils for *Kultur*'

107 MWG I/4, p. 340.

108 MWG I/4, p. 327. For a clarification of the concept of *Arbeitsverfassung* or 'constitution of labour', and the difficulties in translating it, see my comments on section 8.4.

109 MWG I/4, pp. 327–8. Weber is referring here to Friedrich Engels's authorship of the expression 'objective hatred'.

in its levelling of formerly-established middle strata – such as the *Instleute* in the German East – and in how it put nations of different 'cultural standings' (e.g. Germans and Poles, English and Irish etc.) in competition with one another.

Modern economic development had, in addition, changed the nature of social conflict from an atomised opposition into a *collective antagonism*, which brought its own political consequences. Both these issues, i.e., the broadening of social struggle and the danger of a debasement of *Kultur*, explain why Weber stressed the importance of channels of upward social mobility for the urban and rural working classes. What was at stake was the realisation of both the possibilities of cultural ascension that capitalism opened up and, at the same time, the 'integration' of higher-standing workers into a modernised structure of social stratification. Hence Weber's conclusion to the effect that '[c]*lass struggle is here and it is an integrating element of the current societal order* – only the form is up for discussion'.[110]

The form favoured by Weber was a legal and organised one – what he called 'orderly interest representation'[111] – according to which workers channelled their economic grievances through trade unions and other institutional pathways, in line with English developments. But, for that to take place in Imperial Germany, class struggle had to be 'recognised': 'Only with this recognition, does *class struggle* become *legalised* for current society'.[112] Once this process took on proper institutional expression, higher-standing workers would settle into a new status as both carriers of the status quo *and* its subaltern subjects, a situation Weber believed was more in line with modern social conflict under the impersonal 'rule of capital' than the old pair of patriarchal authority and unquestioned obedience.

In a lecture on 'The bourgeois development in Germany' of early 1897,[113] Weber articulated this stance in clear terms. The 'legalisation' of class struggle meant that 'the relationship between employer and worker must also rest on the recognition of legal equality [*Rechtsgleichheit*]' and that 'the labour relation must be conceived commercially [*geschäftlich*]' considering that

> … every salesman has the right to demand the price for his commodities that pleases him and that he believes he can get for them. The commodity

110 MWG I/4, p. 329, my highlights.
111 MWG I/4, p. 345.
112 MWG I/4, p. 329.
113 MWG I/4, pp. 814–18.

> of the worker is his labour output [*Arbeitsleistung*]. He too has the right to sell his commodity at the highest price possible.[114]

Along these lines, Weber criticised employers' outrage at strike action, yet also made clear that the establishment of 'employers' associations' was just as legitimate as an organised labour movement.[115] 'Legalised' class struggle consisted, therefore, in the purely economic dispute over wages and working conditions. It need not take on any political content, provided it was recognised and gained legal form; furthermore, it operated independently of any form of benevolence by employers or a sense of loyalty on workers' part.

Interestingly, Weber's notion of a 'legalised class struggle' echoes, to an important degree, Marx's account of the dynamics of class struggle and impersonal domination under the capitalist mode of production. Yet, just as in the case of his appropriation of Engelsian concepts, Weber operates a subtle reframing of vantage point that, among other consequences, *extirpates the horizon of social transformation* – the overcoming of capitalism – that Marx's account in *Capital* embodies and announces.[116] Significantly, in the particular passage of *Capital* that likely served as a basis for Weber's remarks, the worker speaks in the first person:

> You and I know on the market only one law, that of the exchange of commodities. And the consumption of the commodity belongs not to the seller who parts with it, but to the buyer, who acquires it. To you, therefore, belongs the use of my daily labour-power. But by means of the price that you pay for it each day, I must be able to reproduce it daily, and to sell it again … I demand, therefore, a working-day of normal length, and I demand it without any appeal to your heart, for in money matters sentiment is out of place. You may be a model citizen, … but the thing that you represent … has no heart in its breast. That which seems to throb there is my own heart-beating. I demand the normal working-day because I, like every other seller, demand the value of my commodity.[117]

Though the passage is meant to underscore the call for the 10-hour working day – in line with Weber's 'legalisation of class struggle' – Marx's conceptualisation of the worker as no more than a walking and talking bearer of the

114 MWG I/4, p. 817.
115 MWG I/4, p. 817.
116 See Hudis 2012, pp. 147–68.
117 MEW 23, pp. 248–9 (translation based on the first English edition).

commodity labour-power is ultimately aimed at denaturalising the fact that, under the rule of capital, labouring for the capitalist's benefit is the ultimate purpose of a worker's life. A similar critique underlies Marx's portrayal of reproductive activities and of the need for leisure as mere means of replenishing the capacity to work (for someone else). Though both Marx and Weber see the labour relationship in the capitalist enterprise as having the advantage of dispensing with patriarchal sentimentality (and arbitrariness), the transformation of these parties into mere commodity buyers and sellers, respectively, is interpreted in a fundamentally different manner. While Weber posits this status as the end-goal of the modernisation of economic relations, Marx sees it as a refashioning of labour alienation under a new form and, as such, as a historically contingent step in the pathway to the effective emancipation of labour.[118]

This is not to say, however, that modern social conflict was a purely economic and legal-formal affair to Weber. To him, class struggle also possessed a cultural component: 'Class struggle within the nation is psychologically and morally – let's not fool ourselves – analogous to the struggles between nations'.[119] This meant the legal redressing of class conflict would not suffice for the social 'integration' of higher-standing workers. Their elevation would only be complete if it was accompanied by a (partial) bridging of the cultural abyss between the working classes and their propertied counterparts.

The goal of achieving a higher cultural status was, in this sense, one of only two positive aspects of workers' struggles that Weber actually recognised, the other one being the striving for a better economic standing. Hence the following remark at the Protestant Social Congress: 'I throw no stone at a member of the clergy, who believes the emancipatory struggle of an ascending class is a good and divinely ordained struggle'.[120] Weber seldom associated workers' struggles with a striving for emancipation, but when he did, it was not in recognition of a drive for liberation, but rather of the will to overcome what he perceived as workers' own previous state of resignation, backward subjugation and ignorance.

The question of workers' possible cultural ascent also presents the key to Weber's stance on German Social Democracy. It was during his lecture to the Fifth Protestant Social Congress in 1894 that Weber made his most significant appraisal of the merits and faults of the SPD. This came directly after his remarks on the function of 'social policy', which Weber framed as a modality

118 See the epilogue for my argument that the 'non-alternative' to capitalism continued to structure Weber's understanding of this societal formation into his later works.

119 MWG I/4, p. 330.

120 Ibid.

of state intervention aiming to rearrange social structure, i.e., not in the usual sense of a set of measures meant to address the refractions of the 'social question'.[121] Given that Weber considered social change to be intimately related to *cultural change*, his understanding of the role of 'social policy' also included the task of fostering *Kultur*:

> What seems *valuable* to us in man is self-responsibility, the profound longing for ascension, for the intellectual and moral goods of mankind; this we want to stimulate and support, also where it appears in its most primitive forms [i.e., in workers – V.S.]. We want to shape external conditions ... not, so that individuals may feel more content, but so that under the duress of the inevitable struggle for existence the best in them is conserved, the – physical and ideal – traits that we desire the nation to possess. Now, gentlemen, we are dealing here with value judgements and they are mutable. It is above all an *irrational* element. But this irrational standpoint is, in fact, not only our own, but can also be found, for instance, in the best representatives of socialism.[122]

Culture appears in the passage in Weber's peculiarly polysemic use of the concept. The achievement of *Kultur* is not understood simply in the sense of intellectual cultivation, but also of acquiring a self-responsible and forward-looking stance; the *locus* of culture is the nation and Weber's hierarchy of culture along national and social lines ('primitive forms') is hinted at. Yet, on this particular occasion, and very likely because it involved a contrast with the views of Social Democrats, Weber will stress that *Kultur* also involved an 'irrational element', subsequently described as the decided affirmation of an ideal that goes beyond economic demands. Weber saw here a common trait with socialism's 'best representatives', though it is not clear whom he had in mind. A passage from August Bebel's *The Woman and Socialism*, a work first written in 1879 and which remained a social-democratic 'best-seller' in the 1890s,[123] gives an indication of what might have spurred this favourable assessment of the SPD's relationship to *Kultur*. The passage stems from the preface to the *The Woman and Socialism*'s 1891 edition, that is, the first after the end of the *Sozialistengesetz*, which was also the time Weber likely came into contact with it:[124]

121 cf. MWG I/4, pp. 339–40.

122 MWG I/4, p. 340.

123 See Bonnell 2002.

124 Weber mentions Bebel's work and its concept of an entirely voluntary and reciprocally-desired marriage in an article published in February of 1893 (See MWG I/4, p. 129).

> the fundamental transformation of society should not merely consist in a wide majority living better than it currently does, but in enabling it to partake in all cultural achievements [*Kulturerrungenschaften*]. It is not a question of lowering the level of culture, but of raising it significantly.[125]

In this quote from Bebel, one finds what Weber considered the two contradictory dimensions of Social Democrats' programme. On the one hand, a 'typically philistine' emphasis on 'material goals' [*materielle Ziele*] visible in the call for improving the livelihoods of the wide majority. On the other, Bebel's rejoinder that this process of economic change also had a cultural dimension, i.e., what Weber identified as the 'irrational' standpoint that he and Social Democrats had in common:

> Social Democracy has obviously a mechanical, materialistic jargon. It speaks of the all-encompassing importance of 'knife and fork' questions. But if we take its actual demands we find, however, that behind them is the same irrationalism as in our case. If knife and fork questions are the only things that matter to it, why does [Social Democracy] not leave the polish beast to subsist there, where it has enough to eat, until it perishes without ever having known or desired another existence?[126]

Surprisingly, the example Weber provides for the 'irrational' standpoint he claimed to share with a part of Social Democrats was embodied in an act of internationalism,[127] i.e., a stance he bitterly rejected. Nevertheless, the fact that

---

125 Bebel 1891, p. XIV.

126 MWG I/4, p. 340.

127 Weber's allusion to Social Democrats' solidarity with Polish workers could very well be a reference to Max Quarck, who had reacted to Weber's anti-Polish discourse in a follow-up article to the Verein's conference of March 1893. In it, Quarck raised the question of whether Polish migration could be stopped at all, considering it could be seen as 'a small stream in the unstoppable current which led the Earth's peoples from East to West, to ever higher culture [*Kultur*]' and that it was senseless to fight this, considering that, precisely through this contact, 'Western cultural status could be transmitted to the backward masses' (SpCb II, 28 [10.04.1893], p. 331). This standpoint was not all that distant from Weber's own hierarchy of culture and hardly a gleaming example of Social Democrats' internationalism, but it still angered Weber. Quarck had also shown great scepticism that workers could be infused with nationalist convictions in an effort to turn them against Polish migrants; instead, he argued that only trade unions could regulate employers' attempts to bring in foreign migrant workers to drive down wages (Ibid). Weber's reaction was to brand Quarck's remarks as 'sentimental cosmopolitanism' in a response published in mid-1894 (MWG I/4, p. 416).

Weber saw in it the expression of an 'irrational' ideal, rather than a conscious ethical-political choice, is crucial for his positive assessment. Less clear is where Weber located the driving force of this positive 'irrationalism'. In one passage, he seems to suggest it sprang from workers' themselves, as opposed to the petty-bourgeois elements in the SPD:

> The derision of idealism is nothing more than jargon, ostentation. In the honesty of speaking out the irrational stance of every worker regarding the progress of humanity, we are more youthful than all the senile whiners [*greisenhafte Nörgler*] that have now made it their business to represent socialism.[128]

In this – decidedly Nietzschean – passage, we see Weber both *identify with workers'* yearning to partake in the fruits of human progress, i.e., to ascend in the realm of *Kultur*, and *draw a clear separation* between the rank and file of the SPD and its *déclassé* leadership, with its rudimentary materialism. Again, the idealism expressed by internationalism is not understood as a conscious adhesion of workers to a universalist concept of culture and progress or to cross-border solidarity, but as a product of 'irrationalism' – even if one he saw in a positive light. Considering the fierce competition between 'national economies' that inevitably resulted from their linkage in the world market, any form of internationalism could only be but irrational to Weber, whether the 'mode of economic organisation was capitalist or socialist'.[129]

A short time after he made these remarks, Weber would again refer to himself as an 'honest opponent' of Social Democracy, i.e., as someone who did not outright reject the SPD and its policies. While this statement came after the party's newspaper had briefly incorporated some of his views on the 'rural labour question',[130] his remarks in this occasion are still very much representative of his fundamental stance towards the German labour movement. Weber criticised, namely, the 'philistine illusion' on the part of conservatives that

128 MWG I/4, p. 340.

129 MWG I/4, p. 416.

130 '*Vorwärts* knows we are honest adversaries' (MWG I/4, p. 476). This statement by Weber was made in reference to the fact that the SPD outlet – and its then editor Bruno Schönlank more specifically – briefly espoused Weber's view that at least a part of rural workers would not be drawn to a collectivist solution to the 'agrarian question', favouring an 'individualistic' form of agriculture instead, i.e., the ownership or tenancy of a small plot (see MWG I/4, p. 476, n. 33). This statement appeared in *Vorwärts* immediately after the Verein conference in March 1893, making it very likely that Schönlank was behind it. The debate between opposing stances regarding the solution to the 'agrarian question' would make

> a politically mature labour movement that contributes positively to Germany's greatness … could ever emerge while the class consciousness of [this] ascending social segment was ignored or repressed, preventing it from exercising its free self-determination.[131]

Similarly to his remarks to the Protestant Social Congress, Weber's call for the need to respect the autonomy of workers (and sharp criticism of patriarchal views to the contrary) was predicated on the expectation of their positive contribution to 'Germany's greatness' – i.e., imperial expansion – and 'political maturity' – the surrender of revolutionary and internationalist perspectives. As ever, Weber clearly indicates this applied to the labour aristocracy ('ascending segments') and not workers in general. Another aspect of the passage worth highlighting is the fact that Weber's critique of conservatives was directed at their attempts to repress workers' class consciousness, i.e., it was analogous to Weber's critique of social-democratic leadership for deriding the idealism of its proletarian membership.

In the case of the SPD, however, the issue was compounded by the fact that party cadre mostly belonged to a class fraction Weber utterly despised, namely, the *Spießbürgertum* or – in an approximate translation – the 'philistine' petty-bourgeoisie. According to Weber, the 'social-democratic movement' was, in fact, 'to a great extent a product of the German philistine petty bourgeoisie'. This provenance explained its 'lack of great national power instincts', focus on 'material objectives' and on 'the interests of one's own generation', all of which – in clearly Nietzschean tones[132] – Weber harshly condemned.[133] In the *Antrittsrede* of a year later (May 1895), Weber stressed once more the supposed division between a 'philistine' social-democratic leadership and the party's ordinary rank and file:

> Economically, the highest segments of the German working-class are much more mature than the selfishness of the propertied classes would care to admit and [this highest segment of workers – V.S.] justifiably demands the freedom to represent its interests in an open and organised form of economic power struggle. *Politically*, it is infinitely less

up a central element of the SPD's congresses of 1894 and 1895, where the 'socialist position' – defended by Kautsky – which held that land had to be socialised and not parcelled out, would ultimately be victorious (cf. Lehmann 1970).

131 MWG I/4, p. 476.

132 See Majul 2018.

133 MWG I/4, p. 341.

> mature than the clique of journalists – which seeks to monopolise its leadership – would lead it to believe.[134]

The picture of the impressionable mass on one side and a rabble of agitators on the other is completed with Weber's remark that these '*déclassé* bourgeois' liked to play with 'reminiscences of a century ago', i.e., of the French Revolution of 1789, and especially with the time of the National Convention and Jacobin rule. With the key difference that German petty-bourgeois agitators were 'infinitely harmless', not only because they did not possess the 'catilinarian energy of the *deed*', but because they equally lacked 'even an inkling of the tremendous *national* passion that flowed through the Convention'.[135]

The SPD's adherence to Marxism, in turn, also bore the mark of its petty-bourgeois leadership. In an approving reference to the National-Social Association's goal of winning over a working-class membership, Weber added that this would mean

> the intellectual emancipation of workers, a freedom of thought that Social Democracy does not tolerate, as they pound the dogma of Marx's broken system into the heads of the masses; it would also mean freedom of consciousness, which in [Social Democracy] … only exists on paper, not in reality.[136]

Weber's rare use of the notion of emancipation appears here, symptomatically, not in connection to workers' liberation from oppression or exploitation, but from their own ignorance or, in this case, from the Marxist dogma supposedly force-fed by social-democratic leadership. Clearly, the problem was not with the imposition of certain ideas on the working masses, but with *the kind of ideas* the SPD was propagating; Weber made no attempt to hide the fact that his own political project demanded a reshaping of worker consciousness by political agents from other social classes. Hence, in his closing words to the Protestant Social Congress, Weber called for the formation of Protestant workers' associations,

> … so that the construction [*Herausbildung*] of class consciousness – which will also come to the rural proletariat – is not carried out by the hands of others.[137]

134 MWG I/4, p. 570.
135 MWG I/4, p. 571.
136 MWG I/4, p. 619.
137 MWG I/4, p. 345.

Fostering an adequate form of worker consciousness was a central element of Weber's proto-Fordist project of political transformation for Imperial Germany. Yet the passage is revealing in another key sense; it indicates, namely, that Weber's understanding of working-class culture did not allow for the possibility that workers' own standpoint and experiences could form the basis for their own class consciousness – much less, for that matter, that revolutionary socialism was a (possible) expression of this social vantage point. Even if Weber recognised a limited scope of particular interests that the working class should be allowed to affirm through their own organisations, these interests could never truly frame the fundamental transformation of society and the establishment of another configuration of political rule. This was another facet of the normative aspect of Max Weber's understanding of *Kultur*, whose class content is embodied in its flat refusal of any other modern viewpoints on social life beyond a bourgeois-individualistic framework (and imperialist notions of ethnic and 'racial' superiority).

This insight had a direct bearing in Weber's relationship to German Social Democracy. Because the majority stance in the party before 1914 collided with the nationalist and imperialist ethos Weber believed characterised a 'mature' labour movement, this made the SPD an ultimately unreliable shepherd of the 'labour aristocracy' towards the role he envisioned for it.[138] The issue was not simply that Social Democrats had *politicised* workers in a socialist direction, i.e., expanding their demands beyond strictly corporative economic issues. While Weber lamented the fact that German workers lacked 'the long-standing effort of *economic* education, which the organised struggle for their own interests had impressed upon the English working class',[139] he equally saw a deficit at the cultural front within the German labour movement. Hence Weber's call for a proposed 'Protestant-social labour movement', whose programme he commended for going 'beyond what [workers'] corporative interests [*Berufsinteressen*] required' and for fully embracing an 'idealistic standpoint'.[140]

The trouble with the SPD, therefore, was that it fostered the wrong sort of demands – i.e., demands that were not strictly economic – among its working-class constituents, the wrong sort of *Kultur*. Even if Weber affirmed that the 'degree of political power' and of 'power in the broadest and highest sense of the word' that the working class would be able to yield within 'its *own* state'

138 This assessment was only confirmed, in Weber's eyes, by the fact that the 'reformist' wing of the SPD was unable to assert itself in the mid to late-1890s, see Hoffrogge 2017, pp. 143–51.

139 MWG I/4, p. 571.

140 MWG I/4, p. 341.

was dependent on 'the degree of earnestness and force of their ideals', that is, 'on the degree of courage with which they stood for these ideals', this did not always apply; if the ideals in question were internationalism, the solidarity between skilled and non-skilled workers and a universalistic concept of culture and enlightenment, all of which characterised Social Democracy's programme and ideology around 1900, then Weber refused to recognise their legitimacy.

In this sense, the expanded political role Weber envisioned for the working class did not depend 'on the degree of clamour' with which its members stood for 'material interests, for the knife and fork questions of their own generation'.[141] Rather, it was only the *'resonance of the status of a world power'* that, as had been the case in England and France, would provide the 'chronic political education' the German working class was in need of.[142]

Weber's repeated critical reference to the Chartist notion of 'knife and fork questions', first introduced to German audiences by Friedrich Engels, takes us back to his (subterranean) dialogue with Marx's lifelong friend and collaborator. Here was a fundamental point of disagreement on Weber's part regarding both Engels's account of English developments and prevailing stances in pre-1914 German Social Democracy. Engels had seen in the ascendance of 'knife and fork questions' precisely the transition of Chartism's programme from strictly political to *social* demands.[143] *'Chartism has essentially a social nature'*, he asserted.[144]

Engels posited that at the root of this shift were not the actions of petty-bourgeois agitators, but the fact that 'workers began to see themselves as a class in its entirety' and, consequently, to understand their collective strength. This shift also implied the separation from the bourgeoisie in terms of 'consciousness', i.e., 'the constitution of perceptions and ideas peculiar to workers and their living conditions'. As a result of this process, 'the awareness [*Bewusstsein*] of being oppressed sets itself in, and workers take on a political and social importance'.[145] Friedrich Engels's narrative of the development of class consciousness, therefore, sharply diverged from that of Weber's, considering that, to the former, it was the growing awareness of the *common* interests of the working-class as a whole, by workers themselves, that signalled their

141 MWG I/4, p. 341.

142 MWG I/4, p. 571.

143 'The "knife and fork questions" of the Pastor Stephens were a truth only for a part of Chartists in 1838; it became a truth for all in 1845' (MEW 2, p. 451).

144 MEW 2, pp. 450–1.

145 MEW 2, p. 349.

emergence as relevant political and social actors, as opposed to latter's notion of a *detachment* of a 'higher-standing' segment of 'politically mature' workers.

∴

In retrospect, Friedrich Engels's assessment that 'nationality is annihilated in the worker', while based on a still valid understanding of the world-spanning nature of the capitalist system and of the fact that it would take a cross-border alliance of workers to challenge it, seems less clairvoyant than Max Weber's claim that 'mature' workers would ultimately identify with their nation-state and willingly support imperial expansion. The fate of the SPD in August 1914 would also dramatically lend weight to Weber's stance in this debate.[146]

That said, the aim of this section has been less a comparison of both thinkers' perspectives on workers, than to show how Weber's outlook was sharpened and enriched through his contact and sincere engagement with the work of Engels. This process would, in a way, continue, though in reverse direction, as Max Weber's work challenged an entire new generation of Marxist thinkers, from Georg Lukács, Ernst Bloch and Antonio Gramsci to Walter Benjamin and the Frankfurt School among many others. That is not to say that these thinkers became Weberian through this dialogue, just as Weber did not become a historical materialist through his close reading of Friedrich Engels's work. Unearthing the dialogue between Engels and Weber does not mean arguing for a 'Marxist' Weber. There are other forms of engagement between authors besides adhesion and outright rejection. What Heinrich Heine argued about the relationship of Spinoza to Descartes, i.e., that 'genius fashions itself through another great genius, less by assimilation than by friction', is, as I aimed to show, surprisingly accurate in terms of Weber's relationship to Engels (and to Marx, of course).

The fruitfulness of this dialogue across ideological and class lines becomes evident when Weber's relationship to a fellow bourgeois intellectual, Lujo Brentano, is considered. Though belonging to different generations, Weber and Brentano shared a desire to renew German liberalism and both looked to Britain for inspiration. Yet, their preferred course of action was literally worlds apart. As Detlef Lehnert remarked, Brentano criticised the leading figures behind the National-Social Association for hitting 'the "wrong address"

146 For a nuanced take on the historical path leading up to the SPD majority's support for Germany's entry into war, in a flagrant surrender of the party's previous internationalist viewpoint, see Hoffrogge 2017, pp. 186–93.

in their efforts at political persuasion', considering that 'instead of winning the bourgeoisie for their social ideas, they tried to win over workers for their national perspective'.[147] Brentano would stand firmly by the notion that only the 'idea of the rule of law [*Rechtsidee*]' and 'never the naked power idea' could serve as the 'guiding principle' going forward for social-liberals. In light of future developments, this outlook seems less erroneous than hopelessly naïve. Thus, while Brentano was no doubt more knowledgeable on British history and politics, Weber was the one to have emphasised the centrality of empire for the emergence of Britain as a world power and for the formation of its 'labour aristocracy'. That this insight came at least in part through a dialogue with Friedrich Engels is revealing of the peculiar genesis of Max Weber's outlook in a late nineteenth-century Imperial Germany ripe with social struggle and political transformation. In this sense, Weber's dialogue with Engels is a microcosm of the former's early trajectory.

∴

A final and telling instance where the views of Weber and Engels form an almost perfectly inverted image of each other was in their respective assessments of the future of socialism in Britain. Weber closed his lessons on the labour movement and 'labour question' of 1895 and 1898 with a consideration of the current state of English working-class politics. The most important development of recent years had been the 'participation of unskilled workers in the trade union movement';[148] this was significant considering that it ran counter to Weber's 'ideal-typical' understanding of how the labour movement developed and 'matured', i.e., through the gradual detachment of a well-organised 'labour aristocracy' from the rest of the working masses. A second element of recent English occurrences also seemed to collide with Weber's two-staged understanding of the dynamic of social conflict, namely, that this 'enlargement of the trade union movement went hand in hand with state-socialist ideas'[149] or, as he put it in his notes to these lessons,

> Complications with a *political* labour movement.
> Offspring of the *unskilled* unions. Penetration of continental socialism
> Very questionable subsequent development

147 Brentano apud Lehnert 2012, p. 122.
148 MWG III/4, p. 306.
149 MWG III/4, p. 307.

> Apparently, constitution of a broad group from the less-developed skilled workers and the more highly-developed unskilled.[150]

Weber had to somehow explain why a segment of the working class he had described as lacking both the economic position and degree of consciousness necessary to engage in political action and union organising had done so with surprising success from the late 1880s and throughout the 1890s in Britain. According to Weber, the fact that unskilled workers could not regulate the offer of labour power like skilled ones could – meaning they were more easily replaceable – explained why they turned to the state (rather than to self-help through unions) for the fulfilment of their welfare demands. Weber believed this equally explained the fact that 'continental socialism' had suddenly emerged as a factor in Britain in the late nineteenth century.

Finally, the apparent emergence of a new coalition within the working class – uniting the 'lower' segments of skilled labour and 'higher-standing' unskilled workers – was another phenomenon Weber's initial conceptualisation did not allow for. In Weber's projection there was, after all, no space for the self-organisation and rising consciousness of *unskilled* workers. Weber identified the roots for this in the unfavourable economic situation of the period, which was beneficial for the 'socialist tendency' amongst English workers. This tendency was also behind the proposal to build a 'broad worker's party, in which the unions of the older and newer tendencies would be absorbed'.[151] With Weber's framework to understand such phenomena allowing little space for workers' own agency (particularly in the case of unskilled workers), the question of whether a socialist party would emerge in Britain was reduced to a single overriding factor:

> In any event, the future of the labour movement is dependent on England's international power position. If it regresses, the penetration of Social Democracy is certain.[152]

Hence, if imperial expansion had been the element Weber saw as primarily responsible for the sustained detachment of a 'labour aristocracy' from the rest of English workers, then a partial reversal of this process of 'social differentiation' could only mean that the power of the British Empire had

150 MWG III/4, p. 240.
151 MWG III/4, p. 307.
152 MWG III/4, p. 307.

itself begun to stagnate.[153] In this sense, for all the keen realism that characterised Weber's views of social conflict in England – setting him apart from the rose-coloured accounts of figures like Lujo Brentano – there was still a fundamental bias in his understanding of working-class politics. For, even in light of growing evidence, Weber refused to recognise the primary role of the autonomous agency of workers – above all of unskilled workers – in recent developments of the labour movement in England. This bias was a product of Weber's deep-seated conviction that *Kultur* – and the greater degree of individual autonomy that was its hallmark – was not to be found in the lowest strata of society. Speaking before the Protestant Social Congress, Weber remarked how

> The enlightenment fervour that prevailed twenty or thirty years ago is behind us now; it has been thrown in the rubbish heap. Ever since we consciously faced the crude fact that, for a long time to come and perhaps enduringly, our societal conditions will at most allows us to bread a feeble half-education in the masses, we lost interest in 'enlightenment' for its own sake.[154]

Despite all that separated Max Weber's generation from that of his liberal forefathers, and I have argued throughout this work that the rise of the labour movement was a key factor in the development of his viewpoint beyond a patriarchal stance, it seems it was not enough to uproot a deep-seated conviction regarding the inability of the masses (or at least a broad segment among them) to be permeable to 'enlightenment' and *Kultur*. Since Weber had framed the rise of German Social Democracy not as the expression of a working-class agency that bred its own distinct cultural achievements, but within a narrative of gradual 'maturation' en route to its ultimate convergence with the English prototypical case, no amount of evidence would convince him that workers' autonomous agency could be behind recent processes of social change across the Channel. Thus, in the case of the estimation of the future of the English labour movement and of English socialism, this prevented Weber from recognising what Friedrich Engels characterised in 1892 as 'one of the greatest and most fruitful facts of this *fin de siècle*', one he was 'glad and proud' to have lived to see, namely, 'the revival of the East End of London':

---

153 In his notes to this lesson, Weber makes a direct connection between the '*stability*' of British imperial expansion and a halting of 'social differentiation' (MWG III/4, p. 240).

154 MWG I/4, p. 333.

> That immense haunt of misery is no longer the stagnant pool it was six years ago. It has shaken off its torpid despair, has returned to life, and has become the home of what is called the 'New Unionism', that is to say, of the organisation of the great mass of 'unskilled' workers. This organisation may to a great extent adopt the form of the old Unions of 'skilled' workers but it is essentially different in character … The new Unions were founded at a time when the faith in the eternity of the wage system was severely shaken; their founders and promoters were socialists either consciously or by feeling; the masses, whose adhesion gave them strength, were rough, neglected, looked down upon by the working-class aristocracy; but they had this immense advantage, that *their minds were virgin* soil, entirely free from the inherited 'respectable' bourgeois prejudices which hampered the brains of the better situated 'old' Unionists. And thus we see now these new Unions taking the lead of the working-class movement generally, and more and more taking in tow the rich and proud 'old' Unions.[155]

To his credit, Max Weber did indicate at the end of his appraisal of the current situation in England that he took these latest events, which had so elated the elder Engels, quite seriously. Having previously characterised as optimistic the notion that the emergence of the 'labour aristocracy' had solved the 'labour question', it is nevertheless noteworthy that he would end his diagnosis of the country that constituted the paragon of successful containment of working-class politics with the following words: 'In any event, the "social question" in England is far from being solved and conditions there are just as problematic as on the continent'.[156]

155 MEW 22, pp. 328–9.
156 MWG III/4, p. 307.

Epilogue: The Late Max Weber and the Problem of the Non-existing Alternative to Capitalism

The writings and interventions analysed in this work are not the ones that raised Max Weber to the status of a classic. His report for the Verein für Socialpolitik and most of the material on the 'rural workers' question' quoted in the previous chapters were never widely read or translated and, if so, only piecemeal. Their impact has, therefore, been limited to scholarship *on Weber*, rather than on their subject matter itself. The same applies to the rest of his output from the 1890s, i.e., the writings on the stock exchange and, to a lesser extent, the essay on the 'decline of ancient culture' – which did find some resonance amongst historians of Greco-Roman antiquity. There is no question then that, while impressive in their sheer volume and, especially for today's standards, thematic breadth, Weber's production before the onset of his illness around 1898 would not have sufficed to raise him to posthumous notoriety. A full-blown novel analytical perspective on social life would only emerge with his return to intellectual work (though not to full health or a university post) in 1903. The results of this new phase of production appeared mainly in the journal *Archiv für Sozialpolitik und Sozialwissenschaften*, whose editorship he took over alongside Werner Sombart and Edgar Jaffé in 1904; having distanced himself from academia, the *Archiv* would constitute the main platform for Weber's scholarly engagement until the war. This resumption of activities also coincided with a key thematic shift; religion now played a central role in Weber's historical-analytical efforts; his two-part essay on the *Protestant Ethic and the Spirit of Capitalism* [PE] would be the first major product of this new orientation and, though contemporary German *intelligentsia* took heed of and would continue to hold Weber's work in high regard until his death in 1920, it is Weber's post-war global reception that cemented the canonical standing of his post-1903 writings.[1]

As a result, most of what has been read in the syllabuses of sociology, history and political science courses since the 1950s all around the world belongs to this later, 'mature' phase in Weber's *oeuvre*. Besides the PE and the wider 'sociology of religion' which came to frame it, the posthumously edited *Economy and Society*, the methodological writings and the 'vocation' lectures all stem from this period. Also worth mentioning are Weber's political writings during the First

1 See Derman 2016, Mata 2013, Morcillo Laiz and Weisz (eds.) 2016.

World War and the early Weimar Republic, which, despite constituting interventions 'in the spur of the moment', have attained a canonical status of their own. Finally, the fact that Weber's (partial) recovery from illness kicked off this celebrated phase of production, added a clear biographical break to the intellectual one. This has only contributed to the notion that Weber's first decade of scholarly output, starting with his PhD dissertation on medieval trading companies in 1889, is at best fodder for the historical and biographical pursuits of the most motivated amongst (German-reading) 'Weberologists'. As is the case with many other predominant lines of interpretation of Weber's work, Talcott Parsons helped formulate what would long define the consensus around the status of the 'early' writings:

> the earlier period remained on the whole one of disconnected historical studies with a rather definite materialistic bias. A change of orientation came in rather dramatic fashion with Weber's recovery from the nervous breakdown which forced his retirement from all scientific work ...[2]

Parsons saw further evidence for this 'dramatic' break in the fact that the youthful Weber's preoccupation with '"material" factors' was, as he put it, 'material in the Marxian sense'. This emphasis was supposedly already visible in the 'economic slant' of Weber's doctoral thesis, but found its culmination in his writings on antiquity, though Parsons conceded that their stress on 'material factors' concerned 'military organization rather than the economic in a narrower sense'.[3] It would, however, be unfair to blame the sedimentation of this view within the scholarship on Parsons's intervention alone; his German contemporary – and main editor of Weber's work from the 1950s onwards – Johannes Winkelmann reacted to the proposal of a *Gesamtausgabe* in the 1970s, i.e., the critical edition of Weber's works, letters and materials, by remarking that 'all the relevant texts of scientific importance were already known'.[4]

Finally, the one text from the 1890s that is widely read is Weber's 'Freiburg Inaugural Speech' [*Antrittsrede*] of 1895. A caustic and undeniably nationalist intervention that also marked the racist peak of Weber's anti-Polish agitation, it is framed precisely as the immature, value-laden and methodologically questionable counterpart to the balanced and sophisticated *Objectivity* essay of 1903 (and the substantive contributions that followed it).

2 Parsons 1968, p. 503.
3 Parsons 1968, pp. 502–3.
4 Hanke et al. 2012, p. 69.

While Weber's early production merits the critiques it has drawn from Weberians and non-Weberians alike and if the later production contained important departures with regards to it, positing a rigid 'youthful' vs. 'mature' dichotomy within his work is misleading. The major reason I chose to focus on his writings of the 1890s in this work, aside from the fact that not much scholarship has been produced on them, is precisely because of the many keys they provide to his post-1903 production. In similar terms, though my analysis of Weber's relationship with the German labour movement, Marx's work etc. only encompasses his 'early phase', I am convinced that a consideration of his later production through this prism would equally yield valuable insights. While making good on this claim would mean a whole other monograph (or two …) and years of work, with this epilogue I aim to provide enough preliminary evidence to indicate that the insights contained in previous chapters can provide keys not only to understanding the 'young' Weber, but also the canonical one.

∴

My starting point is a candid balance sheet of Max Weber's efforts at tackling the 'rural labour question' that doubles as an analysis of their political and historical context provided by … Weber himself. His *Editorial Preface* to the publication of the Protestant Social Congress's rural minister survey[5] – undertaken by his doctoral students – is one of the many treasures buried deep in the *Gesamtausgabe*. The fact that the preface dates from 1899 already makes it a significant document, considering it is among the very last pieces Weber published before his illness took an incapacitating turn. Written at a point when he had not only decided to give up his teaching duties and abandon scholarly work but must also confront his utter failure to influence policy on several fronts, the text is uniquely forthright. Max Weber had never refrained from openly expounding his views in the interventions of the 1890s; yet, his awareness of the many conflicting interests that came to bear on his topics of inquiry at this juncture – especially the social and labour 'questions' and the matter of Prussian dominance in Imperial Germany – had not only put objectivity and partisanship in scholarship at the centre of his concerns, but had also led him to adopt a (for his standards) predominantly cautious and measured tone. Politically

5 See Chapter 7 for a detailed discussion of the survey, which was carried out by Max Weber and Paul Göhre in 1892/93 as a follow-up to the Verein's own 1892 landowner survey on the 'situation of rural workers'.

defeated, with a declining interest in his adopted area of academic work (political economy) and suffering from depression, Max Weber no longer seemed to care about the consequences of printing exactly what he thought in the preface of 1899.

His considerations come after a copy of the questionnaire sent to rural ministers[6] and some brief observations on the number of respondents (about 1,000) and their regional distribution.[7] The first remark worthy of note is Weber's explanation for the six-year interval separating the arrival of the last filled-out questionnaires (in mid-1893) and the publication of their analysis in 1899. On the one hand, the gap was the consequence of 'purely personal circumstances'; his editorship and initial efforts to analyse the material himself had been constantly interrupted by the 'appointment to a teaching position, with two subsequent changes of post, including, at one point, the shift to a new discipline' and an illness that was 'slight at first', but proved 'lasting'.[8] There were also the familiar questions of funding the data analysis phase and finding a publisher willing to take on the project. In spite of these difficulties, Weber asserts that he never considered transferring his editorial duties to another scholar – for fear the project would never be concluded – and adds that the 'analysis of individual regions' was eventually carried out by the 'gentlemen of my [doctoral] seminar'. This work transpired, as Weber put it, 'under my supervision and scrutiny' and, apart from interventions directed at fostering a coherent assessment across the individual case studies, 'in full scientific autonomy'.[9]

Weber then explains that the analytical focus on a few provinces in Northern Germany resulted from the 'numerous and workable material' they had yielded. As for Upper Silesia and Posen (in the German Northeast) and both the Rhineland and Westphalia to the West an important hurdle had arisen; because the large '*purely* Catholic areas' of these provinces suffered from 'an obvious lack of respondents', they had to be excluded from consideration.[10] Furthermore, in those areas where there was a 'confessional mix' of Protestant and Catholics material was sparce, because, as confessional statistics showed, 'the strata with the lowest social standing … are carriers of Catholicism', something that is 'especially valid for the countryside' and, therefore, applies 'in particular to

6 MWG I/4, pp. 694–705. I analyse the questionnaire from the Protestant Minister survey in detail in sections 7.2 and 7.3, contrasting it to the Verein's questionnaire.

7 MWG I/4, p. 706.

8 Ibid.

9 MWG I/4, p. 707.

10 Ibid.

rural workers'.[11] But why not fill this considerable gap by sending 'similar questionnaires' to the Catholic clergy? Weber matter-of-factly remarks that he had 'pondered this idea with his Catholic students', but that

> … *for me as a Protestant*, given prevailing circumstances, it would sadly have been a pointless effort; what is more, it would have likely triggered the mistrust of the Ordinariates[12] leading to inconveniences for the clergymen willing to participate in the survey.[13]

It is a well-known fact that Martin Offenbacher's insight into the correlation between confession and social standing in Baden delivered a key building block for Weber's conceptualisation of a 'protestant Ethic'. Weber even referenced his doctoral student in the opening pages of his famous essay,[14] in what is the most direct link between his own agrarian studies of the 1890s and the PE. The quotes above add nothing new in this regard; what is noteworthy about them is how Weber framed his and his students' religious positionality with regards to scholarly work. While his entire approach to the 'rural labour question' was predicated on overcoming one-sided standpoints on the issue, Weber dismisses an effort at overcoming religious, as opposed to class divides, as a futile pursuit. In fact, though he did reaffirm elsewhere in the 1899 *Preface* that obtaining a counterpoint to landowners' views and gaining access to rural workers' perspectives in a 'manner that was the least indirect possible' were key reasons for turning to Protestant ministers as respondents,[15] he somehow never seriously considered the notion of leveraging Catholic clergy towards the same goals. Also telling is the fact that if this extension of the survey was considered at all, it was conceived as a task for Catholic researchers alone, because a Protestant professor was regarded *a priori* as a biased party.

Weber's capitulation in this front indicates that while he held workers' 'ethical-ideal drivers' to be accessible to the bourgeois scholar (given sufficient data and a suitable approach), the views of working-class Catholics were off-limits to a Protestant researcher. The resulting analytical blind-spot harkens back to Weber's analogous refusal to consider the ethical drivers of Polish migrant workers as relevant factors for an assessment of the 'rural labour ques-

11 Ibid.
12 Ordinariates are the administrative organs of Roman Catholic dioceses and archdioceses.
13 MWG I/4, p. 708, my highlights.
14 MWG I/18, p. 126, n. 4 and also pp. 128–30.
15 MWG I/4, p. 708.

tion' in the German East.[16] Thus, while class barriers could be analytically overcome to some extent, religious and ethnic-racial divides could not. The keyword here, as is often the case with Max Weber, is *culture*. The shared cultural status of the bourgeois and the 'high-standing' worker afforded a mutual 'legibility' of subjective drivers; as for relationships structured by 'cultural difference', whose markers were religion and race, but also *class* – if the gap was large enough – such a legibility was lost.

In Weber's post-1903 work, this normative understanding of *Kultur* would come into tension with its formal framing along anthropological and relativist lines. The latter is best expressed in a celebrated quote from his 1904 essay, 'The "Objectivity" of Knowledge in Social Sciences and Social Policy':

> The transcendental precondition of every *cultural science is not* that we find a particular, or indeed any, 'culture' *valuable*, but that we *are* cultural *beings*, endowed with the capacity and the will to adopt a deliberate *position* with respect to the world, and to bestow *meaning* upon it. Whatever this meaning may be, it will become the basis on which we are, in our life, led to *judge* certain phenomena of human existence in common and to adopt a (positive or negative) position with respect to them because we regard them as *significant*.[17]

This take on culture as a fundamental aspect of human beings' relationship to the world was in stark contrast to its normative framing along class and ethnic lines from his earlier writings. Their dissonance notwithstanding, Weber *never fully abdicated* from the earlier (normative) understanding of culture in favour of the latter, anthropological one. Even the most cursory consideration of the PE, i.e., the paragon text of his mature phase, shows this to be the case.

∴

Weber indicates the continuity between his 'rural labour' studies of the 1890s and the PE at the very beginning of his essay – on page 2 of the original 1904 publication to be more precise. After his opening remark on the existence of a link between confession and social standing as per official German statist-

16 See Chapter 10.

17 Weber 2012, p. 119. Here in the excellent translation of the Whimster and Bruun volume of methodological writings.

ics, pointing to the 'starkly *predominant* Protestant character' of capitalists and the 'higher skilled segments of the working class' alike, Weber stresses that this applied

> Not only in those places where the discrepancy of confession coincides with a difference in nationality, and **thus in the degree of cultural development** [*Grad der Kulturentwicklung*], as in the German East between Germans and Poles, but almost everywhere where capitalist development, at the moment of its greatest expansion, had a free hand to alter the social structure and the occupational profile of the population according to its needs ...[18]

The quote above betrays the enduring normative character of Weber's conceptualisation of culture into his 'mature' work in two (subtle) ways. First, in the use of the connective 'thus' [*damit*], which creates a causal relationship between 'difference in nationality' – understood as ethnicity, just as in his earlier writings – and 'degree of cultural development'. Second, in the notion of *Kulturentwicklung* itself which, framed as a sliding scale measured in 'degrees', presupposed a hierarchy amongst different 'cultures' (as in the supposed disparity between ethnic Poles and Germans).

However, the fact that Weber's matter-of-fact example of an instance of 'cultural difference' in the opening of the PE regards ethnic Poles means that the passage can be dismissed as a product of Weber's stubborn 'prejudices', supposedly no different than those of the 'average German' of the age. But this problematic line of argumentation becomes untenable when, further on in the work, Weber returns to the findings of his 'rural labour' studies in an effort to provide empirical evidence for the gap in 'cultural development' between Germans and Poles. The divergence in how the working-class representatives of these ethnicities relate to labour is leveraged by Weber to demonstrate how the struggle of the 'capitalist "spirit"' with its foremost 'opponent', 'traditionalism', plays out 'from below'.[19] Non-coincidentally, the issue of workers' attitudes towards the 'piece-wage' is the chosen example. In his 'rural labour' writings, Weber had found the resistance on the part of workers to this more intensive and exploitative form of labour control to be the starkest evidence for the centrality of 'ethical-ideal drivers' to economic activity; workers' rejection

---

18 MWG I/18, pp. 126–7. I opted for the most literal translation possible. Talcott Parsons's – now much maligned – effort is actually the most precise across extant translations of the PE with regards to this particular passage.

19 MWG I/18, p. 176.

of the 'piece-wage' system had shown their desire for freedom clearly overrode economic incentives.[20] In the PE, on the other hand, Weber emphasises the possible manipulation of piece-wage remuneration by workers who '"by nature"' only desire to 'earn as much as necessary' so as to live 'as they are accustomed to living', i.e., the 'leitmotiv of pre-capitalist economic labour'.[21] Weber does caution against the attempt to stamp out such 'traditionalist' impulses by simply repressing wages;[22] yet, one of his arguments as to why this might fail – 'the efficiency of labour decreases with a wage which is physiologically insufficient' – is symptomatically exemplified with a return (without naming it as such) to his 'intensity of Germanness' scale, that is, his benchmark of cultural level drawn from a (racialised) ethnic cartography of the German East:

> The present-day average Silesian mows, when he exerts himself to the full, little more than two-thirds as much land as the better paid and nourished Pomeranian or Mecklenburger, and the Pole, the further East he comes from, accomplishes progressively less than the German.[23]

The evidence for Weber's use of 'nationality' as an indicator for 'cultural difference' is, however, not restricted to the German/Polish contrast; in fact, it is found throughout the PE and arguably structures its entire argument. One telling example that is harder to dismiss as 'simply' an instance of nationalist or 'anti-Polish' bias are Weber's remarks on the French and 'French culture' in the PE. While relatively sparse, they play a significant role in the work, mostly in terms of aiding in Weber's effort at conceptual definition by means of the negative case. The most relevant remark on the French in the PE follows Weber's key assertion that 'purely mundane rational philosophy' did not flourish only, or even predominantly, in 'highly developed capitalist countries':

> If under 'practical rationalism' a type of life conduct is understood which consciously grasps the world in terms of the worldly interests of the isolated individual, judging it from this vantage point, then this way of life was and is the very much typical peculiarity of the peoples of "liberum arbitrium", such as the Italians and the French are in very flesh and blood.

20 See the detailed analysis in section 8.5, above.
21 MWG I/18, pp. 177–8.
22 MWG I/18, p. 179.
23 MWG I/18, p. 180, here in the Parsons' translation.

> But we have already convinced ourselves that this is by no means the soil in which that relationship of a human being to his "calling" in terms of a task, as was necessary for capitalism, has pre-eminently grown.[24]

In this and other passages of the PE, Weber conjoins France and Italy as nations anchored on a self-referenced kind of individualist personality, running the gamut from the charlatan to the humanist; Thomas Mann arguably forged a character uniting both extremes in *Magic Mountain*'s Lodovico Settembrini. Elsewhere in the PE Weber refers to the Catholicism of the French masses as particularly *lebensfroh* or 'fond of life',[25] suggesting the same brand of 'inner-worldly' individualism flourished lower down the social hierarchy. If, from a hermeneutical perspective, Weber has good reason to exclude the 'Mediterranean' personality type – even in its more rationalist iterations – from the purveyors of *Beruf*, the way he construes the French in the PE cannot but evoke his youth in an Imperial Germany united 'externally' through a war with France, and whose persecution of Catholics – i.e., the *Kulturkampf* – was one of the earliest state-sponsored efforts to unite it 'internally'.[26]

Both vectors intersect in Weber's praise of Werner Wittich's work on the 'struggle of nationalities' in Alsace, published in 1900.[27] Wittich also attributed an 'individualist character' not only to France's 'intellectual culture [*geistige Kultur*]', but also to its 'economic, social and political culture[s]'.[28] In an assessment that Weber would echo in the PE, Wittich concluded that this cultural peculiarity led to a predominance of 'subjective traits' over 'objective institutions', of 'products of individual taste, of craftsmanship or of diligent care', over 'mass production' and so on.[29]

If the French-German rivalry and the status of Alsace as a quasi-colonial space in Imperial Germany informs such comparisons as much as any actual empirical work, the fact that similar constructs characterise Weber's view of Italians point to deeper-seated aspects of his understanding of culture:

> As every factory owner knows, the insufficient 'coscienziosità' of the workers of these countries, say of Italy in contrast to Germany, has been and,

24 MWG I/18, p. 208 – This is a heavily modified version of the Parsons translation.

25 MWG I/18, p. 138.

26 See my analysis of the young Weber's ambivalent stance towards the *Kulturkampf* in section 4.2 above.

27 See MWG I/18, p. 138, n. 15.

28 Wittich 1900, p. 86.

29 Wittich 1900, pp. 85–6.

> to an certain extent, still is one of the main impediments of their capitalist expansion. Capitalism has no use for the practical representatives of undisciplined 'liberum arbitrium' as workers.[30]

The notions of a clearly discernible national character and of the nation as an elementary cultural unit betray, in their centrality to Weber's *Protestant Ethic*, their pre-World War I apex. The reason such recurrent statements – and their connection to Weber's writings of the 1890s – have so often been overlooked or dismissed in the scholarship as evidence for the survival of a normative concept of culture in his mature work corresponds to Weber's own attempts to qualify and relativise them. Italian workers' personality type hampered 'bourgeois-capitalist expansion' only as '*measured* by the standards set by occidental development';[31] in other words, given a specific benchmark, to which supposedly no intrinsic value is attributed, this conduct of life proved unfavourable. If, to go back to the *Objectivity* essay, '"Culture" is a finite section of the meaningless infinity of events in the world' which is 'endowed with meaning and significance' by a human agent, then Weber can claim he 'arrived at this position' – namely, the downgrading of 'Mediterranean' culture – 'by relating that particular culture to his value ideas and finding it "wanting"'.[32] As such, his assertion becomes, in fact, the function of a '*purely logical and formal* circumstance', that is, 'that all historical individuals must by logical necessity be anchored in "value ideas"'.[33]

Hence, by taking *technical* development as a 'value idea' and framing capitalism as a social phenomenon so universal that it becomes 'fate', Weber can argue that appraising ethnicities and personality types according to their 'significance' to this 'particular' cultural macrocosm is a *formal*, rather than a normative operation. This application of Weber's objectivity-paradigm in appraisals of his empirical work, as if the latter was the chemically pure incarnation of his own methodological prescriptions, has been the main bastion of most defences of the formal nature of his understanding of culture. Put shortly, it is the world that is Eurocentric, not the thinker. And majority-Protestant nations (especially Anglo-Saxon countries) are the best at being capitalist (at least until now), raising the 'value-free' question as to why. Regarding this 'virgin birth' perspective on his output, I can only say Weber was not *Weberian* and that you cannot understand him exclusively in his own terms. These final pages offer some hypothesis as to why.

---

30 MWG I/18, p. 173.
31 Ibid, my emphasis.
32 Weber 2012, p. 119.
33 Ibid.

∴

An issue arising out of attempts to translate expressions such as *Kulturbedeutung* (cultural significance) and *Kulturentwicklung* (cultural development) into English and Romance languages casts doubt on the sophisticated elision of partisanship inherent in Weber's late work. In these categories, namely, culture is used as an attributive noun, i.e., as a noun that modifies another noun. This means that, in contrast to other concepts Weber employs such as 'modern culture' [*moderne Kultur*] or 'capitalist culture' [*kapitalistische Kultur*], which suggest that culture is devoid of a content of its own – hence the need for adjectives – in the role of attributive noun, it is *culture* that provides the content of 'cultural *significance*' and 'cultural *development*'. If it were purely formal, it would hardly be able to perform this function. This contradiction at the core of Weber's 'objectivity' paradigm, that is, his imbuing of the formal with a determinate content that renders ostensibly formal operations into (silently) normative ones, is especially pertinent to how Weber articulates his stance towards capitalism in the PE and later writings.

Once more, examining Weber's 'mature' production as a development of, not anathema to, his earlier work provides important keys to support this claim. As I argued in Parts 2 and 3, Weber could only attribute a higher or lower level of culture to specific classes, class segments and ethnicities in his writings of the 1890s by furnishing the concept with a determinate content. While a capacity for autonomy and purposeful activity, on the one hand, and the desire to enjoy the 'goods of this world', on the other, might seem purely formal criteria for assessing one's 'degree of culture', their bourgeois-individualist tinge emerged when the former was tied to the industriousness of the property owner (or of those striving to achieve this status) and the latter to typically bourgeois forms of cultivation. As a result, Weber read workers' 'urge for freedom' and self-reliance in his 'rural labour' studies exclusively through the lenses of bourgeois notions of success and self-realisation.[34] In doing so, he ruled out that this drive could have an altogether different horizon, namely, radically *overcoming* existing social realities, and that cultural elevation and, indeed, new forms of culture, could be rooted in the working-class condition. The fact that the leading elements of the SPD, in line with a majority of its membership, held on to these positions also explains Weber's disappointment with the party by the mid-1890s.

---

34 For a critical analysis of Weber's understanding of *Bildung*, personality and individuality, see Farris 2013, pp. 47–50.

There can be little doubt that Weber continued to understand the relationship of culture, class and labour within a similar framework in his post-1903 major works, not least in the PE. As a contingent 'inner-worldly' byproduct of ascetic Protestants' search for salvation, entrepreneurship emerges in this classic work as the bourgeois anathema to the utopia of labour emancipation. As such, the silent 'flipside' of Weber's hypothesis that the *secularisation* of the Protestant (work-) ethic was capitalism's 'powerful helper',[35] consists in no less than the *sacralisation* of the capitalist societal form.[36] For if the ascetic Protestant derived a tremendous capacity for work, a drive for innovation and a mistrust of established authorities from their peculiar religious sentiment, as Weber argues throughout the PE, the fundamental presupposition for this 'conduct of life' was a relationship to God characterised by absolute subjection. Hence the paradox that ascetic Protestants' 'incredible world-transcending potency'[37] [*weltüberwindende Macht*] – i.e., their ability to intervene in and transform established worldly realities – was inscribed in their complete subservience to an external and objective power. This *ringfencing* of freedom, initiative and, indeed, of the drive to change the world within a horizon of willing subjection to a higher authority was to Weber just as crucial for ascetic Protestantism's functionality to a fledgling capitalist economic order as its dissemination of a rational and methodical conduct of life. And because the subject's fundamental condition of alienation before an unknowable, almighty God is not eliminated with the onset of what Weber called the process of 'secularisation', the eclipsing of religion as a shaper of life conduct only *changes the form* of this alienated relationship, never transcending it. If anything, the 'disenchanted' rule of capital is even more desolate than that of the Calvinist or Puritan God – which opened up (to some) the possibility of salvation:

> The capitalistic economic order of the present day is an immense cosmos into which the individual is born, and which manifests itself to him, at least as an individual, as an unalterable framework [*Gehäuse*] in which he must live. It forces the individual, in so far as he is involved in the system of market relationships, to conform to its economic norms of action. The manufacturer who in the long run acts counter to these norms, will just

35 MWG I/18, p. 181.

36 It is no coincidence then that both Ernst Bloch and Walter Benjamin framed 'capitalism *as* religion' with reference to Weber's work, See Löwy 2013, pp. 127–47.

37 MWG I/18, p. 329.

> as inevitably be eliminated from the economic scene as the worker who cannot or will not adapt himself to them will be thrown into the streets without a job.[38]

Interestingly, Marx portrays the structural imperativeness of the law of value with regards to its societal bearers in very similar terms in his critique of political economy, most notably through the concept of social roles as variable, mutually related 'character masks' assigned by the prevailing relations of domination within a given mode of production;[39] just like Weber, Marx understood the self-reproductive, impersonal manner with which the process of capital valorisation imposes itself on its human agents to be one of the keys to its unprecedented capacity to develop forces of production (and consequently to exploit labour power and gobble up natural resources). But, while Marx 'examine[s] value-production from the vantage-point of both pre-capitalist *and* postcapitalist social relations',[40] the absence of any sensible ('inner-worldly') alternative to the capitalist cosmos in Weber's understanding of modernity[41] means its economic determinations (and societal patterns) invariably harden into *the* cultural norm. As a result, when Weber distils a specific personality type as the privileged carrier of advanced capitalist societies in the imperialist age, it becomes by default the benchmark to assess the cultural standing of a collection of 'others' which, in a manner akin to a set of distorted mirrors, are framed as traditional, unorderly, sentimental and inefficient.[42]

---

38 MWG I/18, pp. 161–62. This, and further quotes from the PE are modified versions of the Parsons translation.

39 In the words of Wolfgang Fritz Haug, with his concept of 'character mask' Marx expresses the 'form in which individuals are positioned towards each other and characterised in opposition to one another through their placement within specific relations of domination' (See 'Charaktermaske', HKWM 2, 1995, p. 442).

40 Hudis 2012, p. 155. In fact, as Hudis stresses, Marx's entire critique of political economy was predicated on the possibility that '[w]ith the creation of a free association of individuals who consciously plan out the production and distribution of the social product, labour ceases to be subject to the dictatorship of … an external, abstract, and impermeable force governing them irrespective of their will and needs' (2012, p. 159). In this sense, not only can the 'character masks' be overcome together with the social relations that forged them but, even within the capitalist mode of production, it is an 'imprint of relations that by no means fully encompasses the concrete individual' (Haug, 'Charaktermaske', HKWM 2, 1995, p. 446).

41 See Löwy 2013, p. 140.

42 The metaphor stems from Josep Fontana's *Europa ante el Espejo* [Europe before the mirror], translated in 1995 as *The distorted past: a reinterpretation of Europe* (Oxford: Blackwell, 1995).

Beyond a Eurocentric or Orientalist warping of perception, this stance results from the equally political, if silent, premise that there is no possible societal form beyond capitalism which does not represent a regression in terms of freedom, technical development and individual self-expression. In terms of Weber's relationship to Marx, here was a lesser-known, 'implicit' critique. As Sara Farris has argued, beyond the rejection of historical materialism's inherent 'one-sidedness' 'as a way of explaining social phenomena', Weber also criticised 'Marx's ideal vision of humanity freed from the prison of vocation and given the ability to determine its own realisation'.[43] Yet, by establishing this closed horizon, Weber hardwired alienation into modern social life, extirpating any possible progressive alternative to its capitalist iteration. To evoke Bolívar Echeverría's conceptualisation, there is no modernity in Weber's paradigm that does not carry its current capitalist form, i.e., no 'alternative' modernity to its capitalist variant is conceivable.[44]

This explains why Weber considered a Puritan faith anchored 'in unconditionally valid norms with absolute determinism' and the 'total transcendence of the otherworldly' [*Übersinnliches*] to be 'significantly "*more modern*"' than 'any doctrine … that also subjected God to the laws of morality'.[45] Being 'more modern' means, therefore, not only the virtue of conducting rational, systematic, inner-worldly activity, but *at the same time* the ultimate submission to objective imperatives. In the framework of the PE, the affirmation of freedom and rationality are only possible within (never beyond) the confines of the established social order. This is what made the 'shell' of capitalist modernity 'hard as steel', a *stahlhartes Gehäuse* in Weber's oft-quoted metaphor. For the imperatives of this societal form manifest themselves even in those organisations ostensibly created to transcend it, like German Social Democracy. Contrary to claims that SPD members' vaunted discipline was an emulation of military conduct, Weber saw its roots

> in the living economic fate of the modern worker, which he experiences at every turn and which he finds once more and must abide to within the party. Party discipline is the reflection of the discipline in the factory.[46]

---

43 Farris 2013, p. 106.

44 'Mercantile socialization', i.e., a socialization based on the *commodity-form*, argues Echeverría, 'is a constituent element of the essence of modernity'. 'On the other hand', he stresses, 'mercantile-capitalist socialization is only distinctive of the particular form [*figura peculiar*] of modernity prevalent today' (2011 [1995], p. 112).

45 MWG I/18, p. 341.

46 MWG I/18, p. 162.

More than a side note, this extemporaneous reference to Social Democracy in a footnote of the PE speaks to what Gangolf Hübinger has called 'the central element of [Weber's] political anthropology'.[47] Weber best articulated it in a letter of 4 August 1908 to Robert Michels:

> There are two possibilities: either (1) 'my kingdom is not of this world' … – *or*: (2) the *affirmation* of culture (that is, of *objective* culture which manifests itself in *technical* etc. 'achievements') along with *adaptation* to the sociological conditions *of all* 'technical phenomena', be they economic, political or of any other kind (this would be embodied *to the furthest extent* precisely in 'collectivist societies'). In the second case, all talk of 'revolution' is farcical, and *any* idea of doing away with the 'domination of man over man' by means of *any* social system, *however* 'socialist', or of *any* form of 'democracy', however ingenious, is a utopia.[48]

In the passage, Weber opposes a drive for emancipation that he frames as fundamentally religious (irrespective of whether its subjects are anarcho-syndicalists or millenarian prophets) and a clearly *resigned* 'affirmation' of culture as expressed in technical achievements. Resigned, because profiting from modern advancements implies endorsing the conditions of their development, i.e., rationalisation, industrialisation, impersonal domination etc. and the social ills that accompany them. But Weber goes further. This passive endorsement equally implies the spontaneous corruption of any utopian impulses:

> Whomever desires to live as a 'modern human being', if only in the sense of having his daily newspaper and [access to] railways, electrics etc., *renounces* all those ideals that obscurely go through his mind; indeed, [he renounces them] as soon as he *abandons* the terrain of revolutionarism *for its own sake* and *in the absence* of any 'goal', indeed in the absence of even the *conceivability* of a 'goal'.

In this utter rejection of an *inner-worldly* horizon of radical transformation, which he banishes to the realm of the inconceivable, the 'realist', dispassionate Weber, reveals himself to be an early harbinger of the non-existing alternative to capitalism, that is, of *anti-utopia*. In Darko Suvin's recent definition:

47 Hübinger 2019, p. 184.

48 MWG II/5, p. 615f. The letter is also accessible online in the *Themenportal Europäische Geschichte* http://www.europa.clio-online.de/2007/Article=279.

> The anti-utopia is a targeted and openly political use of a closed horizon to refute, ridicule, and render unthinkable both the eutopia of a better possible world and the dystopia as awful warning about the writer's and readers' present situation.[49]

Rather than being in conflict with his value-free sociology, Weber's *political anthropology of the absent alternative* informs it on a fundamental level. The resulting understanding of political life exclusively in terms of 'power politics' and endless struggle, with all its ramifications for his social theory, was not, however, a product of purely intellectual influences. As Carl Levy surmised, it was rooted in a particular, even obsessive concern with 'the fate of German power'.[50] As such, it had a historical genesis in the dilemmas of a rising Imperial Germany, a 'classic "late developer"' ripe with contradictions;[51] thus, if the only pathway to ascendancy in the age of empire was the successful leveraging of the forces of capitalist innovation, labour mobilisation and wealth creation, then *surrendering to* and attempting to gain a prominent position *within* this 'cosmos' was the only choice for the nation, a unit outside of which Weber could hardly fathom a functioning advanced society.

Such geopolitical and political-economic macro considerations came to bear, in turn, at the level of the 'modern personality', for which similar imperatives existed. If one was to reject a pathway of 'other-worldly' salvation, the affirmation of purely objective culture became a norm. By tracing back this 'disenchanted' attitude to ascetic Protestants, Weber gave it, however, *more* than a genealogy; he furnished it with a specific *geography*. By fusing Northern and Central Europe as well as the North American colonies into a single cultural space on account of their Protestantism, Weber not only set it apart from a South that was already global, because it started in the Mediterranean and stretched all the way to Asia and Latin America, he also managed to detach it from the transnational breeding grounds of the Enlightenment, with its egalitarian and human rights traditions. Hence, in Weber's classic essay, *the ethic and the ethnic* become two sides of the same coin. The PE's narrative of the rise of

49 Suvin 2019, p. 150.

50 Levy 1999, p. 84.

51 See Mishra 2020 for a recent take on the prototypical status of Imperial Germany as a capitalist 'late-developer'; it is, in fact, this condition which would later catapult the *Reich*'s modernising reformers, such as Max Weber, as the foremost political educators of Americanist-Fordist hegemony, as Jan Rehmann forcefully demonstrated (see Rehmann 2015). This also helps explain Weber's early and enthusiastic reception as the modernising mentor for many nations striving for a way out of 'underdevelopment' in the post-WWII 'Third World'.

reified formal rationality[52] from its humble beginnings in the ascetic morality of fringe Protestant denominations to a cataclysmic shaper of human agency and social life *presupposed* the catastrophe of colonialism, yet still very much silenced it. The PE's obfuscation of settler-colonialism, slavery and imperialist conquest – broken only in the elegiacal references to those 'Puritan tradesmen', who were themselves 'hard as steel'[53] – constitutes, alongside the closed horizon of anti-utopia, the fundamental (and deeply intertwined) partisan gestures of Max Weber's intellectual edifice. It is also where the dividing line separating him from Marx – and other anti-colonial, emancipatory paradigms – is drawn. It is telling, then, that the section of Marx's *Capital* that most closely addresses the questions Weber would raise in the PE – the chapter on so-called 'primitive accumulation' – also contains this passage on Puritans' unspeakable violence against Native Americans:

> But even in the colonies properly so called, the Christian character of primitive accumulation did not belie itself. Those sober virtuosi of Protestantism, the Puritans of New England, in 1703, by decrees of their assembly set a premium of £40 on every Indian scalp and every captured red-skin ...[54]

As for the silence on the role of slavery for the rise of the United States to the status of the world's leading capitalist nation in the 1900s – the scandal of which, as I write this epilogue in the summer of 2020, has been the driving force behind unprecedented mass protests around the globe – W.E.B. Du Bois, a contemporary of Weber,[55] was equally emphatic:

> The Negro question is an inescapable legacy from which America cannot free itself without further ado. It is a debt that has been entered into to the advantage of the Americans living today. The contemporary industrial development of America is based on the blood and sweat of unpaid Negro labour in the seventeenth, eighteenth, and nineteenth centuries.[56]

52 In a similar sense, see Marcuse 1965.

53 MWG I/18, p. 302.

54 MEW 23, p. 781. For this translation of *Capital*, see https://www.marxists.org/archive/marx/works/1867-c1/ch31.htm.

55 For a critical account of how Du Bois interacted with the intellectuals of the Verein für Socialpolitik as a doctoral researcher in 1890s Imperial Germany, see Zimmerman 2012, pp. 104–10. For the context of Du Bois's article publication in the *Archiv* following Max Weber's trip to the United States in 1904, see Zimmermann 2012, pp. 210–12.

56 Du Bois 2006 [1906], in Joseph Fracchia's translation.

The passage comes from an essay originally published in German in the *Archiv* in 1906. The profound contradiction that is Max Weber, the historical individual, is ideally represented by the conjugation of his silences (and resigned affirmations) in the PE and his willing editorship of a radical thinker such as Du Bois. As this work has argued, Weber's relationship to the German labour movement followed the same dissonant tune; the makeup of his work and the magnitude of his contribution to social thought would not have been possible without his confrontation with the SPD, the mass movement it embodied and the ideas of Marx and Engels. Yet throw in his lot with them, he would not.

Carouge GE, Switzerland, Summer 2020

Bibliography and Sources

Albrecht, Heinrich 1902, *Handbuch der sozialen Wohlfahrtspflege in Deutschland. Auf Grund des Materials der Zentralstelle für Arbeiterwohlfartseinrichtungen*, Berlin: C. Heymann.

Aldenhoff-Hübinger, Rita 1988, 'Max Weber und der Evangelisch-soziale Kongreß', Wolfgang Schwentker and Wolfgang J. Mommsen (eds.), Max Weber *und seine Zeitgenossen*, Göttingen/Zürich: Vandenhoeck & Ruprecht, 285–296.

Aldenhoff-Hübinger, Rita 2002. *Agrarpolitik Und Protektionismus: Deutschland und Frankreich im Vergleich, 1879–1914*, Göttingen/Zürich: Vandenhoeck & Ruprecht.

Aldenhoff-Hübinger, Rita 2004, 'Max Weber's Inaugural Address of 1895 in the Context of the Contemporary Debates in Political Economy', *Max Weber Studies* 4, 2: 143–156.

Anderson, Margaret Lavinia 2000, *Practicing Democracy: Elections and Political Culture in Imperial Germany*, Princeton, NJ: Princeton Univ. Press.

Baumgarten, Hermann 1974 [1866], *Der Deutsche Liberalismus: eine Selbstkritik*, edited by Adolf M. Birke, Frankfurt a.M.: Ullstein.

Bebel, August 1891, *Die Frau und der Sozialismus*, Stuttgart, Dietz.

Bebel, August 1995, *Ausgewählte Reden und Schriften*, vol. 6, Berlin: Dietz.

Becker, Frank 2001, *Bilder von Krieg und Nation: Die Einigungskriege in der bürgerlichen Öffentlichkeit Deutschlands, 1864–1913*, München: Oldenbourg.

Bendikat, Elfi 1988, *Wahlkämpfe in Europa 1884 bis 1889: Parteiensysteme und Politikstile in Deutschland, Frankreich und Großbritannien*, Wiesbaden, Dt. Univ.-Verl.

Berger, Stefan 1997, *The search for normality: National identity and historical consciousness in Germany since 1800*, New York: Berghahn.

Bergler, Andrea 2011, *Von Armenpflegern und Fürsorgeschwestern: Kommunale Wohlfahrtspflege und Geschlechterpolitik in Berlin und Charlottenburg 1890 bis 1914*, Stuttgart: Steiner.

Bernet, Claus 2004, 'The "Hobrecht Plan" (1862) and Berlin's urban structure', *Urban History*, 31, 3: 400–419

Bernstein, Eduard 1899, *Die Voraussetzungen des Sozialismus und die Aufgaben der Sozialdemokratie*, Stuttgart: Dietz.

Bernstein, Eduard 1907, *Die Geschichte der Berliner Arbeiter-Bewegung: Ein Kapitel zur Geschichte der Deutschen Sozialdemokratie, 2. Die Geschichte des Sozialistengesetzes in Berlin*, Berlin: Vorwärts.

Bernstein, Eduard 1910, *Die Geschichte der Berliner Arbeiter-Bewegung: Ein Kapitel zur Geschichte der Deutschen Sozialdemokratie, 3. Fünfzehn Jahre Berliner Arbeiterbewegung unter dem Gemeinen Recht*, Berlin: Vorwärts.

Biefang, Andreas 1996, 'Der Streit um Treitschkes "Deutsche Geschichte" 1882/83. Zur

Spaltung des Nationalliberalismus und der Etablierung eines National-Konservativen Geschichtsbildes', *Historische Zeitschrift*, 262, 2: 391–422.

Biefang, Andreas 1999, Review of '*Heinrich von Treitschke. Politische Biographie eines deutschen Nationalisten* by Ulrich Langer', *Historische Zeitschrift, 268*, 2: 504–506.

Biefang, Andreas 2009, *Die andere Seite der Macht: Reichstag und Öffentlichkeit im 'System Bismarck' 1871–1890*, Düsseldorf: Droste.

Birke, Adolf 1974, 'Einleitung' in Hermann Baumgarten 1974 [1866], *Der Deutsche Liberalismus: eine Selbstkritik*, edited by Adolf M. Birke, Frankfurt a.M.: Ullstein.

Bismarck, Otto von 1895, *Fürst Bismarcks Gesammelte Reden*, vol. 3, Berlin: Cronbach.

Bismarck, Otto von 1981, *Die Großen Reden*, Lothar Gall (ed.), Berlin: Severin und Siedler.

Boatcă, Manuela 2013, '"From the Standpoint of Germanism": A Postcolonial Critique of Weber's Theory of Race and Ethnicity', *Political Power and Social Theory*, 24: 55–80.

Boatcă, Manuela 2015, *Global Inequalities Beyond Occidentalism*, Farnham: Ashgate.

Brakelmann, Günter et al. 1982, *Protestantismus und Politik: Werk und Wirkung Adolf Stoeckers*, Hamburg: Christians.

Brentano, Lujo 1872, *Die Arbeitergilden der Gegenwart*, Band 2: Zur Kritik der Englischen Gewerkvereine, Leipzig: Duncker & Humblot.

Bruch, Rüdiger vom (ed.) 1985, 'Bürgerliche Sozialreform im deutschen Kaiserreich', Rüdiger vom Bruch (ed.), *Weder Kommunismus Noch Kapitalismus: Bürgerliche Sozialreform in Deutschland vom Vormärz bis zur Ära Adenauer*, München: Beck, 61–179.

Bruhns, Hinnerk 2009, 'Scholarship and Political Commentary in the Day to Day in the Work of Max Weber: Some Historical Observations on the Theme of Value-Freedom', *Max Weber Studies* 9, 1: 95–121.

Brunn, Gerhard 1986, 'Vom politischen Kellerkind zur Mehrheitspartei: Die SPD in Köln 1875 bis 1914', Brunn, Gerhard (ed.) 1986, *Sozialdemokratie in Köln: Ein Beitrag Zur Stadt- Und Parteiengeschichte*, Köln: Emons, 49–82.

Cioli, Monica 2003, *Pragmatismus und Ideologie: Organisationsformen des Deutschen Liberalismus zur Zeit der Zweiten Reichsgründung (1878–1884)*, Berlin: Duncker & Humblot.

Conrad, Sebastian 2013, 'Rethinking German Colonialism in a Global Age', *The Journal of Imperial and Commonwealth History*, 41, 4: 543–566.

Day, Richard B. and Daniel Gaido (eds.) 2011, *Discovering Imperialism. Social Democracy to World War I*, Leiden: Brill.

Derman, Joshua 2016, *Max Weber in Politics and Social Thought: From Charisma to Canonization*, Cambridge: Cambridge Univ. Press, 2016

Dibble, Vernon K. 1968, 'Social Science and Political Commitments in the Young Max Weber', *European Journal of Sociology* 9, 1: 92–110.

Du Bois, W.E.B. 2006 [1906], 'Die Negerfrage in den Vereinigten Staaten (The Negro Question in the United States)', *CR: The New Centennial Review* 6, 3: 241–90.

Ducange, Jean-Numa 2020, *Jules Guesde: The birth of socialism and Marxism in France*, Cham: Palgrave.

Echeverría, Bolívar 2011 [1995], 'Modernidad y capitalismo: 15 tesis sobre la modernidad', in: *Antología. Crítica de la modernidad capitalista*, La Paz: Oxfam/Presidencia de la Asamblea Legislativa Plurinacional de Bolivia, 67–115.

Eley, Geoff 1976, 'Social imperialism in Germany: Reformist synthesis or reactionary sleight of hand?', in Joachim Radkau, Imanuel Geiss (eds.), *Imperalismus im 20. Jahrhundert: Gedenkschrift für George W.F. Hallgarten*, München: C.H. Beck, 71–86.

Eley, Geoff 1980, *Reshaping the German right: radical nationalism and political change after Bismarck*, New Haven, London: Yale University Press.

Eley, Geoff 1984, 'The British Model and the German Road: Rethinking the Course of German History Before 1914', Blackbourn, David and Geoff Eley, *The Peculiarities of German History: Bourgeois Society and Politics in Nineteenth-Century Germany*, Oxford: Oxford University Press, 39–155.

Engelberg, Ernst 1990, *Bismarck: Das Reich in der Mitte Europas*, Berlin: Siedler.

Escher, Felix 1985, *Berlin und sein Umland: Zur Genese der Berliner Stadtlandschaft bis zum Beginn des 20. Jahrhunderts*, vol. 1, Berlin: Colloquium-Verl.

Faber, Karl-Georg 1966, 'Realpolitik als Ideologie. Die Bedeutung des Jahres 1866 für das Politische Denken in Deutschland', *Historische Zeitschrift*, 203, 1: 1–45.

Falk, Francesca 2011, *Eine gestische Geschichte der Grenze. Wie der Liberalismus an der Grenze an seine Grenzen kommt*, München: Verlag Fink.

Farris, Sara 2013, *Max Weber's Theory of Personality: Individuation, Politics and Orientalism in the Sociology of Religion*, Leiden: Brill.

Fontana, Josep 1995, *The distorted past: a reinterpretation of Europe*, Oxford: Blackwell.

Frenz, Wilhelm and Heidrun Schmidt (eds.) 1989, *Wir Schreiten Seit an Seit!: Geschichte der Sozialdemokratie in Nordhessen*, Marburg: SP-Verlag.

Friederici, Hans Jürgen 1985, *Ferdinand Lassalle: eine politische Biographie*, Berlin: Dietz Verlag.

Frohman, Larry 2008, *Poor Relief and Welfare in Germany between the Reformation to World War I*, New York: Cambridge University Press.

Gagel, Walter 1958, *Die Wahlrechtsfrage in der Geschichte der Deutschen Liberalen Parteien, 1848–1918*, Düsseldorf: Droste Verlag.

Ghosh, Peter 2009, 'From the "spirit of Capital" to the "Spirit" of Capitalism: The Transition in German Economic Thought between Lujo Brentano and Max Weber', *History of European Ideas*, 35, 1: 62–92.

Ghosh, Peter 2014, *Max Weber and the Protestant Ethic: Twin Histories*, Oxford: Oxford Univ. Press.

Gniffke, Kai 1992, *Max Quarck (1860–1930): Eine Sozialdemokratische Karriere Im Deutschen Kaiserreich*, PhD Thesis, Frankfurt a.M.

Göhre, Paul 1891, *Drei Monate Fabrikarbeiter und Handwerksbursche: eine praktische Studie*, Leipzig; Grunow.

Goldmann, Lucien 1952, *Sciences Humaines et Philosophie*, Paris: Presses Universitaires de France.

Gorges, Irmela 1980, *Sozialforschung in Deutschland 1872–1914: Gesellschaftliche Einflüsse Auf Themen- und Methodenwahl des Vereins Für Socialpolitik*, Königstein/Ts.: Hain

Gramsci, Antonio 1966, *Note Sul Machiavelli Sulla Politica e Sullo Stato Moderno*, Torino: Einaudi.

Groh, Dieter 1974, 'Die Sozialdemokratie im Verfassungssystem des Reiches'. Hans Mommsen (ed.), *Sozialdemokratie zwischen Klassenbewegung und Volkspartei*, Frankfurt: Fischer, 62–83.

Guettel, Jens-Uwe 2012, 'The Myth of the Pro-Colonialist SPD: German Social Democracy and Imperialism before World War I', *Central European History*, 45: 452–84.

Hanke, Edith, Gangolf Hübinger and Wolfgang Schwentker 2012, 'The Genesis of the Max Weber-Gesamtausgabe and the Contribution of Wolfgang J. Mommsen', *Max Weber Studies*, 12, 1: 59–94.

Haug, Wolfgang Fritz 2006, 'Marx's Learning Process: Against Correcting Marx with Hegel', *Rethinking Marxism*, 18, 4: 572–584.

Henning, Hansjoachim und Florian Tennstedt (eds.) 1998, *Quellensammlung Zur Geschichte Der Deutschen Sozialpolitik: 1867 Bis 1914, Abt. 2. Von Der Kaiserlichen Sozialbotschaft Bis Zu Den Februarerlassen Wilhelms II (1881–1890), Bd. 3. Arbeiterschutz*, Stuttgart et al.: Fischer.

Henning, Hansjoachim und Florian Tennstedt (eds.) 2003, *Quellensammlung Zur Geschichte Der Deutschen Sozialpolitik: 1867 Bis 1914, Abt. 2. Von Der Kaiserlichen Sozialbotschaft Bis Zu Den Februarerlassen Wilhelms II (1881–1890), Bd. 1 Grundfragen der Sozialpolitik, Die Diskussion der Arbeiterfrage auf Regierungsseite und in der Öffentlichkeit*, Darmstadt: WBG.

Henning, Hansjoachim und Florian Tennstedt (eds.) 2004, *Quellensammlung Zur Geschichte Der Deutschen Sozialpolitik: 1867 Bis 1914, Abt. 2, Von Der Kaiserlichen Sozialbotschaft Bis Zu Den Februarerlassen Wilhelms II. (1881–1890), Bd. 6. Die Gesetzliche Invaliditäts- Und Altersversicherung Und Die Alternativen Auf Gewerkschaftlicher Und Betrieblicher Grundlage*, Stuttgart et al.: Fischer.

Henning, Hansjoachim und Florian Tennstedt (eds.) 2008, *Quellensammlung Zur Geschichte Der Deutschen Sozialpolitik: 1867 Bis 1914, Abt. 2, Von Der Kaiserlichen Sozialbotschaft Bis Zu Den Februarerlassen Wilhelms II. (1881–1890), Bd. 4. Arbeiterrecht*, Stuttgart et al.: Fischer.

Hennis, Wilhelm 1987, *Max Webers Fragestellung: Studien zur Biographie des Werks*, Tübingen: J.C.B. Mohr.

Hobsbawm, Eric J. 1987, *The Age of Empire 1875–1914*, London: Pantheon Books.

Hoffrogge, Ralf 2017, *Sozialismus und Arbeiterbewegung in Deutschland und Österreich*: Von den Anfängen bis 1914, Stuttgart, Schmetterling Verlag.

Hübinger, Gangolf 1984, *Georg Gottfried Gervinus: historisches Urteil und politische Kritik*, Göttingen: Vandenhoeck & Ruprecht.

Hübinger, Gangolf 2019, *Max Weber Stationen und Impulse einer intellektuellen Biographie*, Tübingen: Mohr.

Hudis, Peter 2012, *Marx's concept of the alternative to capitalism*, Leiden: Brill.

Jansen, Christian 2011, 'Bismarck und die Linksliberalen', Lothar Gall (ed.), *Otto Von Bismarck Und Die Parteien*, Paderborn: Schöningh, 91–110.

Joll, James 1955, *The Second International 1889–1914*, London: Weidenfeld and Nicolson.

Jones, Elisabeth B. 2009, *Gender and Rural Modernity: Farm Women and the Politics of Labor in Germany, 1871–1933*, Farnham/Burlington: Ashgate.

Kahan, Alan S. 2003, *Liberalism in Nineteenth-Century Europe: The Political Culture of Limited Suffrage*, Houndmills; New York, N.Y.: Palgrave Macmillan.

Käsler, Dirk 2014, *Max Weber: Preuße, Denker, Muttersohn*, München: Beck.

Kaube, Jürgen 2014, *Max Weber: Ein Leben zwischen den Epochen*, Berlin: Rowohlt.

Kieseritzky, Wolther von 2002, *Liberalismus und Sozialstaat: Liberale Politik in Deutschland Zwischen Machtstaat und Arbeiterbewegung (1878–1893)*, Köln: Böhlau.

Kofler, Leo 1966, *Zur Geschichte der bürgerlichen Gesellschaft. Versuch einer verstehenden Deutung der Neuzeit*, Neuwied, Berlin: Luchterhand.

Kramme, Monika 2015, 'Franz Mehring (1846–1919). Sein Weg als Publizist im Kaiserreich vom Liberalismus zur Sozialdemokratie', Detlef Lehnert (ed.), *Vom Linksliberalismus zur Sozialdemokratie*, Wien, Köln, Weimar: Böhlau Verlag, 39–66.

Ladd, Brian 1990, *Urban Planning and Civic Order in Germany, 1860–1914*, Cambridge, Mass: Harvard Univ. Pr.

Langewiesche, Dieter 1988, *Liberalismus in Deutschland*, Frankfurt am Main: Suhrkamp.

Langewiesche, Dieter 2001, 'Bismarck und die Nationalliberalen', Lothar Gall (ed.), *Otto Von Bismarck Und Die Parteien*, Paderborn: Schöningh, 73–90.

Lasker, Eduard 1910, *Gegen das Sozialistengesetz 1878*, München: Buchhandlung Nationalverein.

Le Rider, Jacques 2008, *L'Allemagne au Temps du Réalisme: De L'Espoir au Désenchantement, 1848–1890*, Paris: Albin Michel.

Lehnert, Detlef 2012, 'Lujo Brentano als politisch-ökonomischer Klassiker des modernen Sozialliberalismus', Lehnert, Detlef (ed.), *Sozialliberalismus in Europa: Herkunft und Entwicklung im 19. und frühen 20. Jahrhundert*, Köln/Wien: Böhlau Verlag, 111–134.

Levy, Carl 1999, 'Max Weber, Anarchism and Libertarian Culture: Personality and Power Politics', Whimster Sam (ed.), *Max Weber and the Culture of Anarchy*, London: Palgrave Macmillan.

Lidtke, Vernon L. 1966, *The Outlawed Party: Social Democracy in Germany, 1878–1890*, Princeton, NJ: Princeton Univ. Press.

Liebknecht, Wilhelm 1891, 'Berathung des Parteiprogramms', *Protokoll über die Verhandlung des Parteitages der Sozialdemokratischen Partei Deutschlands*, Berlin: Vorwärts, 323–360.

Lih, Lars 2008, *Lenin rediscovered: What is to be done? In context*, Chicago: Haymarket.

Lipietz, Alain 1982, 'Towards Global Fordism?', *New Left Review*, I, 132: 33–47.

Losurdo, Domenico 1993, *Democrazia o Bonapartismo: Trionfo e Decadenza del Suffragio Universale*, Torino: Bollati Boringhieri.

Loth, Wilfried 1996, *Das Kaiserreich: Obrigkeitsstaat und Politische Mobilisierung*, München: Deutscher Taschenbuch Verlag.

Löwy, Michael 1970, *La théorie de la révolution chez le jeune Marx*, Paris: Maspero.

Löwy, Michael 1976, *Pour une sociologie des intellectuels révolutionnaires: l'évolution politique de György Lukacs, 1909–1929*, Paris: PUF.

Löwy, Michael 2005, *The theory or revolution in the young Marx*, Chicago: Haymarket.

Löwy, Michael 2013, *La cage d'acier: Max Weber et le marxisme wéberien*, Paris: Stock.

Ludwig, Andreas 2005, *Der Fall Charlottenburg: Soziale Stiftungen im Städtischen Kontext (1800–1950)*, Köln: Böhlau.

Lukács, Georg 1947, *Deutsche Literatur im Zeitalter des Imperialismus*, Berlin: Aufbau.

Lukács, Georg 1954, *Die Zerstörung der Vernunft*, Berlin: Aufbau.

Lukács, Georg 1967 [1943], '*Über Preußentum*', *Schriften zur Ideologie und Politik*, Neuwied und Berlin: Luchterhand, 330–53.

Majul, Octavio 2018, 'Una gran victoria es un gran peligro: Max Weber, Friedrich Nietzsche y el problema del epigonismo', *Tópicos* (México), 54: 263–300

Marcuse, Herbert 1965, 'Industrialisierung und Kapitalismus', Otto Stammer (ed.), Max Weber und die Soziologie heute: Verhandlungen des 15. Deutschen Soziologentages in Heidelberg 1964, Tübingen: Mohr, 161–180.

Marx, Karl and Friedrich Engels 1953, *Karl Marx and Frederick Engels on Britain*, Moscow: Progress Publishers.

Mata, Sérgio da 2013, *A Fascinação Weberiana. as Origens da Obra de Max Weber*, Belo Horizonte: Fino Traço.

Mayer, Gustav 1949, *Erinnerungen: Vom Journalisten zum Historiker der deutschen Arbeiterbewegung*, München: Verl. der Zwölf.

Mayer, Gustav [1911] 1969, 'Die Trennung der proletarischen von der bürgerlichen Demokratie in Deutschland', Hans-Ulrich Wehler (ed.), *Radikalismus, Sozialismus Und Bürgerliche Demokratie*, Frankfurt am Main, Suhrkamp, 108–78.

Mayer, Gustav [1932] 1975, *Friedrich Engels: eine Biographie, Vol. 1, Friedrich Engels in seiner Frühzeit*, Frankfurt a.M.: Ullstein.

Mayer, Paul 1972, *Bruno Schoenlank (1859–1901), Reformer der Sozialdemokratischen Tagespresse*, Hannover: Verlag für Literatur und Zeitgeschehen.

McGowan, Lee 2014, *The radical right in Germany: 1870 to the present*, London/New York: Routledge.

Mehring, Franz 1875, *Herr Von Treitschke, der Sozialistentödter, und die Endziele des Liberalismus: Eine sozialistische Replik*, Leipzig: Genossenschaftsbuchdruck.

Mészáros, István 2010, *Social Structure and Forms of Consciousness*, Vol. 1: The Social Determination of Method, New York: NYU Press/Monthly Review.

Miller, Susanne and Heinrich Pothoff 1986, *A history of German Social Democracy: from 1848 to the present*, New York: St. Martin's Press.

Mitzman, Arthur 1970, *The Iron Cage: An Historical Interpretation of Max Weber*, New York: Knopf.

Möller, Frank 1996, 'Die sich selbst bewußte Massenbeeinflussung. Liberalismus und Propaganda', Gerald Diesener and Rainer Gries (eds), *Propaganda in Deutschland: Zur Geschichte Der Politischen Massenbeeinflussung Im 20. Jahrhundert*, Darmstadt: Primus, 3–22.

Möller, Frank 2003, 'Vom revolutionären Idealismus zur Realpolitik. Generationswechsel nach 1848?', *Historische Zeitschrift*, Beihefte 36: 71–91.

Mommsen, Wolfgang J. 1974, *Max Weber: Gesellschaft, Politik und Geschichte*, Frankfurt am Main: Suhrkamp.

Mommsen, Wolfgang J. 1987, 'Max Weber and German Social Democracy', Levy, Carl (ed.), *Socialism and the Intelligentsia: 1880–1914*, London: Routledge & Kegan Paul.

Mommsen, Wolfgang J. 1989, 'Joining the Underdogs? Weber's Critique of the Social Democrats in Wilhelmine Germany', *The Political and Social Theory of Max Weber: Collected Essays*. Cambridge: Polity Press, Blackwell, 74–86.

Mommsen, Wolfgang J. 1993, 'Max Weber: ein politischer Intellektuelle im Kaiserreich', Rita Aldenhoff-Hübinger, Gangolf Hübinger and Wolfgang J. Mommsen (eds.), *Intellektuelle im Deutschen Kaiserreich*, Frankfurt a M.: Fischer, 33–61.

Mommsen, Wolfgang J. 2004 [1959], *Max Weber und die deutsche Politik*, Tübingen: Mohr.

Mommsen, Wolfgang J. 2005, 'From Agrarian Capitalism to the 'Spirit' of Modern Capitalism: Max Weber's Approaches to the Protestant', *Max Weber Studies*, 5, 2: 185–203.

Mommsen, Wolfgang J. and Wolfgang Schwentker (eds.) 1988, *Max Weber und Seine Zeitgenossen*, Göttingen: Vandenhoeck & Ruprecht.

Morcillo Laiz, Álvaro and Eduardo Weisz (eds.) 2016, *Max Weber en Iberoamérica. Nuevas interpretaciones, estudios empíricos y recepción*, México: Fondo de Cultura Económica/Centro de Investigación y Docencia Económicas.

Müller, Johann Baptist 1971, 'Der deutsche Sozialkonservatismus', Helga Grebing et al. (eds.), *Konservatismus – eine deutsche Bilanz*, München: Kiepenhauer und Witsch, 67–97.

Nelson, Robert L. 2010, 'From Manitoba to the Memel: Max Sering, Inner Colonization and the German East', *Social History*, 35, 4: 439–457.

Nelson, Robert L. 2015, 'A German on the Prairies: Max Sering and Settler Colonialism in Canada', *Settler Colonial Studies*, 5, 1: 1–19.

Netto, José Paulo 1992, *Capitalismo monopolista e serviço social*, São Paulo: Cortez.

Netto, José Paulo 2001, 'Cinco Notas a Propósito da "Questão Social"', *Temporalis*, 2, 3: 41–49.

Nipperdey, Thomas 1993, *Deutsche Geschichte, 1866–1918, Band 2: Machtstaat vor der Demokratie*, München: C.H. Beck.

Nyassi, Ulrike and Helmut Köster 1979, 'Vaterlandslose Gesellen. Sozialdemokratie und Sozialistengesetz in Köln (1878–1890)', Reinhold Billstein (ed.), *Das andere Köln. Demokratische Traditionen seit der Französischen Revolution*, Köln: Pahl-Rugenstein, pp. 135–155.

Oberschall, Anthony 1965, *Empirical Social Research in Germany: 1848–1914*, New York: Basic Books.

Pack, Wolfgang 1961, *Das Parlamentarische Ringen um das Sozialistengesetz Bismarcks, 1878–1890*, Düsseldorf: Droste.

Palonen, Kari 2010, *'Objektivität' Als Faires Spiel: Wissenschaft Als Politik bei Max Weber*, Baden-Baden: Nomos.

Pankoke, Eckart 1970, *Sociale Bewegung, Sociale Frage, Sociale Politik: Grundfragen der deutschen Socialwissenschaft im 19. Jahrhundert*, Stuttgart: Klett.

Paré, Jean-Rodrigue 1999, *Les Visages De L'Engagement Dans L'Oeuvre De Max Weber: La Nation, La Culture et La Science*, Paris: Harmattan.

Parsons, Talcott 1968, *The Structure of Social Action*, Vol. 2, New York: Free Press.

Plessen, Marie-Louise 1975, *Die Wirksamkeit des Vereins für Sozialpolitik von 1872–1890: Studien zum Katheder- und Staatssozialismus*, Berlin: Duncker & Humblot.

Pöls, Werner 1960, *Sozialistenfrage Und Revolutionsfurcht in Ihrem Zusammenhang Mit Den Angeblichen Staatsstreichplänen Bismarcks*, Lübeck: Matthiesen.

Poore, Carol 2000, *The Bonds of Labor: German Journeys to the Working World*, 1890–1990, Detroit: Wayne State University Press.

Prüfer, Sebastian 2002, *Sozialismus statt Religion: Die deutsche Sozialdemokratie vor der religiösen Frage, 1863–1890*, Göttingen: Vandenhoeck & Ruprech.

Pulzer, Peter 1988, *The rise of political Anti-semitism in Germany & Austria*, Cambridge, Mass.: Harvard University Press.

Radkau, Joachim 2005, *Max Weber: Die Leidenschaft des Denkens*, München: Hanser.

Rehmann, Jan 2015, *Max Weber: Modernisation as Passive Revolution*, Leiden: Brill.

Repp, Kevin 2000, *Reformers, Critics, and the Paths of German Modernity Anti-Politics and the Search for Alternatives, 1890–1914*, Cambridge, Mass: Harvard University Press.

Resch, Stephan 2012, *Das Sozialistengesetz in Bayern: 1878–1890*, Düsseldorf: Droste.

Reulecke, Jürgen 1983, *Sozialer Frieden Durch Soziale Reform: Der Centralverein für Das Wohl der Arbeitenden Klasse in der Frühindustrialisierung*, Wuppertal: Hammer.

Reulecke, Jürgen 1985, 'Die Anfänge der organisierten Sozialreform in Deutschland', Rüdiger vom Bruch (ed.), *Weder Kommunismus noch Kapitalismus: Bürgerliche Sozialreform in Deutschland vom Vormärz bis zur Ära Adenauer*, Münich: Beck.

Riesebrodt, Martin 1986, 'From Patriarchalism to Capitalism: The Theoretical Context of Max Weber's Agrarian Studies (1892–93)', *Economy and Society*, 15, 4: 476–502.

Ritter, Gerhard A. and Merith Niehuss (eds.) 1980, *Wahlgeschichtliches Arbeitsbuch: Materialien zur Statistik des Kaiserreichs, 1871–1918*, München: Beck.

Rochau, Ludwig August v. 1972 [1869], *Grundsätze der Realpolitik: Angewendet auf die staatlichen Zustände Deutschlands*, Frankfurt a.M.: Ullstein.

Roth, Guenther 2001, *Max Webers Deutsch-Englische Familiengeschichte 1800–1950*, Tübingen: Mohr Siebeck.

Sachße, Christoph and Florian Tennstedt 1998, *Geschichte der Armenfürsorge in Deutschland. 1. Vom Spätmittelalter bis zum 1. Weltkrieg*, Vol. 1., Stuttgart: Kohlhammer.

Scaff, Lawrence A. 1984, 'Weber before Weberian Sociology', *The British Journal of Sociology*, 35, 2: 190–215.

Scaff, Lawrence A. 1989, *Fleeing the Iron Cage: Culture, Politics, and Modernity in the Thought of Max Weber*, Berkeley: Univ. of California Press.

Scarpa, Ludovica 1995, *Gemeinwohl und Lokale Macht: Honoratioren und Armenwesen in der Berliner Luisenstadt im 19. Jahrhundert*, München: Saur.

Schippel, Max 1891a, Drei Monate Fabrikarbeiter (Part I), *Die neue Zeit: Revue des geistigen und öffentlichen Lebens*, 9 (1890–91), 2, H. 41: 468–475.

Schippel, Max 1891b, Drei Monate Fabrikarbeiter (Part II), *Die neue Zeit: Revue des geistigen und öffentlichen Lebens*, 9 (1890–91), 2, H. 42: 499–506.

Schmoller, Gustav 1866, 'Die Ländliche Arbeiterfrage mit Besonderer Rücksicht auf die Norddentschen Verhältnisse', *Zeitschrift Für Die Gesamte Staatswissenschaft*, 22, 2: 171–233.

Schmoller, Gustav 1890 [1872], 'Rede zur Eröffnung der Besprechung über die Sociale Frage in Eisenach, den 6. Oktober 1872', *Zur Social- und Gewerbepolitik der Gegenwart: Reden und Aufsätze*, Leipzig: Duncker & Humblot, 1–13.

Schmoller, Gustav 1890 [1874], 'Die Sociale Frage und der Preußische Staat', *Zur Social- und Gewerbepolitik der Gegenwart: Reden und Aufsätze*, Leipzig: Duncker & Humblot, 37–63.

Schultz, Ferdinand 1887, *Chronik Der Residenzstadt Charlottenburg: Ein Stadt- Und Kulturbild*, Charlottenburg: Grundmann.

Schulz, Peter 1990, *Nicht die Zeit, um Auszuruhen: Dokumente und Bilder zur Geschichte der hannoverschen Arbeiterbewegung, 1814–1949*, Hannover: Verl. Buchdr.-Werkstätten.

Seager, Frederic H. 1969, *The Boulanger Affair; Political Crossroad of France, 1886–1889*, Ithaca, N.Y.: Cornell University Press.

Seeber, Gustav (ed.) 1977, *Bismarcks Sturz: Zur Rolle der Klassen in der Endphase des Preussisch-Deutschen Bonapartismus 1884/85 bis 1890*, Berlin: Akademie Verlag.

Short, John P. 2012, *Magic lantern empire: Colonialism and society in Germany*, Ithaca: Cornell University Press.

Sombart, Werner 1896, *Sozialismus und soziale Bewegung im 19. Jahrhundert*, Jena: G. Fischer.

Sperber, Jonathan 1997, *The Kaiser's Voters: Electors and Election in Imperial Germany*, Cambridge [etc.]: Cambridge university press.

Strazzeri, Victor 2014, 'A trajetória histórica do "social"', *Serviço Social & Sociedade*, 119: 508–530.

Strazzeri, Victor 2015, 'Max Weber and the "labour question": An initial appraisal', *Max Weber Studies*, 15,1: 69–100.

Strazzeri, Victor 2017, 'Review of "Max Weber, Briefe 1895–1902", ed. Rita Aldenhoff-Hübinger in cooperation with Uta Hinz (Max Weber Gesamtausgabe II/3; Tübingen: Mohr Siebeck, 2015)', *Max Weber Studies*, 17,1: 92–103.

Suvin, Darko 2019, 'On Communism, Science Fiction, and Utopia: The Blagoevgrad Theses'. *Mediations*, 32, 2: 139–160.

Tennfelde, Klaus, 2011 'Bismarck und die Sozialdemokratie', Lothar Gall (ed.), *Otto Von Bismarck Und Die Parteien*, Paderborn: Schöningh, 111–135.

Tennstedt, Florian 1983, *Vom Proleten zum Industriearbeiter: Arbeiterbewegung und Sozialpolitik in Deutschland 1800 bis 1914*, Köln: Bund-Verl.

Tennstedt, Florian 1988 'Hugo Thiel Und Der Verein Für Sozialpolitik', *Zeitschrift Für Sozialreform*, 34, 9: 524–537.

Torp, Cornelius 2005, *Die Herausforderung Der Globalisierung: Wirtschaft Und Politik in Deutschland 1860–1914*, Göttingen: Vandenhoeck & Ruprecht.

Treitschke, Heinrich von. 1875, *Der Socialismus und seine Gönner: Nebst Sendschreiben an Gustav Schmoller*, Berlin: G. Reimer

Ullrich, Volker 2007, *Die Nervöse Grossmacht: Aufstieg und Untergang des Deutschen Kaiserreichs 1871–1918*, Frankfurt am Main: Fischer Taschenbuch Verlag.

Valentin, Veit 1977 [1930], *Geschichte der deutschen Revolution von 1848–1849*, Frankfurt a.M., Wien, Zürich: Büchergilde Gutenberg.

Verein für Socialpolitik 1893, *Verhandlungen der am 20. und 21. März 1893 in Berlin abgehaltenen Generalversammlung des Vereins für Socialpolitik über die ländliche Arbeiterfrage und über die Bodenbesitzverteilung und die Sicherung des Kleingrundbesitzes*, Berlin: Duncker & Humblot.

Vormbaum, Thomas 2011, *Juristische Zeitgeschichte: Darstellungen und Deutungen*, Berlin: Lit.

Weber, Marianne 1984 [1926], *Max Weber: Ein Lebensbild*, Tübingen: Mohr.

Weber, Marianne 1975 [1926], *Max Weber: a biography*, New York: Wiley.

Weber, Max 1984, *Max-Weber-Gesamtausgabe, Band I/3: Die Lage der Landarbeiter im ostelbischen Deutschland*, edited by Martin Riesebrodt, 2 vols., Tübingen: Mohr.

Weber, Max 1986, *Max-Weber-Gesamtausgabe, Band I/2*: Die römische Agrargeschichte in ihrer Bedeutung für das Staats- und Privatrecht, edited by Jürgen Deininger, Tübingen: Mohr.

Weber, Max 1990, *Max-Weber-Gesamtausgabe, Band II/5: Briefe 1906–1908*, edited by M. Rainer Lepsius and Wolfgang J. Mommsen with Birgit Rudhard and Manfred Schön, Tübingen: Mohr.

Weber, Max 1993, *Max-Weber-Gesamtausgabe, Band* I/4: *Landarbeiterfrage, Nationalstaat Und Volkswirtschaftspolitik: Schriften Und Reden 1892–1899*, 2 vols., edited by Wolfgang Mommsen with Rita Aldenhoff, Tübingen: Mohr.

Weber, Max 1994a, *Political Writings*, edited by Peter Lassman and Ronald Speirs, Cambridge: Cambridge University Press.

Weber, Max 1994b, *Max-Weber-Gesamtausgabe, Band II/6: Briefe 1909–1910*, edited by M. Rainer Lepsius and Wolfgang J. Mommsen with Birgit Rudhard and Manfred Schön, Tübingen: Mohr.

Weber, Max 1998, *Max-Weber-Gesamtausgabe, Band I/8: Wirtschaft, Staat und Sozialpolitik. Schriften und Reden 1900–1912*, edited by Wolfgang Schluchter with Peter Kurth and Birgitt Morgenbrod, Tübingen: Mohr.

Weber, Max 2003, *Max-Weber-Gesamtausgabe, Band II/8: Briefe 1913–1914*, edited by M. Rainer Lepsius and Wolfgang J. Mommsen with Birgit Rudhard and Manfred Schön, Tübingen: Mohr.

Weber, Max 2008, *Max-Weber-Gesamtausgabe, Band III/5: Agrarrecht, Agrargeschichte, Agrarpolitik. Vorlesungen 1894–1899* edited by Rita Aldenhoff-Hübinger, Tübingen: Mohr.

Weber, Max 2009a, *Max-Weber-Gesamtausgabe, Band III/1: Allgemeine ("theoretische") Nationalökonomie. Vorlesungen 1894–1898*, edited by Wolfgang J. Mommsen with Cristof Judenau, Heino H. Nau, Klaus Scharfen and Marcus Tiefel, Tübingen: Mohr.

Weber, Max 2009b. *Max-Weber-Gesamtausgabe, Band III/4: Arbeiterfrage und Arbeiterbewegung. Vorlesungen 1895–1898*, edited by Rita Aldenhoff-Hübinger with Silke Fehlemann, Tübingen: Mohr.

Weber, Max 2012, *Max Weber: Collected Methodological Writings*, edited by Hans Henrik Bruun and Sam Whimster, London and New York: Routledge.

Weber, Max 2015, *Max-Weber-Gesamtausgabe, Band II/3: Briefe 1895–1902*, edited by Rita Aldenhoff-Hübinger with Uta Hinz, 2 vols., Tübingen: Mohr.

Weber, Max 2016, *Max-Weber-Gesamtausgabe, Band I/18: Die protestantische Ethik und der Geist des Kapitalismus. Die protestantischen Sekten und der Geist des Kapitalismus. Schriften 1904–1920*, edited by Wolfgang Schluchter with Ursula Bube, Tübingen: Mohr.

Weber, Max 2017a. *Max-Weber-Gesamtausgabe, Band II/1: Briefe 1875–1886*, edited by Gangolf Hübinger with Thomas Gerhards and Uta Hinz, Tübingen: Mohr.

Weber, Max 2017b. *Max-Weber-Gesamtausgabe, Band II/2: Briefe 1887–1894*, edited by

Rita Aldenhoff-Hübinger with Thomas Gerhards and Sybille Oßwald-Bargende, Tübingen: Mohr.

Wehler, Hans-Ulrich 1972, 'Einleitung', Rochau, Ludwig August v. 1972 [1869], *Grundsätze der Realpolitik: Angewendet auf die staatlichen Zustände Deutschlands*, Frankfurt a.M.: Ullstein, 7–21.

Wehler, Hans-Ulrich 1987, *Deutsche Gesellschaftsgeschichte. 1, Vom Feudalismus des Alten Reiches bis zur Defensiven Modernisierung der Reformära 1700–1815*, Vol. 1, München: Beck.

Wehler, Hans-Ulrich 1989, *Deutsche Gesellschaftsgeschichte. 2, Von der Reformära bis zur Industriellen und Politischen "Deutschen Doppelrevolution", 1815–1845/49*, Vol. 2, München: Beck.

Wehler, Hans-Ulrich 1995, *Deutsche Gesellschaftsgeschichte. Von der "Deutschen Doppelrevolution" bis zum Beginn des Ersten Weltkrieges: 1849–1914*, Vol. 3, München: Beck.

Weipert, Axel 2013, *Das Rote Berlin: Eine Geschichte der Berliner Arbeiterbewegung 1830–1934*, Berlin: Berliner Wiss.-Verl.

Wittich, Werner 1900, *Deutsche und französische Kultur im Elsass*, Strassbourg: Schlesier & Schwerikhardt.

Wright, Erik Olin 2002, 'The Shadow of Exploitation in Weber's Class Analysis', *American Sociological Review* 67, 6: 832–853.

Zimmerman, A. 2006, 'Decolonizing Weber', *Postcolonial Studies*, 9,1: 53–79.

Zimmerman, A. 2012, *Alabama in Africa: Booker T. Washington, the German Empire, and the Globalization of the New South*, Princeton, NJ: Princeton University Press.

Index

www.ingramcontent.com/pod-product-compliance
Lightning Source LLC
Chambersburg PA
CBHW062113040426
42337CB00043B/3732
* 9 7 8 1 6 4 2 5 9 9 8 9 3 *